SHAKESPEARE AND THE SECOND WORLD WAR:
MEMORY, CULTURE, IDENTITY

EDITED BY IRENA R. MAKARYK AND
MARISSA MCHUGH

Shakespeare and the Second World War

Memory, Culture, Identity

UNIVERSITY OF TORONTO PRESS
Toronto Buffalo London

ISBN 978-1-4426-4402-1

Printed on acid-free, 100% post-consumer recycled paper with
vegetable-based inks.

Library and Archives Canada Cataloguing in Publication

Shakespeare and the Second World War : memory, culture, identity /
edited by Irena R. Makaryk and Marissa McHugh.

Includes bibliographical references and index.
ISBN 978-1-4426-4402-1 (bound)

1. Shakespeare, William, 1564–1616 – Appreciation.   2. Shakespeare,
William, 1564–1616 – Stage history – 1800–1950.   3. World War,
1939–1945 – Literature and the war.   I. Makaryk, Irena R. (Irena Rima),
1951–   II. McHugh, Marissa, 1980–

PR2970.S53 2012   822.3'3   C2012-903357-X

University of Toronto Press acknowledges the financial assistance to its
publishing program of the Canada Council for the Arts and the Ontario
Arts Council.

University of Toronto Press acknowledges the financial support of the
Government of Canada through the Canada Book Fund for its publishing
activities.

Contents

Illustrations

Acknowledgments

The Editors wish to acknowledge the financial assistance of the Social Sciences and Humanities Research Council of Canada, which provided major funding for *Wartime Shakespeare in a Global Context/Shakespeare au temps de la guerre*, an international bilingual conference that took place at the University of Ottawa in 2009. A small sampling of essays, revised and expanded from that conference, form the basis of this book. We would also like to thanks the Faculty of Arts, the Faculty of Graduate and Postdoctoral Studies, and the Central Administration of the University of Ottawa for additional funding and for their enthusiastic support of this project.

The Editors wish to thank *Comparative Drama* for permission to reprint excerpts from Mark Bayers's 'The Merchant of Venice, the Arab-Israeli Conflict, and the Perils of Shakespearean Appropriation.' For permission to reprint images found in Zeno Ackermann's essay, we thank Bärbel Reissman, Stiftung Stadtmuseum Berlin; Ilse Jung, Landesmuseum für Kultur und Geschichte Berlins, Kunsthistorische Museum (Berlin); Imagno Brandstätter Images; and Österreichisches Theatermuseum, Vienna. For images accompanying Nancy Isenberg's essays, thanks to Biblioteca Museo Teatrale del Burcardo (Rome, Italy). For the photograph of her late husband, Dimitris Myrat as Othello (1942), many thanks to Voula Zouboulaki; and for the advertisement for the production, thanks to the Central Library of Aristotle University, Thessaloniki, Greece. Images in Krystyna Kujawińska Courtney's essay are courtesy of Instytut Teatralny im Zbigniewa Raszewskiego and especially Dorota Buchwald. Illustrations in Alexander C.Y. Huang's essay appear thanks to the People's Government of Jiang'an County, and to Zizhong People's Government, China. For use of the delicate images of the Osiris Players, thanks to Marie Crispin; for their reproduction, to Mary Lou White, Reprographic Supervisor, University of Winchester. For David Low's cartoon, originally published in the *Evening Standard*, thanks to Lorna Scott, University Archivist, University of Gloucestershire, to The Shakespeare Centre Library and Archive, and to Solo Syndication. Many thanks to Petr Pasternak for permission to reproduce the image of Boris Pasternak. All photographs in Katarzyna Kwapisz Williams' essay are by Julia Sielicka-Jastrzębska; thanks to the Museum of the Warsaw Uprising for permission to reproduce them here. Our thanks go also to the Ruth Pincoe for creating the index.

SHAKESPEARE AND THE SECOND WORLD WAR

Introduction: Theatre, War, Memory, and Culture

IRENA R. MAKARYK

> All theatrical cultures have recognized, in some form or another, this ghostly quality, this sense of something coming back in the theatre, and so the relationships between theatre and cultural memory are very deep and complex. Just as one might say that every play might be called [Ibsen's] *Ghosts*, so, with equal justification, one might argue that every play is a memory play. Theatre, as a simulacrum of the cultural and historical process itself, seeking to depict the full range of human actions within their physical context, has always provided society with the most tangible records of its attempts to understand its own operations. It is the repository of cultural memory, but, like the memory of each individual, it is also subject to continual adjustment and modification as the memory is recalled in new circumstances and contexts.
>
> (Roach 2)

Studies of 'ghosting,' repetition, memory, recycling, and 'double-vision,' are particularly appropriate theoretical models with which to approach theatre – and more specifically, Shakespeare – and the Second World War. Herbert Blau's simple but potent remark, 'Where memory is, theatre is' (173),[1] may be extended to include the theatre of war: 'Where memory is, war is.' By its very name, the Second World War draws attention to its presiding 'ghost,' the First World War.[2] Most obviously linked through numerical sequence, the two wars are often inextricably connected in other ways, including the numerous memorials on which the fallen soldiers of the Second World War appear directly underneath those of the First, rather than on a separately dedicated monument.[3]

Similarly, Shakespeare's 'return' in the Second World War was 'haunted' by the extensive uses of his plays in the First.[4] As will be seen in the pages that follow, Shakespeare's role in the Second World War was more complex and nuanced than it was in the Great War, where the Bard was found on stage, in the press, in sermons, in the new medium of silent film, and in propaganda.[5] In the late 1930s and the 1940s, neither the actors nor the public easily took to such jingoistic uses of the Bard. As A.D. Harvey has astutely and wittily observed, 'the second-time-round syndrome' is 'less obviously an advantage in art and literature' (Harvey 273). The Second War, coming so soon after the First, was, for the most part, unable to call upon what Harvey terms 'The Romance of War' – the promise of glory, the opportunity to reveal 'character' through heroic or courageous acts in a war that would be quickly resolved. Such 'Romance' had withered 'under the machine guns of the Somme' (Harvey 63).[6]

Shakespeare presents a fascinating case study of the nexus of problems binding together concepts of collective remembrance, history, war, and national identity. His works – themselves frequently engaged with issues of memory – occupy a prismatic and complex position in world culture: they straddle both high and low, national and foreign, literature and theatre. If cultural memory is defined as comprising 'that body of reusable texts, images, and rituals specific to each society in each epoch, whose "cultivation" serves to stabilize and convey that society's self-image' (Assmann 132), then Shakespeare poses a special challenge, since he forms part of the sanctioned, institutionalized heritage of many different cultures – not just one.

Most, if not all, of the belligerents of the Second World War have, at one time or another, laid claim to Shakespeare and have called upon his work to convey their society's self-image. His works constituted a readily available, malleable, and instantly recognizable part of their cultural inventory of signs and symbols: a 'ghost' of their cultural past, and for some, a ghost whose use was also strongly embedded in the previous war. However, as the essays in this volume will amply prove, the meaning that accrued to that 'ghost,' that sign, was neither single nor simple. In calling up their cultural inventory during wartime, various groups were forced to confront the crisis of their own identity and cultural memory,[7] a confrontation that often involved questioning the extent of their allegiance to that very English author. Shakespeare's complex and ambiguous cultural position was further complicated – and sometimes aided – by intermediaries. Thus, for example, the fact that the Japanese had appropriated Shakespeare from German sources partly mitigated the Bard's unwelcome and problematic English origins.[8]

Fought on every continent except Antarctica, the Second World War offers a unique and temporally limited but geographically inclusive period in which to analyse and probe the vexed interrelations among war, Shakespeare, nationalism, political exigency, collective memory, and collective identity. The social and political upheaval of the war, the sheer number of casualties, the reshaping of borders, the massive movement of refugees, and the central event of the Holocaust reshaped cultural values, paradigms, and mores. We are still living with the consequences today.[9]

Wartime conditions provide especially fertile grounds for testing a variety of theories concerning concepts of culture (in both an anthropological and an aesthetic sense). Classical reflection theories (the assumption of the existence of a collectively shared national identity and distinct features of a national culture), one may posit, are least problematically assimilated during wartime when desire, fear, or both, require collective, not individual, thought and shared, rather than divided, allegiances. Theatre, however, appears to work against such reflexes. As playwright David Edgar observes, 'Theatre invites – indeed requires – the audience to empathize,' to see the world from another, competing perspective, without the comforting guidance of a single narrator or historian (36). Theatre is, of necessity, an interrogative venture that requires audience collaboration, its 'imaginarie Forces' (to employ the Chorus's phrase from *Henry V*), to work for its completion. Theatre's 'imaginary puissance' also lies in the simple fact that it is literally an embodied genre in which actors repeat the action again and again, each time with a difference. Every performance is 'haunted' by the history – and histories – of previous performances. Both this interrogative nature of theatre and its 'haunting' complicate our understanding of the reception of especially difficult plays such as *The Merchant of Venice* (a recurring topic in this book).

The role of theatre and, in particular, Shakespeare, during the Second World War has not yet been examined or documented in any depth, despite the fact that theatrical representations contributed to the war effort from almost the first moments of hostilities.[10] As of the point of writing, there were only about a dozen articles that examined the interplay between Shakespeare, theatre, and the Second World War, although both war studies and reception studies of Shakespeare have seen a remarkable growth during the past two decades.[11] *Shakespeare and the Second World War* is thus the first sustained international, collaborative incursion into this terrain.

The core of *Shakespeare and the Second World War* is formed of invited essays and a small sampling of revised and expanded papers originally presented at the three-day international bilingual conference Wartime Shakespeare in a Global Context/Shakespeare au temps de la guerre, held at the University of Ottawa in 2009 and timed to coincide with the 70th anniversary of the declaration of the Second World War.

This volume does not present a history of Shakespeare during the Second World War nor is it intended to be complete and comprehensive in its geographical reach, although it does include a wide, international perspective on the topic. Rather, *Shakespeare and the Second World War* focuses on the way in which Shakespeare – 'recycled,' re-viewed, and reinterpreted – is illuminated by and simultaneously illuminates the war in various countries around the world. Among the subtexts of the essays that follow is the recurrent notion that Shakespeare, though seemingly infinitely malleable, is not easily snaffled by propaganda, censorship, or ideology. Slithering out of such constrictions, 'local' reinterpretations of Shakespeare's plays often present unintended meanings and gesture at unexpected discourses.

Most of the essays that follow involve examining what Dennis Kennedy has called 'foreign Shakespeare' – that is, Shakespeare in a language other than English and often in an adapted or otherwise transformed mode. The editors and contributors share the view of Julie Sanders who, in her study of adaptation, observed that

> it is usually at the point of infidelity that the most creative acts of adaptation and appropriation take place. The sheer possibility of testing fidelity in any tangible way is surely also in question when we are dealing with such labile texts as Shakespeare's plays. Adaptation studies are, then, not about making polarized value judgements, but about analyzing process, ideology, and methodology. (20)

This last point – analysing process, ideology, and methodology – occupies a central part of the book's discussions about Shakespeare in/and the Second World War. Moreover, as has been argued, above, Shakespeare is a kind of 'sign' or 'symbol' of cultural memory. His works serve functions similar to that of

> myths, fairy tales, and folklore which by their very nature depend on a

communality of understanding. These forms and genres have cross-cultural, often cross-historical, readerships; they are stories and tales which appear across the boundaries of cultural difference and which are handed on, albeit in transmuted and translated forms, through the generations. In this sense they participate in a very active way in a shared community of knowledge, and they have therefore proved particularly rich sources for adaptation and appropriation. (Sanders 45)

As will be seen, Shakespeare frequently served as a point of reference for communal memory and understanding, complicated and problematized by war. Usually instantly recognizable, infinitely referential, but frequently shifting in meaning, Shakespeare's works offer a prismatic lens through which to view – and sometimes to replay on the cultural plane – the ideological and military clashes of the Second World War. If, as has been argued, performance is deeply 'embedded into notions of nationalism, identity and power' and, if 'war is the continuation of politics by other means' (*pace* von Clausewitz), then, 'performance may well be a continuation of war and politics by other means'; so indeed suggest Thompson, Hughes, and Balfour (1–2). In the current climate of anxiety about the imposition of Western values (represented, as has been argued, by Shakespeare) on other cultures, and the daily presence of war around the world, *Shakespeare and the Second World War* also invites us to consider the 'ghosting' qualities of theatre: whether and how these issues may also obtain today.[12]

The following essays also suggest that to imagine a simple pro- and anti-war binary use of Shakespeare is not sustainable. As Thompson, Hughes and Balfour have perceptively noted, 'Theatre in the moment of war creates a time and a conscious space apart from the conflict while paradoxically remaining part of the context. At times, it is part of a resistance against the 'enemy' within the narrative of the conflict. At other times, it seeks to resist war itself by trying to construct a reality beyond competing narratives' (68). Despite the aims of their makers, wartime theatre is rarely consistent with their intentions.

This volume opens with **Werner Habicht**'s essay, 'German Shakespeare, the Third Reich, and the War,' a discussion of the Nazi regime's ambivalent response to Shakespeare, one which became increasingly complex throughout the 1930s and, especially, during the war. Although Shakespeare had been deeply embedded in German literary and theatrical heritage for more than a century, he was also inconveniently English in a time of war with Britain. On the one hand, the Nazis attempted to impose ideological conformity on the theatres and turn them into instruments of political indoctrination and propaganda, including a shaping of national and racial consciousness; on the other, the Nazis perceived themselves as expert carriers of the best of world culture.[13] As Habicht reminds us, the Germans established or subsidized theatres throughout the lands they occupied (including Czechoslovakia, Poland, Belarus, the Netherlands, and France). Indeed, the Nazi regime was perhaps one of the most theatrical of regimes, both in its creation, support, and attempt to control theatres, and in its insistent use of theatrical techniques in staging mass rallies.

Gerwin Strobl has suggested, and Habicht confirms in his essay, that 'Shakespeare's fluctuating fortunes in the Third Reich are more than just a historical curiosity. They go to the heart of the Nazi efforts of "cleansing" the German mind and the wider drive to create a Germany in the Party's image' (Stroble 16). While Habicht touches only lightly on foreign policy considerations (such as Nazi cultural 'accommodation' of Britain up to 1939 and into the early years of the war), he provides a nuanced picture of the way in which prominent theatre artists continued to stage a Shakespeare that did not always cohere with the demands of official ideology. Habicht also alludes to a major theme or undercurrent in many of the essays that follow: the ever inexplicable, paradoxical conjunction of culture and barbarism. Indeed, the long-standing centrality of Shakespeare in German culture often ensured Shakespeare's use and survival in countries as different as Italy and Japan.

Zeno Ackermann's 'Shakespearean Negotiations in the Perpetrator Society: German Productions of *The Merchant of Venice* during the Second World War' takes us deeper into this terrain by focusing on a vexed play that was changed forever by the Holocaust[14] and that continues to spark heated debate with every new production. Ackermann tackles head on both the use that the Nazis made of *The Merchant* as a tool of racial propaganda and, as he puts it, the 'ongoing anxieties that Shakespeare may have been a "Jew-hater."' This essay raises three important questions: (1) How was the reception of *The Merchant* related to Nazi anti-Semitism and the Holocaust? (2) Was there indeed a change in the reception of this play in 1933, when the National Socialist party first came to power in Germany? (3) How much 'Angst' did Shakespeare's character of a thwarted Jewish avenger inspire in the proponents of anti-Semitism?

In the process of dealing with these difficult issues, Ackermann reveals the ambivalent and even contradictory relationship of Nazism to *The Merchant*, which appears to have been a 'problem play' for the theatres of National Socialist Germany. His essay reminds us how performance remembers, supports, but sometimes contradicts the past; it is 'subtly "imbricated" in all aspects of warfare. Performance can help us carry out war and urge us to commit atrocities; it can also be deliberately employed by artists to create a productive tension with other kinds of culture-war relations and seek to prevent, resist and rebuild' (Thompson, Hughes, Balfour 14).

Mark Bayer examines Shylock, one of the key figures of *The Merchant of Venice*, from an entirely different cultural and geographical perspective. His essay, 'Shylock, Palestine, and the Second World War,' discusses the way in which *The Merchant of Venice* variously functioned as a symbol of Zionist ambitions in the region, as a model of and justification for violence against non-Jews, and as a caricature of a number of political figures. In his study of the 'local' meanings of Shakespeare set against the backdrop of world power politics, Bayer examines two applications – one Zionist and the other Arab – of Shakespeare's play to the growing Arab-Israeli conflict. Leopold Jessner's production of *The Merchant* at the Habimah Theatre in Tel Aviv (1936), argues Bayer, is surprisingly employed as propaganda supporting the Zionist cause. In this controversial production, Shylock became an allegory of the long-suffering Jewish people who feel only contempt for the Christian aggressors.

By contrast, writing near the end of the war, Ali Ahmed Bakathir shifted the focus of *The Merchant* onto a local struggle between the indigenous Arab population and the Zionist Jews. As Bayer points out, the characters in Bakathir's adaptation of Shakespeare's play, *The New Shylock* (1945), are fully aware that they are reliving this drama in the present, and that the 'old' Shylock prophetically anticipates the 'new Shylock' who wants more than a pound of flesh. With Bakathir's transformation of the centrepiece of the play, the trial scene, into an international tribunal aimed at determining the future of Palestine, 'the pound of flesh' becomes the issue of sovereignty over the entire country. The play's representation of Arab and Jew is resonant with an ensemble of current stereotypes and longstanding archetypes, thus making it a useful vehicle for distilling some of the complex and volatile Middle Eastern issues of the Second World War that continue to haunt us today.

With **Nancy Isenberg**'s essay, '"Caesar's word against the world": Mussolini's Caesarism and Discourses of Empire,' we turn to Italian

Fascist uses of Shakespeare and, in particular, to Mussolini's use of a Caesarian model of politics and leadership to make of his rule a Modern Roman Empire, and of his persona a Modern Caesar. Shakespeare's *Julius Caesar* was called up to aid and abet Fascist ideological programs, and in so doing to help rally popular consensus for Mussolini's belligerent empire-building intentions. Shakespeare's play also directly or indirectly spawned alternative stage *Caesars* better suited to a changing political climate after Italy's invasion of Ethiopia. Among them was a new play, *Cesare*, written by Mussolini with the help of Fascist playwright Gioacchino Forzano. This adaptation, aimed at celebrating Caesar and regarding him as a hero called to save Rome from decadence, occludes all references to ambiguity and doubt found in Shakespeare's play. Mussolini's penchant for the grandiose and his theatrical use of display, along with his other invented symbols of 'ancient' Rome, were so visually potent that they ironically and falsely influenced the collective imagination worldwide. As one example, Isenberg points to Joseph Mankiewicz's 1953 film that liberally (but unknowingly) used Fascist symbols and visual references, taking them for the ancient Roman.

In places occupied by Italian and German forces during the war, a strict censorship was imposed on all aspects of intellectual and cultural life, including the theatre; yet, as **Tina Krontiris** reveals in 'Shakespeare and Censorship during the Second World War: *Othello* in Occupied Greece,' there were many faultlines in the seemingly rigid totality of censorship and control. The Nazis, and Hitler in particular, held no particular racial prejudice against the Greeks. Although Shakespeare, as an Englishman, could not appear on the stage of the National Theatre of Greece (which had hitherto always awarded the Bard a prominent position), his plays could be found in the private theatres. One of these was a production of *Othello*, purportedly directed by Spyros Melas (but, in fact, by Dimitris Myrat) at the Cotopouli Theatre in 1942. While the reason for Myrat's choice of this specific play is not entirely clear, what is certain is that he aimed through this production to introduce a new, psychologically oriented, and ideologically progressive approach to Shakespearean drama. His Othello was a self-controlled, noble, self-reflexive, dark (but not black) protagonist who sported a kippah-like cap and spoke with a slightly Hebraic accent. Such an Othello, argues Krontiris, was only possible through the mediation of Melas, the Nazi collaborator whose name was identified on the advertisements and the program as the production's director. Aiding in this advancement of an anti-racist interpretation of Othello was Shakespeare's special relation-

ship with German culture (remarked upon above) and the collabora-
tions and the gaps created by the interdependence of Greek nationals,
collaborators, and Nazi occupiers.

The situation in Poland was radically different. **Krystyna Kujawińska
Courtney**'s essay, '"In This Hour of History: Amidst These Tragic
Events" – Polish Shakespeare during the Second World War,' is the
first work to examine Shakespeare's presence in Poland, a country that
found itself trapped between Nazi and Soviet aggression. Theatres were
closed; many actors and writers were killed or sent to concentration
camps while others fled abroad. Literary and scholarly publications
were prohibited. There were no Polish productions of Shakespeare
under Nazi occupation, which aimed to eradicate completely the cultural life (including the education) of all Slavs. Working through hitherto unexplored documents, Kujawińska Courtney has discovered that,
under the auspices of the Secret Theatre Council, Shakespeare moved
underground. In Warsaw and Cracow, his works were secretly read
and performed by Polish national artists and intellectuals. Ironically,
censorship was eased in the Jewish ghettos, perhaps to distract the
inhabitants from their ultimate fate, and thus permission was granted
to stage an adaptation of *Hamlet*. Shakespeare was also found in internment camps, particularly in Murnau, which was close enough to the
Swiss border to serve as a 'Potemkin' camp at which amateur theatricals (including Shakespeare) organized by Polish officers were permitted. Polish soldiers who served with the Allied forces found *Macbeth* a
particularly congenial play. Many highly regarded Shakespeare, some
even perceiving him as a guarantor of European and world cultures.
Less grandly, the Scottish play was adapted as a farcical comedy reflecting on the quotidian life of Polish soldiers in Britain, serving both to lift
up morale and to unify soldiers in exile.

As Kujawińska Courtney's essay suggests, the human losses on
the Eastern front were staggering. Historians estimate that 32 million
military and civilian lives were lost, but even these numbers may not
yet represent a final tally.[15] **Aleksei Semenenko**'s 'Pasternak's Shakespeare in Wartime Russia' turns to *Hamlet* in this context of total war
and strict censorship. In such circumstances, translation often becomes
an aesopic activity, masking yet revealing personal and social-political
realities. Translation also served Pasternak as a sole outlet for a creativity that would otherwise be shackled by censorship. Boris Pasternak's
Hamlet, the most influential of all of his translations of Shakespeare,
served not only stage but also screen (as the script for Grigorii Koz-

intsev's famous film), but provoked much controversy. It still plays a significant role in many aspects of Russian cultural life and may be – as Semenenko claims – the most important Russian work of translation of the twentieth century.

On the Far Eastern front, as elsewhere, Shakespeare elicited complex and ambivalent responses. **Ryuta Minami**'s 'Shakespeare as an Icon of the Enemy Culture in Wartime Japan, 1937–1945' considers the shifting positions of Shakespeare on page and stage in wartime Japan. 'Possessing' Shakespeare had been regarded as one proof of Japan's status as a modern, advanced nation since his first introduction to that country in 1875, but by 1940 the Japanese government had begun an extensive series of prohibitions that included banning not only the use of English words but also performances of American and British music and plays. Yet, as with Germany and Italy, Japan's attitude to Shakespeare was not simply that of antagonism toward an icon of the enemy culture. Some Japanese scholars and theatre artists tried to 'appropriate' Shakespeare while separating him from his birthplace, Britain. One of the reasons that Shakespeare survived the war in Japan was his strong association with German culture. Simultaneously admired and hated, Shakespeare nonetheless retained his status as a symbol of cultural sophistication; his plays, while not staged, were recommended reading, along with Tolstoy's works and Greek myths, for teenage girls.

From Japan, we turn to China. **Alexander C.Y. Huang**'s '"Warlike Noises": Jingoistic *Hamlet* during the Sino-Japanese Wars' shows how, during the 1940s when China was under threat of Japanese invasion, Shakespeare emerged as a weapon of political propaganda. Huang uncovers the competing, yet sometimes collaborative, tension between admiration for Western theatre and the pull of Chinese nationalist sentiment. During a time when the theatre was suspect, the Shakespearean canon was an obvious choice for those who wished to avoid censorship by the Nationalist government. The function of this body of work as a site for social education and its potential for propaganda were seen as compelling reasons to stage public performances. Examining Jiao Juyin's 1942 *Hamlet* set in a Confucian temple in rural China, Huang argues that a special prestige accrued to this production. The unusual location emphasizes how site-specificity may bring unexpected and new cultural, religious, political, or other discourses into an interpretation of the play, thus confirming the value of what has been called 'topoanalysis.'[16]

In addition to the esteem associated with Shakespeare's stature, the sheer ability to stage and attend plays during a time of war was itself perceived as a victorious gesture by the Chinese, as it was by other nationalities, including the British. With **Simon Barker**'s 'Shakespeare, Stratford, and the Second World War,' we turn to the English Midlands, the Shakespearean heartland. Barker's essay describes the wartime context for short seasons of plays staged at the Memorial Theatre in Stratford in order to show how the war years irreversibly transformed the relationship between Stratford and Shakespeare. With its Shakespearean associations, its location in the symbolic centre of England (and its proximity to major targets of enemy bombing), Stratford represented a geographically and ideologically unique place from which to observe the potential destruction of the values it had come to represent.

Peter Billingham's 'Rosalinds, Violas, and Other Sentimental Friendships: The Osiris Players and Shakespeare, 1939–1945' admiringly examines the little-known work of an all-female touring company that brought productions of Shakespeare to non-standard venues and disparate communities. While the composition of the Osiris Players was, at that time, unique, their commitment to taking theatre to wartime citizens of Britain mirrored that of other touring companies including the Adelphi Players, the Pilgrim Players, and the Compass Players. It has been argued that these – and other better known companies (such as the Old Vic) that toured the various nooks and crannies of Britain – in fact constituted the real 'national' theatre (Wolfit). Such groups (both professional and amateur, English and refugee troupes) bringing pared-down productions with none of the conventional trappings to Welsh mining towns, gun sites, factory canteens, and other such locations, created new audiences for theatre; in turn, the players, brought closer to their public, thrived on this synergy. The wartime perambulations of theatre companies revived British theatre and, it has been argued, contributed to the postwar 'unprecedented growth in the size and vigour of alternative and experimental theatre' (Davies 64). In bringing to light information about this all-female company, Billingham's essay offers a neat complement to the recent work of Michael Dobson, who has studied all-male companies in prisoner-of-war camps.[17] Both Dobson and Billingham have begun the necessary process of the restoration of the numerous 'other,' especially amateur, wartime 'voices.'

Anne Russell's essay, 'Maurice Evans's *G.I. Hamlet*: Analogy, Authority, and Adaptation,' examines an unjustly ignored but, in its day, popular production of *Hamlet* (1944) for an audience of American soldiers stationed in Hawaii, close to the geographical reminder of the reason that the United States entered the war: the bombing of

Pearl Harbor. Russell explores the cuts and changes that Evans made to Shakespeare's play about revenge, and demonstrates that Evans's hyper-masculine – rather than hesitating – Hamlet was created to help the GIs more readily identify with the Danish Prince. Adapting the play for practical, as well as aesthetic and ethical reasons, Evans justified his cuts with reference to eighteenth-century theatrical practice. Most notably, in removing the graveyard scene, he hoped to avoid too much direct attention to a physicality and omnipresence of death that would counteract his desire to raise the troops' morale. Despite Evans's intentions to stage a less problematic play, his adapted *Hamlet* nonetheless revealed that the genre of tragedy is difficult to digest in wartime and is particularly resistant to explicit ideological uses.

The last three essays in this book turn more specifically to a consideration of Shakespeare and (rather than during) the Second World War. Today, the war is still experienced very much as a physical presence. In Europe, buildings still retain pock-marks from shelling; entirely new postwar city centres have sprouted up on the ground of destroyed buildings; grim historical plaques in places like the Paris Metro remind us how even innocuous places were scenes of execution; and still-dangerous unexploded shells lurk underneath otherwise pastoral-looking fields. In North America, however, the consequences of the war are decidedly more human than architectural, historical, or geographical. With the huge influx of postwar immigrants and refugees (especially from Eastern Europe), who ultimately reshaped the values and the culture of this country, Canadian demographics changed dramatically. These groups, along with returning soldiers and war brides, also brought with them stories of unimaginable horrors that only began to seep into North American consciousness after the war, especially with the onset and the aftermath of the Nuremberg Trials (1945–9).

Because Canada was never occupied, nor did its citizens experience such devastating attacks (as did the Americans, who felt the full force of the war at Pearl Harbor), the nature of Canadian responses to the Second World War was necessarily of a different order. As **Marissa McHugh**'s 'The War at "Home": Representations of Canada and of the Second World War in *Star Crossed*' shows, the Canadian response has been focused more on the domestic and personal, than on the overtly political or horrific aspects of war. But even this 'local' view of war does not fail to raise the troubling spectre of collaboration with the enemy, at home, on the domestic front.

McHugh focuses on a little known but intriguing Canadian adaptation of *Romeo and Juliet* set in German-occupied Holland. She examines the way in which the playwright (perhaps Patrick Bentley) uses *Romeo and Juliet* to expose the way in which war infects domestic spaces that appear to be far removed from its horror. By transposing the setting from Italy to Holland, a location and a distinct moment when Canada was said to have proved its independence as a nation, the playwright is able to critique the effects of war on a nation's social-domestic relations without undermining the importance of the Second World War in the development of Canadian national identity. This provocative interrogation of a highly celebrated moment of Canadian war history, the liberation of Holland, is set within the context of a universal critique of intolerance and hatred that also necessarily afflicted Canada. Since, among others, the loyalties of Canadian-German families were suspect, the author may have found it necessary to conceal his own domestic German connections. In moving the action of Verona to Holland, but all the while perhaps thinking of tensions in Canada, the author employs the Shakespearean intertext to critique war and 'tribal' affiliations. Less optimistic than Shakespeare, 'Bentley' finds no communal unity or restoration created by the lovers' deaths.

Yet a more personal and visceral response to Shakespeare and the war may be found in **Tibor Egervari**'s contribution to this volume, '*Shakespeare's Merchant of Venice in Auschwitz.*' Egervari, himself a playwright, theatre director, scholar, and survivor of both the Holocaust and Stalinist Hungary, first discovered *The Merchant of Venice* in 1970 on the stage of Canada's Stratford Festival. As elsewhere, the Stratford Festival production of this play raised controversy and dismay, particularly around the question of what it may have contributed to anti-Semitism. (As noted above, these issues are explored in greater detail by Zeno Ackermann and Mark Bayer in this volume.) Egervari's theatrical experience of *The Merchant* centred on its dramatic greatness and particularly on the hugely powerful figure of Shylock. Grappling with what Shylock has come to mean and what Egervari believed that the character both was before the war and should be now, Egervari began a struggle with Shakespeare's work that ultimately resulted in an urge to recreate the play. His essay describes his process of writing *Shakespeare's Merchant of Venice in Auschwitz*: a way of thinking through Shakespeare and the war. Egervari's elation and frustration with Shakespeare's 'ghost,' the 'ghosts' of history, and his own inability to achieve his goals, are markedly part of his personal account of his attempt to deal with the politics and the ethics of representation.

The delicate balance between a critique of war and an admiration for heroism and courage is explored in detail in the concluding essay of this volume: **Katarzyna Kwapisz Williams**'s 'Appropriating Shakespeare in Defeat: *Hamlet* and the Contemporary Polish Vision of War.' Gathering up a number of the themes raised in the other essays, Kwapisz Williams examines what it means to recycle both painful history and Shakespeare in the context of a culture that has traditionally (and for the most part unconditionally) admired heroism and sacrifice for one's country. What she calls the Polish 'national martyrology' is brought to bear upon the interpretation of a specific event, the Warsaw Uprising of 1944, as it appears in a trenchant analysis by Paweł Passini in his production of *Hamlet'44*. This 2008 adaptation of Shakespeare's play is rich in thematic intensity, setting official versions of the past against the memories of ordinary people; national history against family history; collective memory against historical memory; acts of remembrance against memory aids; the need to forget against the need to remember.

Hamlet'44 is remarkable in its forthright attempt to stage questions about the ethics of representation, narrative testimony, and individual and national identity within the context of a war that shattered Eastern Europe. Passini's production may usefully be regarded as what Roger Simon has called a 'difficult return' – that is, 'a form of memorialization where history is allowed to remain problematic and unresolved in the present' (qtd in Thompson, Hughes, Balfour 211) – or what Andreas Huyssen describes as 'productive remembering' (qtd in Thompson, Hughes, Balfour 214), that is, a practice that opens up public debate about strategies of remembering, and appears to encourage new possibilities for engaging with the past. Passini's invoked 'ghosts' – of war, of Shakespeare, of memory – demand the critical interrogation of received ideas, myth, and stereotypes; rather than safely bracketing off the past from the present, they invite its audience to stare history in the face. Adapting *Hamlet*, Shakespeare's best known play, for this purpose, Passini suggests the way in which acts of remembrance may not simply prevent forgetting but may also 'fix' the identity of a community and prevent its recovery.[18]

Kwapisz Williams thus brings us up to the present day, to a world that is englobed by wars and their ghosts. Her essay – like that of McHugh – seems to confirm Sidney Aster's claim that 'the nature of the national experience itself … is the lasting fruit, or poison, of 1945.' Not so much physical destruction, but rather psychological and sociological upheavals are among the most potent reasons for our continuing fascination with the Second World War. Thirty years ago, Aster observed, '[A]ll wars begin as propaganda and end as myth ... It is only by looking again at the 1939–1945 War ... that the balance between myth, illusion and reality can be restored.' Kwapisz Williams similarly suggests that there is no better way to comprehend the terrifying events of war – any war, and the myths created about those events – than by exposure, repetition, and recycling; she also compellingly argues that the best way to understand Shakespeare's texts is by appropriating them to local contexts where, ironically, they become fully revealed.

Notes

1 Other thought-provoking studies on this topic are Marvin Carlson, *The Haunted Stage: The Theatre as Memory Machine* (Ann Arbor: University of Michigan Press, 2001); and Joseph Roach, *Cities of the Dead* (New York: Columbia University Press, 1996).
2 On the literature of the First World War, see Paul Fussell, *The Great War and Modern Memory* (Oxford: Oxford University Press, 2000); and A.D. Harvey, *A Muse of Fire: Literature, Art and War.*
3 This is certainly true of Canadian war memorials.
4 On Shakespeare, commemoration, and the First (Great) War see the work of Clara Calvo and Ton Hoenselaars. I am grateful to both for sharing their essay-overview of the First World War, 'Shakespeare and World War I,' soon to be published by Greenwood Press. Also see Werner Habicht, 'Shakespeare Celebrations in Times of War,' *Shakespeare Quarterly*; and, in the same volume of that journal, Coppélia Kahn, 'Remembering Shakespeare Imperially: The 1916 Tercentenary,' *Shakespeare Quarterly* 52 (2001): 456–78.
5 See Balz Engler, 'Shakespeare in the Trenches,' *Shakespeare Survey* 45 (1993): 105–11 for a discussion of German uses and celebrations of Shakespeare during the First World War, including the German Chancellor's citations from *Henry V* when the troops stood before Calais. On German Shakespeare also see Wilhelm Hortmann, *Shakespeare on the German Stage: The Twentieth Century* (Cambridge: Cambridge University Press, 1998) and Rodney Symington, *The Nazi Appropriation of Shakespeare: Cultural Politics in the Third Reich* (Lewiston, NY: Mellen, 2005).
6 Among the exceptions is Canada, as Jeffrey A. Keshen notes: 'Jingoism and even naïvete were very much evident among volunteers' (22). Keshen suggests that both their age and the fact that some of them were veterans of

the Great War contributed to the idea of war as a site of valour and 'manly' comradeship.

7 The last two decades have seen an explosion of research on the topic of cultural memory and cultural remembrance. Still, an excellent survey of the major trends may be found in Jeffrey K. Olick and Joyce Robbins, 'Social Memory Studies: From "Collective Memory" to the Historical Sociology of Mnemonic Practices,' *American Review of Sociology* 24 (1998): 105–40.

8 On this point, see Ryuta Minami's essay in this volume.

9 An indication of the continuing fascination with the Second Word War can be seen, for example, in the creation of the World War Two Society, established in 2009 'to foster interest in the period of the Second World War and to remember the sacrifice and achievements of the British and Commonwealth Forces between 1939 and 1945.' See the Society's webpage at http://battlefieldsww2.50megs.com/ww2_society.htm. The World War Two Studies Association (an older organization, established in 1967) continues to promote 'historical research in the period of World War II in all its aspects,' and is affiliated with the International Committee for the History of the Second World War. See http://www.h-net.org/~war/wwtsa/.

10 See, for example, Steve Nicholson, *The Censorship of British Drama, 1900–1968*, vol. 2 (Exter: Exter University Press, 2003): 'the role of theatre and the stage during the Second World War has never been documented or subjected to a general analysis' (167). Since then, Rodney Symington and John London have begun to address this lacuna.

11 This list includes Jonathan Baldo, Alan Clarke, Gerd Gemuenden, Werner Habicht, John London, Zoltán Márkus, Irena Makaryk, and Rodney Symington. While little has been written about Shakespeare and the Second World War, there has been a resurgence of interest in studying theatre, war, violence, and conflict, doubtless spurred on by the war in the Middle East and in Afghanistan. The European Shakespeare Research Association (ESRA) dedicated their 2009 conference (held in Pisa) to the theme of Shakespeare and Conflict: A European Perspective. There has also been a renewed interest in the representation of war in Shakespeare's plays. For an overview of the literature, see 'War in Shakespeare's Plays,' *Shakespearean Criticism*, vol. 88, ed. Michelle Lee (Detroit: Thomson Gale, 2005) 239–380. More recent studies include *Shakespeare and War,* eds. Ros King and Paul J.C.M. Franssen (Basingstoke: Palgrave Macmillan, 2008).

12 The world press coverage of director Corinne Jaber's 2005 production of *Love's Labour's Lost* in Kabul, Afghanistan, sparked such a continuing debate about the relationship between Western culture and its 'imposition' on new audiences. For a detailed reconstruction and analysis of this pro-

duction, see Irena R. Makaryk, '"Brief candle"?: Shakespeare in Afghanistan,' *Multicultural Shakespeare: Translation, Appropriation, and Performance* 6 (21)/7 (22) (2010): 81–113.

13 Jonathan Petropoulos, *Art as Politics in the Third Reich* (Chapel Hill, North Carolina: University of North Carolina Press, 1996), examines the aesthetic theories of the Nazis and their habits of art collection. While focusing on visual art, Petropoulos offers a fascinating picture of the way in which the Nazis perceived themselves as arbiters of great art. Many of the same claims can be made about their views of theatre.

14 John London concludes "Non-German Drama in The Third Reich" by asking whether Shakespeare did indeed survive the Nazis 'unscathed' or whether 'a certain approach to Shakespearian drama (and other non-German plays) extended beyond 1945' (252).

15 This figure is approximately equivalent to the current population of Canada. It may be that the finally tally will never be known, since, as Catherine Merridale has observed, under the Soviet regime, 'among the many secrets of this war was its true cost' (127). R.A.C. Parker observes that the 1959 Soviet census showed a deficit of 50 million, extrapolating from the 1939 census what the approximate figures, in stable circumstances, should have been (281). Robert Service calculates that 26 million Soviet citizens perished, and that 1,710 cities and 70,000 villages were destroyed (225).

16 See, for example, Leslie Hill and Helen Paris, eds., *Performance and Place*, Performance Intervention Series (Houndsmills, Basingstoke: Palgrave Macmillan, 2006), especially Hill's Preface and Introduction, for a penetrating analysis of notions of place, space, and 'non-spaces.' The term 'topoanalysis' is originally that of Gaston Bachelard and his experience of architecture; see *The Poetics of Space* (1958) (Boston, MA: Beacon Press, 1994). Also useful, M.A. Carlson, *Places of Performance: The Semiotics of Theatre Architecture* (Ithaca: Cornell University Press, 1989); and G. McAuley, *Space in Performance: Making Meaning in the Theatre* (Ann Arbor: University of Michigan Press, 1999).

17 I am grateful to Michael Dobson for sharing with me the manuscript of his chapter on 'Prisoners' from his book *Shakespeare and Amateur Performance: A Cultural History* (Cambridge: Cambridge Univeristy Press, 2011).

18 On the notion of fixing identity and on issues of remembering, see Thompson, Hughes, Balfour.

Works Cited

Assmann, Jan. 'Collective Memory and Cultural Identity.' *New German Critique* 65 (Spring/Summer 1995): 125–33.

Aster, Sidney. 'The Second World War as a National Experience.' n.d. 27 Sept. 2010. http://www.ibiblio.org/hyperwar/UN/Canada/Natl_Ex[/NatlExp-Intro.html.

Baldo, Jonathan. 'Wars of Memory in *Henry V.*' *Shakespeare Quarterly* 47.2 (Summer 1996): 132–59.

Blau, Herbert. *The Eye of Prey.* Bloomington: Indiana University Press, 1987.

Calvo, Clara. 'Shakespeare as War Memorial: Remembrance and Commemoration in the Great War.' *Shakespeare Survey* 63 (2010): 198–211.

– Calvo, Clara, and Ton Hoenselaars, eds. *Shakespeare and the Cultures of Commemoration.* Special theme issue of *Critical Survey* 22:2 (2010).

Clarke, Alan. 'German Refugee Theatre in British Internment.' *Theatre and War 1933–1945: Performance in Extremis.* Ed. Michael Balfour. New York and Oxford: Berghahn Books, 2001. 86–116.

Davies, Andrew. 'The War Years.' *Theatre and War 1933–1945: Performance in Extremis.* Ed. Michael Balfour. New York and Oxford: Berghahn Books, 2001. 54–64.

Dobson, Michael. *Shakespeare and Amateur Performance: A Cultural History.* Cambridge and New York: Cambridge University Press, 2011.

Edgar, David. 'Making Drama Out of Conflict.' *Conflict Zones.* Ed Carla Dente and Sara Soncini. Pisa: Edizioni ETS, 2004. 31–48.

Gemuenden, Gerd. 'Space out of Joint: Ernst Lubitsch's *To be or not to Be.*' *New German Critique* 89, Film and Exile (Spring–Summer 2003): 59–80.

Habicht, Werner. 'Shakespeare and Theatre Politics in the Third Reich.' *The Play out of Context: Transferring Plays from Culture to Culture.* Ed. Hanna Ščolnicov and Peter Holland. Cambridge and New York: Cambridge University Press, 1989. 110–20.

– 'Shakespeare Celebrations in Times of War.' *Shakespeare Quarterly* 52 (2001): 441–55.

Harvey, A.D. *A Muse of Fire: Literature, Art and War.* London and Rio Grande: The Hambledon Press, 1998.

Hoenselaars, Ton, and Clara Calvo. 'Shakespeare and World War I.' *The Shakespeare Encyclopedia: Life, Works, World and Legacy.* Ed. Patricia Parker et al. Phoenix, AR: Greenwood Publishing (forthcoming).

Kennedy, Dennis. *Foreign Shakespeare. Contemporary Performance.* Cambridge: Cambridge University Press, 1993.

Keshen, Jeffrey A. *Saints, Sinners, and Soldiers: Canada's Second World War.* Vancouver: University of British Columbia Press, 2004.

London, John. 'Non-German Drama in the Third Reich.' *Theatre under the Nazis.* Ed. John London. Manchester: Manchester University Press, 2000.

Makaryk, Irena R. 'Wartime Shakespeare.' *Shakespeare in the Worlds of Com-*

munism and Socialism. Ed. Irena R. Makaryk and Joseph G. Price. Toronto: University of Toronto Press, 2006. 119–35.

– 'World War II.' *The Shakespeare Encyclopedia: Life, Works, World and Legacy.* Ed. Patricia Parker et al. Phoenix, AR: Greenwood Publishing (forthcoming).

Márkus, Zoltán. 'Shakespeare at War: Cultural Appropriations of Shakespeare in London, Berlin, and Budapest during World War II.' PhD Diss. New York University, 2002.

Merridale, Catherine. *Ivan's War: The Red Army 1939–1945.* London: Faber and Faber, 2005.

Parker, R.A.C. *The Second World War: A Short History.* 1989. Oxford: Oxford University Press, rev. ed. 2001.

Roach, Joseph. *Cities of the Dead.* New York: Columbia University Press, 1996.

Sanders, Julie. *Adaptation and Appropriation.* New Critical Idiom. London: Routledge, 2006.

Service, Robert. *Comrades. Communism: A World History.* London: Macmillan, 2007; Pan Books, 2008.

Strobl, Gerwin. 'Shakespeare and the Nazis.' *History Today* (May 1997): 16–21.

Symington, Rodney. *The Nazi Appropriation of Shakespeare.* Lewiston, NY: Edwin Mellen, 2005.

Thompson, James, Jenny Hughes, and Michael Balfour. *Performance in Place of War.* London, New York, and Calcutta: Seagull Books, 2009.

Wolfit, Donald. 'Shakespeare in Wartime.' *First Interval: The Autobiography of Donald Wolfit.* London: Odhams Press, 1954. 192–234.

1 German Shakespeare, the Third Reich, and the War

WERNER HABICHT

In September 1939 the Kammerspiele, one of the two major playhouses in Munich, was to open its season with a new production of *Hamlet*. When the scheduled date approached, the war had begun. One of the restrictions now imposed on public life was a ban on performances of plays by enemy dramatists. Accordingly, a local Nazi functionary hastened to order the cancellation of Shakespeare's tragedy. The director of the Kammerspiele, not entirely persuaded, checked with the Reichsdramaturg (Rainer Schlösser, head of the theatre department of the Ministry of Propaganda) in Berlin, and was assured that Shakespeare was to be treated as a German author. Thus, although delayed by two months, *Hamlet* did reach the stage.

This incident is characteristic of German attitudes toward Shakespeare in general, and of the vagaries and inconsistencies of Nazi cultural practice in particular. For at least a century there had been patriots who objected to the cultivation of the British Bard, especially in times of Anglo-German political friction or war. But invariably more influential patriots succeeded in vindicating Shakespeare, invoking the common Germanic heritage or praising the German spirit for having adopted Shakespeare as a truly national classic. Irritations of this kind had occurred in 1933 when the Nazi regime came to power, assumed control of public institutions, including theatres, and insisted on ideological conformity. Hitler considered the theatre, alongside schools and universities, an indispensable instrument of an education aimed at activating national and racial consciousness of the masses (Ziegler 5). In May 1933 Dr Joseph Goebbels, the newly installed minister of propaganda, told a convention of theatre directors that German drama of the future was to be 'heroic,' 'steely romantic,' 'unsentimentally factual,' and 'national with grand pathos,' or else it would not be at all (Goebbels 36). These catchwords were immediately expanded into programmatic theories, position papers, and hasty projects. Traditional theatres, whether private or supported by the states or cities, continued to function, but there was an effort to turn them into showcases of the new regime. Politically or racially unreliable artists were dismissed, programs were supervised, and restrictions were imposed on non-German plays. The naturalist dramas and experimental performances of classic plays that had galvanized the theatre of the 1920s were now condemned as symptoms of degenerate art. Conservative productions of selected classics were tolerated, at least for the time being, as the 'new' kind of heroic drama had not yet taken on a satisfactory aesthetic shape.

The suitability of Shakespeare's plays did not remain undisputed. Some authors, ready to provide the kind of drama envisaged by Goebbels, objected that Shakespearean emphasis on character portrayal was too individualist to be compatible with the community-oriented ideal – a reservation that persisted throughout the twelve years of the Third Reich. But Shakespeare's Nazi defenders, including scholars and educators, again a potent majority, hastened to offer new interpretations, stressing heroic aspects rather than character problems, and pointing out that as a 'Nordic visionary' Shakespeare advocated the submission of the individual person to higher public values (the state in the tragedies and histories, social structures in the comedies), and that many protagonists of his tragedies and histories were, indeed, Germanic heroes and epitomes of strong leadership, commanding and enforcing their subjects' allegiance. Julius Caesar, Coriolanus, and Ulysses were extolled as supreme examples, and even Hamlet, Richard III, and Macbeth were awarded heroic halos. A new hierarchy of the most valuable plays was proposed, with 'heroic plays' (*Julius Caesar, Coriolanus*) and 'Nordic tragedies' (*Hamlet, King Lear, Macbeth, Richard II*) at the top of the list, followed by 'racial dramas' (useful to enhance an audience's racial consciousness: *The Merchant of Venice, Othello, The Tempest*), and, lastly, 'comedies' pure and simple (*Twelfth Night, The Winter's Tale*) (Schröter 206). Thus Shakespeare performances continued to flourish – not so much because they adopted principles such as these, which would have made them rather boring, but because they were inspired by an imagination released by Shakespearean drama itself.[1]

The situation did not change incisively at the beginning of the war. When in 1940 the dramatist Curt Langenbeck launched his manifesto *Wiedergeburt der Tragödie aus dem Geist der Zeit* [Rebirth of Tragedy from the Spirit of the Time], which rejected Shakespeare's open form, ironic mode, and individualist stance as a model for the 'new' drama (and his own work) and recommended Greek tragedy as a better point of orientation, a good deal of public pro-Shakespearean protest forced him to modify his position. Although enemy dramatists were banned from the stages,[2] an explicit exception was made for Shakespeare. Hence, despite initial irritations, Shakespeare performances and Shakespeare studies could continue in much the same way as before the war. The only other British dramatist who escaped the ban was George Bernard Shaw, both because he was not English but Irish and because his criticism of English society in many of his plays was felt to be in harmony with Nazi attitudes; *Saint Joan* and *The Apple Cart* were favourites, while the anti-heroic *Arms and the Man* was strictly forbidden.

By way of illustration it may be useful to look briefly at the historical and biographical context of the Munich *Hamlet* of 1939 mentioned above. Its producer, Otto Falckenberg, had been director of the Kammerspiele since 1917, when, in the middle of the First World War, he had catapulted himself into prominence with ground-breaking productions of Strindberg's late plays and Shakespeare's *As You Like It*. Falckenberg established a distinctive style, often described as poetic magic, as it explored the rhythm, the musicality, and the imaginative potential of the texts, and presented, as he himself once put it, 'a play as a magic image of real action, just as Cézanne has painted his apples' (Petzet and Falckenberg 327). Under his guidance the Kammerspiele became a centre of progressive theatre art in the 1920s. In 1933, in the early days of the Third Reich, Falckenberg was arrested by the Gestapo. A report from a member of his staff concerning a letter that had reached him from Moscow automatically led to an assumption that he must be a Communist spy, especially since some of his previous seasons had included expressionist and social-critical plays (among them early scripts by Brecht) that the Nazis now condemned as 'degenerate' or 'cultural bolshevist.' Since the allegations turned out to be unfounded (the letter from Moscow was a harmless New Year greeting from a colleague who had emigrated), and since his artistic merits were indisputable, Falckenberg was permitted to resume his position, but he found that several of his top actors had either fled or been dismissed. Although he considered emigration himself, he decided to remain and make an effort to protect his theatre from political perversions. Such an attempt would not have been possible without compromises with the controlling authorities, but he never became a member of the Nazi Party. He increasingly avoided directing modern drama, adamantly refused to stage the propagandist Nazi plays recommended to him (with one unavoidable exception),[3] and turned to classical works that allowed him to pursue the poetic magic of his performance style. His productions included remarkable works by Shakespeare, including *Cymbeline*, *The Winter's Tale* and *Troilus and Cressida*. Such plays, not exactly suited for heroic reinterpretations, were seldom staged elsewhere; he had directed some of them previously but their new versions had a more disturbing impact. For example, *Troilus and Cressida*, which in his production of 1925 highlighting the ironies of war and love had amused audiences, became in 1936 an overwhelming 'verdict on the present time,' as his colleague Hans Schweikart remembered (Euler 140), and Thersites's outcry 'still wars and lechery, nothing else holds fashion' was heard as a sinister prophecy. At the same time Schweikart launched his own series of more popular Shakespeare plays in a more realist style at the competing Munich playhouse, the Residenztheater.

What followed at the Kammerspiele, however, was a series of intrigues by Nazi members of its board of trustees aimed at restricting Falckenberg's directorial competence if not removing him altogether. At last Hitler, who apparently had nostalgic memories of the Kammerspiele, intervened. He had attended the theatre several times before he became dictator, and even after his rise to power had greatly appreciated a performance of a play by Tirso de Molina. Hitler summoned the mayor of Munich, informed him that Falckenberg was one of the three or four most outstanding German theatre artists who deserved to work unmolested, and promised ample funds for a restoration of his playhouse, to make it worthy of the city where the Nazi movement had originated. By the time the restoration was about to begin, however, Hitler had started the war by invading Poland, and the promised funds were diverted to serve martial purposes. At this point *Hamlet* was temporarily removed from the program, and the local Nazis soon resumed their intrigues. Falckenberg, however, remained faithful to his style, as his subsequent wartime productions testify: examples include *A Midsummer Night's Dream* staged in 1940 as a dangerous nightmare rather than a harmless comedy, and a 1942 production of *Othello* that was not entirely compatible with Nazi racist politics. Schweikart's Shakespeare series at the Residenztheater also continued, less provocatively perhaps, with *Twelfth Night* (1941), *The Merry Wives of Windsor* (1942), and a production of *Macbeth* (1942) dedicated to the German army. After the war Falckenberg was again arrested, this time by the American occupation army, doubtless because of the favour temporarily bestowed upon him by Hitler; although he was cleared of Nazi partisanship, he was not permitted to resume directorship of his theatre. Soon thereafter he died.[4] After a brief interim directorship Hans Schweikart became his successor; he remained for the following sixteen years, and the Munich Kammerspiele has kept up its reputation as a progressive theatre up until now.

This is just one example. Comparable stories could be, and have been, told about some of the most prominent theatre artists of the time, notably the directors of the two major playhouses in Berlin – the privileged theatrical centre – both of whom were known for their remarkable Shakespeare productions. Gustaf Gründgens had been appointed to lead the Berlin Staatstheater (controlled by Hermann Göring as Minister President of Prussia) because of his charismatic popularity as an actor, despite his lack of particular Nazi leanings. Heinz Hilpert, favoured by Goebbels, had taken over the Deutsches Theater, despite his previous close association with Max Reinhardt (who as a Jew had to leave the country). As Göring is reported to have remarked, it seemed 'easier to make an artist into a National Socialist than the other way around' (Grange 80). But in fact it was not at all easy. These theatre artists were determined to make use of the freedom they were allowed and occasionally added oppositional touches: for example, in Jürgen Fehling's *Richard III* (1937) at Gründgens's Staatstheater, Werner Krauss's Richard Gloucester, far from being the fascinating 'Nordic' power politician recommended by commentators (including chief ideologist Alfred Rosenberg [306]), was in fact a demonic manipulator, a source of evil, limping on the stage like Goebbels in real life, while Clarence's murderers wore black costumes that resembled SS uniforms.[5] During the war years, however, both Gründgens and Hilpert had to cope with increasing criticism and restrictions by their political masters.

The provincial theatres all over Germany, where regular Shakespeare performances continued (war or no war), tended to conform more readily to the official Nazi ideology. The Berlin theatres, however, commanded special nation-wide attention. The chief reviewer of the official Nazi newspaper, *Völkischer Beobachter*, was convinced that 'thanks to dramaturgic activity and performative energy bordering on the miraculous, the great productions and decisive caesuras in the chronicle of modern theatre took place in the wartime seasons' (Biedrzynski, Preface). This, explained a more independent critic, was so because 'independent of the demands, wishes and proclamations of cultural revolutionaries unfamiliar with the art of the theatre, a new dramatic style resulting from pure dedicated work with the text has crystallized' (Ruppel 22). In fact performances were by no means uniform. For example, near the beginning of the war, the two leading Berlin playhouses offered competing versions of *Richard II*, one directed by Jürgen Fehling, the other by Heinz Hilpert; Richard was played by Gustaf Gründgens and Rudolf Forster respectively. Both directors exhibited, though with radically different approaches and emphasis, the complexities surrounding the confrontation of the suffering king and the active usurper. Fehling individualized the tragedy of Richard; Hilpert universalized the political constellation, revealing the ambiguity of historical processes. Reviewers remained puzzled by the problem of legitimacy and usurpation.[6] A number of impressive, if not disturbing, Berlin Shakespeare productions were to follow. The Staatstheater presented *Measure for Measure* and *As You Like It* in 1940, *Julius Caesar* and *The Merry Wives of Windsor* in 1941, *The Taming of the Shrew* in 1942, and *Othello* in 1944; some of these productions were directed by Gründgens himself, while others were directed by colleagues such as Lothar Müthel or Karl-Heinz Stroux. At the Deutsches Theater Heinz Hilpert went on to produce *King Lear* and *A Midsummer Night's Dream* in 1940, *Antony and Cleopatra* in 1943, and *The Winter's Tale* in 1944. Other Berlin theatres contributed additional Shakespeare plays.

These productions were supported by a special kind of war propaganda, similar to that promulgated at the beginning of the First World War. The continued presence of Shakespeare now needed revised justifications that were somehow compatible with the anti-English war propaganda that began to rage in public. Invoking ethnic kinship would no longer do. A press campaign launched in 1940 applauded and justified wartime Shakespeare performances. For example, a February 1940 issue of *Wille und Macht*, the organ for Hitler Youth leaders, was devoted to this matter. In it Baldur von Schirach, top leader of the Hitler Jugend, asserted that 150 years of German Shakespeare appropriation 'even in the face of the [British] enemy' had proved how open-minded, quality-conscious, and fair German culture was (Preface). In the same issue Herbert A. Frenzel of the Reichdramaturg's staff declared that Shakespeare had become part of world literature, and that thanks to Goethe 'we [the Germans] have shown to the world how world literature ought to be cultivated,' whereas the English had, thanks to Shakespeare, received a 'dramatic impulse, which to make use of and to develop they have been neither capable nor willing' (2).

For, as the dramatist Hermann Burte added, Puritanism and liberalism had fragmented the British nation, while 'Germany is now at the point where Britain was before the battle with the Armada' (7). The tone, which was slightly more moderate than it had been in the First World War, may be attributable to the fact that, after the conquest of France, Hitler still entertained megalomaniac dreams of an ultimate arrangement with Britain by which world dominance could be shared between Germany and the British Empire. Indeed, propaganda was exported into the occupied territories as soon as they were invaded. 'Today,' asserted a theatre historian as late as 1944, 'all over Europe (except for Britain and Russia) the German actor stands close to the German soldier' (Kindermann 51). German theatres were established and subsidized in countries such as Czechoslovakia (Prague and elsewhere), Poland (especially Łódź and Poznań), Belarus (Minsk), the Netherlands (The Hague), and France (Strasbourg, Mulhouse) (Daibler 282). Although these houses were mainly meant to provide entertaining fare such as farces, melodramas, and operettas, the occasional Shakespeare play did come forward. The French in particular were supposed to be in need of an introduction to the Germanic Bard, of whom they allegedly knew next to nothing, even though at the same time the traditional French theatre culture, especially in Paris, was allowed to continue on condition that the Jewish element was eliminated and plays suggesting Resistance ideas (such as Jean Anouilh's *Antigone*) were removed.

When Hitler had to realize that Churchill's rejection of diplomatic attempts aimed at a separate Anglo-German peace treaty was irreversible, Nazi interest in Shakespeare began to dwindle. All Shakespeare (and Shaw) performances were stopped in April 1941 for at least six months. No explicit reason was made public. It seems that the dictator himself had dropped a remark that for the time being (when the German air force was about to lose the 'Battle of Britain') the presence of Shakespeare could have a negative psychological effect. A Shakespeare festival pompously planned for Vienna was cancelled (or postponed, as the official version had it), as was the annual meeting of the German Shakespeare Society in Weimar. Later in 1941 Shakespeare was re-admitted, but from then on each new production required special permission from the censuring authority, who also saw that productions were rationed to one per season on any playhouse's schedule. When Hilpert submitted a program proposal for the 1942–3 season of the Deutsches Theater that contained three Shakespeare plays and three plays by Shaw, he was threatened with 'severe consequences' if he did not change his plans (Wardetzky 341 f.).

Some academic advice in selecting reliable plays was expected from scholars of the humanities. Many of these academics (unless they had to serve in the army) were enlisted in a wartime project devoted to critical research of 'enemy culture.' One section of this project addressed the problem of Shakespeare (Hausmann 297–364); among its printed results were studies explaining which plays had a contemporary importance that consisted of a special 'closeness to National Socialism' unrecognized in England. Other scholars set out to review and revalue the history of Shakespeare's glorious reception in Germany: Professor Wolfgang Keller, editor of the *Shakespeare Jahrbuch*, died in 1943, leaving his work incomplete; Ernst Leopold Stahl's 800-page history of Shakespeare on the German stage, a work of hitherto unprecedented scope and thoroughness despite some traces of Nazi discourse, was published soon after the war as *Shakespeare und das deutsche Theater* [Shakespeare and the German Theatre] (1948). The immediate impact of all this research was predictably minimal.

Hence the number of Shakespeare performances began to decrease and the choice of plays was narrowed down. Comedies were relatively unmolested, with *Twelfth Night* at the top of performance statistics, closely followed by *The Taming of the Shrew*. *A Midsummer Night's Dream* lost its rank as the most popular comedy, divorced from its traditional marriage with Mendelssohn's romantic music owing to the composer's Jewish origin; either the efforts of pure-blooded composers to provide alternative incidental music proved less attractive, or the play turned out to be as gloomy as Falckenberg's production of 1940, with a concept that required the replacement of both the Mendelssohn score and the romantic Schlegel translation for aesthetic reasons (Petzet and Falckenberg 363–9). *The Merchant of Venice* was a special case; it seemed useful for anti-Semitic propaganda, but not everyone was inclined to stage it as such.[7] The English history plays disappeared entirely. There is no record of a performance of *Henry V* during the entire Nazi period – curiously perhaps, since academic critics insisted on praising the hero's ideal kingship and his Germanic self-assurance set off against French corruption. *Richard II*, *Henry IV*, and *Richard III* were staged successfully only during the early part of the war. There was even a production of *Richard III* in occupied Prague in 1941, before this play's replacement by the more acceptable *Macbeth* was recommended. *Macbeth*, as a 'Nordic ballad' about a hero tragically overwhelmed while fighting the English, enjoyed Nazi favour to the very last. So did *Othello* – again curiously, considering its interracial problem, but the moor was invariably presented as an Arabic nobleman rather than as a black African (Bonnell, *Shylock* 173–6). The Cobourg Landestheater even planned an *Othello* for the 1944–5 season, which the Reichsdramaturg approved in August 1944, shortly before all theatres went dark. On the other hand, *Hamlet* performances became less frequent. The politically correct view would have called for an active, heroic, Nordic protagonist, not a procrastinating one, not the tender soul overwhelmed by the enormity of his task as described by Goethe. Apparently not every actor was ready to play Hamlet as ruthlessly 'steely' as did Willy Birgel, a well-known film star at the time, in the Mannheim theatre. Another case in point was *Coriolanus*, whose protagonist had been favourably compared with Hitler during the early years of the Third Reich, praised as an outstanding leader contrasting with the masses misguided by egoistic agitators of a false democracy. But this comparison also caused discomfort; one scholarly commentator described the play as a 'lesson about false leadership' (Heerwagen 241–7). By the time the war began, *Coriolanus* was no longer seen on any German stage. The war play *Troilus and Cressida* had to go because of its lack of heroism, and doubtless also because this play and *Richard III* had by then been convincingly staged as anti-Nazi plays in Switzerland, where many exiled German actors had taken refuge. And when Hilpert staged *Antony and Cleopatra* in 1943, the production elicited the protest of chief ideologist Alfred Rosenberg, who argued that 'a play in which a warlord leaves the battlefield to run after his mistress must be judged as particularly negative' (Drewniak 252).

The Third Reich theatre ended nine months before the downfall of the Third Reich itself. All German theatres were closed on 1 September 1944, when the Allied forces were approaching the German borders. Theatre artists were sent to the army or to work in the arms industry. One of the last Berlin performances, scheduled in the afternoon because the capital was nightly bombed by the British Air Force, was one of *The Winter's Tale*, directed by Hilpert at the Deutsches Theater. This 'romance' may have been intended, like many films of that time, as an escapist diversion from the brutal reality of the war; the Bohemian scenes are said to have been particularly attractive. But in fact the story of Leontes, who in his delusion tears down his own house, was prophetic enough.

After the war, when the Third Reich, German nationalism, and ideas of militant heroism had thoroughly collapsed, many theatres were in ruins. Companies re-emerged within a year or two, if only on provisional stages, now controlled and censured by the military governments of the occupation armies who were determined to eradicate all traces of Nazi influence and recommended modern foreign plays, albeit different ones in the four occupation zones. Shakespeare, too, was revived, with special encouragement in the British zone, and in any case in an unprecedented international context. There was reorientation, but there was continuity as well. For example, the Munich Kammerspiele reopened in October 1945 with *Macbeth*, one of the last plays seen in that city during the war; now, according to the program note (printed on a tiny sheet because of paper shortage), its 'visionary power' was to reflect 'the essence of that inferno through which we have gone in the past twelve years' and to mark a new beginning (Petzet 424). The same could also be said of *The Winter's Tale*, the last Shakespeare play Hilpert had staged in wartime Berlin, and the play with which he began a new career in provincial Germany in 1946. He then took over the playhouse of the small university town of Göttingen, where in the 1950s his numerous Shakespeare productions became legendary. Other theatre artists who had been prominent during the war, though silenced for a while, also made new beginnings in the Western zones, as did Gründgens in Dusseldorf and later in Hamburg. Another notable example was Gustav Rudolf Sellner, whose career had begun within the Nazi context itself. After a period of philosophical self-reflection he resumed his activities at the theatre of Darmstadt, which under his direction became another mecca of Shakespeare performance in the 1950s, most notably because of his *A Midsummer Night's Dream*, which replaced the romanticism of Mendelssohn's incidental music with a more disharmonious score by Carl Orff, combined with images reminiscent of Hieronymus Bosch phantasies, continuing along the sinister lines begun by Falckenberg in 1940. Audience response may have been different from what it had been before, but on the whole the styles and trends of Shakespeare performance, shunning daring experimentation, did not change fundamentally and remained faithful to the dignity of the author's dramatic art. Indeed they tended to be, at least in the Western parts of Germany, restorative and conservative. It was only in the mid-1960s that a new generation, rebelling against ideologies of their elders, began to subject Shakespeare to iconoclastic deconstructions and provocative reconstructions.

Notes

1 Retrospective accounts and documentations of theatre politics in the Third
  Reich with incidental remarks on the role of Shakespeare include Joseph
  Wulf, *Theater und Film im Dritten Reich* (Gütersloh: Mohn, 1964; repr.
  Frankfurt: Ullstein, 1983); Günther Rühle, *Zeit und Theater*, vol. 5 (Frankfurt: Ullstein, 1974) 47–52; Bogusław Drewniak, *Das Theater im NS-Staat*
  245–54; Jutta Wardetzky, *Theaterpolitik im faschistischen Deutschland*; Glen W.
  Gadberry, ed., *Theatre in the Third Reich, the Prewar Years: Essays on Theatre
  in Nazi Germany* (Westport, CT: Greenwood Press, 1995); Henning Rischbieter, ed., *Theater im Dritten Reich* (Seelze-Velber: Kallmeyer, 2000) 297–316;
  Gerwin Stobl, *The Swastika and the Stage* (Cambridge: Cambridge University Press, 2007). On the role of Shakespeare in particular, see Wilhelm
  Hortmann, *Shakespeare on the German Stage: The Twentieth Century* (Cambridge: Cambridge University Press, 1998); Rodney Symington, *The Nazi
  Appropriation of Shakespeare*; Andrew G. Bonnell, *Shylock in Germany* – the
  latter three have extensive bibliographies – and Werner Habicht, 'Shakespeare und der deutsche Shakespeare-Mythus im Dritten Reich,' *Anglistik:
  Research Paradigms and Institutional Policies*, ed. Stephan Kohl (Trier: Wis-
  senschaftlicher Verlag, 2005) 79–111.
2 Nor was it permitted to employ persons of enemy nationality in any theatre, as decreed by the Reichskulturkammer on 23 May 1940. Enemy countries were defined as Great Britain, including the Empire; France, including
  overseas possessions; the Netherlands and Belgium, both including their
  colonies; Egypt; Sudan; Iraq; and Poland (Circular Rp/Bo. 781/40). Russian plays were allowed to enjoy temporary popularity as a result of the
  Hitler-Stalin treaty of 1939, but the ban on these was even more emphatic
  after Germany invaded the Soviet Union; on 9 February 1943 Reichsdramaturg Schlösser ordered that all plays that were even remotely Russian
  or suggested a Russian environment were to be eliminated (Circular T
  6200/500-25,1).
3 The unavoidable exception was a performance of Eberhard Wolfgang
  Möller's anti-Semitic *Rothschild siegt bei Waterloo* [Rothschild's Victory at
  Waterloo], which Falckenberg had to contribute to the party-supported
  Reichstheaterfestwoche festival in 1936; he gave the play a humanist touch
  that is said to have infuriated its author (Pargner 185 f.).
4 In Falckenberg's autobiographical account (Petzet and Falckenberg),
  which was published during the war, references to Third Reich politics
  were carefully avoided. His activities of that period are documented in
  Birgit Pargner, *Otto Falckenberg*, especially 181–213. On the Kammerspiele,

see Wolfgang Petzet, *Theater: Die Münchner Kammerspiele 1911–1972* (1973), especially 246–327 for the detailed eye-witness report by Falckenberg's chief dramaturg.

5 In his memoirs published after the war, the dramatist Sigmund Graff, who was temporarily on the Reichsdramaturg staff, describes Fehling's *Richard III* as 'a terrible blow wielded against the regime' (270). And yet the regime did nothing to stop further performances.

6 For an account of the reception of these productions, see Endriss 303–5.

7 For *The Merchant of Venice*, see Zeno Ackermann's contribution to this volume. See also Bonnell, *Shylock* 119–69.

Works Cited

Biedrzynski, Richard. *Schauspieler, Regisseure, Intendanten*. Heidelberg: Hüthig, 1944.

Bonnell, Andrew G. *Shylock in Germany: Antisemitism and the German Theatre from the Enlightenment to the Nazis*. London and New York: Tauris Academic Studies, 2008.

– 'Shylock and Othello under the Nazis.' *German Life and Letters* 63 (2010): 166–78.

Daibler, Hans. *Schaufenster der Diktatur*. Stuttgart: Neske, 1995.

Drewniak, Bogusław. *Das Theater im NS-Staat*. Dusseldorf: Droste, 1983.

Eicher, Thomas. 'Spielplanstrukturen 1929–1944.' *Theater im Dritten Reich*. Ed. Hennig Rischbieter. Seelze-Veber: Kallmeyer, 2000.

Endriss, Beate-Ursula. *Shakespeare-Inszenierungen in Berlin 1933–1944*. Diss. Freie Universität Berlin, 1994.

Euler, Friederike. 'Theater zwischen Anpassung und Widerstand: Die Münchner Kammerspiele im Dritten Reich.' *Bayern in der NS-Zeit*. Ed. Martin Broszat and Elke Fröhlich. Munich: Oldenbourg, 1979: 2: 90–173.

Goebbels, Joseph. 'Rede des Reichspropagandaministers Dr. Joseph Goebbels vor den deutschen Theaterleitern am 8 Mai 1933.' *Das deutsche Drama* 5 (1933): 28–40.

Graff, Sigmund. *Von S.M. zu N.S.* Munich: Wels, 1963.

Grange, William. 'Ordained Hands on the Altar of Art: Gründgens, Hilpert, and Fehling in Berlin.' *Theatre in the Third Reich, the Prewar Years: Essays on Theatre in Nazi Germany*. Ed. Glen W. Gadberry. Westport, CT: Greenwood, 1995. 75–89.

Hausmann, Frank Rutger. *Anglistik und Amerikanistik im Dritten Reich*. Frankfurt: Klostermann, 2003.

Heerwagen, Heinrich. 'Shakespeares *Coriolanus* als Beitrag zur Führerfrage.' *Politische Erziehung: Monatsschrift des NS-Lehrerbundes* (1936): 241–7.

Herbert A. Frenzel. 'Ist Shakespeare ein Problem?' *Wille und Macht* 2–3.

Hermann Burte. 'Der englische und der deutsche Tag.' *Wille und Macht* 3–9.

Kindermann, Heinz. *Die europäische Sendung des deutschen Theaters.* Vienna: Ringbuchhandlung, 1944.

Langenbeck, Curt. *Wiedergeburt der Tragödie aus dem Geist der Zeit.* Munich: Langen-Müller, 1940.

Pargner, Birgit. *Otto Falckenberg: Regiepoet der Münchner Kammerspiele.* Leipzig: Henschel, 2005.

Petzet, Wolfgang. *Theater: Die Münchner Kammerspiele 1911–1972.* Munich: Desch, 1973.

Petzet, Wolfgang, and Otto Falckenberg. *Otto Falckenberg: Mein Leben – Mein Theater: Nach Gesprächen und Dokumenten aufgezeichnet.* Munich: Zinnen, 1944.

Rosenberg, Alfred. *Der Mythus des 20. Jahrhunderts.* 5th ed. Munich: Hoheneichen, 1933.

Ruppel, Karl H. *Berliner Schauspiel: Dramaturgische Betrachtungen 1936–1942.* Berlin: Neff, 1943.

Schröter, Werner. 'Grundsätzliches zur Deutung fremdsprachlicher Literatur.' *Die Neueren Sprachen* 46 (1938): 199–207.

Symington, Rodney. *The Nazi Appropriation of Shakespeare: Cultural Politics in the Third Reich.* Lewiston, NY: Edwin Mellen Press 2005.

von Schirach, Baldur. 'Shakespeare 1940.' *Wille und Macht* 1.

Wardetzky, Jutta. *Theaterpolitik im faschistischen Deutschland.* Berlin: Henschel, 1983.

Wille und Macht. Führerorgan der nationalsozialistischen Jugend 3 (1 Feb. 1940): 1–25.

Ziegler, Hans Severus. *Das Theater des deutschen Volkes.* Leipzig: Voigtländer, 1935.

2 Shakespearean Negotiations in the Perpetrator Society: German Productions of *The Merchant of Venice* during the Second World War

ZENO ACKERMANN

It may well appear as a self-evident truth that *The Merchant of Venice* provided an ideal pretext for National Socialist propaganda. In his magisterial study on the Shylock topos, John Gross states that the play 'enjoyed special popularity from the outset' of Nazi rule (294). Such notions continue to be influential in the wider cultural sphere. A recent book, in which actor Gareth Armstrong describes his experiences while touring with a solo program on Shylock, provides a dense summary of pervasive clichés concerning the status of *The Merchant* in Hitler's Germany. Referring to ongoing anxieties that Shakespeare might have been 'a Jew-hater,' Armstrong – who is generally entertaining, perceptive, and well-informed – explains: 'The Nazis certainly thought he was. They encouraged productions of the play throughout the Reich during the thirties and the war years, and in Vienna, the Gauleiter commanded a performance on the grounds that "every Jew active in Europe is a danger to European culture"' (46).

In reality, however, the stance of the Nazi bureaucracy and of cultural makers towards the play was much more twisted. Recent scholarship – especially by Thomas Eicher, Jörg Monschau, Rodney Symington, and Andrew G. Bonnell[1] – has pointed out that the beginning of the National Socialist hegemony actually coincided with a notable relegation of *The Merchant of Venice* on the programs of German theatres. Since the end of the eighteenth century the play had always held an important place in the German Shakespeare canon. According to the performance statistics published in the yearbooks of the German Shakespeare Society,[2] *The Merchant* ranked first among Shakespeare plays in 1927; it held third place in 1928, 1929, and 1931, and fourth place in 1932. By 1941, however, the number of performances would reach an all-time low of three shows, staged in a provincial theatre in Bohemia (annexed to the Reich in consequence of the 1938 Munich Agreement): in the listings for that year *The Merchant* held twenty-first place, just ahead of *The Merry Wives of Windsor*. There were still nine new productions during the 1933–4 theatre season, but numbers dropped to usually one or two for the following seasons (Eicher 304). Thomas Eicher attributes these declining numbers to systematic interventions by the administration, claiming that the play was in effect 'stopped' (303–8; quote 304).[3] Indeed, when Paul Rose, manager of the large private Rose Theatre in Berlin, asked for permission to stage the play in the 1937–8 season, the responsible supervisor in the Propaganda Ministry crossed out *The Merchant* on Rose's list – and inserted *Othello* in its place (Freydank 148, 154 note 24).

Most current studies can be seen struggling with such information: while acknowledging the dramatic drop in performance numbers, they tend to focus on the few productions that actually did take place – in effect raising the impression that, after all, the play *was* a seminal tool of Nazi propaganda (cf., for example, Bonnell 171–2). And indeed, as a figure or as a stereotype, Shylock certainly was an important reference point both for the self-image of National Socialists and for their anti-Semitic propaganda. According to the protocols of his table talk, Hitler is said to have declared in July 1942 that Shakespeare's portrayal of Shylock provided a 'timelessly valid characterization of the Jew' (Picker 457, entry for 24 July 1942; my translation). It might even be claimed that significant connections existed between the evolution of the *Stormtrooper* cliché of 'the Jew' during the lead-up to Nazi rule and contemporary representations of Shylock on stage. It is also true that there were several high-profile propagandistic productions of *The Merchant of Venice*. The best known is the 1943 production at Vienna's Burgtheater, in which Shylock was played by Werner Krauss (see fig. 2.1), an actor who had contributed a number of Jewish stock characters to Veit Harlan's notorious propaganda film *Jud Süss* [Jew Süss] (1940). Less well known is the fact that there even were plans for producing a film adaptation of *The Merchant*: Harlan was to direct and shooting was scheduled to commence in November 1944.[4] This might well mean that *The Merchant* was considered fit to serve as the last stand of Nazi propaganda.

In light of these contradictions, it seems that a new and systematic interpretation of the functions of the play under the National Socialist hegemony and within the context of the Holocaust is called for. Such

2.1. Werner Krauss as Shylock in *The Merchant of Venice*, directed by Lothar Müthel, Burgtheater, Vienna, May 1943. Österreichisches Theatermuseum, Vienna.

an interpretation should explain the tensions between the obvious ideological significance of the text and the marked reticence in staging the play. It should also look into the question of when, how, and why this reticence was overcome, so that methodical propagandistic productions finally seemed feasible. Starting from the assumption that *The Merchant of Venice* was, quite literally, a 'problem play' for National Socialist cultural policy, this essay will try to address – provisionally and tentatively – three major questions:

First of all, how was the contemporary reception of *The Merchant* related to National Socialist anti-Semitism and the Holocaust? In trying to suggest answers, the emphasis will be placed on the period between 1939 and 1945. However, it will also be necessary to consider developments before the outbreak of war and during the Weimar Republic. The second key question, or rather set of questions, concerns the vexing but seminal problem of change and continuity. Was there a decisive break in the play's reception history in 1933? Did such a break occur later during the National Socialist period? Was the Shylock portrayed by Werner Krauss in the notorious 1943 production at the Vienna Burgtheater essentially different from his interpretation of the role under (Jewish) director Max Reinhardt in 1921? It will not be possible to pursue all of these questions systematically, but they will always be present in the background of the following interpretations. My third question is really a hypothesis, but since it provides a counterpoint to the assumption that *The Merchant* simply *must* have been a favourite during the 'Third Reich,' I would like to spell it out in the very beginning: How afraid were the Nazis of Shylock? How much 'Angst' did Shakespeare's profoundly ambivalent figure of a thwarted Jewish avenger inspire in the proponents of an eliminatory anti-Semitism?

In voicing such a hypothesis I should be careful to point out that clear-cut generalizations such as 'the Nazis' always carry the danger of obscuring the complexity of historical processes. Recent scholarship on National Socialist society and the Holocaust has emphasized the tangled interplay – the tensions as well as the synergies – between various groups and agents whose dispositions, interests, and intentions need to be differentiated.[5] In trying to understand the interaction of state and society within the ideological framework of the so-called 'Volksgemeinschaft' ('community of the people'), we should be wary of reducing National Socialist rule in Germany to one-directional acts of domination and control. Rather, it may be helpful to follow Alf Lüdtke in approaching National Socialist rule as a set of 'social practices.'[6]

I use the term 'National Socialist hegemony' in order to indicate the dialectic of domination and agency that characterized the political, social, and cultural atmosphere of the so-called Third Reich. Such a conceptualization is bound to change our perspectives on the functions of *The Merchant* within the context of Nazi propaganda. Traditionally, propaganda has often been seen as a simple process of programmed indoctrination, exerted by specific institutions and agreeing to a clear set of intentions. If – and insofar as – National Socialist rule can be regarded as a hegemonic system in the Gramscian sense of the term, however, it is necessary to apply a more open concept of propaganda. According to such a concept, propaganda emerges from complex processes of mediation in which the personal interests and intentions of individual cultural makers are negotiated with – and offer themselves for integration into – the political and ideological programs of the state apparatus. The role of the theatres in National Socialist Germany clearly is a case in point.

Evading Shylock (1933–41)

The relegation of *The Merchant of Venice* after 1933 certainly was not due to a general demotion of Shakespeare and his plays. It is true that there was some discussion about whether the works of Britain's national poet should be allowed to play a pronounced role in German cultural life. Also, it seems that by 1939 the authorities interfered more frequently with the staging of Shakespeare's plays (a process that actually began some time before the commencement of the war); by April 1941 even a short-lived 'ban' on Shakespeare productions may have been in place (Eicher 298–301). Looking at the entire National Socialist period, however, we can see Shakespeare vying with Friedrich Schiller for the place of most often produced playwright (Eicher 297). Indeed, the National Socialist hegemony was able to build on an established discourse of appropriation, according to which Shakespeare's works had been translated or even transplanted into German culture (cf. Symington). The German Shakespeare Society had long since established so-called 'Shakespeare-Pflege' – that is, the 'culture' or even the 'cultivation' of Shakespeare's works on German soil – as a national obligation.[7]

Although it had often been fostered by liberal nationalists such as the eminent Jewish scholar Friedrich Gundolf – whose widely influential study *Shakespeare und der deutsche Geist* [Shakespeare and the German Spirit] was published in 1911[8] – the notion that Shakespeare was somehow inherent in German culture was adaptable to reactionary and even racist readings. A good example of how racist tendencies intruded into German Shakespeare scholarship is provided by the admission of Hans F.K. Günther to the executive board of the Shakespeare Society in 1936. Indeed, Günther was not a Shakespeare scholar but the most highly profiled 'race scientist' in National Socialist academia. In 1937, the new board member was even allowed to present the inaugural lecture at the society's annual meeting. He presumed to talk about 'Shakespeare's Girls and Women' from the perspective of eugenics (see Günther; cf. Strobl).

If Shakespeare could be bent to serve the ends of an ideologue as fierce as Günther, why then was *The Merchant of Venice* at first avoided? Wilhelm Hortmann and Jörg Monschau have suggested that the reticence of theatre managers may have been one reason for the declining performance numbers: expecting that authorities would accept only a radically anti-Semitic interpretation of the issues raised by the play, the less ideologically committed probably abstained. On the other hand, the argument continues, Shakespeare's play also offered considerable difficulties for those who were intent on promulgating anti-Semitic messages (Hortmann 135; Monschau 1–6; Márkus 148). Jessica's role in the plot was the most obvious stumbling block; if this role is viewed from a racist perspective the comedy seems to make 'miscegenation' part of its dramatic resolution. In 1936 author and translator Hermann Kroepelin approached the theatre department of the Propaganda Ministry (the so-called Reichsdramaturgie) to suggest a solution. He explained that it was certainly impossible to publicly stage and condone an instance of mixing 'Aryan blood with Jewish blood.' At the same time, Kroepelin pointed out in his letter, *The Merchant* was a play 'that, on account of its other things, we would not like to do without.' His way out of the dilemma was to have Jessica, at the last possible moment, give in to her father's pleadings and desist from marrying a non-Jew (qtd in Eicher 304; my translation).

A different solution, preferred by the head of the theatre department, Dr Rainer Schlösser, was to insinuate that Jessica really was Shylock's non-Jewish foster-child. According to a list of suggested changes (qtd in Eicher 304–8) compiled by the Propaganda Ministry on the basis of the favoured Schlegel translation, all passages referring to Jessica as a Jew or as the daughter of Shylock were to be either dropped or rewritten. However, Schlösser's version suggests that the union of Jessica and Lorenzo was not the only hurdle that the play presented in the eyes of National Socialist cultural administrators. The adaptation also expunged passages that make the conflict between Shylock and the Christians appear as a conflict between different religious rather than different ethnic or racial groups. Accordingly, Shylock's determined refusal of Bassanio's invitation ('Yes, to smell pork, to eat of the habitation which your prophet, the Nazarite, conjured the devil into! I will buy with you, sell with you, talk with you, walk with you, and so following; but I will not eat with you, drink with you, nor pray with you' [1.3.27–30]) was cut.

The most drastic change in the Propaganda Ministry's adaptation was to delete – entirely! – Shylock's famous monologue in act 3, scene 1. Did Schlösser seek to evade the universalist humanism that can potentially be seen at work in this speech? I believe that there were also different concerns – concerns that relate to the status or stature of Shylock and that take us to the heart of the ambivalent relationships to the play that were at work within National Socialist society. The issue becomes clearer if we turn to the public reception of a production staged exactly at the moment of transition towards the National Socialist hegemony. In September 1932 the Deutsches Theater am Rhein, an illustrious new branch of the Cologne public theatre, was opened with *The Merchant of Venice*, directed by Fritz Holl with Walther Richter as Shylock. The reviews of the new production remind us about the ideological climate that was in place even before Hitler was installed as chancellor some four months later. Walter Schmits, the reviewer of the *Kölnische Zeitung*, described Richter's Shylock: 'His appearance was repulsive and vermin-like rather than terrible. He had a gaunt, sickly pale and grubby face. His thin beard seemed to have been attacked by an unappetizing lichen. His clumsy, fat body shuffled forward, waddling and staggering on its flat feet' (qtd in Weisker 210; my translation). In a manner that is characteristic for this kind of review, the short passage boasts such a wealth of descriptive vocabulary that it is almost untranslatable. This exercise in distilling disgust serves an obvious ideological purpose: dwelling on the supposedly repellent qualities of his body, the description radicalizes Shylock's difference and translates it into the discourse of racism.

However, Schmits's well-nigh ritualistic incantation of abusive terms also has other – one might say 'psychological' – functions. As the reviewer saw it, Richter's performance divested Shylock of all sympathetic traits and consequently freed the audience from nagging doubts concerning the legitimacy of his destruction: 'It goes without saying that the court verdict against such a Shylock failed to have the deep effect that a heroic rendering of the role inspires.' Rather, Schmits continues, 'one was lead to accept, without a split conscience, the sentence against Shylock as the well-deserved punishment for his mean intentions and character' (210). Thus, in spite of – or exactly because of – its fierceness, the review betrays a need to manage insecurities concerning Shylock. It not only struggles with an evidently well-established tradition of empathizing with the Jewish outsider as a victim but simultaneously strives to divest him of heroic might and grandeur. Schmits, one might almost be tempted to say, seems to fight an inferiority complex as well as a 'split conscience.' Indeed, as my first quotation from the review shows, his main point is that Richter's Shylock seemed 'repulsive' ('widerlich') rather than 'terrible' ('schrecklich'). Obviously, Schmits was eager to assure his readers that this Shylock lacked real personal power – that there was nothing to be afraid of.

A review essay in the Shakespeare Society's yearbook for 1933, published after the beginning of Hitler's chancellorship, described Holl's production as 'a clear commitment to theatre as such, to tradition, to a theatre devoted to culture, to the spiritual values of humanity' (Weisker 211; my translation). This statement insinuates that the stage was to be regarded as the site of a fight against fundamental cultural threats – threats that Shylock was taken to represent metaphorically or metonymically. However, the reception of Holl's 1932 production also betrays how powerful Shylock still seemed as an opponent. As I would like to suggest, the nervousness or 'Angst' that he inspired in many proponents of National Socialism and in cultural makers who were willing to contribute to the cultural discourses of National Socialist Germany was due less to the general potentials of Shakespeare's text than to the stage history of the play in Germany, where both Jewish and non-Jewish actors had established a tradition of pronouncedly Jewish Shylocks that were shown to be problematic but powerful personalities.

Alexander Granach – who, interestingly, had played the role in a production directed by Holl at Berlin's Volksbühne in 1924 – offers a particularly significant example of the tendency to render or adopt Shylock as a Jewish hero.[9] Originally from Galicia (then part of Austria, now in Western Ukraine), Granach was born into a Jewish family in 1890, became a student of Max Reinhardt, and soon embarked on an eminent stage and screen career, starring in F.W. Murnau's *Nosferatu*

(1922) among many other films. His success continued even after his flight from Germany, which eventually took him to the United States. Significantly, Granach devoted the concluding chapter of his memoirs – published in 1945 by a German exile publisher in Stockholm – to the figure of Shylock both as a theatre role and as a Jewish role model. Granach talks about the injustice done to Shylock and recounts how, as a teenager, he resolved to devote his 'entire life to slamming this injustice into the face of the world' (421; my translation). When he first played Shylock at the young age of twenty-nine in a 1920 production at the Munich playhouse, the actor based his performance on a tacit private fantasy concerning the character's fate after the verdict. Convinced that 'never can a Shylock alter his faith' (424), the young actor imagined a character who, immediately after the trial, escapes from Venice. Granach's Shylock eventually arrives in Ukraine, where he remarries and becomes the progenitor of an entire tribe of Jews: 'broad-shouldered, hard-working, and hungry for new experiences' (427). Indeed, Granach imagined himself and other Jewish immigrants from Galicia as descendants of this Shylock. According to this fantasy, some of Shylock's offspring became actors and 'discovered their forefather in the work of Shakespeare': 'From their parents and forebears they had learned about Shylock's story of suffering. Now, on account of their kindred heart, they recognized him. And, leaning on Shakespeare's genius, they played the character of their ancestor in a tragic and partisan [Granach's expression is 'parteiisch'] manner' (427).

As an impressive array of scholars – ranging from Hermann Sinsheimer[10] and Edgar Rosenberg to John Gross and James Shapiro – have demonstrated, the figure of Shylock originally evolved as a non-Jewish invention, as an epitome of and a projection screen for the fantasies that an often ignorant majority entertained of Jews and Jewishness. Since the end of the nineteenth century, Jewish actors and directors (such as Jacob Adler in the United States, Maurice Moskovitch in Britain, and Max Reinhardt in Germany) began to make notable contributions to the construction and reconstruction of the Shylock figure. It is evident, however, that their efforts were hampered or defined by the constraints of a non-Jewish discourse of alterity. It therefore seems remarkable that Granach should call on Jews to 'recognize' the Shylock figure as a template of Jewish self-definition. Indeed, one might almost be tempted to argue that the strategy of dealing with an increasingly powerful anti-Semitism by means of adopting and appropriating Shylock constituted a bold attempt at a 'paradoxical intervention' into the discourse.

However, Granach was certainly not the only protagonist of such a strategy. Arnold Zweig's description, published in 1928, of the Shylock played by Jewish actor Rudolf Schildkraut in Max Reinhardt's famous 1905 production, appears to tie in with Granach's Shylock fantasy:

> You will not be allowed to spit into his beard with impunity. It is not a good idea to first mistreat and provoke him, and then to fall into his hands ... To pay back injuries point by point, this is what he is a man for ... Schildkraut's Shylock smells of onions and garlic – and this is a meal and a smell at least as good as slaughtered pigs and goat kids cooked in their mothers' milk ... The right of self-defence clearly is on his side, and he has a tremendous vital power that allows him to strike back even in situations when other types would have long since made an ideal of their serfdom. This is why Rudolf Schildkraut, fidgeting, portly, throaty, has been one of the most potent fascinations and shocks on the German stage. (Zweig 178–9; my translation, cf. Marx, 'Die drei Gesichter Shylocks' 179)

Zweig's description probably constitutes an appropriation of the highly influential performance offered by Schildkraut.

During the 1920s, however, Fritz Kortner quite consciously tried to play the kind of Shylock that Zweig described (see fig. 2.2). In an unpublished essay entitled 'Shylock,' Kortner later spoke of his striving to express the character's 'ethical vehemence' and 'volcanic' energy (qtd in Critchfield 47, note 1; my translation). In his memoirs the actor also commented on the differences between his conception of the role and that of director Jürgen Fehling, as they surfaced during rehearsals for an important 1927 production of *The Merchant of Venice*: 'He, the Aryan with a slight blotch in the generation of his grandparents, wanted to reconcile, emphasizing the individual's tragedy and cutting out the other implications of the play. I, the blotch-less full Jew, wanted to settle the score, exposing the un-Christian hate [of the Christians], and the corruption behind the colourful and carefree façade' (Kortner 379; my translation).

In 1929 Kortner himself became the victim of a campaign that activated common prejudices against Jews for the ends of theatre politics. When Hilde Körber (the wife of Veit Harlan, who would later direct *Jew Süss*) accused Kortner of sexual harassment, reactionary newspaper journalists and politicians tried to use the scandal to destabilize the position of both Kortner and his mentor Leopold Jessner, then manager of the Berlin State Theatre. Having cleared himself of the allegations,

2.2. Fritz Kortner as Shylock in *The Merchant of Venice*, directed by Max Reinhardt, Theater in der Josefstadt, Vienna, 1924.

it was in the role of Shylock that Kortner, after an interval of several weeks, returned to the stage. This seems to have been a deliberate choice: according to Peter Marx, Kortner had purposefully proposed a rerun of Fehling's production of *The Merchant* ('Eine Ohrfeige' 88). The significance of Shylock as a (precarious) reference point for Jewish self-definition in opposition to the rising tide of anti-Semitism is also indicated by an essay published by Jewish author Ernst Simon in 1929 under the title 'Lessing und die deutsche Geschichte' [Lessing and German History]: in light of the decaying Jewish-German symbiosis, Simon called on Jews to take Shylock rather than Nathan as a role model.

Writing after the Second World War, Günther Rühle emphasized the function of theatre in Germany as an institution for defining national and social self-images. 'The language and the gestures of the stage,' Rühle claimed, 'have had a definitive influence on the social life of Germany, where it has been easier to activate the stage for intellectual and political causes than in any other country' (12; my translation). During the first third of the twentieth century Jewish actors had sometimes quite successfully 'activated' the stage – and, specifically, the role of Shylock – in order to assert the presence of Jews in German culture and to counter the theatricality of National Socialist politics with a different kind of theater.[11] This, I would argue, is why the notorious Nazi weekly *Der Stürmer* [The Stormtrooper] 'spat fire' (Kortner 379) at Kortner's impersonation of Shylock – and why this Shakespearean character continued to inspire a certain 'Angst' in the proponents of National Socialism even (or perhaps especially) after their rise to supremacy in Germany.

Both Jewish and non-Jewish actors had contributed to the evolution of Shylock as a staging ground for theatrical figurations – and fictions – of difference. However, it was the actual Jewishness of some among these resilient Shylocks that caught and occupied the imagination of the Nazis. As Richard D. Critchfield observes, 'the name Kortner and Shylock became inseparable in Nazi anti-Semitic propaganda. If Hitler was Germany and Germany was Hitler … then in the eyes of the Nazis Kortner was also Shylock and Shylock was Kortner' (51). Shylock had acquired profoundly ambivalent significations and functions: as a figuration of difference he simultaneously unsettled *and* ratified the fantasies of the Nazis. This is why the administrators of National Socialist cultural policy were so cautious about allowing Shylock to appear on the stage – and, at the same time, it is why they were so eager to make him serve their ends.

Parading Shylock (1942–4)

Two weeks after the November Pogroms of 1938 an article in the NSDAP (Nationalsozialistische Deutsche Arbeiterpartei / National Socialist German Workers' Party) newspaper *Völkischer Beobachter* [The People's Observer] reminded readers of Kortner's Shylock in Fehling's 1927 production. Although the article claimed that Shylock was the only role in which Kortner had truly succeeded – supposedly because he had in fact played himself – it also denounced the production for presuming to emphasize the faults of the Christians rather than those of the Jew. The article concluded: 'How quickly the German people's good nature has led them to forget such ghosts of the past! If the Germans are only now solving the Jewish question, it is the settling of an old account' (qtd in Critchfield 52, note 4; my translation). Critchfield refers to these pronouncements in order to point out the connections that they establish between Kortner's Shylock during the Weimar Republic and the present persecution of Jews and the 'future genocide' (52). Indeed, if the Nazi authorities were showing a conspicuous reluctance to face Shylock on the boards of the theatres, the text from the *Völkischer Beobachter* proposes persecution and murder as the appropriate response to the provocation allegedly offered by Kortner's interpretation of the role. It is against the background of such bewildering semantic regressions – resulting in a destructive jumble of 'Angst' and triumphalism, figuration and fact, theatre and reality – that the stage history of *The Merchant of Venice* during the Second World War must be viewed.

As mentioned above, the performance numbers for the play reached an all-time low in 1941. By that point, however, the stage had already been set for a return of *The Merchant*. In July 1940 the head of the Propaganda Ministry's theatre department presented his suggestions for an adapted version to Goebbels. In his memorandum for the minister, Schlösser explained:

> In agreement with previous instructions, *The Merchant of Venice* has been kept from Berlin theatre programs during the past years. In the meantime, however, a couple of stages in other places have tested out, with my permission, a slightly adapted version ... which creates the impression that Jessica is not the Jew's daughter but merely his foster-child ... Accordingly, I do not see why we should continue to prevent performance of this classic in Berlin, in particular since skilful productions would actually be able to support our fight against the Jews. (qtd in Eicher 308; my translation)

Within three days Schlösser had the minister's approval. Berlin's privately owned Rose Theatre, which had originally planned to produce *The Merchant* in the 1937–8 season, was eventually given permission, but the production premiered only in August 1942. At that point the genocide that had begun simultaneously with the war had long since reached Germany: as of September 1941 German Jews were forced to wear the yellow badge and the first deportations from Berlin (and other major cities) took place in October of the same year.

Other than the show at the Rose Theatre (the only production of *The Merchant* in Berlin during the National Socialist period), during 1942, the play was also staged at the municipal theatres of Görlitz and Göttingen. Indeed, while it would be wrong to claim that the implementation of the Holocaust in Germany was accompanied by an actual wave of *Merchant* productions, it remains a fact that the number of performances rose significantly: while there were only three shows in 1941, the figure for 1942 (72) represents the highest number since 1933, taking *The Merchant* back to fourth place in the Shakespeare Society's ranking. Such data certainly would not support claims that Shakespeare's comedy had turned into a mainstay of National Socialist propaganda. Rather, these figures are significant for suggesting that, in the context of the genocide, the play yet again seemed possible.

In his memorandum to Goebbels, Schlösser had suggested that the amenability of *The Merchant* depended on the skill shown in producing the play ('bei geschickter Darstellung'). But what constituted a 'skilful rendering' of Shakespeare's comedy? The eminently successful[12] and relatively well-documented production by the Rose Theatre may serve as a first example (see fig. 2.3). Considering the history of the production, it is more than probable that Schlösser's adaptation of the play was used. Indeed, a contemporary review spoke of Jessica as Shylock's 'adoptive daughter' (qtd in Bonnell 157). Throughout, there was evidently a strong emphasis on Shylock's Jewishness and on the fundamental otherness of that Jewishness. According to one reviewer, the Shylock scenes evoked a strong 'Ghetto atmosphere'; apparently, settings included the interior of a synagogue (qtd in Endriss 177). Actor Georg August Koch – an active party member and professed anti-Semite (cf. Bonnell 159–61; Rischbieter 86) – did not forsake the opportunity to achieve 'strong effects through his articulation and facial expression' (Papsdorf, Stahl, and Niessen 133; my translation).

Koch's performance included the traditional gesture of actually whetting his knife on the sole of his shoe (Endriss 179). Simultaneously, spectators were invited to identify with the Venetians. As one review

Bühnenbilder auf der Modellbühne zu Shakefpeares »DER KAUFMANN VON VENEDIG«
von Wolfgang Znamenacek im Rofe=Theater 1942   Bild Mitte: Georg Augu t Koch

2.3. Detail from program for production of *The Merchant of Venice*, directed by
Paul Rose, with Georg August Koch as Shylock and stage designs by Wolfgang
Znamenacek, Rose Theatre, Berlin, 1942. Stiftung Stadtmuseum, Berlin.

pointed out, in the trial scene parts of the audience were brought 'close to actively participating in the events on stage' (qtd in Endriss 178; my translation). However, the frequently repeated anecdote that Paul Rose placed extras in the auditorium who hissed and swore at Shylock during act 4 (Wulf 281; referred to by Bonnell 156 and Monschau 68) is hard to substantiate. It may well be a myth, based not only on a misreading of the review in the *Völkischer Beobachter*[13] but also on a misleading conception of the complex workings of anti-Semitic ideology and propaganda during the National Socialist period.

Indeed, I would suggest that arousing outright anti-Jewish aggression was not the main propagandist function of the production. The Rose Theatre's Shylock was evidently meant to be comically, rather than threateningly, 'other.' That the production clung to the old tradition of providing the Jewish character with a long reddish beard (Bonnell 157; cf. Endriss 178) may have been intended as an outward signal for the firm containment of this Shylock within the sphere of comedy. The yearbook of the Shakespeare Society commented: 'In his *Merchant of Venice* at Berlin's Rose Theatre, Paul Rose openly displays his inclination towards comedy, or even towards commedia dell'arte. The play was rendered as a confrontation between clever people rather than as a struggle between law and mercy' (Papsdorf, Stahl, and Niessen 133; my translation). In his pioneering study *Shakespeare on the German Stage*, Wilhelm Hortmann picks up on the notion of commedia dell'arte in order to claim that, in terms of propagandistic efficacy, the Rose production must have been a surprisingly muted undertaking (135 note 41). Indeed, if the stylization of commedia dell'arte would not admit the portrayal of Shylock as a heroic figure of tragic grandeur, neither would there be room for his demonization in the manner of *Jew Süss* or similar propaganda efforts. But this does not mean that Paul Rose's show was not a 'skilful' production according to the requirements of the regime. In the case of *The Merchant*, the most important propagandistic task was not to demonize but rather to downsize Shylock. It is telling that the *Völkischer Beobachter* headed its review of the Rose production 'Shylock at Carnival Time' (Grundschöttel).

In line with the more straightforward mode of propaganda that the party newspaper espoused, Wilhelm Grundschöttel's review was actually slightly critical of the production's mixed tone. As Grundschöttel explained, Rose – 'holding on to the principles of comedy' and 'generously providing caprioles' – had 'run the danger of obscuring the meaning and thoughts of the poet' (my translation). From today's viewpoint, however, it is important to understand that, according to the ideological economy of the so-called 'Volksgemeinschaft' ('people's community'), seemingly 'innocuous' gestures of degradation and exclusion were at least as significant as explicit instigations to murder. Indeed, Paul Rose's staging of the play did not refrain from allusions to the palpable contemporary reality of persecution, segregation, and deportation. Bonnell points out Wolfgang Znamenacek's set design for Shylock's house: 'a small booth-like structure with a pointed-arched window and marked with a yellow star of David on top' (157). I would like to follow Bonnell in reading this as a deliberate allusion to the so-called Judenhäuser – that is, the practice of evicting Jews from their apartments and forcing them to live in specially designated – and increasingly overpopulated – buildings. Since concentrating the victims in such houses constituted a preparation for eventual deportation and murder, the Rose production may actually be interpreted as linking Shakespeare's comedy to the elusively implied reality of the Holocaust.

In a parliamentary address of January 1939 Hitler claimed that 'international financial Jewry' ('das internationale Finanzjudentum') would be to blame for the coming war, predicting that this conflict would result in 'the extermination of the Jewish race in Europe' (qtd in *Verhandlungen des Reichstags* 16). If Jews had thus been defined as Germany's real enemy, the Rose production, staged at a time when the fortunes of war could be seen to be changing, was eager to suggest that this enemy, at least, was already as good as vanquished. Accordingly, a strong emphasis was placed on act 5, evoking the aftermath of conflict and the felicitous reconstitution of society. As Grundschöttel's review in the *Völkischer Beobachter* noted approvingly, the show ended in a fairy tale atmosphere:

> The ending with the idyll of the three loving couples on the terrace, bathed in moonlight, is then steeped in the mood of a summer night, to which [Engelbert] Humperdinck's background music, ceremoniously played on the theatre's newly enlarged organ, was quite well suited; and, in tune with this mood, a mute Puck with a tail, accompanied by four elves, led the play off the stage. (my translation; cf. Bonnell 156–7)

It is evident, then, that the Rose production made bold to combine quite heterogeneous moods and elements. How such stylistic eclecticism connected to the contradictions of National Socialist ideologies and to the immediate historical context of war, deportation, and genocide will become clearer as we turn to the other high-profile staging of *The Merchant of Venice* in this period: Lothar Müthel's production at the Vienna Burgtheater, which premiered in May 1943.

Before a fabulous salary helped to coax him to Vienna as director of the prestigious Burgtheater, Müthel had been a member of Gustaf Gründgens's ensemble at the Berlin State Theatre. Shortly after the war, German Shakespeare scholar Ernst Leopold Stahl claimed that Müthel – who joined the NSDAP in May 1933 – had 'never in any way been a proponent of National Socialist party or art doctrines' (Stahl 709; my translation). Indeed, the director clothed his compliance with the ideological demands of the hour in the mantle of aesthetic historicism. Two days before the premiere, he published an article in the *Neues Wiener Tagblatt* in which he meticulously expounded on his artistic principles. The thrust of the argument was that the new production would restore Shakespeare's original intentions. During the previous decades, Müthel explained, Jews had exerted their 'influence' in order to 'expand' Shylock into 'a leading and even tragic character.' In contrast to this vogue, however, Shakespeare had really intended him as a 'dangerous and cheating buffoon,' an 'idiot with evil intentions' (qtd in Monschau 75–8; my translation).

Müthel referred to 18th-century German actor August Wilhelm Iffland as a historical model of how Shylock ought to be performed on stage. In his memoirs, Werner Krauss would use this lead in order to play down his part in the Vienna production (see fig. 2.4), declaring that he had merely followed Müthel's wish to play Shylock in the manner of Iffland – a wish that the director had allegedly supported with several books from the national library.

Moreover, Krauss implied that his rendering of the role in 1943 had not been much different from the interpretation he had previously offered under (Jewish director) Max Reinhardt (208–9). Theatre critic Herbert Ihering, an admirer of Krauss, was willing to grant him this point: 'In 1943 at the Burgtheater,' Ihering wrote, 'Krauss repeated his Shylock with the same comical drift but *without* the evil ferocity which he had displayed in 1921. In Vienna, Krauss played Shylock as an odd and funny lout who, in the trial scene, fails to grasp why the Doge and the judge should have anything against him' (Ihering 60; my translation and emphasis). As descriptions of Krauss's outward performance at the Burgtheater, these observations may actually be pertinent. They fail to take into account, however, the fact that the comical deflation of Shylock's power – as well as the containment of the horror of his

2.4. Werner Krauss as Shylock (left) and Ferdinand Maierhofer as Tubal in *The Merchant of Venice*, directed by Lothar Müthel. Burgtheater, Vienna, May 1943. Österreichisches Theatermuseum, Vienna.

destruction – were actually the main requirements of Nazi propaganda at this particular moment in history.[14] Siegfried Melchinger – who would become a highly influential theatre critic and theatre scholar after the war – published an enthusiastic review of the Vienna production. Writing in the same newspaper in which Müthel had pronounced his dramatic principles, Melchinger fully ratified the director's claims, calling the production 'less a new interpretation of Shylock than the restoration of the drama as a work of art.' In particular, the review stressed Müthel's truthfulness to the text. As Melchinger professed, the director had 'changed not a syllable and made hardly any cuts' (my translation). At first sight, it may seem surprising that the surviving prompt book for the Burgtheater production confirms this latter claim: apart from minor omissions that kept open the possibility that Jessica is not really Shylock's daughter, not too many changes had been made in the Schlegel translation; in contrast to the Propaganda Ministry's suggestions (see above), Shylock's great monologue was left untouched.[15]

In fact, it is likely that the ideological value of *The Merchant of Venice* as performed at the Burgtheater in 1943 did not really depend on the massive propagandistic interventions that most of the later commentators seem to have taken for granted.[16] Rather, the particular ideological strategy with which Müthel complied consisted in appropriating a seemingly authentic version of Shakespeare's work into the social and historical context of a Vienna whose Jewish inhabitants had recently been expelled or deported. In such an environment, seemingly unobtrusive shifts in articulation and accentuation were probably sufficient to make an Elizabethan comedy sanction a totalitarian politics of deportation and murder.

According to Melchinger, the production not only presented the play in the proper format of comedy but also did justice to its 'fairy tale' qualities. Thanks to these features, Melchinger argued, Müthel managed to integrate the heterogeneous elements of the play into a convincing whole. To describe this feat of integration, the reviewer used the term 'Bindung,' which can mean 'binding together' as well as 'tying down.' Melchinger wrote: 'The laughter is carried from one sphere to the next. When Shylock appears, there is no longer the merest hint of seriousness. And even Shylock's merriness does not stick out in comparison to that of the other characters. Here, too, everything remains *bound* to the centre of the play' (my translation and emphasis). Jörg Monschau offers an interesting – and, I believe, pertinent – interpretation of the ideological subtext inherent in Melchinger's essay: 'By

"Bindung" Melchinger really meant drowning out Shylock. This was realized by the seamless, inconspicuous, and collective transition from general mirthfulness to the group derision of an involuntarily comical clown, who was still the enemy but had somehow lost the stature of a serious opponent.' As Monschau observes, this stance indicates a shift from previous anti-Semitic propaganda: 'What Melchinger describes as the gist of the performance already smacks of the arrogance of the victor' (Monschau 80; my translation).

According to such an interpretation, there was a direct and real connection between the genocide and the Vienna production. Contrary to ordinary expectations, however, the most important link was not in the accentuation of the familiar clichés of the demon Jew (though many reviewers certainly sought and found these clichés in Krauss's interpretation of Shylock).[17] Rather, the connection between the Holocaust and the Burgtheater's production of *The Merchant of Venice* consisted primarily in the degree to which that production built on and ratified the pastness of the Jewish presence in Austria and Germany. Not even the most indifferent member in the audience could have been unaware of the disappearance of Vienna's 200,000 Jewish inhabitants. Up to the end of 1941 many had been able to emigrate; almost all of the remaining 60,000 Jews were deported between October 1941 and October 1942. Judging from Melchinger's review, expulsion, deportation, and genocide shimmered through the surface of the Burgtheater production with the irreversibility and the intangibility of archetypes. It seems incredible that Melchinger should have spelt out these connections – but it is difficult to read the following sentence in any other way: 'Behind the Jew we can see the wicked man of the fairy tale, the unearthly man-eater, the bogey man, who, just like the witch, will finally have to be shoved into the oven' (Melchinger; my translation).

During the Second World War theatre was one of the truly important devices of cultural policy on the home front, but it was also a means for keeping up the morale of fighting troops, and it served as a tool for cultural pretension in occupied territories. Due to the memoirs of Inge Stolten, a member of the Minsk German Theatre, we know of a production of *The Merchant of Venice* that premiered there in September 1943, at the time when the so-called German Ghetto in Minsk was being liquidated. Stolten comments: 'I was in the place where that was being realized which Hitler, Himmler, and their coterie had planned such a long time ago: the "final solution of the Jewish question"' (87; my translation).[18] In fact, the program notes for the production claimed 'contemporary relevance' for the play, stating that 'we in the East experience the Jewish-Aryan race problem more immediately than the people back home' (qtd in Stolten 85–6). Stolten, who mentions that a bomb went off during one of the shows (100–1), does not describe the production in detail. I think it unlikely, however, that its primary function was to increase the audience's hatred of Jews. Rather, it may be assumed that the performance was devised to offer German administrators and Reichswehr men – as well as the 'well-behaved SS officers,' each of whom, Stolten surmises, 'might himself have taken part in the murders' (86) – a modicum of emotional relief in the context of ongoing killings and deportations. In such a context the 'romance' aspects of the play – the scenes of social reconstruction in a Belmontian realm of music and female beauty that follow on Shylock's sudden exit – must have been of particular relevance. Like Müthel's production at the Burgtheater several months earlier, *The Merchant* in Minsk was probably less an instigation to genocide than a veiled acknowledgement and simultaneous displacement of the murders committed while Shylock trod the boards of the theatre.

Following an order by Goebbels, all German theatres shut down by the end of August 1944.[19] Only a few weeks later Veit Harlan contacted the Propaganda Minister to discuss a film version of *The Merchant of Venice*.[20] The role of Shylock was to go to Werner Krauss, who had played Shylock at the Burgtheater and with whom Harlan had already collaborated in the production of *Jew Süss*. As Bonnell points out, '[i]t is perhaps a comment on Joseph Goebbels' priorities as Nazi Germany approached total defeat that he embraced this concept' (167). It is indeed startling to find a propaganda apparatus bent to churn out lavish film productions even after defeat had become inevitable. More interesting, however, is the question of why *The Merchant* was chosen as the basis for such a terminal effort. As plans for *The Merchant* project were being finalized, Harlan was completing *Kolberg*, a film set during the time of the Napoleonic Wars, about a besieged town that held out against all odds. Such a story might have served to spur on Germans to desperate acts of resistance, but Shakespeare's play is hardly suited to similar ends. It is possible that the *Merchant* film was intended to communicate a kind of legacy that the faltering Nazi empire was to leave behind. If so, Shakespeare's problematic comedy must have been intended not as a call to arms but as a pretense to some sort of victory. Indeed, the film project seems to corroborate my argument that the place of *The Merchant* within the psycho-ideological economy of the so-called *Volksgemeinschaft* was significantly different from that of the film documents (such as *Jew Süss* or *Der ewige Jude* [The Eternal Jew]) that tend to determine our understanding of National Socialist anti-Semitism. Rather than paving the way to segregation and murder, the propagandistic efficacy of National Socialist *Merchant* productions presupposed the Holocaust as both an 'open secret' and a fait accompli.

Notes

This essay emerged from a research project headed by Professor Sabine Schülting at Freie Universität Berlin. Under the title 'Shylock und der (neue) "deutsche Geist,"' the project investigates the German reception of *The Merchant of Venice* from 1945 to the immediate present. Our focus is on the functions of the Shylock figure within German discourses of remembrance. See the project website at http://www.geisteswissenschaften.fu-berlin.de/v/shylock/.

1 On the reception of *Merchant* in National Socialist Germany, see esp. Eicher 302–8; Monschau 19–25 and 68–87; Symington 244–51; and Bonnell 119–69. See also Márkus 148–54; Hortmann 134–7; Endriss 170–80; Ledebur 213–18; Drewniak 250–1; and Wulf 280–3.
2 See the section 'Theaterschau: Statistischer Überblick' in the various volumes of the *Shakespeare Jahrbuch*. These reports generally refer to the year preceding publication. From 1942 to 1945, however, publication of the yearbook was interrupted. The 1946 issue contains the statistics for 1941 and 1942; there are no statistics for 1943 and 1944.
3 It seems, however, that only a limited number of concrete cases of intervention against planned productions of *The Merchant* are actually documented.
4 See the more detailed discussion of the film project at the end of this essay.
5 See Frank Bajohr, 'Vom antijüdischen Konsens zum schlechten Gewissen: Die deutsche Gesellschaft und die Judenverfolgung 1933–1945,' Frank Bajohr and Dieter Pohl, *Der Holocaust als offenes Geheimnis: Die Deutschen, die NS-Führung und die Alliierten* (Munich: Beck, 2006) 15–79. See also Peter Longerich, 'Davon haben wir nichts gewusst!' *Die Deutschen und die Judenverfolgung 1933–1945* (Berlin: Siedler, 2006).
6 Cf. Alf Lüdtke, 'Funktionseliten: Täter, Mit-Täter, Opfer? – Zu den Bedingungen des deutschen Faschismus,' *Herrschaft als soziale Praxis: Historische und sozial-anthropologische Studien* (Göttingen: Vandenhoeck and Ruprecht, 1991) 559–90.

7 See Ruth Freifrau von Ledebur, *Der Mythos vom deutschen Shakespeare: Die Deutsche Shakespeare-Gesellschaft zwischen Politik und Wissenschaft 1918–1945* (Köln: Böhlau, 2002). (Eds.: For the influence of this book on Japanese appreciation of Shakespeare see Ryuta Minami's essay in this volume.)
8 There is a persistent cliché that Gundolf, who taught German literature at Heidelberg, was the admired teacher of Joseph Goebbels, perhaps even the supervisor of his dissertation. While it is an intriguing fact that the paths of Goebbels and Gundolf crossed, there is little evidence for such close contact. Goebbels's diaries speak only of a single meeting; he saw the professor in his office, apparently intending to discuss a possible dissertation. It seems that Gundolf declined, so Max Freiherr von Waldberg – another Jewish professor – supervised Goebbels's work. For these facts, see Michael Petrow, *Der Dichter als Führer? Zur Wirkung Stefan Georges im Dritten Reich* (Marburg an der Lahn: Tectum, 1995) 69–71. For the argument that Gundolf can be seen as a sort of mediator between Stefan George, on the one hand, and National Socialist cultural politics, on the other, see Franz Leschnitzer's 'George–Gundolf–Goebbels,' which was published in Moscow in 1934 (*Internationale Literatur* 4.4: 115–34).
9 I am indebted to Professor Irmela von der Lühe (Freie Universität Berlin) for alerting me to Granach and his autobiography.
10 Significantly, Sinsheimer had completed his original manuscript in 1937, that is, prior to his flight from Germany. The text actually passed the censor and, if the approaching war had not halted the project, might have been printed for circulation in Germany.
11 This perspective can also be applied to Ernst Lubitsch's *To Be or Not to Be* (1942). On the film and its references to *Merchant*, see Elisabeth Bronfen, 'Man wird weder als Frau noch als Jude geboren: Was wir von Lubitsch über den *Kaufmann von Venedig* lernen können,' *Shylock nach dem Holocaust: Zur Geschichte einer deutschen Erinnerungsfigur*, ed. Zeno Ackermann and Sabine Schülting (Berlin: de Gruyter, 2011) 201–17.
12 As of the end of 1942 the Rose production had reached fifty performances – clearly more than any other Shakespeare production of that year (see statistics in *Shakespeare Jahrbuch* 80/81 [1946]: 113–21).
13 The passage 'and Paul Rose had the voice of the people rise from the gallery, with outraged cries and hisses' (Grundschöttel; my translation) does not refer to the audience on the balconies of the theatre but to the Venetian populace placed on a gallery on stage. (For information on the stage setting of this production, see Endriss 178.)
14 Cf. Habicht: '[E]ven Werner Krauss's impersonation of the Jew in Müthel's notorious Viennese production of 1943 did not differ substantially from the

one he himself had played under Max Reinhardt in the twenties. But it did now create a macabre effect deriving from the context of organized anti-Semitism and the holocaust' (117).

15 I am indebted to Ludwig Schnauder (University of Vienna) for providing me with a copy of the prompt book from Müthel's production. Cf. Ludwig Schnauder.

16 See, for example, Oliver Rathkolb, *Führertreu und gottbegnadet: Künstler-eliten im Dritten Reich* (Vienna: Österreichischer Bundesverlag, 1991), who has argued that the Burgtheater production constituted nothing less than a brutal 'ideological (i.e. anti-Semitic) rape of the original text' (162; my translation).

17 The most notorious quotation comes from Richard Biedrzynski's 1944 book *Schauspieler, Regisseure, Intendanten*: 'And then, suddenly, as if it were an uncanny shadow, something revoltingly alien and astonishingly repel-lent drags itself across the stage: a marionette jingling its ducats, wearing a black gaberdine and a garishly yellow synagogue shawl – the Shylock of Werner Krauss' (qtd in Wulf 282; my translation).

18 On occupational politics and the Holocaust in Belorussia, see Christian Gerlach, *Kalkulierte Morde: Die deutsche Wirtschafts- und Vernichtungspolitik in Weissrussland 1941 bis 1944* (Hamburg: Hamburger Edition, 1999); see especially 738, on the Minsk production of *The Merchant*.

19 Due to the theatrical activities of German prisoners of war, Goebbels's order was not the end of the stage history of *The Merchant* in the context of the war. Bonnell has information on a production organized in Septem-ber 1944 at Tatura Camp 3 in Victoria, Australia. Apparently, the program notes contained racist quotations by Alfred Rosenberg and Hans F.K. Günther (Bonnell 165–6; 221 note 252). See also Krystyna Kujawińska-Courtney's contribution to this volume, which discusses a 1943 produc-tion by Polish officers in a prisoner-of-war camp at Murnau, Germany, in 1943.

20 On the film project, see Bonnell 167–9 and Harlan 199–205. See also Dorothea Hollstein, *Jud Süss und die Deutschen: Antisemitische Vorurteile im nationalsozialistischen Spielfilm* (Frankfurt am Main: Ullstein, 1983) 175–82. In contrast to Bonnell and Holstein, Harlan suggests that the idea of pro-ducing a film version had come from Goebbels. Characteristically, Harlan spells out the dialectics of National Socialist propaganda in order to place himself firmly on one side of the issue and Goebbels on the other: while the director would have liked to produce a harmless comedy, it is claimed, the Propaganda Minister 'absolutely wanted a horrifying representation' (203; my translation).

60   Zeno Ackermann

Works Cited

Ackermann, Zeno, and Sabine Schülting, eds. *Shylock nach dem Holocaust: Zur Geschichte einer deutschen Erinnerungsfigur*. Conditio Judaica 78. Berlin: de Gruyter, 2011.

Armstrong, Gareth. *A Case for Shylock: Around the World with Shakespeare's Jew*. London: Nick Hern, 2004.

Bonnell, Andrew G. *Shylock in Germany: Anti-Semitism and the German Theatre from the Enlightenment to the Nazis*. London: Tauris Academic Studies, 2008.

Critchfield, Richard D. *From Shakespeare to Frisch: The Provocative Fritz Kortner*. Heidelberg: Synchron, 2008.

Daiber, Hans. *Schaufenster der Diktatur: Theater im Machtbereich Hitlers*. Stuttgart: Neske, 1995.

Drewniak, Bogusław. *Das Theater im NS-Staat: Szenarium deutscher Zeitgeschichte, 1933–1945*. Dusseldorf: Droste, 1983.

Eicher, Thomas. 'Spielplanstrukturen 1929–1944.' *Theater im 'Dritten Reich': Theaterpolitik, Spielplanstruktur, NS-Dramatik*. Ed. Henning Rischbieter. Seelze-Velber: Kallmeyer, 2000. 285–486.

Endriss, Beate-Ursula. *Shakespeare-Inszenierungen in Berlin 1933–1944*. Diss., Freie Universität Berlin, 1994.

Freydank, Ruth. 'Die Klassiker als Herausforderung an eine Vorstadtbühne.' *Das Rose-Theater: Ein Volkstheater im Berliner Osten 1906–1944*. By Michael Baumgarten and Ruth Freydank. Berlin: Edition Hentrich, 1991. 126–54.

Granach, Alexander. *Da geht ein Mensch: Autobiographischer Roman*. Stockholm: Neuer Verlag, 1945.

Gross, John. *Shylock: Four Hundred Years in the Life of a Legend*. London: Chatto & Windus, 1992. *Shylock: A Legend and Its Legacy*. New York: Simon & Schuster, 1992.

Grundschöttel, Wilhelm. 'Shylock im Fasching: Paul Rose inszenierte den *Kaufmann von Venedig*.' *Völkischer Beobachter* (2 September 1942): n.pag.

Günther, Hans F.K. 'Shakespeares Mädchen und Frauen: Ein Vortrag vor der Deutschen Shakespeare-Gesellschaft.' *Shakespeare-Jahrbuch* 73 (1937): 85–108.

Habicht, Werner. 'Shakespeare and Theatre Politics in the Third Reich.' *The Play out of Context*. Ed. Hanna Sčolnicov and Peter Holland. Cambridge: Cambridge University Press, 1989. 110–20.

Harlan, Veit. *Im Schatten meiner Filme*. Gütersloh: Mohn, 1966.

Hortmann, Wilhelm. *Shakespeare on the German Stage: The Twentieth Century*. Cambridge: Cambridge University Press, 1998.

Ihering, Herbert. *Werner Krauss: Ein Schauspieler und das neunzehnte Jahrhundert*. Ed. Sabine Zolchow and Rudolf Mast. Berlin: Vorwerk 8, 1997.

Kortner, Fritz. *Aller Tage Abend*. 1959. Berlin: Alexander Verlag, 1991.

Krauss, Werner. *Das Schauspiel meines Lebens: Einem Freund erzählt*. Stuttgart: Henry Goverts, 1958.

Ledebur, Ruth Freifrau von. 'Der deutsche Geist und Shakespeare: Anmerkungen zur Shakespeare-Rezeption 1933–1945'. *Wissenschaft und Nationalsozialismus: Eine Ringvorlesung an der Universität-Gesamthochschule Siegen*. Ed. Rainer Geissler and Wolfgang Popp. Essen: Die Blaue Eule, 1988. 197–225.

Márkus, Zoltán. '*Der Merchant von Velence: The Merchant of Venice* in London, Berlin, and Budapest during World War II.' *Shakespeare and European Politics*. Ed. Dirk Delabastita, Jozef De Vos and Paul Franssen. Cranbury, NJ: Associated University Presses, 2008. 143–57.

Marx, Peter W. 'Die drei Gesichter Shylocks: Zu Max Reinhardts Projekt eines metropolitanen, liberalen Theaters vor dem Hintergrund seiner jüdischen Herkunft.' *Max Reinhardt und das Deutsche Theater: Texte und Bilder aus Anlass des 100-jährigen Jubiläums seiner Direktion*. Ed. Roland Koberg, Bernd Stegemann, and Henrike Thomsen. Blätter des Deutschen Theaters 2 (2005). Berlin: Deutsches Theater / Henschel, 2005. 51–9.

– 'Eine Ohrfeige und ihr Echo: Die Harlan-Kortner-Kontroverse 1929. Oder: Skandal als kulturelle Traumarbeit.' *Politische Künste*. Ed. Stephan Porombka, Wolfgang Schneider and Volker Wortmann. *Jahrbuch für Kulturwissenschaften und ästhetische Praxis* 2 (2007): 77–90.

Melchinger, Siegfried. '*Der Kaufmann von Venedig*: Müthels Neuinszenierung im Burgtheater.' *Neues Wiener Tagblatt* (17 May 1943): n.pag.

Monschau, Jörg. *Der Jude nach der Shoah: Zur Rezeption des Kaufmann von Venedig auf dem Theater der Bundesrepublik Deutschland und der Deutschen Demokratischen Republik 1945–1989*. Diss., Ruprecht-Karls-Universität Heidelberg, 2002. 10 Feb. 2010. http://www.ub.uni-heidelberg.de/archiv/3530/.

Müthel, Lothar. 'Zur Dramaturgie des *Kaufmann von Venedig*.' *Neues Wiener Tagblatt* (13 May 1943): n.pag.

Papsdorf, Werner, Ernst Leopold Stahl, and Carl Niessen. 'Shakespeare auf der deutschen Bühne 1940/42.' *Shakespeare-Jahrbuch* 78–9 (1943): 128–37.

Picker, Henry. *Hitlers Tischgespräche im Führerhauptquartier*. Stuttgart: Seewald, 1983.

Rischbieter, Henning. 'NS-Theaterpolitik.' *Theater im 'Dritten Reich': Theaterpolitik, Spielplanstruktur, NS-Dramatik*. Ed. Henning Rischbieter. Seelze-Velber: Kallmeyer, 2000. 9–278.

Rosenberg, Edgar. *From Shylock to Svengali: Jewish Stereotypes in English Fiction*. 1960. London: Peter Owen, 1961.

Rühle, Günther. *Theater für die Republik*. Frankfurt am Main: Fischer, 1967.

Schnauder, Ludwig. '"The poor man is wronged!" Die Figur des Shylock in Inszenierungen am Burgtheater.' *Die Rezeption anglophoner Dramen auf Wiener Bühnen des 20. Jahrhunderts.* Ed. Ewald Mengel, Ludwig Schnauder, and Rudolf Weiss. Trier: WVT, 2010. 119–47.

Shakespeare, William. *The Merchant of Venice.* Ed. M.M. Mahood. The New Cambridge Shakespeare. Cambridge: Cambridge University Press, 2003.

Shapiro, James S. *Shakespeare and the Jews.* New York: Columbia University Press, 1996.

Simon, Ernst. 'Lessing und die deutsche Geschichte.' *Jüdische Rundschau* (22 Jan. 1929). Rpt. in *Brücken: Gesammelte Aufsätze.* Heidelberg: Schneider, 1965. 215–19.

Sinsheimer, Hermann. *Shylock: The History of a Character; or, The Myth of the Jew.* London: Victor Gollancz, 1947.

Stahl, Ernst Leopold. *Shakespeare und das deutsche Theater: Wanderung und Wandelung seines Werkes in dreiundeinhalb Jahrhunderten.* Stuttgart: Kohlhammer, 1947.

Strobl, Gerwin. 'The Bard of Eugenics: Shakespeare and Racial Activism in the Third Reich.' *Journal of Contemporary History* 34.3 (1999): 323–36.

Symington, Rodney. *The Nazi Appropriation of Shakespeare: Cultural Politics in the Third Reich.* Lewiston, NY: Edwin Mellen, 2005.

Verhandlungen des Reichstags: Stenographische Berichte 460 (1939–42): 16.

Weisker, Jürgen. 'Theaterschau: Shakespeare auf der deutschen Bühne 1932/33.' *Shakespeare-Jahrbuch* 69 (1933): 200–25.

Wulf, Joseph. *Theater und Film im Dritten Reich: Eine Dokumentation.* 1964. Frankfurt: Ullstein, 1989.

Zweig, Arnold. *Juden auf der deutschen Bühne.* Berlin: Welt-Verlag, 1928.

3 Shylock, Palestine, and the Second World War

MARK BAYER

Today the Arab-Israeli conflict has taken on a sense of inevitability, but matters were different during the 1930s and 1940s. Rather than the harbinger of a seemingly endless regional conflict, Arabs and Jews in Palestine saw considerable opportunity to advance their territorial interests through the Second World War and the radically altered global power structure that it promised. Shifting patterns in international relations also brought considerable risks, different adversaries, and new forms of propaganda. It is in this climate that Shakespeare, and especially *The Merchant of Venice*, first emerged as an important form of political signification in the Middle East, allowing that play to function variously as a symbol of Zionist ambitions in the region, a model of and justification for violence against non-Jews, and a caricature of a number of political figures.

Two of the earliest applications of Shakespeare's play to the emerging Arab-Israeli conflict, one Zionist and one Arab, were produced in the years leading up to and during the Second World War. In 1936 Leopold Jessner, an accomplished German (Jewish) director fleeing Nazi persecution, first staged *The Merchant of Venice* in Hebrew at Tel Aviv's Habimah Theatre. Jessner chose to foreground the play's political implications for a Jewish audience well aware of the anti-Semitism the play contained. Arabs also noticed the utility of Shakespeare's play for commenting on contemporary politics. Near the end of the war Ali Ahmed Bakathir wrote a two-part play entitled *Shyluck Al-Jadid* (1945), or *The New Shylock*, to depict the conflict in Palestine, reimagining the possibilities of the play for Arab propaganda. When we consider these plays now, we do so knowing the tumultuous postwar history of the region, easily recognizing the stereotypes and political rhetoric that have fuelled animosity between Arabs and Jews and have plagued attempts at peace. When read in their moment, however, these plays disclose more specific anxieties about the war and its aftermath. I want to highlight this considerably more localized context to interpret these adaptations, understand the issues that animated Middle Eastern politics during this period, and appreciate again the plasticity of Shakespeare's plays as propaganda.

Politically, the Arab-Israeli conflict has its origins in Europe. Tensions in the Middle East during the two world wars and the years in between were largely caused by decisions made in London and Berlin, not Jerusalem or Cairo. Great Britain first weighed in on the nascent conflict between Jews and Arabs in Palestine on 2 November 1917 with the issuance of the Balfour Declaration. This brief letter from British Foreign Secretary Arthur James Balfour to Lord Rothschild, President of the Zionist Federation, gave Imperial Britain's blessing to the Zionist dream of creating a Jewish homeland in Palestine. Following the war, when the Crown undertook Mandatory control of Palestine, it seemed certain that a resolution to the regional crisis would ultimately be brokered by Great Britain. The Balfour Declaration is significant not just because it raised the political stakes in Palestine and heightened tensions between Arabs and Jewish immigrants, but also because it did so by integrating the fate of Palestine with the arc of European politics, forcing both sides to follow the affairs of the great powers. As we shall see, the Balfour Declaration became the major point of contention in the region over the next two decades, both politically and aesthetically.

The Balfour Declaration was extremely ambiguous: it promised that 'his Majesty's government view with favour in Palestine the establishment of a national home for the Jewish people,' but only if this home does nothing to 'prejudice the civil and religious rights of existing non-Jewish communities in Palestine' (Laquer and Rubin 16). In subsequent years the British would spend tremendous political energy trying to reconcile this conflicting language to suit their geopolitical interests, incensing Arabs and Zionists alike. While violence escalated and both sides adopted more organized and effective forms of political resistance, British authorities qualified the Balfour Declaration in two White Papers. The first, issued by Winston Churchill in 1922, pleased the Zionists at the expense of Arabs by allowing for increased Jewish immigration to Palestine. The second White Paper, issued in 1939, seemed to reverse the previous policy statement, severely curtailing immigration. With war looming, the British were willing to risk alienating the

Zionists in order to preserve stability in the Middle East. The Balfour Declaration, a source of so much contention, was never implemented in any meaningful way, and was rendered moot when Zionists declared the State of Israel in 1948.

How did Shakespeare's play come to be implicated in this dispute? There are, of course, obvious reasons why *The Merchant of Venice* would offer rich possibilities for anti-Zionist propaganda at any time because of the characterization of Shylock. Following the first Arabic translation by Khalil Moutran in 1922, many in Palestine and across the Arab World noted the anti-Semitism and imagined its utility for an inchoate struggle with the growing number of Jewish immigrants to the region, self-proclaimed Zionists intent on carving out a Jewish homeland in the region, presumably to the detriment of the indigenous inhabitants. As early as 1919 Aref Dajani, picking up on a sentiment latent in *The Merchant*, noted '[I]t is impossible for us [the Arabs] to make an understanding with them [the Zionists] or even to live with them ... because they always arrive to suck the blood of everybody' (qtd in Morris 91). Moutran's translation and Dajani's reference appeared only a few years after the Balfour Declaration, again underscoring the importance of this document in the history of the region.

Although it is not difficult to understand the potential efficacy of *The Merchant of Venice* for Arabs, it is more puzzling to imagine how the play might resonate as propaganda supporting the Zionist cause. Indeed, many openly questioned (and still do question) the desirability of staging such a notoriously anti-Semitic play in the new Jewish homeland at all. Nevertheless, the 1936 production of *The Merchant* was the first play in Hebrew to be staged at the new Habimah theatre.[1] Realizing that the production of a play renowned for its anti-Semitism would raise eyebrows, Jessner took pains not to mitigate the play's political implications, but to foreground them, arguing that *The Merchant*, like the theatre in which it was staged, could 'serve ... as a vehicle of propaganda for the *Eretz-Israeli-an* conception [that is, as propaganda supporting a sovereign Israeli state]' (3; italics in original). Jessner's Shylock was intended as an allegory of the long-suffering Jewish people highlighting their perseverance, suffering, and contempt for their Christian aggressors. Shylock and his fellow Jews are forced to wear the Nazi yellow badge for identification and are accompanied by cries of 'Hep-Hep,' a traditional anti-Semitic cry of abuse. Shylock bears his burden with dignity. The careful, measured delivery of his lines in the trial scene illustrated for Avraham Oz not so much his belligerence, but the moral superiority of the Jews over their persecutors (60–2). Perhaps to augment the play's appeal for multiple segments of the Jewish audience, two actors – Aharon Meskin and Shimon Finkel – alternated as Shylock on successive nights: the former 'a proud and angry spokesman for his people,' and the latter more dignified and ironic (Kohansky, 'Shakespeare' 83). Either way, audiences of the play's forty-seven performances could not miss the political implications, as Shylock 'was played as a sort of national hero' (Kohansky 'Hizkiyahu's new Shylock' 39).

The public controversy that arose in the aftermath of the production – Jessner, along with Shakespeare and the theatre troupe, were forced to defend the performance in a mock trial – clearly intimated the shapes that the play would take over the next several decades. Reactions to Jessner's production ranged from those who felt Shylock should be portrayed as a quiet victim, stalwartly striving for safety and stability for himself and his family, to those who believed the character should actively and violently confront his aggressors. These attitudes towards Shylock had little to do with critical approaches to Shakespeare. Opinions on the play were fairly precise analogues to the views of Jewish settlers who felt grateful to have arrived in Palestine, especially during such a turbulent period for Jews who remained in Europe, and counselled peaceful coexistence with the indigenous inhabitants, or to 'Revisionists' who urged rapid Zionist expansion and eventual statehood, even through military force. Despite detractors who thought the director could have gone further in producing a Shylock with the 'full right to accuse' his Christian adversaries, Jessner hoped to placate both ends of the political spectrum – partly by casting both Meskin and Finkel as Shylock. Jessner claimed that sympathetic Shylocks went some measure in favourably representing the Jewish community, and at the same time insisted that the production ultimately 'does not present a tolerant Shylock, but Shylock the warrior' (qtd in Abend-David 131).[2]

Jessner's decision to stage the play in the first place, and to use it to confront anti-Semitism, undoubtedly came out of his own experience as a socialist Jew in Germany during Hitler's rise to power, which ultimately forced him to leave the country. His aesthetic and political ideas had been formed in Germany and had at least as much to do with European socialist politics in the prewar years as with Zionist expansion in the Middle East. Jessner's work as a director, always politically motivated, rested on the principle that drama should disclose 'the undisguised essence of things' rather than obscuring social realities through opulent spectacle (Hortmann 56–64). His numerous Shakespearean productions at the Königliches Schauspielhaus through the 1920s sought to reveal the objective reality sedimented in the drama in order to comment on underlying social conditions. These same values also permeated his production of *The Merchant of Venice* at the Habimah by suggesting that Shylock's ostracization from Venetian society signified an enduring state of affairs for all Jews.

Jessner's production of *The Merchant* coincided with the Arab revolt of 1936, a series of violent, nationwide altercations following a period of growing rancour between Arabs and Jews in Palestine and rising tensions between European powers. Most worrisome to Arabs was the massive and increasing influx of Jewish immigrants to Palestine. During the 1920s about 4,500 new immigrants arrived each year, a level endorsed by the 1922 White Paper. In 1932, however, 10,500 Jews arrived, and numbers increased to 30,000 in 1933, 42,000 in 1934, and 62,000 in 1935, most fleeing Germany and Eastern Europe after Hitler's rise to power and the terror initiated by Stalin. By 1939 the Jewish population of Palestine had reached nearly 500,000, compared with just below one million Arabs. Immigration on such a large scale proved disastrous for the economy, making it nearly impossible for underskilled Arabs to find work, especially since the growing number of Jewish firms naturally preferred to hire from the growing Jewish labour pool. Inflation compounded the economic crisis as prices rose an astonishing 50,000% between 1914 and 1945 (Morris 122–3). Cultural differences exacerbated the obvious religious divide. Jewish immigrants, nearly all of whom were European, sought to transplant a mercantile and semi-industrialized ethos onto a largely agrarian economy. The antecedents of the Arab revolt, therefore, are intimately tied to European politics in the years prior to the Second World War, again reminding us that the emerging conflict in the Middle East must be understood in the larger context of global politics.

The revolt itself began in April 1936, occurring in gradually escalating stages that included not only strikes, shop closures, nationalist demonstrations, and violence against Jewish homes and businesses but also attacks on telephone lines, traffic, railroad bridges, and other targets controlled by the British colonial authorities, adding a second dimension to the struggle. The first phase of the revolt ended six months after it began, leaving 200 Arabs, 80 Jews, and 28 British dead, and relations among, and within, the three groups were dire as growing nationalist sentiments frayed traditional relationships that revolved around families, tribes, and clans.

The contradictory and equivocal British response to the Arab uprising satisfied neither Arabs nor Jews, and foreshadowed events to come
in Palestine and the function of Shakespeare's play as propaganda. Initially, the British recognized the intractability of the issues that divided
the two sides. A report published in 1937 by a commission led by Lord
Peel abandoned any dream of harmonious relations between Arabs and
Jews and advocated partition of the country. The Jews were to be given
a state comprising Galilee, the Yezreel Valley, and the area along the
coast around Tel Aviv; the remaining area – with the exception of Jerusalem, Bethlehem, and a corridor linking them to the sea that would
remain under British control – was left to the Arabs to be absorbed into
Transjordan (Laquer 42). While many (though certainly not all) Zionists
accepted the deal, Arabs overwhelming rejected it, again plunging the
population into revolt.

The British were reluctant to forcibly suppress the renewed rebel-
lion fomented by the Peel Commission report,[3] realizing after the German annexation of Austria in March 1938 the importance of keeping
the Middle East calm, given the increasing likelihood of another global
conflict. A policy statement issued in November 1938 announced that
'His Majesty's Government ... has reached the conclusion that the political, administrative and financial difficulties involved in the proposal
to create independent Arab and Jewish States inside Palestine are so
great that this solution of the problem is impracticable,' thus revoking
the Peel Commission report and the resulting partition plan (Laquer
and Rubin 43). This time, many (though not all) Arabs applauded the
report, while Zionists overwhelmingly rejected it, especially the
proposals to curtail Jewish immigration and acquisition of land. This
decision reflected Britain's strategic priorities – which hinged on the
appeasement of the Arab population in Palestine and throughout the
region to safeguard oil resources and the route to India, however much
individual ministers might have sympathized with the historical plight
of the Jews. C.H. Bateman, a member of the commission that handed
down the report, conceded that the Jews 'have waited two thousand
years for their "home" ... They can afford to wait a bit until we are better able to help them get their last pound of flesh' (qtd in Cohen 68).

Feeling abandoned by the European powers and surrounded by hostile Arabs, many Palestinian Jews viewed their plight as similar to that
of Shylock. Like Shylock, many Zionists now believed the exercise of
force was necessary to achieve their goals. Vladimir (Ze'ev) Jabotinsky,
the father of Revisionist Zionism, born in tsarist Odessa in 1880, had

for years advocated the use of irresistible force against any adversary, Arab or British, who stood in the way of achieving the Zionist dream of a Jewish state in Palestine. 'Settlement,' he argued, 'can only develop under the protection of a force that is not dependent on the local population, behind an iron wall which they will be powerless to break down' (qtd in Shlaim 13). His rhetoric began to sound eerily similar to that of Shylock: in a speech of 16 June 1933 he declared that '[n]othing less than a merciless fight would be acceptable.' Revisionist doctrine was predicated on the need to avenge a long history of anti-Semitism, making the connection to Shylock natural and the terminology of blood vengeance productive. A few years later, another Revisionist, Uri Greenberg, believed that the Promised Land could not be achieved through politics, diplomacy, or any kind of judicial process, but only through force of arms. In language eerily similar to *Macbeth*, he argued:

> Double blood for blood
> Double fire for fire …
> For thus races repay their enemies
> Throughout the generations. (qtd in Shavit 213–14)

Like other Revisionists, Jabotinsky relished the role of Shylock and even impersonated him. In testimony before the 1937 Peel Commission, in words that would not be forgotten by Arabs, he demanded, 'give us the pound of flesh, we will never let go of the pound of flesh' – that is, the promise in the Balfour Declaration ('Judaism 101').

The British, well aware that their succession of policy reversals on Palestine was unlikely to ameliorate tensions in the colony, convened a series of meetings in London in late February and early March 1939, in an attempt to find common ground between Jews and Arabs on the future of Palestine. These meetings, known as the St James conference, had little chance of succeeding. Neither side was willing to concede any ground and the British had in any case decided that the current status quo was in their interests now that war with Germany seemed inevitable. Jabotinsky and other Revisionists protested the talks and the resulting White Paper by launching a series of terrorist attacks against British targets carried out by a group known as IRGUN, a Hebrew acronym for the National Military Organization in the Land of Israel (Bell 48–53). Arabs invoked Shylock. The popular Egyptian magazine *Al-Thaqafa* [Culture] ran a long story entitled 'The Modern Shylock' [Shaylock al-Hadith] timed to coincide with the breakdown of the St

James conference. The piece compared Chaim Weizmann and the rest of the Jewish negotiators to the Shakespearean character: 'all he wanted was that pound of flesh, to cut off his enemy's body, and he will not renounce one penny of it … and that is also the position of the Zionist leaders regarding Palestine in the twentieth century' (42). Unlike later applications of this trope to current events, this article holds out hope for peaceful coexistence, while recognizing that this goal is impossible without compromises on both sides, something the author feels Zionist leaders have failed to entertain at the expense of the Jewish people. The article concludes: 'they [the Zionists] still cry out every day, demanding their pound of flesh in Palestine, and alleging that in their hands is a contract that gives them this right. But if they hear the call of peace and brotherhood, they would be closer to achieving their great aim in the world' (44).

The metaphor of the contract, so prominent in Shakespeare's play, became especially conspicuous during the Second World War. As war ravaged Europe and much of the rest of the world, Palestine remained relatively quiet, at least militarily. The issues that animated Palestinians and the Jewish settlers in the region revolved primarily around legal and political questions, namely land, immigration, and the legal authority of the 1917 Balfour Accord. Neither Zionists nor Palestinian nationalists were willing to press the British mandatory government for concessions that might disrupt the status quo in favour of their adversaries, and since British intentions remained ambiguous, the future of the region remained uncertain. Most Jews, while continuing to press their political claims in Palestine, were reluctant to urge an expansion of the conflict that might siphon British resources from the war against Germany. David Ben-Gurion explained that 'we shall fight the war against Hitler as if there were no White Paper, and fight the White Paper as if there were no war' (qtd in Gelvin 119). More radical Jews founded a group known as LEHI, 'the Freedom Fighters of Israel,' led by Avraham Stern, who saw Britain as the enemy and even tried to establish an anti-British alliance with the Nazis. Though isolated and unpopular during the war, the 'Stern gang' (as it was known) received the support of more mainstream Zionist groups in early 1944, once the defeat of Germany seemed certain.

In the absence of overt political connections or military might, Jewish efforts in the region focused on the purchase of as much land as possible, making eventual political control seem more or less assured. The rapid and widespread acquisition of land and the consequent eviction

of Arab tenants was so damaging to the Palestinian nationalist movement that many treated it as an issue of 'life or death' (Morris 123).
In this way, *The Merchant of Venice* and its explicit focus on property
seemed appropriate, not just as a general caricature of alleged Jewish
traits but also as a description of the prevailing situation in Palestine
during these years. The ravenous acquisition of land by Zionist settlers in an attempt to dispossess the indigenous inhabitants of property
rights and to pave the way for a Jewish State is one of the central motifs
in Ali Ahmed Bakathir's *The New Shylock*. Native to Yemen, Bakathir
(1910–69) was a versatile translator, dramatist, and poet who, in addition to rendering *Romeo and Juliet* and parts of *Twelfth Night* into Arabic
verse, wrote many plays, poems, essays, and even a nineteen-book epic
on the theme of Arabic nationalism inspired by the spectre of Zionism
(Al Shetawi 17). Modern readers of *The New Shylock* will immediately
recognize the stereotypes that have made Shakespeare's play so notorious. After all, the anti-Israeli invective of Bakathir's two-part play, set
in 1940s Palestine, is hardly subtle and relies on a precise, yet highly
imaginative and sometimes embellished, analogical understanding
of the plot of *The Merchant of Venice* as a guide to Zionist impostures.
Readers in the months and years following its publication in Cairo in
late 1945, however, would appreciate a significantly more nuanced
political commentary.

In Bakathir's play, Shylock is the head of a large Zionist organization
with links to several fictional Zionists: Jack, the president of a Jewish
land-acquisition committee, and Joseph, the leader of a terrorist group
reminiscent of Zionist paramilitary units such as IRGUN and LEHI but
allied with the Yishuv, the official Zionist leadership. The '3,000 ducats' bonded to Antonio is replaced by '5,000 pounds' lent interest-free
(but guaranteed by property) to Arabs, while the 'pound of flesh' is
analogized, through a series of multi-layered metaphors, to the Balfour
Accord. *The New Shylock* begins not with the overt political commentary that eventually saturates it, but with an evocative domestic situation. Rachel (Shylock's niece, the Jessica figure) visits the home of her
lover, Abdullah Fayyad (the Lorenzo figure, and owner of vast tracts
of land near Beersheba). The contrast between the innocent, muscular,
and conservatively-dressed Abdullah and the seductive Rachel, 'a tall
blonde girl, fully blossomed … wearing a sky blue silk dress that is
so tight on her body that it is close to being ripped' could hardly be
more pronounced (1.1 sd.).[4] Her appearance is clearly designed to prey
on widespread cultural fears and an emerging stereotype that Jewish

women actively sought to use sex appeal to corrupt the morality of unsuspecting and vulnerable Palestinian youth as a ploy in a larger economic and political agenda, leading many Arabs to insist that 'love is more dangerous than hate' (Shipler 270).

A mutual friend, Khalil Dawwas, wearing 'an elegant gray suit, now worn with age,' sketches this opening scene, lamenting 'who would have believed that Khalil, of the al-Dawwas family, would walk one day without a single pound in his pocket, when he once never left the house with less than 100?' (1.1). He has lost all his property in an ill-advised sale to Shylock. Khalil's statement is neither fear-mongering – an implicit condemnation of avaricious Jews – nor an attempt to build pathos for dramatic effect. Arabs in the 1940s would have known many who had been reduced to poverty in just the same way. The play thus tries to alert Arabs of the political consequences of private business transactions, how 'a boy [Khalil] from his own noble and patriotic family contributes to the country's crisis. The lands that we own in this stricken country are not ours: they are a trust in our hands for the Arab nation' (1.1).

Many reading or witnessing *The New Shylock* would likely not be familiar with Shakespeare's *The Merchant of Venice*, but would nevertheless be acutely aware of the particular historical situation that Bakathir's adaptation traces, suggesting that the play resonated differently for its original audience, for whom it was at least partially a condemnation of Arab greed. After disclosing and repudiating the impostures of young Arab men, the play turns to the Zionists who have actively worked to bring about this situation. The audience realizes that Rachel is in fact acting at the behest of her Uncle Shylock to foreclose on the Fayyads' land. Another lawyer, Mikhail Jad (the Bassanio figure), warns Abdullah that:

We're in a contest [jihad] fought not only by fighters, but by every person in this nation – young or old, male or female. We are fighting today, son, to stop whatever land we still have from slipping into the Jews' hands. We stand today in the face of the Jewish gold that flows into our country from all Jewish organizations worldwide; it attacks our weak points with its deadly weapons and its demonic temptation. (1.1)

The deadly weapons Abdullah speaks of are not bombs or tanks, but wealth. The gold that Shylock so covets in Shakespeare is again a key image here, and an important means of ingratiating himself in a society that sought to exclude him. As tempting as it is for us to read this as the same kind of stereotyping that has made Shakespeare's play so disputatious, for Arabs in the 1940s Bakathir's portrait of Arab-Jewish land transactions was highly plausible. Bakathir, through Shakespeare, is describing a visible reality that gains purchase beyond its rehearsal of a well-known calumny against all Jews as a race.

In *The New Shylock* the Jewish purchase of Arab property is hardly a benign business transaction, but the harbinger of the loss of political rights. Mikhail is the head of a Jerusalem municipality, a post that he relinquishes out of exasperation with the Jewish members of the council. He claims that 'this presidency has become an impotent position that is of no use to me or my country ... I have endured their harassment for a long time in order to keep this pro forma position for the Arabs, but they have gone too far with their arrogance' (1.1). In this detail, Bakathir was quite possibly drawing directly from current events. On 21 June 1945 the Cairo daily *Al-Ahram* [The Pyramids] reported that 'four of the Arab members on the municipal board for Al-Kudos region lost their membership in reference to the 47th code of the constitution of the municipality law because of their absence from the board for over three months' (['al Kudos Municipality'] 3). The Arab members of the forum were protesting the sale of land to the Zionists, demonstrating how real estate transactions, exactly as Mikhail feared in the play, would lead inevitably to diminished political representation. The board eventually came to be controlled by Zionists, who used the body as an organ to promote Jewish land ownership throughout Palestine. On 27 August 1945 the same newspaper attested to the effectiveness of the Zionists' strategy, reporting that Jews had spent over £10 million annually to buy Arab lands' (['The Project'] 4). Other Arabs had picked up the metaphor even earlier. King Abdul Saud, of Saudi Arabia, wondered how 'a merchant (that is, a Jew) [could] come and take Palestine out of our hands for money' (qtd in Morris 178). Arabs felt that Jews were trying to use their wealth – at a time when all discretionary funds throughout the world were being poured into the war effort – to conjure a state into being, just as Shylock uses his wealth to intervene in the Venetian economy and legal system.

The Zionists in *The New Shylock* recognize the impediments to the creation of a Jewish State in the face of these international developments. Cohen, Shylock's lawyer, understands that 'we can't judge clearly in these exceptional circumstances. The [British Mandatory] government is too busy for us and everyone else right now, with its life and death struggle.' Cohen of course is referring to the pressures of the Second World War and the vexing situation it created for the Zionists. The 1939 White Paper that Jews unanimously rejected remained official policy in Palestine and severely curtailed immigration and land-purchasing operations, forcing Zionists to adopt new tactics. Shylock advocates violence coupled with the continued accumulation of property through foreclosure and usury. The lawyer and his client discuss one reluctant seller:

COHEN: This Sheikh Saad, is he the one who refused to sell his village in the Sarawa Valley?
SHYLOCK (*regains his vigour*): Yes, that's the one; he died tonight with his entire family!
COHEN: I guess that would make it easier for the company to buy his land.
SHYLOCK: Yes, Sarawa Valley will be in our hands by tomorrow. But poor Zegnakh!
COHEN: Did he do that on our orders, Mr. Shylock?
SHYLOCK (*turns left and right*): Of course, Mr. Cohen. (1.2)

Shylock, with his darting movements and maniacal eyes, combines the quintessential stage villain with the Zionist operator who uses wealth and economic coercion to achieve political goals, a figure many Arabs might have encountered themselves or heard about from others as word of Jewish activities spread throughout Palestine. Zegnakh is Shylock's hired gun. Wearing a long black coat and prominently displaying his pistol, he is somewhere between the timeless vice figure and the contemporary Zionist gangster. In his modern incarnation Zegnakh is a member of the Stern gang, the shadowy paramilitary group that believed in using any means necessary to bring about a Jewish State and evict Arabs from Palestine.

Shylock and his cronies are here made to represent the radical fringe of the Zionist movement, suggesting to Arab audiences that these groups were in fact more prominent in the decision-making process than they really were. For Shylock, as for many members of the Stern gang and other Revisionists, the enemy was not Hitler and the Nazis, but the Arabs and British. Shylock feels that there is 'no doubt' that, 'if we had a choice,' it would 'have been in our interests to support Germany,' and therefore free Palestine of British influence and unpopular British policies. Neither were some historical Zionists disturbed by the connection with the Nazis (1.4). Jabotinsky wasn't much troubled when

Ben-Gurion referred to him as Vladimir Hitler, believing that, for Zionists, fascism might provide more useful models than the socialism of
Weizmann and more mainstream settlers (Shavit 368).

Shylock's flirtation with political violence is not restricted to his
attempts to acquire land. He believes that violent activities should be
extended to other arenas in the conflict to 'show our annoyance at the
British government and declare our objection to its policies.' He captures something of the demonic energy of his Shakespearean predecessor in exclaiming 'I want to smell the blood, and to feast my eyes on its
redness.' Like the Stern gang, Shylock envisions an ambitious program
of terrorist activity throughout the region. 'Political assassination,' he
argues, 'should not be in Palestine alone, but in other countries as well.
We have to cause a major episode in Egypt' (1.4). Shylock's wish had
already come to pass. On 6 November 1944 in Cairo, LEHI assassinated
Lord Moyne, the ranking British diplomat in the region, an event that
outraged Churchill and certainly brought the Zionists worldwide recognition. LEHI, like Jabotinsky, believed the real enemy of the Jews and
Zionism was not Hitler and the Nazis, but Britain and her imperialist
policies that would never allow a Jewish state. And although Stern's
politics did not reflect the official policy of Zionist leaders, their dramatic terrorist operations throughout the war years made them the
most visible Zionist group (Bell 62–5).

Like all productions of *The Merchant of Venice*, the centrepiece of
Bakathir's play is the trial scene, and its central figure is Shylock. As in
Shakespeare's play, where a routine loan occasions a much more wide-
ranging debate on the extent and jurisdiction of the law, the issues at
stake concern significantly more than land. In *The New Shylock* the trial
is transformed into an international tribunal charged with determining
the future of Palestine at the expiration of the British mandate in 1947.
The 'pound of flesh' represents not just land holdings of individual
property owners but sovereignty over the entire country; this, indeed,
is how many Zionists preferred to interpret the Balfour Declaration (the
metaphorical 'contract' of the play), even though it had been significantly qualified in the White Papers of 1922 and 1939.

Arab audiences witnessing the play would have been familiar with
the extensive debates concerning these documents over the previous
decade, a war of words that, in this region, was significantly more acute
than the military conflict that absorbed the rest of the world. For Arabs
in the 1940s, the Balfour Accord symbolized not the intervention of
foreign powers in determining the fate of Palestine (as it is typically

interpreted today), but yet another example of the Zionists' penchant for legal and diplomatic manipulation of the West. While Shylock views the Balfour declaration as 'a bill of rights for Jews in Palestine' (2.1), the Arabs in the play interpret it as a fortuitous convergence of British geopolitical strategy during the height of the First World War with what at that time were grandiose Zionist territorial aspirations. In Bakathir's play the Balfour agreement is something '[the Zionists] took [akhathna] from her [Great Britain]' through their own treacherous agency;[5] it is just another reason for Arabs to distrust their Jewish neighbours. During the trial Shylock makes the case to the assembled delegates that the Balfour agreement is legally binding, constituting in itself full legal justification for an embryonic Jewish state. He is adamant that as the Balfour Accord is a binding contract, 'we won't accept anything other than what's in this pact' (2.2), just as his Shakespearean predecessor claimed the 'due and forfeit of my bond' (4.1.36).

Because the Balfour Declaration was highly ambiguous, Arabs discounted its promise to establish a Jewish home in Palestine and instead preferred to concentrate on the caveat, which promised that any action taken would not negatively affect the larger Arab population. Arabs in *The New Shylock* insist that a Jewish state that does not infringe on Arab rights and aspirations is equivalent to cutting a pound of flesh without shedding blood. In light of this ambiguous language, and in the absence of any formal mechanism to implement the policy, the Balfour Accord was largely symbolic, and the battle surrounding it was largely one of interpretation. Bakathir's suggestion in this play is that Shakespeare might function as a guide to decipher the Balfour Accord and the resulting political impasse in the decades since 1917, something that the British government failed to do to anyone's satisfaction.

Like his unrelenting predecessor, when implored by General Swords to show mercy, not to 'cut off Palestine from the heart of the Arab World' (another allusion to excising the pound of flesh without drawing blood) and to consent to a less acrimonious settlement, Shylock vigorously insists on a literal understanding of the law and the full transfer of power to the Jews. He asks the court 'What is the law but a form?,' even admitting that his logic might be 'twisted' (2.1), just as his Shakespearean counterpart realizes his own actions are not rational (Gross 67). This Jerusalem trial, then, essentially takes the same form as its Venetian counterpart, with Shylock arguing for the law as an absolute construct that fully sanctions his individual desire for vengeance, while the president of the tribunal argues that 'the law also has a justice-achieving soul.' There is of course one important distinction that Mikhail Jad (a Palestinian Christian) points out: 'Antonio owned what he was given, unlike the Balfour Accord' (2.2). In seeing the Balfour Accord as more than it was, Shylock commits an error that Arabs frequently levelled against Zionist leaders. Arabs instead saw the Balfour Declaration as an indeterminate policy document coerced from the British during the turbulent days of the First World War from a representative, Lord Balfour, himself of Jewish descent. General Swords again reminds Shylock that '[w]e only gave the Balfour Accord to the Jews to win them over to our side in our war for freedom against the German oppressors' (2.2).

For most Western observers of the Arab-Israeli conflict today, the Balfour Declaration and the statements qualifying it are too imprecise and historically too distant to retain a decisive place in the political history of the region. In any case, there was simply too much going on during the war to pay much attention. Unconcerned with the potential ramifications of the debate, the Earl of Winterton, an MP and leading British anti-Zionist, no doubt expressed a common attitude when he claimed that 'we cannot understand how outbursts between the Arabs and Jews will cause serious damage to the allies' (qtd in Laquer 508). Focus on the axis powers meant that the debate over Palestine during the war was largely ignored by the allies, just as this phase of the Arab-Israeli conflict is largely forgotten to modern commentators who concentrate on the events of 1948 and after. Not so for Arabs. Egyptian President Gemal Abdel Nasser confessed in a 1960 speech that 'the first elements of Arab consciousness began to filter into my mind as a student in secondary schools, wherefrom I went out with my fellow schoolboys on strike on December 2nd of every year as a protest against the Balfour Declaration [which] gave the Jews a national home usurped unjustly from its legal owners' (qtd in Laquer and Rubin 89).

During the war, however, neither side was willing to tread too heavily on the British and the documents that articulated their policy in the Middle East. Aside from extremists on both sides, Arabs and Jews assumed that the future of the region, for better or worse, would ultimately be shaped by Britain and her allies. For this reason, Bakathir's play is just as concerned with courting the British and cultivating a favourable opinion of them among Arabs as it is with demonizing the Zionists. British public opinion after the war did gradually turn towards the Arabs and away from the Zionists, especially with the election of the Atlee government in 1945 and the increase in terrorist attacks against British targets. In *The New Shylock* General Swords, the British envoy, is a staunch ally of the Palestinians. He notes that 'it is because of her strong friendship with the Arabs that Britain was the first country to officially recognize the existence of the Arab League, because our long experience in governing countries has taught us that it would be a mistake to disregard reality' (2.1). British imperialism was fine, and worthy of defence as long as it served Arab interests. And although Bakathir may seem to be straying far from Shakespeare to directly address topical political concerns, by pitting both Arab Palestinians and the British Mandatory government against Shylock, his play essentially creates the same ambience of isolation that dominates *The Merchant of Venice*. Shylock, feeling trapped, becomes increasingly belligerent, retreating to the text of his bond, vowing 'there will be no reconciliation between us until the founding of a Jewish country in Palestine, according to the contract that's in our hand, and we won't settle for half-solutions' (2.2).

This, I think, is where the true value of Shakespeare's play as propaganda emerges for Bakathir and the Arabs. Bakathir's point is not simply that the negative traits of Shakespeare's Shylock persist in the Zionists of wartime Palestine, but that *The Merchant of Venice* is actually a prophetic allegory of events that came to pass. Not unlike the mock trial occasioned by Jessner's Hebrew production of the play, Bakathir's fictional trial is essentially a debate about the meaning of *The Merchant* in light of Zionism, and his characters are fully aware that they are reliving Shakespeare's play in the present. Mikhail outlines the precise extent to which *The Merchant* is an appropriate analogy to contemporary affairs in Palestine. Addressing the tribunal, he notes that

> [I]t is a strange coincidence ... that this opponent of mine shares a name with the Venetian Shylock that the great poet, Shakespeare, drew in his immortal story, and that they are both demanding the same thing. The only difference is that old Shylock wanted to claim the life of a noble Venetian merchant, but the new Shylock's demand concerns the life of a noble people of about seven million ... Shakespeare was not wrong, and is the greatest poet who was aware of the secrets of the human spirit. (2.1)

Mikhail presents his tendentious application of the play as fact, implying that the analogy is beyond cavil, that Shylock is representative of all

Jews, and that certain traits supposedly embodied by fictional Jews in the sixteenth century are timeless.

Contrary to what we might expect, Shylock does not protest the unfavourable comparison with his namesake. He deliberately invokes his earlier Shakespearean incarnation, inviting the audience to appreciate a direct allusion to current events rather than a vague analogy to cultural stereotypes. He explains to the court that *The Merchant* is 'an example I set up as a demand for our right ... You [the British] promised us a pound of flesh, so give us that pound' (2.1). Shylock, of course, is remarkably similar to Shakespeare's Shylock. Arabs, however, might have appreciated a significantly more recent allusion. Mikhail reminds the delegates that 'this Jew demands the pound of flesh, just like one of the radical Zionist leaders has said before him when he was called to testify in London in 1937' (2.1), recalling the language of Jabotinsky's testimony before the Peel Commission. Mikhail also reminds us that the name Shylock was not necessarily an insult for Zionists who relished the role of the defiant victim even as Arabs turned those same characteristics to their advantage.

It is somewhat bizarre that Bakathir's characters and historical figures in Palestine would cling to Shakespeare's play as a harbinger of the Arab-Israeli conflict. Given that both Arabs and Jews recognized Shylock as a plausible analogue to Zionists fighting for a Jewish state in Palestine, partially evacuating the utility of the story as propaganda, we must wonder what purpose these adaptations of and allusions to *The Merchant of Venice* ultimately serve. *The New Shylock* suggests that the answer might not lie in anything intrinsic to the play, but in Shakespeare's perceived cultural authority. Bakathir's play ends with the utter demise of the Jewish State seven years in the future, a wish fulfilled for many Palestinians but hardly a plausible outcome given the growing strength of the Zionists and the weight of global public opinion behind them following the war. Bakathir deflects this fantastical ending onto Shakespeare. When General Swords thanks the court for its recommendations, Mikhail avers, insisting '[y]ou must thank William Shakespeare ... Shakespeare presented the only solution to the international problem of Judaism.' The final words of the play, spoken (tellingly) by General Swords, offer a kind of benediction that again invokes Shakespeare as prophet. 'How right Shakespeare was,' he exclaims, 'as if he saw the future from a transparent screen' (2.3). Though obviously not as blatantly political, Jessner's decision to stage *The Merchant of Venice* as the first play at the Habimah suggests a similar belief in the long-term cultural authority of Shakespeare to attract attention and comment on current affairs. Shakespeare's value as a cultural signifier might have seemed even more pronounced to Arabs and Jews during the Second World War because of the British Mandatory Government and the (probably mistaken) assumption that Shakespeare might be effective in swaying opinion in Whitehall.

Finally, what do these episodes ultimately tell us about the reception of Shakespeare's play? *The Merchant of Venice* and the Arab-Israeli conflict are, I think, understood similarly. Both raise difficult and painful questions; both are thought to be monolithic and intransigent testimony to the persistence of racism, intolerance, and the violence they spawn: *The Merchant* is invariably anti-Semitic, and the conflict between Arabs and Israelis has always been (and for many, always will be) a cycle of violence followed by recriminations. Combining the two makes both seem even more pernicious. Thinking about *The Merchant* during the Second World War in the Middle East alerts us to the fact that Shakespeare's play poses different questions that vary with time and place and are not reducible to broad moral, political, or ideological categories. Properly understanding either the political conflict between Arabs and Jews or the appropriation of Shakespeare in that context forces us to investigate the more mundane work of propaganda as it inflects the parochial debates of the day.

Notes

I would like to acknowledge the diligent assistance of Youmna Dbouk, Melissa Whitney, and especially Deema Kaedbey who translated *The New Shylock* into English for me. Some parts of this essay first appeared in 'The Merchant of Venice, the Arab-Israeli Conflict, and the Perils of Shakespearean Appropriation,' *Comparative Drama* 41.4 (2008): 465–92. I thank the editors for permission to reprint this material.

1 The Habimah, founded in Moscow in 1917, later became the national theatre of Israel.
2 For a more extended discussion of this production, see Oz 60–3.
3 The Peel Commission was charged with clarifying the Balfour Declaration and redirecting British policy in the region. Its report, issued in 1938, proposed to partition Palestine, including a small Jewish State. The report was rejected by both Zionists and Arabs, and was, in any case, reversed by the findings of the Woodhead Commission in 1939.

4 Because my translation of the play is unlineated, references are to act and scene.
5 The Arabic 'akhathna' means 'took' in a very visceral and literal sense, as to physically 'seize' an object rather than 'acquire' it through negotiation or exchange.

Works Cited

Abend-David, Dora. *'Scorned My Nation:' A Comparison of Translations of* The Merchant of Venice *into German, Yiddish, and Hebrew*. New York: Peter Lang, 2003.

'al Kudos Municipality.' *Al-Ahram* [Cairo]. 21 June 1945: 3.

Al-Shetawi, Mahmoud. '*The Merchant of Venice* in Arabic.' *The Journal of Intercultural Studies* 15 (1994): 15–25.

Bakathir, Ali Ahmed. *Shayluck Al-Jadid*. Cairo: Lajnat al-Nasher lil-Jamiiyi, 1945.

Bell, J. Bowyer. *Terror Out of Zion: IRGUN, Zvai Leumi, LEHI, and the Palestine Underground, 1929–1949*. New York: St Martin's, 1977.

Cohen, Michael Joseph. *Palestine, Retreat from the Mandate: The Making of Policy, 1936–45*. London: Paul Elek, 1978.

Gelvin, James. *The Israel-Palestine Conflict: One Hundred Years of War*. Cambridge: Cambridge University Press, 2005.

Gross, Kenneth. *Shylock is Shakespeare*. Chicago: University of Chicago Press, 2006.

Hortmann, Wilhelm. *Shakespeare on the German Sage: The Twentieth Century*. Cambridge: Cambridge University Press, 1998.

Jessner, Leopold. 'Of the Eretz-Israeli Theatre and Its Purpose.' *Bamah* May 1934: n.pag.

'Judaism 101.' Great Leaders of Our People. OU.org. n.d. 4 Feb 2010. http://www.ou.or/about/judaism/rabbis/jabotinsky.htm.

Kohansky, Mendel. 'Hizkiyahu's New Shylock.' *The Jerusalem Post*. 24 March 1972: 39.

– 'Shakespeare on the Hebrew Stage.' *Ariel* 9 (1964): 79–99.

Laquer, Walter. *A History of Zionism*. 3rd ed. London: Tauris, 2003.

Laquer, Walter, and Barry Rubin. *The Israel-Arab Reader: A Documentary History of the Middle East Conflict*. New York: Penguin, 1976.

Morris, Benny. *Righteous Victims: A History of the Zionist-Arab Conflict*. New York: Random House, 1999.

Oz, Avraham. '*The Merchant of Venice* in Israel.' *Foreign Shakespeare*. Ed. Dennis Kennedy. Cambridge: Cambridge University Press, 1993.

'Project of Mr. Alawi to Save the Lands, The.' *Al-Ahram* [Cairo]. 27 Aug. 1945:
    4.

Shakespeare, William. *The Norton Shakespeare*. Ed. Stephen Greenblatt et al.
    New York: Norton, 1996.

Shavit, Yaacov. *Jabotinsky and the Revisionist Movement 1925–1948*. London:
    Frank Cass, 1988.

'Shaylock al-Hadith.' *Al-Thaqafa* 12 (1939): 41–4.

Shlaim, Avi. *The Iron Wall: Israel and the Arab World*. London: Allen Lane, 2000.

Shipler, David K. *Arab and Jew: Wounded Spirits in a Promised Land*. London:
    Penguin, 1986.

Winterton, Earl of. 'The Future of Palestine.' *London Sunday Chronicle*. 1 Oct.
    1945, 14.

4 'Caesar's word against the world': Caesarism and the Discourses of Empire

NANCY ISENBERG

On 10 June 1940 Italy declared war on England. The events leading up to that act of aggression are directly related to Italy's expansionist campaign in North Africa that not only violated the agreements of the League of Nations but also challenged the balance of power among colonizing nations in that part of the world, like England, which reacted by taking coercive measures against Italy.

This essay examines the two decades of Mussolini's dictatorship leading up to 1940 from the perspective of the Duce's use of a Caesarian model of politics and leadership to make of his rule a Modern Roman Empire, and of his persona a Modern Caesar.[1] My focus is, not surprisingly, on Shakespeare's *Julius Caesar*. Twice during Mussolini's Regime, this play was called up to aid and abet Fascist ideological programs, and in so doing to help rally popular consensus for Mussolini's belligerent empire-building intentions. On several later occasions, it also, directly or indirectly, spawned alternative stage *Caesars* that were better suited to a changing political climate after Italy's invasion of Ethiopia.

Mussolini's dictatorship began officially in late October 1922 when he gathered 30,000 troops and moved them spectacularly on a three-day march down to Rome. The march had been staged, even in its itinerary, to replicate one of the great legends associated with Julius Caesar: his 'March on Rome' in 49 BC when, after leading his legions into Italy across its northern boundary then marked by the river Rubicon, he is said to have remarked 'the die is cast' – there is no turning back. Mussolini fully identified his own march with Caesar's in its purpose, as Maria Wyke puts it, 'to uproot a rotten republic and establish a new dictatorial order for the benefit of the people' ('Film Style' 61).[2]

4.1. Fascist parade in the Avenue of the Empire, Rome, 1930s.

The political rhetoric that accompanied the Fascist march capitalized heavily on the historic analogy. For example, a pamphlet entitled *Le due marce su Roma. Giulio Cesare e Benito Mussolini* [The Two Marches on Rome. Julius Caesar and Benito Mussolini], published shortly after the event, draws the correlations between the 'two profound crises of social decomposition, in some ways similar to each other ... The first ... marked with the end of the old aristocratic parties, the triumph of democratic monarchy and of Julius Caesar. The second, nearly two thousand years later ... is characterized by the collapse of revolutionary socialism and the Fascist victory of Benito Mussolini' (Vezio 5).[3]

It must be acknowledged before going any further that Mussolini's appropriation of Caesar and Roman history was by no means original. Throughout history, as Wyke explains, Caesar has been proposed alternately 'as conqueror or civilizer, founder or destroyer, democrat or autocrat, murderer or victim ... [and] deployed to legitimate or undermine the authority of kings, to justify or denounce the coups of generals, to launch or obstruct revolutions' (*Caesar* 17).[4] The coining of the term 'Caesarism' can be traced back to the second half of the nineteenth century around the time of Napoleon III, who like his uncle before him posed as a new Caesar, and who conducted his own 'opération Rubicon,' as his coup d'état in 1851 – with no river crossing – was dubbed (Baehr 6 and 103–4). And, as we know, Mussolini's was not the only dictatorship in his own time to look to ancient Rome and its conquering armies for models of military prowess and discipline, and iconographic symbols. Nonetheless, Mussolini's appropriation of ancient Rome, supported by the unique historic-geographic lineage it could claim, stands out among the others as the most powerful and all encompassing manipulation.

Between 1924 and 1925 at least thirteen new translations of Shakespeare's *Julius Caesar* appeared in print throughout the Italian peninsula, and there are at least forty surviving editions, including new translations and reprints, published during Mussolini's twenty-year rule. That Shakespeare's work might find a place in Italian Fascism's program of cultural propaganda is not in itself remarkable, but the publication numbers here are. According to statistics on illiteracy and poverty in Italy in the early twentieth century, both the reading skills of the majority of the population and their disposable income – for the purchase of books, for example – were either nil or extremely limited.

The explanation lies in the important educational reform that took place in 1923, and that among other things extended the leaving age for students to fourteen. The prolonged education of young people would not only improve the levels of literacy in Italy and combat the nation's cultural and linguistic fragmentation, but also provide the place and time for forging a national identity and pride. While the study of ancient Roman history was prescribed by the Ministry of Education across the entire thirteen year curriculum, Shakespeare's *Julius Caesar* was included as a standard text in the middle school (Galfré 237).

At that time Shakespeare was a very well established cultural icon in Italy. The abundance of Shakespeare's borrowings from ancient and renaissance Italian history, culture, and geography to provide source, story, and setting for so many of his works earned Italy a privileged placed in the Shakespeare canon.[5] In return, Shakespeare's plays became attractively assimilable into Italian culture: they were translated, read, performed, discussed, and appropriated into new works and artistic media, with those for the operatic stage being perhaps the best known.[6] Thus the prominent place of Shakespeare in the school curriculum comes as no surprise, nor does the choice of *Julius Caesar*, given the political climate.

In favour of *Julius Caesar* it could be argued that, stylistically, it was considered one of Shakespeare's most accessible plays. Aside from the quibbling of the artisans in the opening scene, the dialogue appears, in large part, straightforward. Furthermore, sexual innuendos, off-colour jokes, and lewdness have no place in this play – aspects of the text that surely played an important part in its selection as a school text, in Italy as elsewhere in Europe and North America. But more important in the context at hand were *Julius Caesar*'s roots in great Latin texts and its re-creation of a chapter in the life of the greatest of Roman heroes. Youngsters with their impressionable minds fired up by all the glorified facts about the Regime's effulgent legacy would read Shakespeare's *Julius Caesar* and, according to plan, come to adore the legendary Roman hero and through him their current day ruler.

However, as Ernest Schanzer recognized looking back from the 1950s, the play's 'stylistic simplicity, coupled with an absence of bawdy lines' led to the belief that 'it ought to be' and then to the conviction that 'it *is* a simple play,' which it most certainly is not (297). Surely when it was introduced nationwide into the Italian middle school program, the bureaucrats who chose it were blind to the text's many complexities, ambiguities, and contradictions that to our eyes today are clearly in conflict with Fascism's use of Caesar. But as the play's critical history illustrates, whether Caesar is the Man of Destiny or a boastful tyrant, whether Brutus's deed is laudable or foul, or whether Antony is sincere or calculating has been argued differently in different times and by different audiences (Schanzer 297–8).

Shakespeare's text would have exposed the entire school population to a Caesar who nearly drowned in a swimming race (1.2.99–114), who 'fell down in the market-place, and foam'd at mouth' (1.2.249–50), and who, when struck with fever, 'did shake,' whose 'coward lips did from their colour fly,' who groaned and cried then 'as a sick girl' for a drink (1.2.120–7). We might ask today why no potential threats to Mussolini's public image and popular appeal were perceived in such lines spoken by Cassius's as 'It doth amaze me / A man of such a feeble temper should / So get the start of the majestic world, / And bear the palm alone' (1.2.127–30), or 'What trash is Rome, / What rubbish, and what offal, when it serves / For the base matter to illuminate / So vile a thing as Caesar!' (1.3.108–11).

But the many lines that raise doubts seem not to have posed a problem because the text was not read in full but rather studied in extracts (Galfré 217) that would surely have slanted the perspective on the whole; as Cicero remarked to Casca, these were indeed 'strange-disposed' times in which 'men [might] construe things, after their fashion, / Clean from the purpose of the things themselves' (1.3.34–5).

A glance at the preface to one of the school texts illustrates how the young readers were guided through their study of the play, making sure they focused on and appreciated how Caesar's spirit 'powerfully dominates the entire drama,' that they appreciated his devotion to 'saving' and 'consolidating' the empire, that they understood, drawing analogies with their own time, that 'the republican regime which was falling to pieces could only come to an end with Caesar – or rather Caesarism – stepping in ... to save – or rather consolidate – the empire,' and that they admired how he 'held the fate of Rome and the World in his hand' (Muccioli 9). The same preface continues acknowledging the alleged negative traits in Shakespeare's Caesar, disproving them one by one:

We cannot affirm that Shakespeare had an unjust concept of Caesar, for in this play and in parts of others he has given proof of being fully aware of the high moral and intellectual qualities of Caesar. He makes Cassius himself ... admit to Caesar's nobility when he has him declare that Caesar would not be a wolf, if he did not think the Romans were sheep; he would not be a lion, if the Romans were not hinds … Elsewhere Shakespeare defines Caesar as a true man, celebrated for his values, prudence and wisdom which has an incomparable social, political, intellectual and moral greatness. (Muccioli 9–10)

The disproving continues in the notes to the text. One such note, for example, explains that neither Plutarch nor Suetonius mentions the near-drowning episode; rather, 'Caesar was a competent swimmer because both Plutarch and Suetonius recount how he saved his commentaries by holding one hand out of the water while swimming in the port of Alexandria' (Muccioli 36). The note to Cassius's 'It doth amaze me' speech stresses that the episode occurred when Caesar was quite young and points out that Cassius's amazement is directed at the way Caesar managed 'in the competition for power, for honour and glory to overtake more notable and more powerful men in Rome: august majesty of the world' (Muccioli 38).

Supplementary texts on the subject of Caesar in relation to Mussolini, circulated among students and teachers alike, also helped silence the 'disturbances' in Shakespeare's script. One such school book, innocently and simply entitled *Giulio Cesare*, reveals its true purpose in the cover image, which depicts a black profile silhouette of a well-known bust of Caesar: shadowing the silhouette, as if projected by it, is a profile of Mussolini (see fig. 4.2).

The preface to this book illustrates how 'the obvious similarities between the political directions and glorious deeds of the creators of the Roman and Fascist Empires must be attributed to Divine Will' (Guarnieri xii–xiii). It also makes a point of noting what is missing in Shakespeare's *Julius Caesar*: that 'breath of pure Romanness that makes of Caesar and Rome one indivisible symbol – eternal and universal – of wisdom, power, and glory' (Guarnieri xi).

The classroom rhetoric was strong but the street rhetoric – both verbal and visual – was even stronger. With all the Roman props and theatrics introduced into Fascism's self fashioning – the eagle, the lictor symbol, the military salute and marching style, Mussolini's appellation as Duce, and the very term 'Fascism' – how could students, as they read Shakespeare's *Julius Caesar*, not see themselves as the direct heirs of ancient Rome with Mussolini as their Caesar? How could they not identify with characters who, as they were repeatedly told in the introductions to their texts, 'speak only about Caesar, fight only for him, win or lose for him'? (Cesareo 4).

4.2. Cover illustration for the book *Giulio Cesare* by Lyno Guarnieri (Roma: Società italiana edizioni e rappresentazioni, 1938) showing a profile of Mussolini as a shadow of a well-known bust of Caesar.

Such forceful affirmations about fighting only for Caesar, winning or losing for Caesar worked not only towards coercing youthful minds into an unwavering admiration of their Duce and his politics, but also towards indoctrinating the youngsters into the ideology of the *Balilla*, a parascholastic youth institution created not only to fascistize the younger Italians (ages 8 to 18) through moral education but also to provide them with premilitary instruction, preparing them to take up arms to fight for their Duce and his beliefs. In this regard, one cannot help contemplating certain phrases in Shakespeare's text that, appropriated into the Fascist context, must have generated locally appropriated references. The 'havoc' that 'let slip the dogs of war' and gave way to 'domestic fury' and 'civil strife' invoked by Antony might well even have offered a legitimizing analogy for the *squadristi* (political gangster squadrons) that had helped sweep Mussolini into power, and later for the Blackshirts who helped him maintain it. Both militia groups took justice into their own hands and went about crushing voices of dissent with violence and destruction. That same Shakespearean 'havoc' might also have worked as an admonition against treacherous designs on Mussolini's life, and as a reminder of the hell that would break loose in the event of an assassination. Similarly, Shakespeare's 'rag tag people,' the 'common herd,' learning that they are Caesar's heirs could offer another legitimizing analogy – this one for the Roman legacy that Mussolini claimed for his own 'common herd.'

In the construction of a national patriotic culture, it seems that Shakespeare's *Julius Caesar* was seen as useful almost exclusively as written text, not in performance. But on just one occasion this drama stepped off the printed page, to play a part in Mussolini's expansionist campaign.

As Giuseppe Finaldi describes it, Italy's holdings abroad, inherited from the preceding liberal government consisted of 'three small territories (Eritrea, Somalia, and [for a time] Libya) plus a scattering of not very vital islands in the Mediterranean.' The territories of Italy's liberal colonial empire were not of great strategic importance. And as Finaldi reminds us, 'Liberal Italy's Roman Empire was made up of the scraps left over after the choice pickings had gone to the other European powers' (78). At the end of 1934, an incident between Italian and Ethiopian soldiers just inside the Ethiopian borders served as pretext for increased aggression on Italy's part. Ethiopia, like Italy, was a member of the League of Nations. The British minister of the League intervened and tried to negotiate with Mussolini, but without success. The Italian invasion began in October 1935, and on 9 August 1936 the Duce appeared on the balcony of the Palazzo Venezia, in the centre of Rome to proclaim Italy an Empire.

Expansionism had been part of Mussolini's program from the start. He wanted Italy to be respected as the 'bastion of Latin civilization in the Mediterranean' (qtd in Giardina 293) and considered as competition by other European colonizing nations, like England and France. Furthermore, he envisioned new territories that would be able to absorb some of the human excess of his overpopulated country. But perhaps most importantly, as Mussolini expounded in a famous speech several months before his March on Rome, 'Italy ... feels the irresistible attraction of the Mediterranean that opens the way to Africa. A twice millennial tradition calls Italy to the shores of the black continent whose venerable relics display the Roman Empire' (qtd in Giardina 219).

As always, theatrics seem – at least in part – to have determined the agenda. Monumental Rome, as Mussolini's personal stage, would for starters require a more imperial look. The planning began in the mid-1920s when Mussolini first called for an urban renewal that would, as he put it, 'weed out' everything that had grown up around the Mausoleum of Augustus, the Theatre of Marcellus, the Capitoline Hill, and the Pantheon in the 'centuries of decadence' so that the two-thousand-year-old monuments of Italian history could 'giganticize in the necessary solitude' (qtd in Giardina 231). The fact that this plan involved the destruction of 'medieval, renaissance, and baroque buildings, churches ... and squares' and even of other ancient Roman remains did not matter (Giardina 232).

In July 1931 stage two of the renovation went into operation, to open up an artery that would connect Piazza Venezia and the Coliseum. The new avenue, at the cost of further demolition and human displacement, would join two monumental spaces, one representing the glory of ancient Rome, and the other the virtues of the *Risorgimenti* (the nineteenth century 'Resurgence' that unified the city states of Italy into one nation) – two glorious pasts claimed as the foundations of Fascism. The Avenue of the Empire was inaugurated in October 1932. At the time, the term 'Empire' was still a reference only to ancient Rome, in homage to the archeological sites of the Roman forum, the Palatine hill, and the Trajan market flanking the Avenue, but Mussolini would not be satisfied until the toponomastic reference was extended to modern Rome and the Fascist state as well.

Once completed, with its monuments 'giganticized in their necessary solitude,' the Avenue of the Empire was the ideal ambience for

4.3. Production photograph of the funeral scene from *Giulio Cesare*, directed by Ferdinando Tamberlani, Basilica of Maxentium, Rome, Italy, 1935. Reproduced by permission of the Biblioteca Museo Teatrale del Burcardo, Rome, Italy.

a performance that would rally support and approval for Mussolini's African campaign. Although there was already a tradition of open-air performance in Roman amphitheaters in Italy, in the summer of 1935, for the first time ever, the Basilica of Maxentius, one of the most imposing monuments of the Forum-Palatine complex, became not just the backdrop but the very stage for a theatrical production of Shakespeare's *Julius Caesar* (see figs. 4.3 and 4.4).

The event took on all the solemn greatness of its setting – the three main archways were drowned in limelight when the action was centred in that area, and plunged into blackness when it was not; choral scenes, like the Lupercal procession, took over the entire architectural expanse. Huge shadows danced over the towering brick walls behind the arches during the final battle scene. The overall impression – with the imposing setting, the intense play of bright light, shadow, and darkness, and the choreography that moved human masses intricately across the

4.4. Production photograph from *Giulio Cesare*, directed by Ferdinando Tamberlani, Basilica of Maxentium, Rome, Italy, 1935. Reproduced by permission of the Biblioteca Museo Teatrale del Burcardo, Rome, Italy.

expansive performance space – was of 'majesty and grandeur.' In such an atmosphere, the politically most 'dangerous' scene, Caesar's assassination, played in the central arch, could be read only as a tragedy for mankind (Sestiti 128).[7]

The production, which ran for five days, was sponsored and promoted by the Opera nazionale dopolavoro (the National Workers' Recreational Club), a powerful Fascist organization that at the time of the production claimed close to eighty percent of workers among its members. The event was intended as an invitation to spend one of the hottest evenings of the summer out of doors in a privileged setting not normally frequented by the working class, and to enjoy an exceptional offering of theatrical entertainment of the sort not normally addressed to blue-collar audiences, at a very affordable price. For these workers, an evening spent amidst spectacular archeological ruins, watching a performance that re-enacted a piece of their cultural history, was in

itself perceived as a powerful piece of rhetoric that reiterated Mussolini's call 'not to nostalgic contemplation of the past, but *hard preparation
for the future*. Rome is our point of departure ... our myth. We dream of
a Roman Italy, that is wise and strong, disciplined and *imperial*' (emphasis added; qtd in Giardina 219).

It is not surprising to learn that, in the opinion of one reviewer, the
casting choice for Caesar was inaccurate. The actor's physical appearance contrasted disturbingly with that of the Roman leader's, as one
could easily see by observing the statue on display only metres away
on the Avenue of the Empire. The actor was 'not lean, muscular and
wiry, but rather a paunchy fellow with a thick neck' (Contini 4). It
would seem the actor had been chosen to resemble Caesar's modern
would-be counterpart.

In view of the timing – barely two months before the official invasion
of Ethiopia – and collocation – in the newly imperial setting – the event
did indeed provide an opportunity to mould a consensus for Mussolini's imperialist ambitions.[8] Reading about that invasion today, there
is truly nothing to be proud of. The atrocities carried out by the Italians
were unimaginably cruel and horrific. But in 1935 its reading in the Italian context was restricted to signs of importance, power, and respect on
the international map of expansionism, and to the rebirth, after fifteen
centuries, of the great Roman Empire. Exactly one year after the Maxentius performance, Mussolini declared Italy's (re)new(ed) imperial
status, in celebration of which marble maps of the Ancient and Modern
Roman Empires were mounted on the Basilica's boundary walls skirt-
ing the Avenue of the Empire. Any previous doubts about the significance of the setting of the Maxentius *Julius Caesar* were surely erased by
the stone markers of the 'rebirth' of the Roman Empire.   .

Achille Starace, the president of the National Workers' Recreational
Club was credited with the idea for the Maxentius event (Contini 5).
Starace, an ardent supporter of Mussolini who had led a squadron of
Blackshirts in the famous March on Rome, was, at the time, also President of the National Fascist Party. Shortly after the production he took
a leave of absence from politics to participate, in his capacity as army
colonel, in the invasion of Ethiopia.

When the Maxentius proposal landed on the desk of the chief (and
sole) official censor, Leopoldo Zurlo, he felt he had no choice but to
explicitly argue in its favour. He was in no position to oppose a project
promoted by someone as powerful as Starace, and in which Mussolini
had reportedly 'taken a personal interest.'[9] But in his report Zurlo did

tactfully signal some of the play's 'shortcomings' by embedding them in a brief literary discussion. His report pointed out the play's 'major defect' – the role of Brutus is too well developed for a play entitled *Julius Caesar* – and went on to consider the doubts 'raised by others' about a play in which 'a formidable man who had taken over as solitary ruler is assassinated, at the hands of a virtuous man, exclusively for the love of freedom of the people.' 'Some have argued,' Zurlo continued, 'that Shakespeare belittled Caesar, but ... elsewhere Shakespeare praised Caesar's greatness.' Zurlo declared the accusation that Shakespeare's Caesar is effeminate to be another falsehood because 'Caesar is thus described by the vile and deceiving conspirator Cassius.' Finally, Zurlo argued, Brutus was mistaken in thinking that Caesar was a menace to freedom, 'for his death brought about the end of Roman *virtù*.' Brutus had been deceived by that 'foul speculator Cassius.' Zurlo tried to demonstrate that 'Shakespeare expresses the futility of the crime and condemns it, even if it was carried out by a virtuous man' (178–80).

Zurlo was not, contrary to expectation, a zealous party bureaucrat, but in his own words 'an honest anti-fascist' who carried out his work as 'a loyal civil servant.' In his memoirs he explains that he could gauge the reactions of the audience more accurately than could a party supporter in good faith who 'would have gobbled up every word written in praise of Fascism, thus running the risk of disgusting the audience' (16). Having earned his appointment as official censor on the strength of this conviction, he was thus able on the one hand to negotiate with authors and directors, inviting them to make initial cuts, and, on the other, to argue with his superiors in favour of maintaining certain contradictions in their scripts.

Zurlo had been appointed by the national chief of police who, Zurlo later revealed, shared his own anti-fascist beliefs but had 'known how to put on an impenetrable official mask.' Furthermore, Zurlo lived with the vice-chief of police, for whom he declared a 'brotherly friendship.' Accusations by informants that the relationship was homosexual – a gross legal and moral offence – were ignored by the authorities (Benadusi 193–4). As I see it, this trio quietly working together was able to preserve a minimum of cultural dignity on the Italian stage during a time of political repression.

According to the practice established by Zurlo, someone from the Workers' Recreational Club made the initial cuts in the Maxentius script:[10] approximately forty-five percent of Shakespeare's lines are penciled out. Many of these cuts seem to be aimed at simplification of the text for a poorly educated or illiterate working-class audience. Often the large chunks that were removed conveniently incorporated politically offensive or dangerous lines; out went lofty reflections, dialogues peripheral to the action of the main plot, elaborate and indelicate accounts of portents, negative vibrations in the macrocosm, and much of the detail that nuanced character and motive. Dialogues among the conspirators are mostly eliminated and, where unavoidable, reduced to the bare minimum for plot coherence. Brutus's part and character are both considerably downsized. However, although the near-drowning narrative and the reference to Caesar's 'coward lips' in the fever narrative were cut, for example, the comparison to 'a sick girl' and the epilepsy narrative that left Caesar 'foaming at the mouth' remained in the text. Cassius's provocative question to Brutus – 'Why should [Caesar's] name be sounded more than yours?' (1.2.141) – survived censorship, as did the references to Rome as 'trash,' 'rubbish' and 'offal' (1.3.108–9). These and other propagandistically questionable lines had been allowed to slip through the net.

A document in the Censorship Office archives dating from October 1935, two months after the Maxentius event, announces the preparation of a new theatre adaptation of Shakespeare's *Julius Caesar*, this time an opera composed by Gian Francesco Malipiero, scheduled to premiere in Genoa at the Teatro Carlo Felice in February 1936. This document and other archival records regarding Malipiero's work strongly suggest that political attitudes towards Shakespeare's work in performance had radically changed in those sixty days following the Maxentius production.

In a report dated 6 October, shortly after he received Malipiero's libretto, Zurlo takes care to mention that, before proceeding, he had consulted with His Excellency Dino Alfieri, Undersecretary of State in the neo-Ministry of Press and Propaganda (which had just taken over the Censorship office from the Ministry of the Interior and was headed by Mussolini's son-in-law). Zurlo notes that he had shown Alfieri the report drawn up the preceding summer in regard to the Maxentius proposal and that 'His Excellency agreed it would not be possible to prohibit the libretto' (Archivio, Presidenza, 3/2–12.5855).

I believe we should be reading between the lines of Zurlo's remark a reference to the suddenly changed international and national scenes: in only three days the Italian military advance in North Africa had officially become the invasion of Ethiopia; England and France were in the process of publishing heavy sanctions against Italy; Italy responded with retaliatory measures that included prohibiting the performance of works produced in the sanctionist countries; the Inspectorate for the Theatre, however, was arguing for certain exceptions, among which were plays by Shakespeare (Ferrara 34).

Malipiero's *Giulio Cesare* was caught up in the middle of all this. He had chosen a Roman subject in an attempt to get back in the good graces of the Duce after Mussolini had personally banned his previous opera after its opening night.[11] With the most unfortunate timing of its completion, coinciding with the escalation of international tensions, Malipiero worked hard to win the Duce's appreciation for his new effort. A telegram to the composer on 12 October from Mussolini's Cabinet confirms that the Duce was pleased to receive a copy of the opera and sent his thanks. A note from the Cabinet office to Mussolini informed him that the Special Commissioner for the Teatro Carlo Felice was pressing for an official government representation on opening night, and the Undersecretary of State Alfieri was hence ordered by Mussolini to perform this duty. On 7 February 1936 Malipiero sent the following telegram to Mussolini: 'On the eve of *Giulio Cesare* I express my gratitude to His Excellency and inform him that the Teatro Carlo Felice has prepared a most beautiful performance.' That same evening, he also sent off a note on hotel stationery to Alfieri thanking him for coming. Alluding perhaps to Brutus's navigation metaphor ('There is a tide in the affairs of men, / Which, taken at the flood, leads on to fortune; / Omitted, all the voyage of their life / Is bound in shallows and in miseries. / On such a full sea are we now afloat; / And we must take the current when it serves, / Or lose our ventures.' 4.3.217–23), Malipiero added: 'Let us hope there will not be contrary currents, or to be more precise, further subterranean attacks. We are still far out at sea [an Italian expression meaning 'to be far from the solution to a problem'], but that does not mean that we are in a storm. Navigating is in any case a noble undertaking' (Archivio, Presidenza, 3/2–12.5855).

The libretto for Malipiero's *Giulio Cesare* is essentially a very heavily cut version of Shakespeare's text, reduced to approximately thirty percent of the original, with the addition of several choral sections and, for the ending, a Latin hymn to Rome from Horace.[12] A summary comparison of these cuts with those of the Maxentius script reflects the difference in venue and audience. Here, instead of the over-simplified characterizations produced in Rome, in spite of the severe cuts, we find many of the complexities and ambiguities that Shakespeare had created. Furthermore, Shakespearean ponderings and contemplations lend themselves extremely well to operatic arias and choruses. Not surprisingly, the assassination scene was ordered to take place offstage (Malipiero 1).

By the end of the 1930s Shakespeare's play could no longer be bent to serve Fascist politics. The tensions between Italy and England had escalated dramatically, due to Italy's alliance with Germany. Furthermore, a continuous weakening of popular support for Mussolini made the play's ambivalence about Caesar's greatness intolerable. Mussolini had been careful to counter the physical defects of Shakespeare's Caesar by widely circulating images of his determined square jaw, leadership qualities, physical strength, and confident swimming skills, but there was no erasing the double reading of the conspirator's motives and, worse, of Caesar's assassination. The 'bleeding business' of this scene, in times of increasing violence at home and abroad, along with a series of attempts on the Duce's life, was much too a 'bleeding business.' Such times called for a play that would rectify the threats posed by Shakespeare's text.

Mussolini himself stepped in as playwright in collaboration with Giovacchino Forzano, an important opera librettist and dramatist of the time. *Cesare* was their third concerted effort. The play opened at the Teatro Argentina in Rome in April 1939, and ran through hundreds of performances throughout Italy and abroad (Dunnett 257).[13] One critic compared the production, from the perspective of its scenic effects and massive crowd scene, to what Italy's finest opera stages or cinema screens could offer (Lodovici 200). Only outside Italy, however, was Mussolini's collaboration on the play allowed to be officially acknowledged.[14] Having found no explanation for this, I can only surmise that it was thought, in such dire times, that Mussolini ought not to be distracted from his political responsibilities.

Mussolini and Forzano's *Cesare*, as described by Griffiths, 'comprises a series of *tableaux* that portray Julius Caesar first as the man of destiny called to save Rome from decadence, then as the hero who safeguards the imperial destiny of Rome through the defeat of the decadent Egyptians, and finally as the architect of a new Rome whose work is tragically cut short' (Griffiths 345–6). In place of scenes that express doubt over the celebration of Caesar there is a re-enactment of the people's call for his help that led to his march on Rome. There are no scenes that explore the right or wrong of Caesar accepting the crown. Here we have Caesar consolidating the strength of Rome by dominating unrest in far away Egypt. Instead of a staged assassination scene at the Senate, here

4.5. Production photograph of map scene from *Cesare*, a play by Giovacchino Forzano and Benito Mussolini. Teatro Argentina, Rome, Italy, 1939. Reproduced by permission of the Biblioteca Museo Teatrale del Burcardo, Rome, Italy.

we have a Roman port scene, set against an imposing backdrop map of the expanding Empire. News of the assassination reaches the peasant crowds, who love their Caesar unquestioningly, and for whom they are about to abandon their beloved Italy for the shores to Africa, to give birth to new Roman settlements.[15]

The epilogue to this study lies in the reversal of influence. Orson Welles's long-running 1937 *Julius Caesar* at the Mercury Theatre in New York, set in contemporary Fascist Italy, comes immediately to mind, but the reversal goes beyond that. Mussolini's staging of his regime as a New Roman Empire universally but falsely impacted the collective imagination worldwide of ancient Rome. There was a general misunderstanding that the Fascist present was a vehicle for comprehending ancient Rome, whereas in truth, Fascism's *Romanità* was in large part a contemporary invention, taking only minimal inspiration from visual and textual remnants of the past (Giardina 233). Joseph Mankiewicz's

1953 film, starring Marlon Brando, John Gielgud, and James Mason, helped to propagate this misconception through its recurring visual references to Mussolini's *Romanità*. Maria Wyke, in her discussion of the film, points out how Mankiewicz utilizes 'specific memories of the ancient Roman rituals which the Italian ... [regime] had variously borrowed and restaged.' She mentions 'the eagles which litter the film ... [symbolizing] simultaneously Roman dictatorial and imperial power *and* its appropriation and widespread display as part of Fascist ideology.' She also points out how the 'dictator's initial procession to the stadium where he will reject the crown of kingship recollects Italian military parades that were regularly overseen by Mussolini,' and how the 'ubiquity of Calhern's images as Caesar ... recalls the proliferation of images of Mussolini and Caesar that colonized the lives of Italians under the regime' ('Film Style' 61–2).

In Mankiewicz's film, even the camera angle in the funeral orations scene – attentive to the vertical distance between the orators looking down and the mob looking up – seems to be mirroring Mussolini's famous balcony 'performances' (see figs. 4.6 and 4.7).

Maddalena Pennacchia (passim) discusses the staging of Antonio's funeral oration in Shakespeare as an experiment with new mediatic tools. Mussolini, for all his horrific defects, was remarkably innovative when it came to moving the masses and using mass media. A journalist before beginning his political career, he founded both *Il popolo d'Italia*, the leading newspaper under his dictatorship, and the Istituto Luce for the distribution of newsreels and documentaries in movie theatres. Filling Piazza Venezia to overflowing for his appearances from the balcony of Palazzo Venezia, and simultaneously filling all the other major piazzas of Italy where crowds listened to his voice on radio broadcast, amplified by loudspeakers, and filming these turnouts so they could be shown in every cinema theatre in the country and appear in photographs across all six columns of the front pages of newspapers, was certainly several notches up from Antony's working the mob on Shakespeare's stage, but Mussolini's initial inspiration may very well owe something to Shakespeare's Antony, just as the funeral oration scene in Mankiewicz's film may well be derived, in part of Mussolini's balcony 'performances.'

Here then is a summary reconstruction of how 'Caesar's word against the world' was appropriated from Shakespeare in Mussolini's Fascism, first as a cog in the machinery that fascistized Italy's younger population, then as a stepping stone in the path to Empire, and, ultimately, when the drums of war were rolling, as an embarrassing and

4.6. Mussolini addressing a crowd from the balcony of Palazzo Venezia, Rome, Italy, 1940, from a clip published by the Istituto Luce, Rome, Italy.

4.7. Marlon Brando as Mark Antony in the oration scene from film of *Julius Caesar*, directed by Joseph Mankiewicz, 1953.

then dreaded model of what must not be seen or heard, and of how in the wake of this, Mussolini's Fascism would be remediated into the performance of Shakespeare's *Julius Caesar*.

Notes

1 This essay has its roots in a group research project on Shakespeare and Rome coordinated by Maria Del Sapio, involving members of the Department of Comparative Literature at the University of Rome Three. Many of the essays published in relation to this research – especially those in *Identity, Otherness and Empire in Shakespeare's Rome*, ed. Maria Del Sapio (Farnham and Burlington: Ashgate, 2009) and *Questioning Bodies in Shakespeare's Rome*, eds. Maria Del Sapio, Nancy Isenberg, and Maddalena Pennacchia (Göttingen: Vandenhoeck and Ruprecht Unipress, 2010) – although not explicitly cited here, have silently contributed to the fabric of this paper.

2 There was one small detail in Mussolini's March on Rome, overlooked at the time, that distinguished it from Caesar's: Mussolini did not march with his troops, but rode by train down to Rome, getting off only occasionally to be photographed marching alongside his men for the benefit of the press.

3 Here and elsewhere, unless otherwise specified, all translations from Italian are mine. Mussolini articulated a model for a new 'mass society' in explicit opposition to the threateningly fast-spreading Soviet *class*-based model, earning him in the early years of his rule the identity of a great statesman of international stature. This is repeatedly documented in the British and American press, in newsreels projected in the cinema houses on both sides of the Atlantic, in statements of praise by such leaders as Churchill and Roosevelt.

4 See also by Wyke, 'Sawdust Caesar: Mussolini, Julius Caesar, and the Drama of Dictatorship,' *Uses and Abuses of Antiquity*, eds. Michael Biddiss and Maria Wyke (Bern and New York: Peter Lang, 1999) 176–9.

5 For further discussion on the cultural exchange between Shakespeare and Italy, see for example Nancy Isenberg, 'Shakespeare's Rome in Rome's Wooden "O,"' *Shakespeare and Rome. Identity, Otherness and Empire*, ed. Maria Del Sapio, 175–87; Agostino Lombardo, 'Shakespeare in Italy,' *Proceedings of the American Philological Society* 14:4 (Dec. 1997): 454–62; Michele Marrapodi, *Shakespeare, Italy and Intertextuality* (Manchester and New York: Manchester University Press, 2004); Giorgio Melchiori and Michele Marrapodi, eds., *Italian Studies in Shakespeare and His Contemporaries* (Newark: University of Delaware Press, 1999).

6 These extend well beyond the better known operas by Vicenzo Bellini, Gioachino Rossini, and Giuseppe Verdi. See the excellent bibliography at http://pages.unibas.ch/shine/home.html, reachable through the 'adaptations' link in the sidebar.

7 Sestiti's comments derive from reviews in *Giornale d'Italia* by Antonelli and in *La Stampa* by Diego Angeli.

8 Newspaper announcements and reviews confirm that the *Julius Caesar* performances were immediately followed by a production of *Coriolanus*, also at the Basilica, although there is no trace of it in the surviving inventory of the Censorship Office. The war theme in *Coriolanus* makes it an appropriate mate to *Julius Caesar* in line with the political agenda discussed here.

9 In a letter written several years later to Mussolini's private secretary, Fernando Tamberlani, the director of the Maxentius production, recalled how the Duce had taken a personal interest in it (Fernando Tamberlani, letter to Nicolò De Cesare, Ministry of the Interior. 22 Dec. 1942. Archivio, Segreteria, Rome). Unfortunately I have been unable to shed more light on that statement and give substance to Mussolini's 'interest.'

10 The script for the Maxentius production was a copy of Raffaello Piccoli's translation of *Julius Caesar* (Firenze: Sansoni, 1924).

11 Herein hangs a tale that is outside the scope of this paper but, briefly: the opera in question, *La favola del figlio cambiato* [The Tale of the Changed Son], was based on a story by Luigi Pirandello, whose impatience with bourgeois ideals and behaviour was faithfully represented in Malipiero's work, and irritating to upholders of Fascism.

12 Gian Francesco Malipiero, 'Giulio Cesare,' *L'Armonioso Labirinto: Teatro da musica 1913–1970*, ed. Marzio Pieri (Venezia: Marsilio, 1992) 225–69.

13 I am indebted to Dunnett's essay for my initial interest in both the Maxentium production and the Mussolini-Forzano collaboration. Another Fascist theatre script about Caesar is Nino Guglielmi's *Giulio Cesare, dramma* (Roma: Edizioni Fascismo, 1939), which for reasons of space I am forced to treat only summarily in this note. As Guglielmi points out in his preface, '[t]he imminent performance of a 'Giulio Cesare' by another author [i.e., Mussolini] has led me to postpone the debut of my work to the 1939–40 theatre season.' Guglielmi chose Caesar as his subject 'because never in the history of the world – and especially in the history of Italy – were there periods so rich with references and analogies as the Cesarean period and the Mussolinian.' Guglielmi admits to taking Shakespeare as his starting point, and explains that in order to avoid comparisons, his play ends where Shakespeare's begins; in his treatment of the conspiracy and the

Ides of March, he did in fact borrow from Shakespeare, but in so doing his
intentions were to give those scenes a new interpretation (Guglielmi 9–11).

14 See for example the Preview in the *New York Times* 25 April 1939 where the
'avowed author was Giovacchino Forzano' but 'unofficially, it is understood that a relatively new playwright named Benito Mussolini collaborated with Signor Forzano on this opus. Signor Mussolini is thought, in
Rome, to have a bright future' (22).

15 Giovacchino Forzano and Benito Mussolini, 'Cesare,' *Mussolini, autore
drammatico*, ed. Giovacchino Forzano (Firenze: G. Barbèra, 1954) 325–512.

Works Cited

Baehr, Peter R. *Caesar and the Fading of the Roman World: A Study in Republican-
ism and Caesarism*. New Brunswick, NJ: Transaction Publishers, 1997.

Cesareo, G.A. Preface. *Giulio Cesare*. By William Shakespeare. Trans. G.A.
Cesareo. Messina and Rome: Principato, 1924. 3–5.

Contini, Ermanno. '"Giulio Cesare" di Shakespeare.' Prev. of *Giulio Cesare*
directed by Ferdinando Tamberlani. *Il Messaggero* 1 Aug. 1935: 5.

– '"Giulio Cesare" di Shakespeare.' Rev. of *Giulio Cesare* directed by Ferdinando Tamberlani. *Il Messaggero* 2 Aug. 1935: 4.

Dunnett, Jane. 'The Rhetoric of *Romanità*: Representations of Caesar in Fascist
Theatre.' *Julius Caesar in Western Culture*. Ed. Maria Wyke. Malden, MA:
Blackwell, 2006. 244–65.

'Ferdinando Tamberlani.' Carte ordinarie. Ms and TS Archivio Centrale di
Stato in Rome. Segreteria particolare del Duce, 548.138.

Ferrara, Patrizia. *Censura teatrale e fascismo (1931–1944). La storia, l'archivio,
l'inventario*. Roma: Ministero per i beni e le attività culturali. Direzione gen-
erale per gli archivi, 2004.

Finaldi, Giuseppe. *Mussolini and Italian Fascism*. Harlow: Pearson Education,
2008.

Galfré, Monica. *Una riforma alla prova. La scuola media di Gentile e il fascismo*.
Milan: Franco Angeli, 2000.

Gian Francesco Malipiero. *Giulio Cesare*. MS and TS. Archivio Centrale di Stato
in Rome. Presidenza del Consiglio dei Ministri 1934–36, 3/2 12.5855.

'Giulio Cesare' (production at Maxentius Basilica). MS, TS, and Print. Archivio
Centrale di Stato in Rome. Presidenza del Consiglio dei Ministri 1934–36,
158/2880.

Giardina, Andrea. 'Ritorno al futuro: La romanità fascista.' *Il mito di Roma
da Carlo Magno a Mussolini*. By Andrea Giardina and André Vauchez. Bari:
Laterza, 2008. 212–96.

Griffiths, Clive. 'Theatre under Fascism.' *A History of Italian Theatre*. Ed. Joseph Farrell and Paolo Puppa. Cambridge: Cambridge University Press, 2006. 339–48.

Guarnieri, Lyno. *Giulio Cesare*. Roma: Società italiana edizioni e rappresentazioni, 1938.

Guglielmi, Nino. Preface. *Giulio Cesare*. By Nino Guglielmi. Rome: Edizioni Fascismo, 1939. 9–14.

Lodovici, Cesare Vico. '"Cesare" di Forzano.' Rev. of *Cesare* written by Giovacchino Forzano (and Benito Mussolini). *Scenario* 8. 5 (May 1939): 200–1.

Malipiero, Gian Francesco, 'Né con il duce né contro il duce.' Unpublished TS. 21 Sept. 1945. 25 Oct. 1992. http://www.rodoni.ch/malipiero/ducegfm.html.

Muccioli, Alessandro. Introduction and Notes. *Giulio Cesare*. By William Shakespeare. Ed. and trans. Alessandro Muccioli. Firenze: Battistelli, 1924. 5–20.

Pennacchia, Maddalena. 'Antony's Ring: Remediating Ancient Rhetoric on the Elizabethan Stage.' *Identity, Otherness and Empire in Shakespeare's Rome*. Ed. Maria Del Sapio. Farnham and Burlington: Ashgate, 2009. 49–60.

Schanzer, Ernest. 'The Problem of *Julius Caesar*.' *Shakespeare Quarterly* 6, 3 (Summer 1955): 297–308. 8 Apr. 2010. http://www.jstor.org/stable/2866616.

Sestito, Marisa. *Julius Caesar in Italia*. Bari: Adriatica, 1978.

Shakespeare, William. *Julius Caesar*. Ed. T.S. Dorsch. London: Routledge, Arden, 1994.

Vezio, Tulio. *Le due marce su Roma. Giulio Cesare e Benito Mussolini*. Mantua: Edizioni Paladino, 1923.

Wyke, Maria. *Caesar. A Life in Western Culture*. Chicago: University of Chicago Press, 2008.

– 'Film Style and Fascism: *Julius Caesar*.' *Film Studies* 4 (Summer 2004): 58–74. 10 May 2009. http://www.manchesteruniversitypress.co.uk/uploads/docs/040058.pdf.

Zurlo, Leopoldo. *Memorie inutili: censura teatrale nel ventennio*. Roma: Edizioni dell'Ateneo, 1952.

5 Shakespeare and Censorship during the Second World War: *Othello* in Occupied Greece

TINA KRONTIRIS

Censorship has always being used by states to regulate people's political beliefs, sexual attitudes, moral and ethical norms, and even religious practices. In times of war the imperative for regulating public thought and behaviour increases because of the need for national propaganda which is deemed crucial to the outcome of the war. At such times censorship regulations become more stringent. This is certainly true of the Second World War, the producer of the largest censorship operations ever. Although traditionally the arts have been thought to transcend the worlds of politics and war, they were certainly not exempt from regulatory measures in the years 1939–45. Along with cinema, theatre was a very closely monitored form of art presumably because of its recognized direct influence upon the audience. The kinds of censorship and degree of vigilance exercised by country states during the Second World War depended on various factors, such as a country's position in relation to the war (what side of the war it fought on), its degree of independence (whether it was an occupied or a free state) and the social, ideological, and national concerns of the ruling system in effect before and during the war. In England, for example, the censors of the Lord Chamberlain's Office showed an increased concern over matters of public morality, responding to a conservative call for an exemplary ethos that Britain should display in the eyes of its Allies, especially the Americans, who were likely to see theatrical performances in London (Aldgate 19).

Discussions of censorship have generally focused on the power that exercises control,[1] when in fact censorship is a practice characterized by a power-resistance relationship. In his influential book *Domination and the Arts of Resistance* (1990), James Scott studies the dialectical interaction between the powerful and the powerless and suggests that although they are unequal in their capacity to enforce policy, both sides are constrained by the conditions of their interactive setup.[2] Scott observes that the powerful and the powerless behave differently in each other's presence than among members of their own group, and he posits the existence of two types of discourses or 'transcripts,' as he calls them: the 'public transcript,' which is the self-constructed image of the powerful 'as they would have themselves seen' (18), and the private or 'hidden transcript,' which 'represents a critique of power spoken behind the back of the dominant' (xii). The powerful can also have a hidden transcript in so far as the motives and aims of their hegemonic rule are articulated privately but never avowed in front of outsiders or wider audiences. On the basis of this distinction between a public and a hidden transcript, Scott discerns four varieties of political discourse and resistance among subordinate groups (18–19). First, there is the appropriation of the flattering self-portrait of the dominant power. In their official rhetoric, the latter will often incorporate various sensitivities (humanitarian, democratic, anti-racist, etc.) to present themselves as rulers with noble aims ('good guys'). Second, there is the hidden discourse and action – taking place 'offstage' – where the subordinates, away from the fear or intimidating gaze of power, can express feelings and thoughts that must normally be held back in the presence of the representatives of power. Third, there is a type of public discourse, created through disguise and anonymity, that appears harmless on the surface but is intended to convey a double meaning while concealing the identity of the originator of the discourse (this discourse includes rumours, jokes, stories, songs, rituals, codes, etc.). Finally, there are acts of challenge and open defiance, acts that cause the rupture of the seal, the '*cordon sanitaire*,' between private and public transcripts (201).

This concept of a dialectical relation between power and resistance that is constituted by hidden and public discourses and practices is especially suitable in explaining the operation of oppositional theatre under conditions of severe censorship in Nazi-occupied countries during the Second World War. Nazi censorship restricted the choices of theatre artists, who, in turn, developed strategies of resistance that enabled them to do more than the official Nazi policy allowed. In the rest of this essay I wish to examine one instance of theatrical censorship – that imposed on Shakespeare, England's national playwright, by the Axis powers that occupied Greece from 1941 to 1944. Using as a case study a performance of *Othello* in Athens at the heart of the Occupation period, I shall try to investigate the conditions of censorship under which the play came to be staged and the use of this Shakespearean play by a Greek theatre company both as a form of resistance against Nazi ideologies and as a means of combating artistically the debilitating conditions of the Occupation. In the process I hope to shed light on the interrelationship of foreign dominance, cultural politics, resistance, and collaboration.

When the German troops invaded Athens on 26 April 1941 all forms of public life froze. There was no official ban against performances (the state-controlled National Theatre was ordered to carry on as usual), but fear kept both audiences and actors at home, so the theatres shut down for a few days. When they reopened, they had to comply with new, emergency regulations. According to a circular published by the German and Italian occupying forces in July 1941 (Dizelos 454–5), censorship was to be exercised on all plays scheduled for performance, and all shows were limited to a two-hour span; evening shows were to begin at 7:00 p.m. so that the spectators could return home before curfew time. Ten days prior to the opening of a performance, the theatre company was obliged to submit the play script for inspection to the members of three separate censoring committees – the German, the Italian, and the Greek.[3] Theatre companies were also obliged to invite the censors to attend the dress rehearsal that included full costumes and complete sets. In their various circulars, which were eventually incorporated into a law, the occupiers specified all the restrictions and forbade, among other things, the staging of plays written by authors of Allied countries and the use of words such as 'English,' 'American,' 'Australian,' 'Soviet,' that directly referred to the Alliance.[4] Punishment for the violation of censorship rules ranged from a steep fine to closure of the theatre and/or the arrest of the company members (Dizelos 455).

Shakespeare, as an Englishman, was certainly at the top of the banned-authors list, which explains his general absence from the Greek stage during the Occupation period. He is noticeably absent from the National Theatre of Greece, an institution that in prewar times staged a Shakespeare play at the opening of each new season. Of course, Shakespeare's absence from the Greek National Theatre during the Occupation is not surprising. A play by the national poet of England on the national stage of an Axis-occupied country carried an obvious symbolism of English superiority, intolerable to the occupying powers. In their resistance to censorship, private theatre companies in Greece would often camouflage English and American plays by chang-

«ΕΛΕΥΘΕΡΟΝ ΒΗΜΑ»

ΤΕΤΑΡΤΗ, 13 Μαΐου 1942

ΟΘΕΛΛΟΣ

Σκηνοθεσία:
ΣΠΥΡΟΥ ΜΕΛΑ

Μουσικὴ
ΜΑΝ. ΣΚΟΥΛΟΥΔΗ

Σκηνογραφίαι: Ἐνδυμασίαι :
Γ. ΑΝΕΜΟΓΙΑΝΝΗ

ΣΗΜΕΡΟΝ 7 μ. μ.
«ΠΡΩΤΗ»

ΚΟΤΟΠΟΥΛΗ

5.1. A facsimile of the advertisement for a production of *Othello* at the Cotopouli Theatre, Athens, Greece, 1942. The caption reads: '*Othello*/ Directed by Spyros Melas/ Music by Manolis Skouloudis/ Sets & costumes by G. Anemoyiannis/ Today 7 p.m. "First"/ Theatre Cotopouli.' Scanned by the Central Library of Aristotle University, Thessaloniki, Greece.

ing the titles and attributing them to unknown French authors (Dizelos 457–8; Georgopoulou 298–301). Shakespeare, the master of counterfeiting, did not go in disguise. In the one and only time that he appeared in Greece during the Occupation he did so under his own name – or, at least, under the name of his play. On 13 May 1942 an advertisement of *Othello* appeared on the entertainment page of the daily newspaper *Elefthero Vima* (see fig. 5.1).[5]

This advertisement appears to be the same as similar postings for prewar shows, except for the total absence of the name 'Shakespeare,' which would have been prominently displayed. There is one more irregularity: the advertisement names Spyros Melas as director, but the artist who actually instructed the actors in their roles and directed the play, 35-year-old Dimitris Myrat, is missing. Yet, as we shall see below, these are small matters if we consider the fact that *Othello* is one of Shakespeare's best known plays and as such is closely associated with the Bard's name in the public consciousness. Why was such a play staged in the middle of the Occupation period?

Conditions were hard for the Greeks during this period.[6] Lack of food, an uncontrolled black market, a chaotic political situation, and an astronomical inflation rate that rendered the national currency valueless were the main features of the Occupation. Death from starvation was the biggest problem, as famine reigned supreme in the urban areas, especially in the first year of the German invasion. During the winter of 1941–2 people starved to death by the hundreds. Whatever food supplies the country had put away were consumed by the German army, which pillaged storehouses and requisitioned any stock held in shops; at the same time large quantities of farm produce and raw materials (such as cotton and sole leather) were shipped to Germany (Mazower 24). Hitler and his ministers were totally unconcerned about the grave consequences of such actions.[7] These hard economic conditions, along with the enforcement of strict censorship, posed problems of survival for the theatre as well. The elimination of plays by authors of Allied countries, together with the periodic shut downs incurred by the occupying powers (ostensibly for reasons of public health), made it extremely difficult for theatres to operate and created high unemployment among actors. Even construction materials for stage sets and props became scarce, as products such as nails, boards, and canvas were used up in the war effort. Indeed, it is surprising that in such conditions the theatre survived at all, yet survive it did, as there was a demand for all kinds of entertainment, especially revues. Also, despite the hard times, there developed a sense of optimism among artists and intellectuals, who proved very productive in this period.[8] This optimism was largely inspired by the resistance that Greeks throughout the country had shown against their Nazi occupiers. Many actors enlisted in the National Liberation Front (a widely active underground resistance organization), creating a special branch in the area of the theatre (Papadouka 41; Georgopoulou 292–8). While most theatre companies struggled to stay afloat, mounting 'light' comedies and catering to an audience of low expectations, a few, including the Cotopouli Theatre company (which produced *Othello*) set higher goals.

Dimitris Myrat, a member of the Cotopouli Theatre company and its artistic director in early 1942, staged Shakespeare's *Othello* apparently as a way of combating the crippling effect of this dire atmosphere.

In the spring of that year the Katerina Theatre had mounted an innovative production of Ibsen's *A Doll's House*. The staging of these two plays by leading private companies signalled a turn towards quality productions in the midst of the Occupation. Why Myrat chose to stage *Othello* specifically, and to cast himself in the title role, is not clear from the available evidence. Having played several youthful roles in Shakespearean productions during the 1930s, perhaps he wanted now to try his talent in the more mature and challenging role of the Moor who kills his beautiful, aristocratic wife out of jealousy. Or, possibly, he may have thought this play would pass censorship more easily on account of its 'domestic' theme. What Myrat certainly aimed for in his production of *Othello* was the introduction of a new, psychologically oriented and ideologically progressive approach to Shakespearean drama, hoping thereby to initiate the uplifting process in the Greek theatre. In an interview with a theatre critic during the rehearsal process, the young actor-director appears to have stated that he wished to steer away from previous interpretations of the play in Greece. 'I formed the impression,' says the critic, that 'he [Myrat] was fully conscious of his mission and took care to understand the innermost soul of the tragedy … to advance his interpretation on surer ground, different from the one established by the various *Othellos* that his older colleagues have presented to the Greek public from time to time' (Rodas 2).

Using the 1623 Folio version of the play, in which Othello refers to himself as a 'base Iudean' (5.2.348), the multilingual Myrat created a humble, self-controlled general whose slightly Hebraic accent, kippah-like cap, and very dark (but not black) skin associated him with Syria or Palestine (see fig. 5.2).

He stressed the human side of Othello – not the heroic or the jealous one – thus portraying a Moor of Hebraic origin who, though possessed by the passion of jealousy, is able to exercise self-control and engage in self-reflection before he takes his final decision to murder his wife.[9] Myrat's Othello was in contrast to the Moor of uncontrollable passion and primitive instincts that had appeared on the Greek stage up to that time.

Changes were accordingly introduced by Myrat in teaching the role of Iago to the lesser-known actor Christos Tsaganeas, who appeared as a psychologically disturbed man. Tsaganeas's distorted facial expression and bizarre movements on stage were intended as symptoms of his unbalanced mental condition. Iago's evil was thus to be understood in psychopathological terms. Although Myrat did not entirely succeed

5.2 Dimitris Myrat as Othello, Cotopouli Theatre, Athens, Greece, 1942. Reproduced with the permission of Voula Zouboulaki, widow of Dimitris Myrat.

in convincing his critical audience of this interpretation, or in creating a wider stir,[10] he did, nevertheless, offer an antiracist view of *Othello*. In the context of the Occupation such an interpretation acquires a special significance as a subtle act of resistance against the Nazis, who persecuted Blacks and Jews.

Myrat's production of *Othello* would probably not have been allowed without the mediation of the playwright and theatre critic Spyros Melas, the Nazi-collaborator who was displayed as director on both the advertisement and the printed program. Normally, the play script would be presented to the censors by either the theatre owner or the director of the production, but Dimitris Myrat, a socialist sympathizer involved in underground resistance activity,[11] was altogether the wrong person to negotiate the censorship matter. The diplomatic and inventive Melas was much better suited for the job on account of his personal qualities, his high reputation as an intellectual (he was member of the prestigious Athens Academy), and his favourable disposition towards the occupiers. From the first days of the Occupation Melas had published pro-Axis articles in the daily press, urging his compatriots to show 'sincere and active cooperation with the victor' (Melas 1),[12] an attitude for which he was later expelled from the Association of Greek Writers. His collaborative disposition as well as his contributions to the Nazi literary magazine *Quadrivio*, published weekly by the Italian forces,[13] endeared him to both sides of the Axis powers and enabled him to negotiate theatrical matters with them.[14] Melas had never directed a Shakespeare play nor dealt with Shakespeare in any other way. During the Occupation years he worked on commission for various theatre companies, rewriting and adapting scripts so that they would pass censorship. It is reasonable to suppose that Cotopouli Theatre hired him to update a 1915 translation by Constantinos Theotokis and to make cuts in the text so as to fit the play into the two-hour performance limit imposed by the Occupation authorities. All the available evidence suggests a hidden transcript: the theatre company's presentation of Melas as 'director' and the basic reason for hiring him were the connections he offered with the Axis powers and the greater chance he had in getting the play approved by the censors. Evidently, then, *Othello* had passed censorship as an exception to the rule.

Such an exception may have been facilitated by the privileged position Shakespeare held within German culture. From 1797, when Schlegel started translating Shakespeare, to 1915, when Gerhart Hauptmann made the famous statement, 'there is no nation, not even the British, which is more entitled to call Shakespeare its own than Germany' (qtd in Hortmann 3) the idea of 'unser [our] Shakespeare' had taken a strong hold on German culture. It was this assimilation of Shakespeare into a common Germanic heritage that enabled stagings of the Elizabethan dramatist even during the war years, albeit not without problems, contradictions, and disagreements (see Ackermann and Habicht in this volume). As the 1946 issue of the German scholarly periodical *Shakespeare Jahrbuch* shows, a great number of Shakespeare plays were performed in the years 1939–45, including some, such as the Histories and *Othello*, that had been ostensibly banned (Mühlbach 113–21).[15]

Of course, in occupied countries citizens were more restricted in their actions, and rules of censorship were more rigidly applied, but this was not always and not uniformly true. The severity of the occupying power depended on the significance of the country to the overall German plans and the degree of cooperation on the part of the occupied country. Generally speaking, the Germans and the collaborationist governments, in their attempt to minimize resistance, relaxed control on artists or writers if these individuals did not directly challenge their authority and power. In France, for example, during the first two years of the Occupation the Nazis allowed artists a surprising degree of freedom, permitting them to display works that 'would have exposed them to harsh recrimination in Germany' (McCloskey 18). This policy was part of the Nazis' public transcript, which aimed to distract the attention of the French from the atrocities committed daily by the occupiers. This relative leniency did not apply when a country tried to protect Jewish artists. In fascist Spain, where Franco maintained a semblance of independence from Hitler, the Germans attempted to withdraw from circulation *Poetry at Hand*, published in December 1940 by German-Jewish émigré Franz Werfel (Bowen 138).[16] The same policy was maintained in occupied Greece, where the Germans had a reputation for being more lenient than the Italians in matters of censorship,[17] and there is no doubt that policy came from Berlin, not Rome.

Finally, in explaining the exception of Shakespeare's *Othello* from the rules of censorship in occupied Greece, we must look into the 'faultlines' – assailable points of the dominant power's control system.[18] There were several faultlines in the system of the occupiers that created opportunities for the occupied or conversely made things more difficult. One of these was the latent antagonism between the German and Italian forces. Greek author Yiorgos Theotokas wrote about this matter in his diary notebook: 'The Germans show contempt for the Italians in a pointed way. It is obvious that vis-à-vis the first the Italians have a *complexe d'inferiorité*, full of wily animosity. The Italians spread this whisper about the Germans: they are barbarians' (Theotokas 261).[19] There was also antagonism between the Italians and the Greeks. The latter, who had defeated the Italians at the Albanian border in the first phase of the war, invented a series of jokes or satirical stories about them and lost no opportunity to ridicule the 'spaghetti masters' and their Duce.[20] As a faultline within the occupying power block, antagonism usually worked against the occupied as it made it more difficult for them to break the censorship system. In the case of Shakespeare, however, antagonism may have challenged the Italians to show off their cultured side, since the Elizabethan dramatist was universally recognized as a high-art symbol. Alternatively, or additionally, the antagonism here may have been offset by the mediation of Spyros Melas, who contributed to the Italians' self-constructed image of cultural superiority by writing articles for their *Quadrivio*, as stated above.

Another faultline in the power system, more negotiable by the powerless, was the process of mediation in the censoring mechanism itself: the occupiers had to rely on Greek collaborationists for reading the scripts – a form of dependence that essentially transferred the censoring authority to the Greek readers working for the German and Italian committees. Such readers, whose principles of collaboration were more material than ideological, were not infrequently susceptible to corruption. What was placed on the table along with the text sometimes determined whether the play would be allowed. One theatre owner describes in her memoirs the following scene at the office of the German censorship committee, where the reader was a self-indulgent medical doctor who had studied in Germany: 'Before he would start reading we would put on the table, right in front of him, a bottle of wine and a fancy cake. We would let him eat and drink, while we did not dare touch either the wine glass or the cake. We were afraid that we might incur his displeasure and cause him to reject the play' (Manolidou 46). Such incidents evince the vulnerability of the occupying powers that were necessarily constrained by their unfamiliarity with the Greek language as well as by the unavailability of 'proper' collaborators.

In the final analysis, the kind of censorship exercised was a political decision on the part of the Germans, who determined the degree of cultural intervention in each country. Heinz Kindermann, Germany's most influential man in 'theatre science' in the last years of the war, spoke high-mindedly about a German theatre that carried 'the message of German humanity' to people from 'Paris and The Hague to Vilnius and Lublin, from Trondheim to Athens' (qtd in Hortmann 17–18). Apart from its glaring distance from the reality of inhuman acts committed daily by the Axis powers, such a statement was also at variance with Germany's cultural policy and practice in each occupied country. In France, Hitler apparently aimed at cultural domination, as evidenced by the fact that his men moved quickly after the armistice to take control of French art and also by the fact that a few months after the invasion Joseph Goebbels, the German minister of propaganda, personally oversaw all cultural activity in the occupied part of France (McCloskey 21).[21] In occupied Poland the Führer showed no higher aims than the humiliation or physical extinction of artists and intellectuals (as Krystyna Kujawińska Courtney reveals in her essay in this volume). For Greece he harboured no particular passion or racial prejudice. Mark Mazower, a historian who has written extensively on the Second World War in Greece and the southern Balkans, contrasts Hitler's attitude towards Poland and Greece: 'Greece and Poland were very different cases so far as the Germans were concerned. Greece was less important strategically, less contemptible racially. From Hitler downwards there was nothing but admiration on the German side for the way the Greeks had fought' (18).

In occupied Greece this positive attitude of the Germans towards the Greeks is evidenced by the fact that German officers showed a genuine interest in classical Greek culture. They attended a performance of *Oedipus* at the ancient Herodeion a few months after the invasion and did not react when the audience provocatively applauded a group of wounded soldiers who came in just before the start of the performance wearing hospital pajamas (Theotokas 271). The German authorities pressed the National Theatre (over which they had direct control) to mount German plays, but the evidence suggests that the Greek artists working for this state institution did not often give in to German pressure.[22] Overall, in Greece the degree of German intervention in matters of culture appears to have been minimal. This is not perhaps as surprising as it may appear. If the Germans who implemented Nazi policy in Greece could not keep the Greeks from starving to death or, worse yet, could not refrain from consuming their food, how could they propagandize German culture? Undoubtedly, Nazi cultural policy in Greece was weighed against Hitler's higher priorities in the region. The Führer had never actually intended to invade Greece, nor did he have any long-term plans for this small country in the southern Balkans (Mazower 18).

His real target was the invasion of the Soviet Union and in 1941 he was preparing a move in that direction. The invasion of Greece had been necessitated by an unexpected turn of events, namely, the humiliating defeat of Mussolini's forces by the Greek army at the Albanian border. Once Hitler had restituted the prestige of the Axis by invading Greece, there was no reason for him to waste valuable resources. Additionally, Greek resistance ran high and the gain from suppressing it would not answer the cost.

The staging of Shakespeare's *Othello* in occupied Greece could be inscribed in any combination of the above transcripts. It provides evidence that no system of power is unbreakable by resistance and that, in our study of the Second World War, the 'good guys,' the devoted patriots who fought for their country's freedom, cannot always be clearly separated from the 'bad guys,' the collaborationists who sought to befriend the enemy for personal gain. In conditions of war and occupation by a foreign military power, collaboration with the dominant power and resistance against it necessarily occur side-by-side in everyday social life, yet because such acts constitute part of the hidden transcript, they shall never come to full light.

Notes

1 See, for example, George Roeder, Jr, who discusses the careful monitoring of the visual representation of the Second World War by the Roosevelt administration, which withdrew or released images of death so as to regulate public reaction to the war.

2 Foucault's idea of power as 'the multiplicity of force relations immanent in the sphere in which they operate' (Foucault 92) and his proposition that 'there is no binary and all-encompassing opposition between rulers and ruled at the root of power relations' (94) may be applied to peacetime societies but not to wartime situations or totalitarian states. Scott's Gramscian approach to social anthropology helps to explain political practices used especially in situations where ideological or other types of control are of immediate concern to the state.

3 Play scripts were submitted in duplicate to the members of the censoring committees. One copy would be returned to the theatre company with indications about required cuts or changes; the other copy would be kept on file.

4 References to conditions of the Occupation (especially hunger and lack of food) were banned, as were references to mountains and the country-

side because they signified freedom and resistance. Likewise, the use of national Greek costumes on stage was forbidden because they symbolized national independence.

5 Translations from the Greek here and throughout are mine.

6 For an excellent, comprehensive study of the conditions in the period 1941–4, see Mazower, especially chapters 3–6.

7 Günther Altenburg, Hitler's official representative in Greece, was especially alarmed by the starvation deaths and was sensitive to the criticism that was being levelled at the Germans. He wrote to Hitler about the problem, saying that Germany was taking food out of the country instead of bringing it in and that Greece must be helped economically and not be allowed to fall into political and military chaos (Mazower 24, 27). However, the Führer did not show any special concern about the matter and the German Ministry of Food and Agriculture was opposed to sending supplies to Greece (Mazower 27).

8 The establishment in 1942 of the influential Art Theatre by the later renowned Greek director Karolos Koun is an example of creative, resistance-inspired work in this period.

9 When the Cotopouli company restaged *Othello* later in 1951 and took the production on tour to Egypt and Cyprus, Myrat, who played the black general again, wrote a review of his performance, which he published anonymously in a Cypriot daily and later reprinted under the title 'Self-Criticism of an Othello.' In this review article Myrat analyses the character of Othello, whom he describes as a noble, self-possessed man with a primitive inner core. He states that Othello must be portrayed as a 'self-controlled man,' not as 'an enraged beast' (Myrat 75) and considers the general's behaviour in the fourth act as an outbreak of his primitivism, a momentary loss of self-control. The interpretation of 1942 agrees with that of 1951 on many points, but not on the issue of Othello's colour; Myrat presented Othello in the earlier performance as a dark-skinned 'Iudean,' but in the later one as a Negro (79).

10 The Occupation conditions short-circuited the usual route of reception. Whereas normally four or five critics would review a Shakespeare production, this time only Michalis Rodas appears to have written a review, in which he expresses his disappointment at the results of Myrat's studied effort. The production did not enjoy a continuous run. Performances ceased four days after the show opened because all theatres were closed down for a three-week period by order of the occupying powers due to the threat (or ostensible threat) of an epidemic. Performances of *Othello* resumed in February 1943, but by that time public attention had been lost.

11 According to Olympia Papadouka, an actress who participated in and later wrote about the Resistance, Myrat was the secretary of the theatre branch of the National Liberation Front (Papadouka 325).

12 See also Yiorgos Theotokas, 'I periptosi tou Spyrou Mela' [The case of Spyros Melas], *Nea Estia* 44 (1948): 953–6.

13 *Quadrivio* advertised itself on its pages as the organ of 'the New Order' and actively sought contributions from well-known Italian and Greek authors. This publication was a propagandistic attempt (a 'public transcript') on the part of the Nazis to show their good face, while at the same time it may also have been part of the 'private transcript' between the Italians and Germans, with the former showing off to the latter. *Quadrivio* was published by the Italian forces in Athens as a supplement of *Tiveris*, a pro-Nazi daily paper that circulated in Rome in 1933–43.

14 Theodore Kritas, a former actor who worked as theatre manager in the occupation years, records an instance when Melas had asked the Italian commander to intervene on his behalf in a squabble he had with a specific theatre company (Kritas 195–7).

15 Publication of the *Shakespeare Jahrbuch* was suspended from 1940 to 1945. When it resumed in 1946, the journal offered an overview of Shakespeare performances in Germany and Austria during the war years.

16 Through their embassy in Spain, the Germans claimed that the book was politically dangerous. After an exchange of correspondence on the matter, Franco's Falange did not comply with the German request, 'most likely because Werfel's book was already in circulation and Germany did not have a strong argument against it remaining so, other than the author's Jewish heritage' (Bowen 138).

17 Greek author Yiorgos Theotokas comments on the cruelty of the Germans, but says that they were not as passionate about matters of secondary importance to them as the Italians were. He records in his diary for 26 September 1943, after the departure of the Italian forces: 'German censorship is much more liberal than the Italian. Today we write whatever we want as long as we don't criticize Germany's hegemonic struggle' (430).

18 According to Alan Sinfield, a 'faultline' is a flaw in the political structure caused by a disjunction between the ideological and military power (Sinfield 40). I use this critical term here not to suggest an ideological rift between the two Axis powers, but rather to indicate the points of cultural friction, which rendered their ostensibly unified power breakable and exposed its hidden transcript to the occupied.

19 On the animosity between the Germans and the Italians, see also Mazower 84.

20 The German soldiers would recount with pleasure the story of a Greek shoe black who mocked the carabinieri on the street by raising his arms high and calling out 'Bella Grecia,' the phrase the Italian soldiers had used at the Albanian border when they surrendered to the Greeks (Mazower 60).

21 McCloskey suggests that Hitler was envious of French culture and antagonistic towards Paris as the embodiment of high European art. 'Hitler had toyed with the idea of destroying Paris altogether,' she writes, but he changed his mind after a visit to the French capital, which he decided to let stand 'as a diminished and humiliated relic soon to be surpassed by the grandeur of the new Berlin' (21).

22 During the Occupation period the National Theatre staged plays by Sophocles (*Oedipus*), Molière (*The Miser, The Misanthrope,* and *Tartuffe*), Euripides (*Iphigenia at Tauris, Medea,* and *Hecuba*), Goldoni (*The Fan*), Dimitris Horn (*To Fyntanaki* [The Novice]), Goethe (*Faust*), Schiller (*Louisa Miller*), Calderón (*The Phantom Lady*), Kornaros (*Abraham's Sacrifice*), Levidis (*The Shepherd and the Nymph*), Ibsen (*A Doll's House*), Lessing (*Minna von Barnhelm* and *Emilia Galotti*), Synadinos (*In the Heat of the Summer*) Terzakis (*The Big Game*), and Bogris (*The Engagement*).

Works Cited

Aldgate, Anthony, and James C. Robertson. *Censorship in Theatre and Cinema.* Edinburgh: Edinburgh University Press, 2005.

Bowen, Wayne. *Spain during World War II.* Columbia: University of Missouri Press, 2006.

Dizelos, Thalis. 'Theatro stin Antistasi.' *Epitheorisi Technis* 15 (1965): 452–62.

Foucault, Michel. *The History of Sexuality,* vol. 1. Trans. Robert Hurley. Harmondsworth: Penguin Books, 1984.

Georgopoulou, Barbara. '1940–1947.' *Somateio Ellinon Ethopoion: Ogdonta Chronia, 1917–1997.* Ed. Chrysothemis Stamatopoulou-Vassilakou. Athens: Sbilias, 1999. 283–324.

Hortmann, Wilhelm. *Shakespeare on the German Stage: The Twentieth Century.* Cambridge and New York: Cambridge University Press, 1998.

Kritas, Theodoros. *Opos tous Gnorisa.* Vol. 1. Athens: Kastaniotis, 1998.

Manolidou, Vaso. *Vaso Manolidou: Anamneseis.* Athens: Educational Foundation of the National Bank of Greece, 1997.

Mazower, Mark. *Inside Hitler's Greece: The Experience of Occupation.* New Haven, CT: Yale University Press, 1993.

McCloskey, Barbara. *Artists of World War II.* Westport, CT: Greenwood Press, 2005.

Melas, Spyros. 'Energitiki.' *Kathimerini* [Athens], 7 May 1941: 1.

Mühlbach, Egon. 'Statistischer Überblick.' *Shakespeare Jahrbuch* 80/81 (1946): 113–21.

Myrat, Dimitris. 'Autocritiki enos Othellou.' *Opse oi Myloi ton Theon*. Athens: Kastaniotis, 1998.

Papadouka, Olympia. *To Theatro tis Athinas: Katohi, Antistasi, Diogmoi*. Athens: Sbilias, 1999.

Rodas, Michael. 'Theatrikai Zymoseis.' *Elefthero Vima*, 2 May 1942: 2.

Roeder, George, Jr. *The Censored War: American Visual Experience during World War Two*. New Haven: Yale University Press, 1995.

Scott, James C. *Domination and the Arts of Resistance: Hidden Transcripts*. New Haven: Yale University Press, 1990.

Sinfield, Allan. *Faultlines: Cultural Materialism and the Politics of Dissident Reading*. Oxford: Clarendon Press, 1992.

Theotokas, Yiorgos. *Tetradia Imerologiou, 1939–1953*. Ed. Dimitris Tziovas. Athens: Estia, 2005.

6 'In This Hour of History: Amidst These Tragic Events' – Polish Shakespeare during the Second World War

KRYSTYNA KUJAWIŃSKA COURTNEY

Despite the generally acknowledged stable value and/or hierarchical position of Shakespeare in Polish history, there have not, so far, been any studies about his role in the Second World War. In fact, the existing vast and increasingly diverse works on Polish theatre, drama, and poetry either mention only in passing, or utterly omit, any references to him or his works at that time.[1] I, too, was convinced that there had been no place for Shakespeare during this time, when the most significant responsibility of the Poles centred on their survival of unbearable atrocities and ghastly hardship. My archival research has, however, made me modify this initial assumption. 'In this hour of history, amidst these tragic events,' as Stanisław Baliński, a Polish poet exiled in London (1941), called that time in his poem 'Shakespeare's Sky' (Baliński 151), the value of Shakespeare was sustained and transmitted.[2] In fact, Shakespeare's presence in Polish culture during the Second World War could be treated as a lens reflecting the diverse forms of Hitler's and Stalin's persecution inflicted upon the Poles in the period from 1939 to 1945.

On 1 September 1939, Germany attacked Poland from the west, thus beginning the Second World War in Europe. On 17 September the Soviet Red Army invaded the eastern part of the country, pursuant to the Molotov-Ribbentrop Pact signed in Moscow on 23 August 1939. Caught in the powerful grip of two malevolent aggressors, Polish forces were not prepared to mount a significant defence on both fronts. Though officially the Polish government never surrendered, by 1 October Nazi Germany and the Soviet Union had completely overrun the country. On 8 October Nazi Germany incorporated the western part of Poland (Pomerania, Poznań, and Silesia) into the Third Reich; the rest of the occupied area was designated as the *Generalgouvernement* (a colony ruled from Crakow by Hitler's friend, Hans Frank). The Soviet Union seized the eastern parts of the Polish Republic (mainly Belarus and Western Ukraine), which included such important Polish cultural and educational centres of that time as Lviv (Polish: Lwów) and Vilnius (Polish: Wilno).

Though the policies of Nazi Germany and the Soviet Union evolved during the course of the war, the occupying powers intended to carry out both the genocide of the Polish people (classified by the Germans as *Untermenschen* [subhuman]), and the annihilation of their culture, so that Poland would 'cease to exist not merely as a place, but also as an idea' (qtd in Knuth 86). 'The maltreatment of the Poles,' as British historian Niall Ferguson astutely indicates, 'was one of many ways in which the Nazi and Soviet regimes had grown to resemble one another' (423).[3]

Disoriented by the whirlwind of war, many people initially fled the German invasion for the eastern parts of Poland. There, they were met by the Red Army, which eventually installed a government in Vilnius as the capital of the newly created Lithuanian Soviet Socialist Republic (1940). Poles who found themselves under Soviet occupation underwent the ruthless Sovietization (and Russification) of their political, social, and cultural life. Physical extermination constituted one of the most significant elements of the systematic extermination of the Polish intelligentsia and cultural elites: this plan included both mass murders and deportations to Siberia or other Asian territories of the Soviet Union. As an element of superficial 'normalization,' the Soviets initially permitted Polish theatres to open, but they were bound by Communist indoctrination.[4] It was in this environment that Państwowy Teatr Dramatyczny [State Dramatic Theatre], a Polish theatre in Vilnius, presented *Twelfth Night* (29 January 1941) – the only theatrical production of a Shakespearean play in Poland during the Second World War.

Even the title of the play indicates that the production was subject to severe Soviet censorship. Staged under its original title, *Twelfth Night*, the production broke with the traditional religious connotation in Polish culture, where, for centuries this play had been known as *The Night of the Three Magi's Visitation*. Before the premiere *Prawda Wileńska* [Vilnius Truth] (28 January 1941), a Polish daily regarded by Polish intellectuals as an official organ of Soviet propaganda, established Shakespeare's affinity for communist dogma: 'Soviet culture is an international, human culture in the most significant meaning of the word. All works of human thought, regardless of when, in what nation and at which geographical latitude they were produced, belong nowadays to the Soviet Union. One can find [in Soviet culture] all the best ever produced over the epochs and ages' (4).

In *Czerwony sztandar* [The Red Standard], another pro-Soviet daily, Shakespeare was presented as a fighter 'against all kinds of [aristocratic] villainy and evil, reprimanding with his sharp words the hypocrites and prudes who drape themselves in the gowns of stylized mendacity.' In that critic's opinion, Malvolio, 'a typical bourgeois,' was rightly punished for his puritanical cynicism and moral corruption. Further, the critic believed that in *Twelfth Night* Shakespeare revealed himself as 'a social satirist' who ridiculed the capitalist system and glorified Soviet ideology (Dan 4).

So far, no documents have been found that could indicate the extent to which Leopold Pobóg-Kielanowski, the director of this production, was pressured to make his interpretation of the play comply with Soviet ideology. One can only presume that, on the one hand, he had to deal with the censor's prescriptions, while on the other he faced the need to express Polish patriotism.[5] Trying to satisfy both goals, Pobóg-Kielanowski located his interpretation of *Twelfth Night* in the tradition of commedia dell'arte, and thus in 'popular Renaissance culture' (Pobóg-Kielanowski 4). The action took place in two separate spaces: one presented the lyrical, poetic layer of the play, and was interspersed with excerpts from Polish national poetry (Jan Kochanowski, 1530–1584; Ignacy Krasicki, 1736–1801; Franciszek Karpiński, 1741–1825); the other showed the comic prose scenes to which popular Polish songs and ballads were added (Maliszewski 226). To stress the commedia dell'arte dimension of the performance, Pobóg-Kielanowski introduced a clown who 'supervised' and commented upon the action.

Though this spatial and thematic division of the action was designed to fulfil both Polish patriotic and Soviet ideological expectations, it worked against the coherence of the play. As some reviewers rightly observed, the separation destroyed the Shakespearean interdependence of high and low comedy that turns them into inseparable commentary on each other (Hernik Spalińska 161–3). Despite an aggressive promotional campaign, the performance was strongly criticized by the Polish cultural elite, whose representatives saw the production as a profanation of Shakespeare's art, since its '*ludic* nature' overwhelmed the philosophical dimension of the play (Valeska 4).[6] At the same time, however, Sovietized Polish critics praised the performance. Wasilij Romanowicz Sitnikow, Head of the Agitation and Propaganda Department of the Vilnius City Party Committee, admired 'the ideological conception of the performance' and wished that the 'theatre collective' would produce more such artistic achievements (5). The play was 'wholeheartedly recommended' as entertainment for the Vilnius 'working class' (Umru 5).

Throughout the war there were no Polish productions of Shakespeare's plays in the territories under German occupation, where the anti-Polish politics of the *Urząd Polityki Rasowej* (Racial Politics Department/Office) (*Rassenpolitisches-Amt*) had been enforced since their creation on 23 November 1939.[7] These Nazi policies were aimed at the cultural genocide of Slavs, including Poles. Places of learning and culture – universities, schools, libraries, museum, theatres, and cinemas – were either closed or designated *'Nur für Deutsche'* [Only for Germans]. Thousands of university professors, teachers, lawyers, artists, writers, priests, and other members of the Polish intelligentsia were arrested and executed or transported to concentration camps (Leszczynski).[8] The reasoning behind this policy was clearly articulated by a Nazi Gauleiter (district governor): 'In my district, [any Pole who] shows signs of intelligence will be shot' (qtd in Knuth 87).

Opportunities for Poles to experience their culture were severely restricted: no theatres, cinemas or cabarets; no access to radio, press or libraries; no sale of Polish books; and generally no education. Under the control of the German propaganda machine, in some cinemas the Polish people were allowed to see Nazi German movies, preceded by propaganda newsreels. Theatres faced a similar situation. Since the Germans forbade productions of any 'serious' spectacles, propaganda pieces were boycotted by the underground; actors were discouraged from performing in them and warned that they would be labelled as collaborators if they failed to comply.

The Polish Government in Exile in Great Britain created the Polish Underground State, an underground administration that operated in Poland throughout the war; it was the only political entity of this kind in the territories occupied by the Germans in Europe. Despite the real threat of severe retribution, respective units of the Polish Underground State encouraged and organized Polish cultural activities, including publications, academic research, secret art exhibitions, live concerts, and theatrical activities.[9] Especially significant for the preservation of Polish culture was the role of the Department of Education and Culture, and the Department for the Elimination of the Effects of War (Salmonowicz 233).

Beginning in 1940 the underground theatres, found mainly in Warsaw and Cracow, were coordinated by the Secret Theatre Council (Braun 27–9).[10] Underground actors (among them Karol Wojtyła, later Pope John Paul II), many of whom officially held mundane day jobs, secretly presented poetry readings and performed plays written by Polish national artists. These activities were intended to preserve and sustain Polish culture and its national values, and to inspire resistance to a systematic anti-Polish policy that posed the threat of total cultural annihilation. There was, however, no place for Shakespeare in the theatre.

Ironically, restrictions on cultural performances were eased in the Jewish ghettos, where the Germans wished to distract their inhabitants and prevent them from grasping their eventual fate (Sakowska 121–8). Marek Edelman, the last surviving military leader of the heroic Jewish Uprising in the Warsaw Ghetto in 1943, recalls that it was relatively easy to receive permission for theatrical activities. Even when the Nazi regime imposed censorship on a given play, the work would be performed under a different title. 'For example,' Edelman observes that, '[Since] Shakespeare was forbidden, *Hamlet* was staged as *Danish Prince. The Danish Prince. Looked Through and Revised by David Rubinstein'* (Edelman, Assuntino, Goldkorn 38). Unfortunately there are no extant documents describing this intriguing theatrical event.

On the Aryan side of the ghettos in Poland, Shakespeare had to move underground, where theatre professionals, academics, and translators resisted, each in his or her own way, the vindictive and gloomy Nazi dictatorship.[11] For example, Karol Wierciński, a famous prewar Polish director who actively worked as a member of the Secret Theatre Council, prepared to stage *Troilus and Cressida* in Warsaw. On a piece of cardboard (which his widow bequeathed to the Polish Academy of Science Institute of Arts after the war) Wierciński scribbled his 'ideal' casting of the play that included actors who were not in Warsaw at that time, thus optimistically suggesting that the production would take place in a liberated Poland (Marczak-Oborski, *'Troilus'* 28–9).

Escaping Nazi persecution, actor Jacek Woszczerowicz spent the war hiding in an obscure village. Shakespeare's works were the only books he managed to take into his perilous seclusion. Reading and rereading the entire canon, Woszczerowicz formulated his concept of politics as the ruthless operation of a Grand Mechanism of History (independently from Jan Kott) that he later used in his production of *Richard III* (1960).[12] Eminent prewar Polish Shakespeare scholars also embraced Shakespeare throughout the war years. In Cracow Professor Roman Dyboski not only taught courses but also wrote about Shakespeare in his study of British and American literatures.[13] In Vilnius, and later in Cracow, Professor Władysław Tarnawski worked on his translation of the whole Shakespeare canon. Because of his involvement in the underground university, Professor Andrzej Tretiak, one of the most innovative and challenging of Polish Shakespeare scholars, was captured and executed in Warsaw (Stanisz 135).

Shakespeare also shared the fate of the Polish officers who were interned in German Army camps during the September 1939 campaign. Since the Murnau camp was located closest to the Swiss border, where various organizations monitoring compliance with the Geneva Convention on the treatment of the soldiers were situated, this camp became a *Musterlager* (model/exemplary camp) frequented by Red Cross organizations from neutral countries (Dębicki 296–7). To give an impression of 'normality,' Polish prisoners of war were allowed to organize an amateur theatre; Shakespeare's plays became part of the repertoire (see fig. 6.1).

As the memoirs of the interned indicate, life behind barbed wire – guarded by German soldiers from watchtowers, enduring hunger, constant assemblies, alarms, disease, and no contact with the outside world – led to degenerative boredom and depression. The aim of the theatrical events, organized by historians, lawyers, clerks, teachers, professional soldiers, and other enthusiasts of the arts and culture, was primarily of a moral and social character (Marczak-Oborski 111–12).[14] These productions provided meaningful activity for many prisoners who, with real artistic gusto, created highly original artistic costumes, props, and stage designs from such unpromising material as sacks, paper, cardboard boxes, white paint, glue, and pieces of metal (Surynowa-Wyczółkowska 4). With time, the Polish 'theatre,' as one officer noted in his memoirs, was 'supported by the camp headquarters, since the Germans also willingly attended the performances' (qtd in Piekarski 226).

Although the repertoire was dominated by Polish theatricals – mainly musical concerts, variety shows, cabaret, and operettas, intended to lift the national feelings of the interned – the officers also ventured into classical dramas by authors such as Aristophanes (*Birds*), Beaumarchais (*Le mariage de Figaro*), and G.B. Shaw (*Caesar and Cleopatra, Man and Superman,* and *Heartbreak House*). It was the productions of Shakespeare's *The Merchant of Venice,* staged in June 1943, and *Twelfth Night,* in February 1944, that constituted – as one of the directors recalled – 'a real challenge' (Piekarski 265).

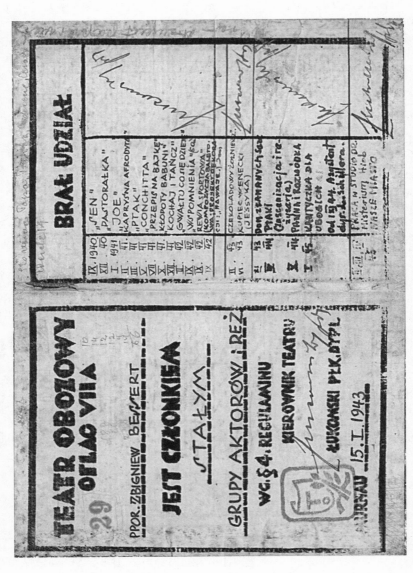

6.1. Document from one of the actors of the prisoner-of-war camp, Professor Zbigniew Bessert, attesting to the many activities of the theatre group in Murnau.

Of the two productions, *The Merchant of Venice* is described slightly more comprehensively in the scanty extant sources, but it is still unfortunately impossible fully to reconstruct all the details.[15] The statement that 'the romantic plot of the comedy was more exposed' (as noted in the memoir of Zdzisław Jaeschke, one of the interned prisoners of war in the camp), is, in fact, the only interpretive opinion we have. None of the interned officers made reference to the interpretation of Shylock, though it seems highly improbable that this Murnau director could have been permitted to deviate from official Nazi anti-Semitic ideology.[16] The mounting of the scenes presented 'insurmountable difficulties' that were solved by 'minimalist' stage designs 'against which colourful costumes evoked an impression of vivid, almost vibrant, smudges.'[17] The actors were praised for their delivery of blank verse, the mastery of which required them to organize more rehearsals than usual (Jaeschke 119).[18]

Though no reference or details exist concerning the presentation of female roles in *The Merchant of Venice*, they must have posed a problem since, as in Elizabethan England, one distinctive feature of the Murnau theatre company was that there were no female actors. Wiesław Mirecki's reminiscences about the moments 'when our Eves were born,' may be treated here as a comment on the production of *The Merchant of Venice*. The 'potential Eves' had to overcome such problems as their psychological attitude to their roles, their fear of emasculation as a result of voice training, and the necessity of shaving their legs and growing their hair out, to say nothing of the challenges connected with their costumes and make-up (81–5; 88–90 and 141–4).

There is no space here to narrate the complicated and tragic tale of the Polish soldiers who remained in the field through all five years of bloody fighting in nearly every major campaign on the European fronts, but Shakespeare's absent presence as their indefatigable companion highlights one dimension of their political, social, and cultural challenges. Shakespeare's plays were never staged by the theatre companies that performed for the Polish Allied Forces fighting on the Eastern Front, on the side of the Red Army. Under the commanding officers recruited from the Polish Communist organizations, the ordinary soldiers were mainly offered various forms of light entertainment (sketches, satire, cabaret, sentimental songs, folk dancing), sometimes permeated with patriotic and Communist ideological doctrine (Kiec).[19]

The situation was different, however, in various divisions of the Polish army that became a part of the Allied forces in the West (for

6.2. Production photograph from *Twelfth Night*, Murnau prisoner-of-war camp, Bavaria, possibly June 1944. Reproduced with permission from the Instytut Teatralny in Zbigniewa Raszewskiego.

6.3. Antoni Libner(?) as Shylock. The actor in white tights (left) is Roman Owidzki; the other actors have not been identified. Production photograph from *The Merchant of Venice*, assumed to be the premiere. Murnau prisoner-of-war camp, Bavaria, 1944. Reproduced with permission from the Instytut Teatralny in Zbigniewa Raszewskiego.

6.4. Antoni Libner(?) as Shylock, with Tadeusz Kubalski, Jerzy Romanski, Adam Nizankowski (order unknown); the remaining actors have not been identified. Production photograph from *The Merchant of Venice*, assumed to be the premiere, Murnau prisoner-of-war camp, Bavaria, 1944. Reproduced with permission from the Instytut Teatralny in Zbigniewa Raszewskiego.

6.5. Michal Lesniak and Wieslaw Pisarczyk (order unknown). Production photograph from *The Merchant of Venice*, assumed to be the premiere, Murnau prisoner-of-war camp, Bavaria, 1944. Reproduced with permission from the Instytut Teatralny in Zbigniewa Raszewskiego.

example, troops that fought in France, Great Britain, Africa, and Italy). Shakespeare strongly influenced those Polish soldiers – poets who found themselves in Britain, especially the Polish Air Force squadrons stationed in Scotland.[20] Some referred to Shakespeare as the guarantor of European or world civilization. For example, in his poem 'A Meeting with Shakespeare' (1941) Wawrzyniec Czereśniewski, a great admirer of Shakespeare (who 'in Warsaw had all [his] wise books, but they all went up in flames'), presents himself as a 'military globetrotter' who converses with the great dramatist about the future of Europe. In this poem his recollection of Shakespeare's poetic power ('Lord of the purest poetry') is interrupted by news from Poland:

... on the banks of the Warta River again people were shot ...

6.6. Andrzej Markiewicz, Aleksander Zaar, and Adam Nizankowski (order unknown). Production photograph from *The Merchant of Venice*, assumed to be the premiere, Murnau prisoner-of-war camp, Bavaria, 1944. Reproduced with permission from the Instytut Teatralny in Zbigniewa Raszewskiego.

... on the banks of the Wisła River people were taken to camps ...
Killed ...
... every day plaintive groans are heard from Poland
Every day, night, every morning. (1156)

At the conclusion of this fictitious conversation, Shakespeare comforts the poet, promising that Prospero (European civilization) would eventually defeat Caliban (Nazi Germany).

Macbeth, a story about the overthrow of a bloody despotic tyrant, became the favourite Shakespeare play among Polish emigrants in Britain. In his poem 'Do Szekspira' [To Shakespeare] (1941), Jan Lechoń deftly explicates why the play was so popular at that time:

We will go safely with you [Shakespeare], since we don't
Doubt the power of predictions and prophesies.
Not the power of steel
But the one who destroys the haughty and the arrogant;

And, as in *Macbeth*, the forest will march like soldiers
And they will kill the murderer.   (176–8)

There was also an attempt to turn *Macbeth* into light entertainment. In 1942 Adam Bunsch wrote *Poprawki do 'Makbeta. Komedii w trzech aktach* [Corrections to 'Macbeth. A Comedy in Three Acts].[21] His version of the Scottish play is a phantasmagoric response to Macbeth's soliloquy 'Is this a dagger which I see before me' (*Macbeth* 2.1) and the scene following King Duncan's murder (*Macbeth* 2.2).[22] Bunsch imagines six Polish soldiers stationed in Macbeth's castle: Lieutenant Bunio, Major Bieński, Cavalry Captain Funio, Officer Cadet Lulo, Sergeant Bodzio, and Elder Lancer Wacio. They deal with the psychologically disturbed Macbeth and Lady Macbeth, who see ghosts and are visited by witches. Treating Shakespeare's play as an accessible source of knowledge about Scottish culture – its social hierarchy, historical traditions, and manners – Bunsch draws attention to the problems that the Polish army encountered in exile. It is a study in highbrow Scottish detachment from real life and the contemporaneous political situation that the Poles faced as soldiers of the Allied forces in Britain.

The play opens with Macbeth's soliloquy, delivered in prose, and with his wife's stated intention to besmear the faces of King Duncan's guards with blood. However, instead of finding Duncan's body in his bedroom, Lady Macbeth finds Lieutenant Bunio in bed wearing a gas mask pierced by a dagger. Her appearance collapses the division between Shakespeare's dramatic fiction and the reality of the Polish soldiers in Scotland. Appalled by Macbeth's treatment of his wife, Bunio says:

As far as this Macbeth goes, even when I was reading the play in high school, I did not like him … Couldn't he do the job himself? Did he have to use a woman to help him, and such a woman, to boot … ? Here [in Britain] they don't know how to appreciate and respect women. Please, look at your hands. How beautiful they would be if they were respected! I am sure that after each murder you had to scrub the floors, carry water, while caustic lye and spiky brush harmed this blooming beauty given to you by nature. And he was, for certain – as he is doing now – waiting behind the door – until you finished, instead of doing the job himself or hiring adequate maids. (171)

Using all the typical Polish methods of seduction, the lieutenant kisses

Lady Macbeth's hands, pays her innumerable compliments, praises her devotion to home and family values, and even manicures her finger nails and paints 'bloody' stains on her hands to mislead her husband. Eventually enamoured, Lady Macbeth pleads with him to murder her husband.

As the encounter between Macbeth and the Polish soldiers reveals, Macbeth does not realize what the real war means. He lives, as the lieutenant tells him, in the past: 'You can only follow the old-fashioned ways, all kinds of novelty upsets you. You will be able to understand the events that took place yesterday only the day after yesterday; you will never be able to comprehend the events of today' (176). In comic and frequently farcical situations, the officers criticize all the possible stereotypical Scottish vices: stinginess, insularity, obsession with tradition, and social hierarchy as well as a lack of openness towards other cultures and their values. Although the Polish officers crave contact with women, Lady Macbeth does not fulfil their needs. As the 'quintessential' Scottish woman, she pales in comparison with Polish women: she does not know how to dress elegantly and sexily, she has an old-fashioned hair style, and, ultimately, she simply is not a Polish woman.

Losing his grip on reality, Macbeth treats Major Bieński as Banquo and plans his murder. Later, during supper, he treats him as Banquo's ghost. At the same time Lieutenant Bunio convinces himself that he has really killed Macbeth, who is lying on the floor in a pool of red wine. The witches and Hecate become upset with the Poles who ridicule their prophesies, and meanwhile Lady Macbeth reconciles with her husband, leaving the lieutenant to the mercy of the vengeful powers that besiege the castle. The play concludes with Bunio rushing into a fight and literally losing his head, after which an alarm, summoning him to a drill, awakens him from his drunken nightmare.

As this summary suggests, Bunsch's farcical play replaces Shakespeare's tragedy with its stylistic and moral sophistication. Its main significance emerges primarily from its intertextuality, the specific and often complex encounters it reveals between *Macbeth*'s original play and the situation of Polish soldiers in Britain during the Second World War. Combining physical comedy, bad punning, and modernized popular language, the play was addressed to a well-defined audience who could appreciate not only its carnivalesque structure and message but also the cultural references and the anarchic treatment of the original text. Although, unfortunately, there are no documents registering the play's reception by Bunsch's military companions, we might posit, from our current privileged position, that the comic rendition of *Macbeth* had a double goal: it was to evoke laughter at British idiosyncrasies and lift up the morale of the Polish soldiers in exile.[23] Here, Shakespeare and his universal appeal fulfilled the role of a catalyst, juxtaposing the political and cultural similarities and discrepancies of these two nations united in a highly tragic historical situation.

In addition to the uses discussed above, wartime Polish Shakespeare also served as a strategy for dealing with national phobias and bigotry, including narrow-mindedness and prejudice against Jews that could already be detected in certain Polish circles during the late 1930s. Roman Brandstaetter, who escaped from Nazi occupation to Palestine, appropriated Shakespeare's *The Merchant of Venice* in *The Merchant of Warsaw* (1941).[24] Staged on 27 October 1941 in Tel Aviv, the play evoked a heated controversy. Brandstaetter was accused of both anti-Polish and anti-Semitic propaganda. As an unfaltering patriot, the playwright defended himself, explaining that his work was 'the fruit of his faith in Poland as a law-abiding country that has to fulfil a special historic mission.' It was, he maintained, 'the result of his faith in social justice' (qtd in Frister 152–3). Yet the insulting campaign directed against Brandstaetter continued, and the production was prematurely terminated.

Another instance of the political appropriation of Shakespeare for expressing Poland's postwar ideological choices may be found in Britain. In 1942, after her visit to the Piccadilly Theatre, where she saw John Gielgud's Macbeth, Polish prose writer and art historian Stefania Zahorska (1890–1961), known by her pseudonym 'Pandora,' published a long article entitled 'Makbet Na Emigracji' [Macbeth in Exile] in *Wiadomości Polskie* [Polish News], a Polish weekly issued in London (1).[25] Gielgud's production made her realize the extent of the cultural distance between the concept of *Realpolitik* in Shakespeare's and her own time. Zahorska localized Shakespeare's play in the context of contemporary political issues, advocating a new social and political future for Poland. Her experiences in prewar Poland and her life in exile during the war made her realize that the 'contemporary Macbeth' would need a pragmatic ideological explanation of his crimes:

> The Macbeth of our times ... could not talk about the murdered King Duncan, that he was a good and gentle ruler who should have lived and reigned. Our Macbeth would be shouting through loudspeakers and the radio that Duncan was a traitor, that he was a national disaster, that he, Macbeth, is the true saviour of the country, that he is the personification

of all the possible elements of the 'preservation-of-the-state,' that his deed should be ranked first in the 'hierarchy' of state goals. (1)

Categorically rejecting any optimistic reading of the ending of Shakespeare's tragedy, Zahorska drew attention to Malcolm's self-incrimination (*Macbeth* 5.2), which she treated as proof that even 'Shakespeare probably doubted whether Malcolm might be better than Macbeth' (1). If Macbeth 'survived the fifth act, surely he would be happy to know that a large portion of his own thoughts, feelings, desires, and methods had been appropriated by his hostile successor' (1).

Sensitive to political struggles in prewar Poland, where many progressive politicians and social activists were imprisoned in camps (for example, the camp in Bereza Kartuska) (Miłosz 383), and where the government changed hands more than thirty times between 1918 and 1939, Zahorska called upon her readers to change the Polish political system after the war. 'Today's war,' she proclaimed, 'is the war against all dictatorships at large'; it should embrace all possible forms of class struggle everywhere in the world where the 'peasants and workers' had been abused and exploited for centuries.

Poland would become a truly liberated country after the war only if power was assumed by the 'working classes.' Considering the idea of the Grand Mechanism of History in the context of social injustice, Zahorska warned that this injustice could create 'Malcolm, or rather Malcolms … and each of them will continue Macbeth's methods.' Further, drawing attention to the repetitiveness of politics in real life ('Macbeth dies on the stage only once, but the Macbeth of history will have to die many times'), she stressed the play's social, political, and cultural dimensions, the results of which affected many human lives over the centuries. In comments seeming to be a call for political and social revolution, Zahorska remarked that 'However difficult the first part of the postwar period will be in Poland, this is the way we should go; we must follow [this path]. And the moment will come when Macbeth, the usurper and tyrant, will die forever. And a wave of history will grind the greedy crowd of Malcolms, the successors, into sand' (1).

Clever and insightful as Zahorska's interpretation of *Macbeth* was, it lacked the depth of Jan Kott's understanding of the Grand Mechanism of History, which he demonstrated in his *Szkice o Szekspirze* [Notes on Shakespeare] (1961), known internationally as *Shakespeare Our Contemporary* (1965): all totalitarian regimes, including the working-class regime, generate their Macbeths and Malcolms. Zahorska herself must have modified her point of view since she never returned to Communist Poland, choosing instead to criticize and comment on its political solutions from a distance and as an emigrant. The Communist regime in Poland, however, is a different story in which Shakespeare – as 'the most popular of Polish poets' – unceasingly played a different but still very significant role.

Notes

1 We can find no references to Shakespeare in Polish culture in, for example, Marta Fik's well-researched essay 'Szekspir w teatrze polskim: Lata 1918–1989' [Shakespeare in the Polish Theatre: 1918–1989] (1997); or Kazimierz Braun's *Teatr polski (1939–1989). Obszary wolności – Obszary zniewolenia* [Polish Theatre 1939–1989. Spaces of Freedom – Spaces of Enslavement] (1994) (25–42).

2 If not otherwise indicated, all translations from Polish are mine.

3 Judith Olsak-Glass shares his opinion, maintaining that 'the prisons, ghettos, internment, transit, labour and extermination camps, roundups, mass deportations, public executions, mobile killing units, death marches, deprivation, hunger, disease, and exposure all testify to "the inhuman policies of both Hitler and Stalin"' and 'were clearly aimed at the total extermination of Polish citizens, both Jews and Christians. Both regimes endorsed a systematic program of genocide.'

4 Something of the atmosphere of the Vilnius and Lviv (Lwów) theatres is recalled by Jan Kreczmar, an eminent Polish actor. In his reminiscences, he describes his friends and their artistic achievements during the war but makes no reference to the political issues that affected theatrical life in the territory occupied by the Soviet Army (Kreczmar 234–41). In 1963, when his essay appeared in print, all information about the Soviet invasion of Poland in 1939 was censored.

5 Leopold Pobóg-Kielanowski (1909?–88) was a well-known artist in the Polish theatrical circles before the Second World War. He was an actor (from 1923), a director (from 1932), and scholar (PhD in humanities, Vilnius University, 1928). He had also worked as an assistant to Gaston Baty in Paris (1933). In other words, he was a highly qualified professional who knew European culture and theatre very well. After working in the Vilnius theatre, Pobóg-Kielanowski managed to escape to Warsaw where he served as a soldier in underground organizations. In 1944–5 he performed forced labour in Germany. He later escaped to Italy and then to Poland (Braun 41).

6 Hanna Ordonówna (1902–50), a famous Polish prewar actress and singer, stressed the ludic (popular) aspects of Shakespeare's *Twelfth Night*, sharing with readers her interpretation of the role of Viola, which she played in this production (4).

7 For a detailed presentation of Ukrainian productions of *Hamlet* (21 September 1943) in Lviv, see Irena R. Makaryk, '*Wartime Hamlet*,' *Shakespeare in the Worlds of Communism and Socialism* (Toronto: University of Toronto Press, 2006) 119–35.

8 This was true of Ukrainians, as well, since Slavs as a whole were regarded as *Untermensch*.

9 I would like to thank Prof. Albin Głowacki, specialist in the history of the Second World War, especially the Eastern Front, in the faculty of history and philosophy at the University of Łódź, for clarifying differences in the political situation during the Second World War among Poland and other Eastern and Central European countries.

10 Four large companies and more than forty smaller groups were active throughout the war; underground acting schools were also created (Braun 30–1).

11 Kazimierz Braun mentions that the great director Juliusz Osterwa prepared a new translation of *Hamlet* in which he transformed the play into a contemporary idiom and action; he viewed the plot as a commentary on the philosophical and ethical problem of the Second World War. At the same time, Czesław Miłosz translated *As You Like It*, which was staged in 1946 (33).

12 The roots of Woszczerowicz's interpretation went back to Nazi totalitarianism, but with the current political climate (specifically the political shuffle of the Polish and Soviet political bureaus after Stalin's death) his 1960 production of *Richard III* was seen as an indirect commentary on the Communist totalitarian regime. See Kujawińska Courtney, 'Influence or Irrelevance: Jan Kott and the Multicultural Shakespeare Context' (194–6).

13 The monograph was published after the war.

14 Marczak-Oborski maintains that Polish theatrical activities had a political dimension: they undermined Nazi propaganda and evoked a feeling of insubordination (*Teatr czasu wojny* 112).

15 *The Merchant of Venice* at Murnau was directed by Czesław Szpakowicz; Włodzimierz Wołoszanowski composed the incidental music (Piekarski 265).

16 See Werner Habicht in this volume. For a detailed reading of the complex relationship between Nazi ideology and the figure of Shylock see Zeno Ackermann, also in this volume.

17 Antoni Dębicki recalls that in *The Merchant of Venice* the officer playing the

part of the Duke had a 'magnificent costume based on Bellini's painting.' Since he sat on a throne throughout the whole act, his colleagues prepared only the front part of the costume: his back showed his own camp clothes (298).

18 There are even fewer references to the production of *Twelfth Night* but the scanty extant scraps of information also confirm its success. One officer noted in his diary: 'At 4:30 p.m. I went to see for *Twelfth Night* or *What You Will* for the second time. It was the last performance. Colonel Skubisz was singing in English because it is the fashionable language nowadays. His songs received three encores. The theatre was filled to its capacity. Even the passages were overcrowded' (Jakubowski 377).

19 The aim of these performances was not only to entertain, but also, and most importantly, to educate and to evoke patriotic feelings. They were of a pragmatic rather than artistic nature and frequently turned into patriotic manifestations, especially when they coincided with national holidays or anniversaries of significant national events.

20 There were about 200,000 Polish soldiers, sailors, and airmen stationed in Scotland from 1940 to 1947 ('Archives Hub: Polish Armed Forces in Scotland Project').

21 Bunsch (1896–1969) was a painter, playwright, teacher, and soldier; he had participated in the September campaign in 1939 and, like thousands of other Polish soldiers, came to Scotland through Hungary and France (Dajnowska).

22 All quotations from the play come from Adam Bunsch, 'Poprawki do *Macbeta*.'

23 The first and only time that the play was staged in Poland was a performance in early 1980, by students from the technical high school where Bunsch taught before the Second World War at the Bielsko-Biała Teatr Polski (Bielsko-Biała Polish Theatre).

24 The text of Brandstaetter's *Merchant of Warsaw* is, unfortunately, lost, but there is a detailed description of it in an article by Frister (148–50).

25 In 1924–5 Zahorska was the director of the art section in the *Przegląd Warszawski* [Warsaw Review], and a permanent collaborator of *Wiadomości literackie* [Literary News]. While in exile in London, she co-founded the Polish Writers Association Ltd. and wrote several political and philosophical novels about human existence in the twentieth century, including *Stacja Abbesses* [Station Abbesses] (1952), *Ofiara* [A Victim] (1955), and *Ziemia przepojona gniewem* [The Soil Overflowed with Anger] (1961). See Zahorska, '*Makbet* z Gielgudem' [*Macbeth* with Gielgud], *Wiadomości polskie* [Polish News] 35 (1942): 2.

Works Cited

Anon. 'William Szekspir.' *Prawda Wileńska* 26 (1941): 4.

'Archives Hub: Polish Armed Forces in Scotland Project.' *Archives Hub.ac.uk.* n.d. 8 Aug. 2009. http://www.archiveshub.ac.uk/news.

Baliński, S. 'Niebo Szekspira.' (1941). *Wiersze zebrane.* London: Stowarzyszenie Pisarzy Polskich, 1948. 149–52.

Braun, K. *Teatr polski (1939–1989). Obszary wolności – obszary zniewolenia.* Warsaw: Wydawnictwo Naukowe: Semper, 1994.

Bunsch, Adam. 'Poprawki do *Macbeta.*' *Dramat.* Vol. 2. Cracow: Wydawnictwo Literackie, 1970. 166–98.

Czereśniewski, W. 'Spotkanie z Szekspirem.' (1941). *Poezja Polski walczącej (1939–1945).* Ed. Jan Szczawiej. Warsaw: Państwowy Instytut Wydawniczy, 1974. 1155–6.

Dajnowska, A. "Mistrzowie mniej znani, Śląski 'Swięciszek: – Adam Bunsch.'" *Sztuka.pl.* n.d. 4 Aug. 2009. www.sztuka.pl/index.php?id.

Dan, A. 'Wieczór Trzech Króli.' *Czerwony sztandar* 177 (1941): 4.

Dębicki, A. 'Teatr obozowy w Murnau.' *Pamiętnik teatralny* 1/4 (1963): 296–313.

Drewniak, B. *Teatr i Film Trzeciej Rzeszy.* Gdansk: Wydawnictwo Morskie, 1972.

Edelman, M., R. Assuntino, and W. Goldkorn. *Strażnik: Marek Edelman opowiada.* Cracow: Znak, 1999.

Ferguson, N. *The War of the World.* New York: Penguin Press, 2006.

Fik, M. 'Szekspir w teatrze polskim lata 1918–1989.' *Teatr* 137 (1997): 22–31.

Frister, E. '*Kupiec warszawski* – debiut dramaturgiczny Romana Brandsteattera.' *Żydzi w lustrze dramatu, teatru i krytyki teatralnej.* Ed. Eleonora Udalska. Katowice: Wydawnictwo Uniwersytetu Śląskiego, 2004. 145–59.

Gross, J. *Shylock.* New York: Touchstone Book, 1992.

Hernik Spalińska, J. *Życie teatralne w Wilnie podczas II wojny światowej.* Warsaw: Instytut Sztuki Państwowej Akademii Nauk, 2005.

Jaeschke, Z. 'Teatr obozowy.' *Lambinowski rocznik teatralny* 11 (1987): 110–27.

Jakubowski, B. *Oflag VII A In Murnau.* Ms. 81. Archive WIH AON. Nr II/52/7.

Kiec, I. *Teatr służebny polskiej emigracji po 1939 roku.* Poznań: Wydawnictwo Uniwersytetu Poznańskiego, 1999.

Knuth, R. *Libricide: The Regime-Sponsored Destruction of Books and Libraries in the Twentieth Century.* New York: Greenwood Publishing Group, 2003.

Kott, J. *Szkice o Szekspirze.* Warsaw: PIW, 1961.

– *Szekspir współczesny.* Warsaw: PIW, 1965.

Kujawińska Courtney, K. 'Influence or Irrelevance: Jan Kott and the Multicultural Shakespeare Context.' *RuBriCa's Studies: A Collection of Essays.* Ed. Irina S. Prikhod'ko. Moscow: Polygraph-Inform, 2006. 193–208.

Kurnakowicz, J. 'Po Czkawce byłby dobry Falstaff.' *Prawda Wileńska* 26 (1941): 4.

Kreczmar, J. 'Teatr Lwowski w latach 1939-1941.' *Pamiętnik teatralny* 1–4 (1963): 234–41.

Lechoń, J. 'Do Szekspira.' (1941). *Poezje*. Wroclaw: Ossolineum, 1990. 176–8.

Leszczyński, S. 'Program zniszczenia polskiej inteligencji.' University of Linz, Germany 12 Feb. 2009. Unpublished paper. http//www.gussen.org.pl.

Maliszewski, A. 'Teatr Wileński w latach 1939–1945.' *Pamiętnik teatralny* 1/4 (1963): 214–33.

Marczak-Oborski, S. *Teatr czasu wojny. Polskie życie teatralne w latach II wojny światowej (1939–1945)*. Warsaw: Państwowy Instytut Wydawniczy, 1967.

– 'Troilus i Kresyda w Warszawie … 1940 roku.' *Teatr Polski* 13 (1965–6): 28–9.

Milosz, C. *The History of Polish Literature*. New York: Macmillan, 1969.

Mirecki, W. *Jeniecka Melpomena*. Warsaw: Wydawnictwo Artystyczne i Filmowe, 1981.

Olsak-Glass, J. 'Review of Piotrkowski's Poland Holocaust.' *Poland's Holocaust Saramatian Review*. n.d. 15 Apr. 2008. http://www.ruf.rice.edu.

Ordonówna, H. 'Ludowość Szekspira.' *Prawda Wileńska* 26 (1941): 4.

Piekarski, S. *Polskie teatry jenieckie w Niemczech 1939–1945*. Warsaw: Departament Społeczno-Wychowawczy Ministerstwa Obrony Narodowej Dom Wojska Polskiego, 2001.

Pobóg- Kielanowski, L. 'Szekspir – jakim go widzi reżyser.' *Prawda Wileńska* 26 (1941): 4.

Sakowska, R. *Ludzie z dzielnicy zamkniętej. Z dziejów Żydów w Warszawie w latach okupacji hitlerowskiej, październik 1939–marzec 1943*. Warsaw: Polskie Wydawnictwo Naukowe, 1993.

Salmonowicz, S. *Polskie Państwo Podziemne*. Warsaw: Wydawnictwa Szkolne i Pedagogiczne, 1994.

Sitnikow, W.R. 'Teatr Polski dobrze pojmuje swoje zadania.' *Wileńska* 26 (1941): 5.

Stanisz, E. Polskie kierunki szekspirologicznej myśli krytycznej w dwudziestoleciu miedzywojennym. Diss. University of Łódź, 2007.

Surynowa-Wyczółkowska, J. 'Leon Schiller w Niemczech.' *Wiadomości* 29/30 (1958): 1–18.

Szczawiej, J. *Poezja Polski walczącej (1939-1945)*. Warsaw: PIW, 1974.

Umru, D. 'Przedstawienie to można polecić pracującym.' *Prawda Wileńska* 26 (1941): 5.

Valeska, A. 'Karnawałowe przedstawienie.' *Prawda Wileńska* 26 (1941): 4.

Zahorska, Stephanie. 'Makbet na emigracji.' *Wiadomości polskie: Polityczne i literackie* 39 (1942): 1.

7 Pasternak's Shakespeare in Wartime Russia

ALEKSEI SEMENENKO

Boris Pasternak's translations of Shakespeare now belong to the classics of Russian literature. Most of his translations, beginning with *Hamlet* in 1940 and ending in 1951 with *Macbeth*, appeared during the Second World War. In this essay I will attempt to recreate the semiosphere – the crucial cultural, artistic, and political subtexts and contexts – of these translations, focusing on three aspects of Pasternak's Shakespeare: his translations in the context of war and the Stalinist period; his ethos as a translator and his understanding of Shakespeare in the context of his historiosophy; and his deliberate incorporation of Shakespeare in his own creative work, with *Hamlet* as the central text. From a broader perspective, I will also show that the Shakespearean context provides valuable insight into understanding the figure of Stalin both during the war and in the postwar period.

Shakespeare during the Great Terror

Pasternak began translating Shakespeare in the late 1930s, the apogee of the period known as Stalin's Great Terror: the wave of arrests and public trials of 'the traitors of the Motherland' (Zinov'ev and Kamenev in 1936, Bukharin in 1937). In addition to members of the Communist Party, Stalin's purges also extended to the Red Army, peasants, ethnic minorities, and other sectors of Soviet society.[1] Writers and poets did not escape this fate; during this period the arrested included Boris Pilniak (Pasternak's neighbour in Peredelkino), Osip Mandelstam, Isaak Babel, Nikolai Zabolotskii, and Vsevolod Meyerhold, to name just a few. Pasternak himself was an extremely suitable candidate for prosecution, especially when, in 1937, he refused to sign the

7.1. Boris Pasternak. Portrait by Alexander Less. 1954. Reproduced courtesy of Petr Pasternak.

petition of the Soviet writers demanding the death penalty for the former Marshal Mikhail Tukhachevskii. These petitions had become a routine ritual accompanying every process against those accused of anti-Soviet activity, and Pasternak's demonstrative refusal was regarded as suicidal. Although he was not repressed, he was aware that his future and the future of his family were uncertain. The essence of terror was its total unpredictability: even those loyal to the regime were not guaranteed escape from repressions or death, and the position of those that were held in suspicion by the authorities was much more precarious.

This was the context in which, in 1939, the theatre director Vsevolod Meyerhold commissioned Pasternak to translate *Hamlet*. By that time the renowned nineteenth-century translations of *Hamlet* by Nikolai Polevoi and Andrei Kroneberg had become obsolete, and the then new translations by Mikhail Lozinskii (1933) and Anna Radlova (1937) probably did not satisfy the director's taste. As Pasternak confessed in a letter to his father, his work on the translation of *Hamlet* saved him 'from many things,' and he 'would have gone insane' without it (E. Pasternak, *Boris* 543). Pasternak is referring here to the tragic events of 1939: Meyerhold was arrested in June and several weeks later Meyerhold's wife, the actress Zinaida Raikh, was murdered. Pasternak's mother died in

August, a week before the beginning of the Second World War. Thus Shakespeare – and *Hamlet* in particular – served Pasternak both as a virtual 'safe haven' from reality and as an instrument of self-reflection. Some of the most significant works of Russian literature were created as a result of this 'dialogue' between Pasternak and Shakespeare.

Translation vs Creation

In the late 1930s and 1940s translation became, for many writers, almost the only means of making a living; aside from Pasternak, Anna Akhmatova, Marina Tsvetaeva, and Mikhail Zoshchenko shared this situation (see Friedberg 114, 193–4). After 1937 Pasternak was unable to publish any major works and therefore turned to translation as an alternative to individual creation. There were periods when Pasternak referred to his practice of translation as an unfortunate necessity or even as a burden that hindered him from his own creative work. For example, in a letter of 30 September 1947 to the well-known and influential Soviet Shakespeare scholar Mikhail Morozov, Pasternak wrote, 'I am a translator not by good fortune but through misprision, and if conditions were better I ought not to be translating at all' (transl. in Barnes 249). Yet, despite these comments, Pasternak did not turn to translating Shakespeare for purely economical reasons; as I will show, Shakespeare strongly resonated with Pasternak's own oeuvre.

Apart from several Shakespeare sonnets, Pasternak translated eight plays by Shakespeare. Here is the concise chronology of these translations:

1939–40   *Hamlet* (first published in 1940).
1941–2   *Romeo and Juliet* (first published in 1944).
1942   *Anthony and Cleopatra* (first published in 1944).
In 1942   Pasternak also published an article entitled 'My Translations' which, as Christopher Barnes correctly observes, is an implicit response to the literary fraternity led by Alexander Fadeev 'who claimed that translation work was an unpatriotic act of ideological retreat in time of war' (198).
1943   British Embassy congratulates Pasternak for his translation of Shakespeare.
1944   *Othello* (first published in 1945).
1945   Both parts of *Henry IV* (first published in 1948).
1947   *King Lear* (first published in 1949).

1949–50   A two-volume edition of Shakespeare in Pasternak's trans-
          lation is published.
1950   *Macbeth* (first published in 1951).

During the 1940s Pasternak also wrote several texts in which he outlined
his principles as a translator and his understanding of Shakespeare. The
two main principles of his method may be formulated as creative freedom and naturalness of language: Pasternak did not accept literal(ist)
or equivalence-oriented translation and argued that a translation must
be produced by an author who has experienced the impact of the original text before the actual act of translating (Pasternak, 'Zametki' 165).
In one of his letters from 1942 he asserts that his translation principles
are those of the nineteenth century, when translation was considered a
literary task of such height that it did not allow for 'linguistic exercises'
(in other words, he opposes literalist, 'word-for-word' translations)
(*PSS* 9: 287).[2] In the case of Shakespeare, he states, 'total freedom of the
mind' is needed (*PSS* 5: 45). Pasternak also emphasizes the importance
of the liveliness and naturalness of language – 'A translation must produce an impression of life, not of literariness [*slovesnost'*]' – and argues
that the translator must avoid stylization and expressions that are not
part of his artistic vocabulary (*PSS* 5: 72).

Pasternak focused on producing a modern and theatre-oriented text
in translation. Here are his well-known remarks in the preface to the
first edition of *Hamlet*:

> Instead of translating words and metaphors I turned to the translation of
> thoughts and scenes.
> The work should be judged as an original Russian dramatic work
> because apart from its accuracy, equilinearity with the original, etc., it
> contains more of that intentional liberty without which there can be no
> approach to great things. (*PSS* 5: 43–4; trans. in Barnes 170; the first sen-
> tence is in my translation).

It must be noted that Pasternak's description accurately reflects his
practice: his translations of Shakespeare (and not only of Shakespeare)
do sound like modern Russian dramatic works and bear the distinct
influence of Pasternak's poetics. Nonetheless, the degree of the translator's involvement in each translation varied: if *Hamlet* was fully 'appropriated' as one of the most important works for Pasternak himself (see,
for example, Gladkov, *Vstrechi* 51), he was much less engaged in some

of his other translations. For example, in correspondence with Olga Freidenberg during the summer of 1944, he confessed that he had been translating Shakespeare 'half-consciously' (*PSS* 9: 379); to Alexander Gladkov, he mentioned on several occasions that he wanted to give up the practice of translation (*Vstrechi* 100). In another letter to Freidenberg in 1947, Pasternak bitterly wrote, 'I once translated well and it was to no good; the only way to take revenge is to do the same badly and carelessly fast ... I do not care about *Lear* and about how good – or how bad – my translation will be. It does not matter at all now' (*PSS* 9: 501). These strong statements should not be taken too literally, of course; we must remember that, at that time, Pasternak was focused entirely on his novel *Doctor Zhivago*, and any other task was considered unessential.

Pasternak's situation was aggravated by the fact that each of his Shakespeare translations was scrutinized and edited. Mikhail Morozov became a sort of a 'private critic' (and censor) of Pasternak's Shakespeare. On the one hand, he helped Pasternak with publishing (and thus legitimized his work), but, on the other, his approach was the complete antithesis to Pasternak's: he urged the writer to maintain an almost literal 'accuracy,' a concept most alien to Pasternak. Morozov's critique of Pasternak's translation of *Hamlet* provoked a very negative reaction in Pasternak who, in a letter to Anna Naumova, wrote that Morozov's advice drove him to desperation (*PSS* 9: 287). Although Morozov was impressed with the translation of *Romeo and Juliet* and praised the translation of *Anthony and Cleopatra* as the best of all of Pasternak's translations, Pasternak continued to experience the strong control of editors that was no less intense during the 1940s and 1950s. Referring to this practice of 'supervised translation,' Pasternak wrote in 1953 that, at the time of total terror, he was forced to make his translations almost literal in meaning not because the editors cared much about the conformity of the translations to the original but because they needed someone to blame, 'if something happens' (*PSS* 9: 754). On the other hand, Pasternak also acknowledges elsewhere that, due to such numerous revisions, the final version of his *Hamlet* translation would ultimately have a lasting value of thirty to fifty years (*PSS* 9: 642). This perspicacious remark suggests that Pasternak realized that some of his translations would become canonical texts of Russian culture.

Hamlet, Hamlet, and Pasternak

Pasternak's work on Shakespeare translation is closely connected with his cooperation with theatres. For Pasternak at that time the theatre presented an opportunity for his work to appear, if not in print, then on stage. However, this connection is also marked by a constant struggle between Pasternak's view of the text and the director's will. The history of the *Hamlet* production at the Moscow Art Theatre (MAT) clearly reflects this complex relationship between the poet and the theatre.

Pasternak's first attempt at a translation of *Hamlet* dates back to 1924, but his efforts at that time represent only a bare beginning (*PSS* 7: 538). As noted above, he began translating *Hamlet* in 1939 at Meyerhold's request and continued the work even after Meyerhold was arrested. Vladimir Nemirovich-Danchenko, one of the founders of the MAT, learned about the new translation of *Hamlet* from Vsevolod Ivanov, and in November 1939 Pasternak was invited to present his translation at the MAT. After hearing Pasternak read several excerpts, Nemirovich-Danchenko cancelled his contract with Anna Radlova,[3] a translator with whom he previously had agreed to work. Thus began the long and unfortunate history of the MAT production of *Hamlet*.

As in his other translations, Pasternak's poetics is explicit in *Hamlet*; the play is written in a vivid expressionistic manner and characterized by an eclectic combination of contemporary idioms, Russicisms (including archaisms), and technical terminology (argotisms). These features drew major criticism in the 1940s (and still do even today),[4] and led to another, no less important aspect of the work: Pasternak's translation went through about twelve different editions (E. Pasternak, 'K istorii' 10). The reasons for these various redactions are quite ambiguous. First, Pasternak's original text was corrected at the insistence of Nemirovich-Danchenko and his actors. Pasternak was eager to see his *Hamlet* at the MAT and quite readily acceded to the demands of the troupe, although he was sometimes irritated by their apparent misunderstanding of his text. In his opinion, Meyerhold's experimental, avant-garde theatre, for which he had written his original translation, was 'more Shakespearean' than the 'realistic' MAT (E. Pasternak, *Boris* 542–3). As a result, the MAT redaction of *Hamlet*, which was released in 1941 by Goslitizdat (the state publishing house), differed significantly from the original version. In the unpublished preface to the translation, Pasternak explained that the corrections were due to 'the pressure of necessity,' and asked readers 'with understanding and taste' to turn to the 1940 journal variant (E. Pasternak, *Boris* 544). But this was by no means the last redaction of the text. In the next edition (published by Detgiz in 1942) the text endured further changes, and each of the subsequent editions, up to the posthumous edition of 1968, also differ from each other.

It would be all too easy to claim that all the post-1940 variants are 'distorted' and not authentic. First of all, multiple variants of the same work are a characteristic feature of Pasternak's poetics (Lotman 91), and it is hard to believe that all alterations to the text were merely 'mechanical.' In 1953, before sending his translation to the stage and film director Grigorii Kozintsev, the creator of the first Russian cinematographic *Hamlet* (1964), Pasternak wrote to him to say that, after so many years of continuous changes, he himself did not know which version to choose as the best or the most 'authentic.'

Translation as Escapism

The pressure that Pasternak experienced over a period of twenty years was reflected in the text of the translation. As Vladimir Markov notes, in Pasternak's translations of 1947 and 1951 there are five lines of Hamlet's soliloquy 'To be or not to be' that have nothing in common with Shakespeare's original but a lot to do with Pasternak's situation (505–6).

Shakespeare's text:
For who would bear the whips and scorns of time,
The oppressor's wrong, the proud man's contumely,
The pangs of dispriz'd love, the law's delay,
The insolence of office, and the spurns
That patient merit of the unworthy takes.

Pasternak's translation:
А то кто снес бы *ложное величье*
Правителей, невежество вельмож,
Всеобщее притворство, невозможность
Излить себя, несчастную любовь
И призрачность заслуг в глазах ничтожеств.[5]

[And who would bear the false grandeur
Of the rulers, the ignorance of the grandees,
The common hypocrisy, the impossibility
To express oneself, unhappy love,
And the illusoriness of merit in the eyes of the unworthy.]

Such phrases as 'the false grandeur of the rulers,' 'common hypocrisy,'[6] and 'the impossibility of expressing oneself' especially warrant our attention: these are the words not of the Danish prince but of Pasternak himself, or rather, Pasternak disguised as Hamlet. Another obvious reference to Pasternak's situation is his translation of Hamlet's line, 'Why, look you now, how unworthy a thing you make of me!' as 'Смотрите же, с какой грязью вы меня смешали!' (literally, 'Look what dirt you have cast at me!'), connoting not only humiliation but also defamation. Thus the soliloquy becomes a 'lyrical confession camouflaged as a translation' (Markov 506) and Hamlet becomes the translator's alter ego.[7]

In the same volume as his translation of *Hamlet*, Pasternak also included a translation of Shakespeare's Sonnet 66, which is thematically closely linked to the 'To be' soliloquy:

Tired with all these, for restful death I cry:
As, to behold desert a beggar born,
And needy nothing trimmed in jollity,
And purest faith unhappily forsworn,
And gilded honour shamefully misplaced,
And maiden virtue rudely strumpeted,
And right perfection wrongfully disgraced,
And strength by limping sway disabled,
And art made tongue-tied by authority,
And folly, doctor-like, controlling skill,
And simple truth miscalled simplicity,
And captive good attending captain ill.
Tired with all these, from these would I be gone,
Save that to die I leave my love alone.

Измучась всем, я умереть хочу.
Тоска смотреть, как мается бедняк,
И как шутя живется богачу,
И доверять, и попадать впросак,
И наблюдать, как наглость лезет в свет,
И честь девичья катится ко дну,
И знать, что ходу совершенствам нет,
И видеть мощь у немощи в плену,
И вспоминать, что мысли заткнут рот,
И разум сносит глупости хулу, ·

И прямодушье простотой слывет,
И доброта прислуживает злу.
Измучась всем, не стал бы жить и дня,
Да другу трудно будет без меня.

Shakespeare's sonnet may be read almost completely as Pasternak's description of his own situation, but in his translation there are also several meaningful alterations. The phrase 'art made tongue-tied by authority' becomes more acute: 'thought is gagged.' Also, in the last two lines of the poem, Pasternak interprets 'tired' with the verb *измучиться*, which refers to suffering and martyrdom,[8] and substitutes 'love' for the more neutral 'friend,' thus obliterating the theme of love.

Destiny and self-sacrifice

It is erroneous to believe, however, that for Pasternak Shakespeare was only a means to express himself under the disguise of translation. The most conspicuous feature of his translation of *Hamlet* is his interpretation of both *Hamlet* the play and Hamlet the character. Pasternak himself wrote that *Hamlet* 'is not a drama of characterlessness, but one of duty and self-sacrifice' (*PSS* 5: 75).

The following crucial summary of Pasternak's understanding of the philosophy of the play is revealing: 'It is far more important that the will of fate elects Hamlet to be the judge of his own time and the servant of a more distant one. *Hamlet* is a drama of exalted calling, imposed heroic task, entrusted destiny' (*PSS* 5: 75; transl. in Barnes 171). Here we can see motifs that are essential to Pasternak's oeuvre as a whole: the motif of duty and self-sacrifice (as opposed to the cliché of Hamlet as a will-less hero), and the motif of predestination, following one's calling.

As is widely known, Pasternak's *Hamlet* is closely linked with his novel *Doctor Zhivago*, which he began writing around 1945,[9] and also with his neo-Christian philosophy. The most evident connection is the poem 'Hamlet' in the collection of Zhivago's poetry, in which the motif of self-sacrifice becomes especially pronounced:

Гул затих. Я вышел на подмостки.
Прислонясь к дверному косяку,
Я ловлю в далеком отголоске
Что случится на моем веку.
На меня наставлен сумрак ночи

Тысячью биноклей на оси.
Если только можно, Авва Отче,
Чашу эту мимо пронеси.
Я люблю твой замысел упрямый
И играть согласен эту роль.
Но сейчас идет другая драма,
И на этот раз меня уволь.
Но продуман распорядок действий,
И неотвратим конец пути.
Я один, все тонет в фарисействе.
Жизнь прожить – не поле перейти.

[The noise subsides. I walk onto the stage.
Leaning on the doorway
I try to guess from the distant echo
What is to happen in my lifetime.
Darkness of night, thousandfold, is focused on me
Down the axis of each opera-glass.
If it may be, I pray Thee, Abba, Father,
Let this cup pass from me.
I love Thy stubborn purpose,
And I consent to play this part.
But now another drama is in progress,
So leave me this time uninvolved.
But the order of action has been settled
And there is no turning from the road.
I am alone, all drowns in [the Pharisees'] hypocrisy.
To live a life is not a stroll across the field.][10]

Here the words of Christ are repeated almost literally: 'Abba, Father, / Let this cup pass from me.' A number of scholars have discussed the theme of Hamlet as Christ in Pasternak's translation (see Nilsson 193; France 202; Clayton 460), and Pasternak himself unequivocally points out this analogy, especially when he equates Hamlet's 'To be or not to be' soliloquy with the Gethsemane prayer (*PSS* 5: 76). Thus Pasternak's Hamlet becomes a messiah, a judge of his time,[11] and a minister of the future epoch; the main motifs of *Hamlet* the play become predestination and self-sacrifice. The same motifs are accentuated in another of Zhivago's poems as well, especially the motif of the judge of the times:

Ты видишь, ход веков подобен притче
И может загореться на ходу.
Во имя страшного ее величья
Я в добровольных муках в гроб сойду.

Я в гроб сойду и в третий день восстану,
И, как сплавляют по реке плоты,
Ко мне на суд, как баржи каравана,
Столетья поплывут из темноты.

[You see, the passage of the centuries is like a parable
And can catch fire while in movement –
In the name of its terrible greatness
In voluntary torments I shall descend into the grave.

I shall descend into the grave and rise on the third day,
And, as rafts floating down a river,
As a convoy of barges, *the centuries*
Will float to me for judgment, out of the dark.]

(trans. in Livingston 113)

These motifs in their messianic context are prevalent in Pasternak's oeuvre as a whole. They constitute a certain neo-mythological theme that can be generally described as a plot in which the messiah-like hero sacrifices himself for the sake of an approaching epoch. His death makes it possible for the new age to come, and his sacrifice turns out to be one of the mechanisms of history. This theme is frequently found in Pasternak's poetry written between 1918 and 1959; examples include *Лейтенант Шмидт* [Lieutenant Schmidt] (1926–7), *Мельницы* [The Mills] (1915, 1928), *Я понял, все живо* [I Have Realized, Everything Is Alive] (1935), *Нобелевская премия* [The Nobel Prize] (1959) (see Semenenko, 'Gamletovskii'). The theme also appears in his translations (*Hamlet*, Pedro Calderón's *El príncipe constante*, Heinrich von Kleist's *Prinz Friedrich von Homburg*) and in his novel *Doctor Zhivago*.

To Act, To Live

Pasternak's poem 'Hamlet' portrays the character as an actor who is forced to play his part not on stage but in life. This image, and the 'histrionic' theme in general, appears in several of his texts and is central to

Слепая красавица [The Blind Beauty], an unfinished play that Pasternak was writing during the last year of his life. This play was intended to depict the fate of an artist under oppression, telling the story of the serf actor Petr Agafonov. Again, it is hard not to see an obvious allusion to Pasternak's own situation, and it is not surprising that the protagonist expresses many Pasternak's own views. For example, in one draft Agafonov almost literally cites Pasternak's statement that *Hamlet* is a play about predestination and a task imposed by fate, and that Hamlet is thus allotted the false role of avenger (*PSS* 5: 187). As we see, Pasternak once again unites the topics of fate and acting through a reference to Shakespeare's text.

The image of an actor is also central in the poem *'О знал бы я, что так бывает'* [O Had I Known That Thus It Happens] (1932):

Но старость – это Рим, который
Взамен турусов и колес
Не читки требует с актера,
А полной гибели всерьез.

Когда строку диктует чувство,
Оно на сцену шлет раба,
И тут кончается искусство,
И дышат почва и судьба.

[But older age is Rome, demanding
From actors not a gaudy blend
Of props and reading, but in earnest
A tragedy, with tragic end.

A slave is sent to the arena
When feeling has produced a line.
Then breathing soil and fate take over
And art has done and must resign.]

> (trans. Lydia Pasternak Slater in Pasternak, *Poems* 60)

In Pasternak's idiom, the image of the actor playing his part is not so much a common metaphor for life (most famously reflected in *As You Like It*, 'All the world's a stage, / And all the men and women merely players') but rather a reflection of the theme of destiny. To play a part means to accept one's fate, whatever the end. (Note that in Pasternak's original, what is expected from the actor is 'a real death in earnest.' In Slater's translation the line becomes smoother: 'A tragedy, with tragic end.') Rome stands for the oppressing State that demands the death of the Poet. The image of merciless Rome is frequent in Pasternak's oeuvre: as early as 1932, in a letter to his parents, Pasternak wrote: 'this is the eternal cruelty of wretched Russia; if she gives her love to someone, the chosen one cannot be saved. He appears, as it were, on the Roman arena, owing her a show for her love' (*PSS* 8: 586).

Pasternak's Rome is not Christian but pagan, ruled by tyrants (Griffiths and Rabinowitz 269), and thus is located outside of the bounds of history. For Pasternak, 'prehistoric' is synonymous with 'non-Christian' because history, and time itself, began with Christianity, with the New Testament. Several characters in *Doctor Zhivago* express the same idea, reflecting Pasternak's views on the essence of history and the development of the human spirit: Nikolai Nikolaevich states that 'history as we know it now began with Christ' and that 'there was no history in this sense in the classical world' (Pasternak, *Doctor* 19). In another passage, Sima opposes the Old and the New Testaments as two epochs, in which the former is the epoch of deafening events of nations lead by their leaders, and the latter is the time of inspiration and quiet private events:

> Something in the world has been changed. Rome was at an end. The reign of numbers was at an end. The duty, imposed by armed force, to live unanimously as a people, as a whole nation, was abolished. Leaders and nations belonged to the past. They were replaced by the doctrine of personality and freedom. (369–70)

For Pasternak, this understanding of history was essentially Shakespearean. He would refer to the period of the late 1930s as 'the Shakespearean times,' meaning that Russia had become a subject of history instead of being its object (Bykov 582). But if the 1930s, the pinnacle of the Stalinist regime, were the years when the hegemony of the State was absolute, the war seriously shook this seemingly steadfast colossus.

Pasternak accepted the Second World War as a fateful event, as a thunderstorm that brought to an end the unbearable expectation of the inevitable catastrophe, and his historiosophy is vividly reflected in his notes on Shakespeare. For example, Pasternak describes Othello and Iago precisely in terms of the dichotomy of history and non-history: 'For Shakespeare, the black Othello is a man of history and a Christian, and it is even more significant that he is opposed to the white Iago, an unconverted prehistoric beast' (*PSS* 5: 80). Pasternak also describes *King Lear* as written in the language of the Old Testament and set in pre-Christian barbaric times. In *King Lear*, he explains, all that is good is quiet and indistinct but evil is very logical, reasonable, and eloquent. Pasternak describes both *King Lear* and *Romeo and Juliet* as quiet tragedies in which love (in a broad sense, including love for one's neighbour and love of truth) is the main victim (*PSS* 5: 88). We find here the same opposition of quiet 'private events' to 'deafening,' oppressive Rome.

My last example is a passage from *Henry IV, Part Two* (3.1.83–9) that Pasternak copied out in 1942 (Barnes 198), in which the Earl of Warwick expresses the idea, crucial to Pasternak, that the life of a private person reflects the course of history:

> *There is a history in all men's lives,*
> Figuring the nature of the times deceas'd;
> The which observ'd, a man may prophesy,
> With a near aim, of the main chance of things
> As yet not come to life, which in their seeds
> And weak beginnings lie intreasured,
> Such things become the hatch and brood of time.

As I have sought to demonstrate by all these examples, for Pasternak Shakespeare appeared as a sort of an artistic mirror that, in the times of oppression and war, revealed and made more palpable the essential motifs of Pasternak's own oeuvre. It is not uncommon in the history of world literature for the 'alliance' of an author with the Bard to inspire the former to produce some most original work. It is therefore not unreasonable to speculate that if it had not been for Shakespeare we probably would have never seen *Doctor Zhivago*, the novel that Pasternak considered the highpoint of his work.

Shakespeare vs Ivan the Terrible

Shakespeare in general, and *Hamlet* in particular, have been considered ideologically 'inappropriate' by many rulers in different periods, and the history of Russian Shakespeare in the 1940s is no exception. In the concluding part of this essay, I would like to situate Pasternak's interest in *Hamlet* by examining a broader issue: how Shakespeare became topical at the height of Stalin's cult of personality.

The unfortunate fate of *Hamlet* in wartime Moscow has already been mentioned: the production at the Moscow Art Theatre was halted first due to the outbreak of the war, then by the deaths of Nemirovich-Danchenko in 1943 and his successor Vasilii Sakhnovskii a year later. Finally, in February 1945, the production was definitely cancelled, apparently on Stalin's verbal order.

According to a wide-spread rumour, the production was shut down in 1940 after Boris Livanov, the leading actor, attending one of the infamous all-night banquets in the Kremlin, asked Stalin how to play Hamlet. Stalin is said to have replied that the play was decadent and needn't be played at all. This legendary response continues to be popular because it fits in the vein of the mythology surrounding Stalin; it was reported by, among others, Isaiah Berlin, who worked at the British Embassy in Moscow in 1945–6. Livanov himself, however, disavows it. A conversation with Stalin about Hamlet did take place in 1940, but Stalin did not make any negative comments about the tragedy. As Dmitrii Bykov correctly remarks, if Stalin had made such a statement in public, *Hamlet* would have disappeared not only from the theatres but also from print (586–8). It seems that before the war became reality for him, Stalin had nothing in principle against the Danish prince.

It is not known whether Stalin was directly responsible for cancelling other Shakespeare productions in Pasternak's translation in Moscow, but other works were also not staged: *Anthony and Cleopatra* at the Moscow Art Theatre, *Othello* at the Theatre of Revolution, and *Romeo in Juliet* at the Malyi Theatre. On the other hand, Pasternak's *Hamlet* was still produced in the provinces: in 1941 in Voronezh, in 1942 in Yerevan and Novosibirsk, and in Vitebsk in 1946 (E. Pasternak, *Boris* 558; Makaryk). This fact suggests that Stalin just did not want to see a play he disliked 'right under his nose' in Moscow.

Pasternak was extremely distressed about the whole situation concerning his Shakespeare translations and especially about the *Hamlet* production at the MAT. On 25 August 1945 he wrote a most peculiar letter to Stalin that is remarkable for its tone. It little resembles a letter to a cruel and unpredictable ruler; rather, it is full of grumblings and petty complaints about such problems as the condition of Pasternak's apartment and his ill health. The letter begins with an ironic understatement, 'The life of my family is pretty difficult sometimes' (*PSS* 9: 407). Then Pasternak changes the subject and comes to his concrete request concerning the cancelled Shakespeare productions. He directly asks Stalin to influence the theatres or, to be more precise, he asks if the Art Committee could hint to the theatres that they might stage whatever they wanted without 'additional authorization.' For example, writes Pasternak, his *Hamlet* has been cancelled in favour of 'the modern play *Ivan the Terrible*' (*PSS* 9: 408).

By calling the play about Ivan the Terrible *modern*, Pasternak ironically refers to the ongoing campaign of mythologization of the first Russian tsar. It is interesting that Pasternak mentions this mythologization already in 1941 when he bitterly writes to Olga Freidenberg that 'the new, openly demonstrated passion' is for Ivan the Terrible, the Oprichnina,[12] and cruelty, and this has become the main topic of all artistic endeavours (*PSS* 9: 203).

Indeed, during the 1940s Stalin launched a large-scale campaign 'aimed at changing the historical image of Ivan's rule (from "repressive" to "progressive") – with an eye to Stalin's own epoch' (Tsivian 12). The close attention paid to Ivan the Terrible was manifested, among other things, in the awarding of Stalin Prizes: for example, the awards for 1946 went to Sergei Eisenstein's *Ivan the Terrible, Part One* (1944), to Alexei N. Tolstoi (posthumously) for his drama of the same title written in 1943, and to Georgian actor Akakii Khorava for his portrayal of Ivan in V. Solov´ev's production Великий государь [The Great Tsar]; and in 1948 Valentin Kostylev received a Stalin Prize for his trilogy about Ivan the Terrible written in 1943–7. There is reason to believe that Stalin's unprecedented attention to Ivan the Terrible was provoked by the shock that he personally experienced by the outbreak of the war: several testimonies point to the fact that, during the first months of the war, Stalin seemed to be virtually paralyzed (Makaryk 119). The new campaign for the 'rehabilitation' of Ivan IV was necessary in order to reestablish the authority of the supreme ruler; here, ironically, Shakespeare became Stalin's main antagonist.

Apart from Pasternak's translations and his letter, to which Stalin never responded, there is one more text that provoked Stalin's irritation and reminded him of the Danish prince: the second part of Sergei Eisenstein's film *Ivan the Terrible*. The two parts of Eisenstein's film significantly differ from each other, and Stalin was the first to notice the transformation from victorious epic into tragedy. On 25 February 1947 Eisenstein and Nikolai Cherkasov were invited to the Kremlin where Stalin, together with Zhdanov and Molotov, clearly expressed their dislike of Eisenstein's portrayal of Ivan. Stalin was very specific in his instructions: he described Ivan as 'a great and wise ruler' who was very cruel because he *had* to be cruel (Eisenstein 161). Remarkably,

Stalin identified Ivan the Terrible and Lenin as the two greatest rulers of Russia (because both introduced a monopoly on foreign trade), implying that he himself was the third (160). Eisenstein's depiction of Ivan was far removed from, if not opposite to, this description. Definitely irritated, Stalin compared Eisenstein's Ivan with the indecisive Hamlet (160). It is hard to believe that this comparison is coincidental; it seems to reveal the essential opposition not only of two characters but also of two models of history.

As is widely known, Eisenstein's understanding of history as reflected in *Ivan the Terrible, Part Two* is based, among other factors, on the Shakespearean model of tragedy. Eisenstein's *Ivan* differs markedly from the 'traditional' historical films, in which the historic events serve as a background for the characters' lives. For Eisenstein, the relation is precisely the opposite: history comes first, and only then the character and his psychology (Thompson 199; Lary 144). As James Goodwin argues,

> Eisenstein insisted that the historical Ivan was not insane and that his film's characterization avoids the psychological dualism of a split personality. Ivan's character is divided, but the divisive forces do not originate in personality alone. The film presents a pathology not of the individual per se but of the *polis*. In autocracy, politics and personality form a historical unity. (186)

Thus Eisenstein's focus on Shakespearean tragedy, in which psychology and history are fused, made Ivan the Terrible a tragic character of the Shakespearean type. But the real mote in Stalin's eye was that this understanding of history was directly antithetical to his own idea of Ivan and, by extension, of his own rule. Stalin certainly knew that hundreds of loyal panegyrics were not enough in order to promote his myth as one of the greatest rulers of Russia. There is a great irony in the fact that Stalin's attempts to create out of himself the mythical Ivan the Terrible, the man who *makes* history, were confronted by the texts of Pasternak and Eisenstein, texts that were based essentially on Shakespearean discourse in which tyrants are *objects* of history.

Notes

1 Editors' note: For the classic study on this era, see Robert Conquest, *The Great Terror: Stalin's Purge of the Thirties* (New York: Macmillan, 1969).

2 All references to *Polnoe sobranie sochinenii*, the eleven-volume edition of Pasternak's works (2003–5) are given as *PSS* followed by a volume number.

3 Anna Radlova (1891–1949) was a poet and translator; her translation of *Hamlet* was published in 1937. Briefly, Radlova's *Hamlet* is characterized by stylistic eclecticism: the unsystematic combination of literalist translation with free renditions of the original. The contrast between the stylistic registers in the translation was the main reason why Radlova's translation was eventually labelled 'vulgar' by many reviewers.

4 Pasternak's translations are usually criticized for being 'deviant,' 'not accurate,' etc. Quite expectedly, Pasternak's version is usually compared to some 'correct' version – which turns out to be a heavy interlinear translation – and is thus denounced as 'wrong.' This approach, which reduces the act of translation to some imagined equivalence between the source text and the target text, totally neglects the interpretive multiplicity of the artistic text. As I have shown elsewhere (Semenenko, *Hamlet*), Pasternak's translations proved to be vital exactly by virtue of the interpretive and creative power of the translator.

5 All emphasis in the cited poems is mine.

6 Cf. Pasternak's letter of 12 September 1941 to Zinaida Pasternak, in which he wrote that he longs for Russia's victory but cannot wish victory to stupidity, vulgarity, and falsehood (*PSS* 9: 249), a phrase for which he could very easily be accused of treason and 'defeatism.'

7 On Pasternak's association with Hamlet, see Gladkov, 'Zima' (435), Barnes (166, 373), Stříbrný (98).

8 As Manfred Pfister shows, under oppressive regimes many authors used Sonnet 66 as a means of expressing their dissident voices. The last line was often omitted or changed in order to underline the political implications of the sonnet.

9 The surviving fragments from the prototype of the novel – the drama *Этот свет* [This World] – bear the distinct influence of Shakespeare.

10 This translation is based on the translations given in Barnes (187) and B. Pasternak, *Doctor* (467).

11 As Susanna Witt has shown, the criminal theme is emphasized in the translation as well, especially in relation to Claudius. Thus the role of Hamlet as a judge becomes more evident (150–3).

12 The Oprichnina (1565–72), a period in the reign of Ivan IV, is associated with political repressions, executions and terror, enforced by the Oprichniki, the tsar's personal 'troopers,' who violently put out sedition and any opposition.

Works Cited

Barnes, Christopher. *Boris Pasternak: A Literary Biography*. Vol. 2. Cambridge: Cambridge University Press, 1998.

Bykov, Dmitrii. *Boris Pasternak*. Moscow: Molodaia gvardiia, 2005.

Clayton, J. Douglas. 'The Hamlets of Turgenev and Pasternak: On the Role of Poetic Myth in Literature.' *Germano-Slavica* 2.6 (1978): 455–61.

Eisenstein, Sergei. *The Eisenstein Reader*. Ed. Richard Taylor. Trans. Richard Taylor and William Powell. London: BFI Publishing, 1998.

France, Anna Kay. 'Boris Pasternak's Interpretation of Hamlet.' *Russian Literature Triquarterly* 7 (1973): 201–26.

Friedberg, Maurice. *Literary Translation in Russia: A Cultural History*. Philadelphia: Pennsylvania State University Press, 1997.

Gladkov, Aleksandr. 'Zima v Chistopole.' *Literaturnoe obozrenie* 4 (1978): 103–11.

– *Vstrechi s Pasternakom*. Paris: YMCA-Press, 1973.

Griffiths, F.T. and S.T. Rabinowitz. 'Stalin and the Death of Epic: Mikhail Bakhtin, Nadezhda Mandelstam, Boris Pasternak.' *Epic and Epoch: Essays on the Interpretation and History of Genre*. Studies in Comparative Literature 24. Lubbock: Texas Tech University Press, 1994. 267–88.

Goodwin, James. *Eisenstein, Cinema, and History*. Urbana: University of Chicago Press, 1993.

Lary, N.M. 'Eisenstein and Shakespeare.' *Eisenstein Rediscovered*. Ed. Ian Christie and Richard Taylor. London: Routledge, 1994. 140–50.

Livingstone, Angela. *Boris Pasternak: Doctor Zhivago*. Cambridge: Cambridge University Press, 1989.

Lotman, Mikhail. *Mandel´shtam i Pasternak (popytka kontrastivnoi poetiki)*. Tallinn: Aleksandra, 1996.

Makaryk, Irena R. 'Wartime *Hamlet*.' *Shakespeare in the Worlds of Communism and Socialism*. Ed. Irena R. Makaryk and Joseph G. Price. Toronto. University of Toronto Press, 2006. 119–35.

Markov, Vladimir. 'An Unnoticed Aspect of Pasternak's Translations.' *Slavic Review* 20.3 (1961): 503–8.

Nilsson, Nils Åke. 'Life as Ecstasy and Sacrifice: Two Poems by Boris Pasternak.' *Scando-Slavica* 5 (1959): 180–98.

Pasternak, Boris. *Polnoe sobranie sochinenii [PSS]: S prilozheniiami: v 11 tomakh*. Moscow: Slovo, 2003–5. T. 1–11.

– *Doctor Zhivago*. Trans. Max Hayward and Manya Harari. London: Harvill Press, 1996.

– *Poems of Boris Pasternak*. Trans. Lydia Pasternak Slater. London: Unwin Paperbacks, 1984.

– 'Zametki perevodchika.' *Znamia* 1/2 (1944): 165–8.

Pasternak, Evgenii. 'K istorii perevoda *Gamleta*.' *Gamlet Borisa Pasternaka: Versii i varianty perevoda shekspirovskoi tragedii*. Ed. Vitalii Poplavskii. Moscow and St Petersburg: Letnii sad, 2002. 5–11.

– *Boris Pasternak: materialy dlia biografii*. Moskva: Sovetskii pisatel', 1989.

Pfister, Manfred. 'Route 66: The Political Performance of Shakespeare's Sonnet 66 in Germany and Elsewhere.' *Shakespeare-Jahrbuch* 137 (2001): 115–31.

Semenenko, Aleksei. *Hamlet the Sign: Russian Translations of* Hamlet *and Literary Canon Formation*. Stockholm: Almqvist and Wiksell International, 2007.

– '"Gamletovskii kontekst" Borisa Pasternaka.' *Scando-Slavica* 51 (2005): 31–48.

Shakespeare, William. *The Complete Works*. Ed. W.J. Craig. London: Oxford University Press: 1914.

Stříbrný, Zdeněk. *Shakespeare and Eastern Europe*. Oxford: Oxford University Press, 2000.

Thompson, Kristin. *Eisenstein's Ivan the Terrible: A Neoformalist Analysis*. Princeton, NJ: Princeton University Press, 1981.

Tsivian, Yuri. *Ivan the Terrible: Ivan Groznyi*. London: BFI Publishing, 2002.

Witt, Susanna. "Perevod kak mimikriia: *Gamlet* Pasternaka." *Swedish Contributions to the Thirteenth International Congress of Slavists, Ljubljana, 15–21 August 2003*. Lund, 2003. 145–56.

8 Shakespeare as an Icon of the Enemy Culture in Wartime Japan, 1937–1945

RYUTA MINAMI

Can he that speaks with the tongue of an enemy be a good counsellor, or no?

Henry VI:2 (4. 5.170–2)

At the beginning and the end of the preface to his *Eibungaku no hanashi* [Tales of English Literature], Yamato Yasuo, a well-established professor of English, repeated the following jingoistic passage: 'Down with the Yanks and the Brits! They are our enemies. Seize Shakespeare! He is ours as well (1, 3).'[1]

It seems somewhat strange that a leading scholar of English could both decry the Britain and the United States and also write an introductory history of English literature for students, claiming Shakespeare – a cultural icon of Britain – for the Japanese. Yet this somewhat self-contradictory slogan vividly reflects the sentiments shared by other Japanese scholars of English studies and by the general public. Japan witnessed sporadic but harsh anti-English measures taken by the governmental and non-governmental institutions; these acts were meant not only to stir up hostility among the general public during the Pacific War but also to respond to the already existing antagonism toward the English-speaking Allies (Oishi 20). Under such adverse circumstances, most Japanese scholars of English could do little but support the nation's cause by emphasizing the necessity and utility of English studies.

Peter Firchow recently discussed the tragic conflict between vocation and national identity that German scholars of English literature experienced during the First World War. During the late 1930s and the early 1940s most Japanese scholars and teachers of English faced a similar conflict, and many opted for nation over profession, though not in equal measure. In this sense Yamato's jingoistic and naïve slogan illustrates the ambiguous position of Shakespeare in wartime Japan where anything English or American was likely to be driven out of daily life. Unlike in Germany and Italy, Shakespeare was not performed on stage during the last five years of the war.[2] Shakespeare in wartime Japan was something to be read, discussed, and imagined as a socio-political product distinct from the Japanese stage. This essay will examine how Shakespeare became both an icon of the enemy culture and an object of desire in wartime Japan.

Shakespeare had played a significant part in Japan when it was establishing itself as a modern, westernized nation state in the late nineteenth century. In an introductory scene added to the first Japanese adaptation of Shakespeare's *The Merchant of Venice* in 1885, one of the Japanese characters discussing the values of Western literature states that Shakespeare is an important means for Japan, a 'half-civilized nation,' to become a fully civilized modern nation state.[3] Similarly, in the preface to the first translation of *Hamlet*, published in 1905, the translator Tozawa Kôya remarked: 'Japan is now preparing to meet the Baltic Fleet, and isn't Japan equal to Elizabethan England, which was ready to beat the Spanish Armada?' Comparisons between rising Japan and Elizabethan England were preferred to comparisons between Japan and modern England, and were repeated in various discourses on nationalistic appropriation of Shakespeare around the turn of the twentieth century. By the 1930s Shakespeare had become an indispensable part of cultural literacy for Japanese elites and intellectuals, and Shakespeare's plays were often referred to in newspaper articles or noted by statesmen in various socio-political contexts. One example can be found in a newspaper caricature published by the *Asahi* on 7 December 1932. This cartoon (see fig. 8.1) shows Baron Shidehara, Minister of Foreign Affairs, Hamlet-like in his hesitation to step in as the Acting Prime Minister after the Prime Minister had been seriously injured by a right-wing assassin. Rather than finding this caricature offensive, Sidehara, who was well-read in English, seems to have enjoyed the connection, and commented in an interview shortly thereafter that he appreciated being compared to Hamlet. As English was not (and is not) the language used in daily life in Japan, it is noteworthy that the famous quotation – 'To be or not to be' – is given in English as well as Japanese.

"*To be, or not to be, —
that is the question: —*"

シデハラ・ハムレット！
舵ふるか、
舵へぬか？
それが疑問ぢや……」

8.1. Cartoon of Baron Shidehara, Minister of Foreign Affairs as Hamlet: 'To be or not to be.' *Asahi* 7 (December 1932).

In a similar reference to Hamlet that same year, a newspaper derisively compared the General Assembly of the League of Nations to the Prince, referring to the length of time the Assembly took to determine the cause of the Manchurian incident (Furugaki 2).[4] Nearly a decade later, in July 1941 – and less than six months before the outbreak of the Pacific War – Fukuhara Rintarô, a leading scholar of English, referred to Shakespeare and compared Japan to Elizabethan England in a newspaper article asserting the significance of studying English literature in Japan. It is noteworthy that in spite of his final statement – 'It is Japan that will soon defeat the Invincible Fleet' – he compared Japan to Shakespearean England, despite the fact that Britain was one of Japan's enemy countries.

Further, Shakespeare's significant cultural status in early twentieth-century Japan is succinctly illustrated by the following comment on the first Japanese translation of Shakespeare's plays. In *Nippon Eigaku Hat-*

tatsushi [The Development of English Studies in Japan] (1933), Take-mura Satoru proudly writes:

> In general, almost all the first- or second-rate civilized nations in the world possess the complete Shakespeare canon in translation. As far as I know, Germany has about ten different German versions of Shakespeare, France has eight or nine, Russia four or five, Spain, Italy, Holland, Poland, Swe-den, Denmark, and Hungary have at least one or two translations of his complete works respectively ... I am afraid Japan was the only first-rate nation that had not had Shakespeare's complete works in Japanese. But now thanks to the publication of Dr Tsubouchi's translation of Shake-speare's complete works, Japan has managed to go beyond the level of China, Turkey, Persia, and other second- or third-rate countries. Japan can rank with the Great Powers in the world. (210)

Here the 'possession' of Shakespeare in the vernacular is seen as a proof of a civilized nation. It must be noted that, at the time of publication, Japan was already in a state of war. Also, Takemura's insistence that the Empire of Japan had already become a first-rate nation actually reflects the atmosphere of the nation that, in the previous year, had invaded China in defiance of the great Western powers and had established the puppet state of Manchukuo. Yet the socio-cultural importance of Shake-speare as an object of such nationalist appropriation might have become difficult to maintain when Japan started a war with America and Brit-ain. The hostile relationship between these countries problematized, and even jeopardized, the hitherto established position of Shakespeare as an indicator of cultural sophistication suitable for a first-rate modern nation.

In his autobiography *Twischen Inn und Themse* [Between the Inns and the Thames Rivers] (1936), Alois Brandl writes, 'No segment of the Ger-man population was hit as hard by the World War as the aspiring troop of *Anglicists* who already numbered in the thousands' (qtd. in Firchow 61). This was equally true of the many Japanese scholars and teachers of English during the Second World War, of whom there were more than one thousand; the English Literary Society of Japan was founded in 1928 with about 1,000 members, and the Shakespeare Association of Japan was established in the following year. Writing about German scholars of English, Firchow remarks that the 'majority of Anglicists seem instead to have used their specialized knowledge chiefly to find real or imaginary weaknesses in literary and cultural armor' (62). Unlike their German counterparts in the First World War, most Japanese Anglicists in the 1940s neither made 'use of their professional expertise to defend the English against attack in the popular press' nor proceeded 'to sling literary hate and mud' (62). There were some scholars, such as Yamato Yasuo, who launched a war of words, but the majority of Japanese scholars of English merely insisted that English literary studies and English language teaching could be important weapons for the Japanese Empire. Soon after the imperial declaration of war in December 1941, leading scholars of English published articles in newspapers and magazines arguing that English should be studied more than ever so that the Japanese could understand English-speaking people and their culture. They also insisted that their expertise in Anglo-American culture and society would serve to develop the culture of a 'Greater East Asia Co-prosperity Sphere' (Oishi 10–12; Miyazaki 11–22). One possible reason for Japanese English scholars' prompt and somewhat desperate responses was that they were likely to be regarded as worse than useless, and even harmful, because of their knowledge of the United States and Britain.[5]

It should be noted that, in the first half of the 1940s, the Japanese government tried to dispose of anything related to America and Britain. The brief chronology presented in table 8.1 (pp. 173–6) reveals how desperately the Japanese government tried to eradicate anything English or American from the country even before the Pacific War broke out. Although most of the prohibitions against anything English seem ridiculous today, they were seriously regarded at the time; indeed, the government's actions appear extensive and decisive. In 1942, for example, as many as 1,492 teachers of English at girls' higher educational institutions (equivalent to women's colleges) were made redundant on a two-month notice. This measure clearly suggests that the teachers' knowledge of English was regarded as a threat to the government's anti-American and anti-British propaganda. In his essay entitled 'The root of our enemy lies in the English language' military analyst Mutô Teiichi insisted that:

English, this abominable enemy language, must be expelled by all means. I simply don't understand why some Japanese admire and cling to English when our country is struggling to destroy Britain and America. It is a shame that Japanese contains too many borrowings from the enemy language, such as *nyûsu* [news] and *anaunsâ* [announcer]. They should be discarded.[6]

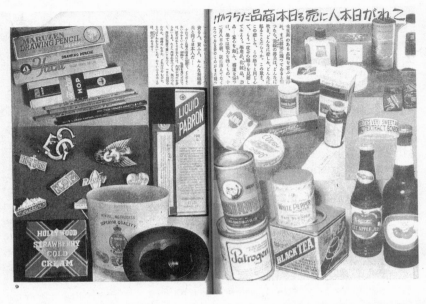

8.2. Photographs of Japanese products with English names or words: 'Are these Japanese products made for Japanese people?' *The Photographic Weekly Bulletin* 257 (3 February 1943), 5–6.

As if in response, on 3 February 1943 the *Shashin Shûhô* [The Photographic Weekly Bulletin], which was published by the Cabinet's Information Board in order to provide extensive publicity for national policy in a straightforward and accessible manner, bitterly criticized Japanese products with English names and words (7–8; see fig. 8.2); the preceding pages of the same issue decried the use of English words in signboards. The hostility expressed toward the United States and Britain may also be seen in the Great East Asia Society of Literature, founded in 1942; the main theme at the annual conferences of the Society (held for three consecutive years, 1942 to 1944) was either critical re-evaluation (that is, devaluation) or annihilation of American and British culture.[7]

In spite of or because of such difficult circumstances, the Japanese elite and intellectuals continued to make an exception for Shakespeare. In an article in the *Asahi* on 8 January 1941, Shakespeare plays, including *Romeo and Juliet*, are found on the list of recommended books for teenage girls, along with Tolstoy's works and Greek myths ('Naniwo Yomuka' 4). How could it be that Shakespeare continued to be both desired and denounced?

There are at least two notable characteristics of the discourses on the nationalist appropriation of Shakespeare in wartime Japan: one is the frequent reference made to Thomas Carlyle's *On Heroes, Hero-worship, and the Heroic in History* (1841) as a way of disqualifying Britain as the sole possessor of Shakespeare; the other is a marked tendency to identify Shakespeare as part of German culture. When Yamato concluded his slogan with 'He is ours *as well*,' he knew that his readers would immediately understand his implicit reference to Carlyle's famous passage and to the British colonies in Asia.

Carlyle's *On Heroes* was one of the most popular books among Japanese students in higher education. The first Japanese translation was published in 1898, and at least three other versions were published and re-printed during the next thirty years (1912, 1914, 1922, 1923, and 1933). The majority of the elite and intellectuals of the 1930s had read Carlyle either in English or in Japanese, and were familiar with the following passage:

> For our honour among foreign nations, as an ornament to our English Household, what item is there that we would not surrender rather than him? Consider now, if they asked us, Will you give up your Indian Empire or your Shakespeare, you English; never have had any Indian Empire, or never have had any Shakespeare? Really it were a grave question. Official persons would answer doubtless in official language; but we, for our part too, should not we be forced to answer: *Indian Empire, or no Indian Empire; we cannot do without Shakespeare! Indian Empire will go, at any rate, some day; but this Shakespeare does not go, he lasts forever with us; we cannot give up – our Shakespeare!* (148; emphasis added)

One year before Yamato wrote his preface, Hakuchô Masamune, a novelist, playwright, and critic, wrote an article, 'Indo ka Saôka' [Indian Empire or Shakespeare], which was published in the *Yomiuri* on 6 July 1940. In it he writes:

> Imagine you say to an Englishman today, 'Since your country has the honour of having produced Shakespeare the best poet-playwright in the

world, you wouldn't care about India and other colonies at all.' No Englishman would agree with you. The Englishman is more likely to say that he would rather give up the rights to publish or perform Shakespeare's plays in order to secure all the colonies. He would rather wish to have a Wellington or a Nelson, and not a Shakespeare today. (1)

Masamune suggests that the British Empire was declining in national power and thus implied that Britain was no longer entitled to enjoy the exclusive possession of Shakespeare.[8] This kind of 'disqualification' of Britain as the home of Shakespeare was further emphasized in 1943 when the American government's prohibition of the performance of *The Merchant of Venice* was reported by newspapers and magazines. Explaining how the Americans came to ban the performance of the play, the front page column of the *Yomiuri* on 4 September 1943, concludes that:

> Britain once had Carlyle, who said 'Indian Empire will go, at any rate, some day; but this Shakespeare does not go, he lasts forever with us; we cannot give up our Shakespeare!' But Britain had already let American soldiers enter India the other day. And now Britain let the Jewish Americans obliterate Shakespeare from the stage. I wonder how the British are feeling now! (1)

If Britain were not eligible for ownership of Shakespeare, who, they wondered, would be entitled to 'take possession.' The answer was Germany. Since the early 1930s, along with recurrent ironical references to Carlyle, both Shakespeare productions in Germany and German studies of Shakespeare had been frequently reported and praised in the press, as if 'Shakespeare' were a German Bard. Showing how thoroughly Shakespeare had been 'de-anglicized' in Germany, a country allied with Japan (see Habicht, 'Topoi' and 'Shakespeare'), the Japanese press suggested the possibilities of owning Shakespeare in the then anti-British Japan.

Interestingly enough, on 30 December 1939, the *Taiwan Nichi-Nichi Shimpo* [Taiwan Daily News] published an article entitled 'Recent Shakespeare Studies in Germany,' introducing Brandl's *Twischen Inn und Themse*. Although the writer seems to have mistaken this autobiography of an English professor at one of Berlin's universities for a biography of Shakespeare, what is to be noted here is that news about

German studies on Shakespeare was circulated through Japan and its colonies in the popular press; in contrast, it seems there was almost no coverage of their British counterparts even before the onset of the Pacific War. On 13 September 1941, the front-page editorial of the *Yomiuri* maintained that it was German literati such as Goethe, Christoph Wieland, and Gotthold Ephraim Lessing that 'taught' English people the greatness of Shakespeare. The editorial also pointed out that the German Shakespeare Society (Deutsche Shakespeare Gesellschaft) was the oldest society of its kind in Europe, with a history of some 80 years. The editorial column concludes with the statement that in Germany Shakespeare's plays were performed more often than plays by other dramatists even though they were written by the playwright of their enemy country. One of the last newspaper articles about German Shakespeare was a review by Watanabe Mamoru published in *Yomiuri* on 21 January 1944, of the latest production of *The Merchant of Venice* presented at the Burgtheater in Vienna. The review, which includes a stage photograph (a rarity at this time in Japan), praised the production and maintained that German people believed that Shakespeare must not be monopolized by Britain.

We may certainly assert that, in the imagination of the Japanese during the 1930s and early 1940s, Shakespeare was considered a part, not only of British, but also of German culture and German classics, a fact that seems to explain why more than 10,000 copies of Friedrich Gundolf's *Shakespeare und der Deutsche Geist* were sold in Japanese translation between 1941 and 1943. Since the number of scholars of English literature in Japan at the time was about 1,000, the enormous sales suggest that Gundolf's book enjoyed a larger readership than usual of books on English literature.

The early and successful appropriation of Shakespeare in Germany ensured the possibility of the Japanese appropriating the English playwright as a 'Japanese Bard,' or at least, the bard of an allied country. It is significant that the subject of the Shakespearean study published just before Gundolf's *Shakespeare* was the reception of Shakespeare in Japan (see table 8.1, pp. 173–6), thus emphasizing how long the two allied countries had possessed Shakespeare and linking them once again. Japanese Shakespeare remained proof that Japan was a culturally enlightened and civilized nation, though this Shakespeare was a safe socio-cultural as well as political product made, for the most part, in Germany.

Table 8.1. Chronology comparing anti-English measures and major events with Shakespeare publications and productions
All Japanese names are given in the Japanese order, that is, family name followed by given name.

Date	Prohibitions and important events	Publications of books on Shakespeare	Productions of Shakespeare plays
1937 January			*The Merry Wives of Windsor* trans. Mikami Isao and Nishikawa Masami; dir. Senda Koreya; [Shin Tsukiji Company].
July	Marco Polo Bridge incident (July 7) begins the second Sino-Japanese war.		
September		Aleksandr Aleksandrovich Smirnov, *Shakespeare: A Marxist Interpretation*, trans. Magami Yoshitarō (Tokyo: Bieidō).	
1938 February		A.C. Bradley, *Shakespearean Tragedy*, part 1, trans. Nakanishi Shintarō (Tokyo: Iwanami Shoten).[1]	
May–June			*Hamlet* trans. Mikami Isao and Okahashi Hiroshi; dir. Yamakawa Yukiyo and Okakura Shirō; [Shin Tsukiji Company].
December			*Hamlet* Mikami Isao and Okahashi Hiroshi; dir. Yamakawa Yukiyo; [Shin Tsukiji Company].

Table 8.1. Chronology comparing anti-English measures and major events with Shakespeare publications and productions
All Japanese names are given in the Japanese order, that is, family name followed by given name (*continued*).

Date	Prohibitions and important events	Publications of books on Shakespeare	Productions of Shakespeare plays
1939			
March		Stendhal, *Racine et Shakespeare*, trans. Satô Masaaki (Tokyo: Aoki Shoten).[2] Nakanishi Shintaô, *Sheikusupia Joron* [An Introduction to Shakespeare] (Tokyo: Kenkyusha). A.C. Bradley, *Shakespearean Tragedy* (2), trans. Nakanishi Shintarô (Tokyo: Iwanami Shoten), translation of the last four chapters.	
November		Nakanishi Shintarô, *Hamlet* (Tokyo: Kôbundô Shoten).	
1940			
January			*Hamlet* partial production, dir. UchimuraNaoya; [Bungaku-za Company].
March	Ministry of Home Affairs bans the use of English stage names.		
May–June			*A Midsummer Night's Dream* adapted and dir. Katô Tadamatsu [Takarazuka Revue Company].
September	Ministry of Railways bans English songs at stations.	Toyoda Minor, *Shakespeare in Japan* (Tokyo: Iwanami Shoten).	
October	Ministry of Education bans the use of English names or words for names of schools.		
November	Ministry of Finance bans the use of English words for names of tobacco products.		

Table 8.1. Chronology comparing anti-English measures and major events with Shakespeare publications and productions
All Japanese names are given in the Japanese order, that is, family name followed by given name (*continued*).

Date	Prohibitions and important events	Publications of books on Shakespeare	Productions of Shakespeare plays
1941			
January	Ministry of Foreign Affairs bans the use of English at press conferences for foreign correspondents.	Friedrich Gundolf, *Shakespeare und der Deutsche Geist*, part 1, trans. Takeuchi Toshio (Tokyo: Iwanami Shoten).[3]	
June		Friedrich Gundolf, *Shakespeare und der Deutsche Geist*, part 2, trans. Takeuchi Toshio (Tokyo: Iwanami Shoten).	
July			Dazai Osamu, *Shin Hamlet* [New Hamlet] A closet drama. Parodic adaptation, published by Bungeishunjūsha, Tokyo.
December	Japanese attack on Pearl Harbor (7 Dec.) begins the Pacific war. The government bans the use of the term 'Far East' in both Japanese and English. Throughout 1941 police in large cities ban the use of English names for coffee shops and restaurants.		
1942			
March	All foreign university teachers of English are fired.		
September	English becomes an optional subject at girls' high schools. Many of the 1,492 full-time teachers of English fear they will become redundant.		

Table 8.1. Chronology comparing anti-English measures and major events with Shakespeare publications and productions. All Japanese names are given in the Japanese order, that is, family name followed by given name (*continued*).

Date	Prohibitions and important events	Publications of books on Shakespeare	Productions of Shakespeare plays
October	The Metropolitan Police Department bans the use of English at table-tennis matches.		
	The botanical garden in Kyoto removes English signs for plant names.		
	Through 1942 many companies change their names to remove English words.		
1943			
January	*Japan Times* changes its name to *Nippon Times*.		
	The Ministry of Home Affairs and the Cabinet Information Board ban the performance and the sale of recordings of more than 1,000 English songs.		
February	English words are banned from magazine titles.		
	The Cabinet Information Board bans English signs and signboards.		
March	Japan Baseball Association bans the use of English baseball terminology.		
	East Asia Medical Society bans the use of English and Dutch.		
April	Tombow Pencils stops using abbreviations H (hard) and HB (hard black) to indicate grades of pencil lead.		
May	Patent Office bans the use of brand names that suggest American and British words.		

Table 8.1. Chronology comparing anti-English measures and major events with Shakespeare publications and productions All Japanese names are given in the Japanese order, that is, family name followed by given name (*concluded*).

Date	Prohibitions and important events	Publications of books on Shakespeare	Productions of Shakespeare plays
June	Ministry of Education bans the use of sol-fa system for naming the notes of musical scales.	Walter Alexander Raleigh, *Shakespeare*, trans. Takeuchi Kouki (Tokyo: Hokkō Shobō).[4]	
September		Friedrich Gundolf, *Shakespeare: Sein Wesen und Werk*, trans. Oguchi Masaru and Asai Masao (Tokyo: Chikuma Shobō).	
1944 January	Ministry of Education announces the deletion of *God Save the King* from English textbooks. Ministry of Education announces that references to enemy countries should be deleted from textbooks of all subjects.		
1945 August	Atomic bombs are dropped on Hiroshima (Aug. 6) and Nagasaki (Aug. 9); Imperial Japan surrenders.		

1 A.C. Bradley's *Shakespearean Tragedy* (1905) was first translated into Japanese in March 1923 by another Japanese scholar of English, and had been the single most influential critical work on Shakespeare's plays since its publication in Japan. While Nakanishi's new translation was favourably received, Bradley's book itself was not a new addition to Shakespeare studies in Japan. This first volume contains only the first six chapter's of Bradley's work; the remaining four chapters were published in a second volume in March 1939.

2 Works on Shakespeare by authors such as Schiller, Goethe, Turgenev, Tolstoy, Coleridge, and Emerson were translated into Japanese in the early twentieth century. Because the Japanese regarded France as less of an enemy than Britain or the United States, official censorship and repression of French literature and culture was not as strict or severe as that of its English and American counterparts.

3 This first volume contains a translation of only the first two chapters; the second volume, containing chapter 3, was published in June 1941. Print runs for both volumes were high: 10,000 copies were printed for the third issue of volume 1; 5,000 copies were printed for the second edition of volume 2.

4 Sir Walter Alexander Raleigh's *Shakespeare* was first introduced to Japanese scholars in 1935 in a translation by Kashiwagura Shunzo of the first chapter plus a summary of the rest of the book. Takeuchi Kouki's translation is based on the 1907 edition.

Notes

All the Japanese names are given in the Japanese order, that is, family name followed by given name, except in cases where the names of Japanese authors are published in Anglicized form in the original. A macron (^) over a vowel indicates that the pronunciation is lengthened. All translations of quotations from Japanese books and articles are mine unless otherwise indicated.

1 As the first two sentences of this passage had become one of the common slogans often put up on school blackboards during the Pacific War, it probably sounded hackneyed.

2 This lack of Shakespeare performances is partly due to the fact that most stage productions of Shakespeare's plays were given by *shingeki* [new drama] companies, most of which were forced by the government to disband because of their leftist leanings. For details about *shingeki* and Shakespeare performances in Japan, see table 8.1. Also, see Sasayama, Mulryne, and Shewring; Minami, Carruthers, and Gillies.

3 On the importance of this adaptation of *The Merchant of Venice* in the modernization of Japan, see Yoshihara.

4 The Manchurian incident was part of the conquest and pacification of Manchuria by the Guangdong Army (Japan's field army in Manchuria) from September 1931 to January 1933. On 18 September 1931 the Guangdong carried out a secret bombing raid on the rails of the South Manchuria Railway (the Liutiaogou incident). They then accused the Chinese troops in Mukden (now Shenyang) of destroying the tracks and made a sudden attack on the main Chinese garrison in Mukden. By the dawn of 19 September they had gained control of the city. In December 1931 the League of Nations appointed a five-man commission, headed by the Earl of Lytton II, to determine the causes of the incidents of 18–19 September. The Lytton Report, submitted on 2 October 1932, stated that Japan was the aggressor, but the General Assembly of the League of Nations did not officially determine the causes until February 1933, when the Lytton Report was finally adopted. The newspaper article, which was published more than two months after the submission of the Lytton Report, illuminates Japan's general concerns about the decision of the League of Nations.

5 The then Japanese government found teachers of English somewhat suspicious and dangerous in part because quite a few of them had studied or spent some time in the United States or Britain, and in part because many of them were well informed about British and American conditions. Cf. Miyazaki Yoshizo, *Taiheiyô-sensou to Eibun-gakusha* [The Pacific War and English Scholars] (Tokyo: Kenshusha, 1999) 23–7.

6 Mutô Teiihchi, 'Tekishoku no Kongenwa Eigo da' [The root of our enemy lies in the English language], *The Houchi Newspaper* 7 March 1942. The passage is taken from Oishi's 'Japanese Attitudes' (8). The English translation is by Oishi but is quoted here with a slight alteration. It is to be noted that 'news' and 'announcer' had become Japanese words (*nyûsu* [news] and *anaunsâ* [announcer]) well before 1942.
7 The hostility against America and Britain was powerfully set out, especially in the second and third Annual Meetings of the Society in 1943 and 1944; see Haga.
8 The front-page news headline for that day was 'Next year's plan for wartime finance is announced.' The fact that Masamune's article was printed just below this top story indicates a wartime atmosphere, even though the attack on Pearl Harbor was a year and a half in the future.

Works Cited

Carlyle, Thomas. *On Heroes and Hero-Worship and the Heroic in History*. World Classics 62. London: Oxford University Press, 1935.
'Chikatte Eibeibunka Senmetsu' [A pledge to annihilate American and British cultures]. *Asahi* 26 Aug. 1943, Tokyo evening ed.: 2.
'Doitsu no Sheikusupia Kenkyû' [Recent Shakespeare studies in Germany]. *Taiwan Nichinichi Shimpô* 30 Dec. 1939, Taipei morning ed.: n.pag.
'Eibeibunka wo Samon' [Inquiries into American and British cultures]. *Yomiuri* 17 Sept. 1944, Tokyo morning ed.: 4.
Firchow, Peter Edgerly. *Strange Meetings: Anglo-German Literary Encounters from 1910 to 1960*. Washington: Catholic University of America Press, 2008.
Fukuhara, Rintarô. 'Chiteki Seifukuyoku' [The desire for intellectual conquest]. *Asahi* 5 July 1941, Tokyo morning ed.: 4.
Furugaki, Tetsurô. 'Rijikai Tsuini Hamlet' [The General Assembly has finally become a Hamlet]. *Asahi* 27 Dec. 1932, Tokyo morning ed.: 2.
Habicht, Werner. 'Shakespeare and Theatre Politics in the Third Reich.' *The Play Out of Context: Transferring Plays from Culture to Culture*. Ed. Hanna Sčolnicov and Peter Holland. Cambridge: Cambridge University Press, 1989. 110–20.
– 'Topoi of the Shakespeare Cult in Germany,' *Literature and Its Cults: An Anthropological Approach*. Budapest: Argumentum, 1994. 47–65.
Haga, Mayumi. 'Eibeibunka no gekimetsu' [The destruction of American and British Cultures]. *Asahi* 25 Aug. 1943, Tokyo morning ed.: 4.
Ishikawa, Tatsuzô. 'Bungakusha no Teishin' [The devotion of literati]. *Asahi* 25 Aug. 1943, Tokyo morning ed.: 4.

Masamune, Hakuchô. 'Indo kaSaôka' [India or Shakespeare]. *Yomiuri* 6 July 1940, Tokyo evening ed.: 1

Minami, Ryuta, Ian Carruthers, and John Gillies, eds. *Performing Shakespeare in Japan*. Cambridge: Cambridge University Press, 2001.

Miyazaki, Yoshizo. *Taiheiyô-sensou to Eibun-gakusha* [The Pacific war and Japanese scholars of English]. Tokyo: Kenshusha, 1999.

'NaniwoYomuka' [What to Read]. *Asahi* 8 Jan. 1941, Tokyo morning ed.: 4.

Oishi, Itsuo. 'Japanese Attitudes toward the English Language during the Pacific War' [In English]. *Seikei Hogaku* 34 (1992): 1–20.

Saitô, Takeshi. 'Daitôa Bungakusha Taikai: Kyôei Bunka no kakuritsue' [The Great East Asia Society of Literature: Towards the establishment of the culture of a greater East Asia co-prosperity sphere]. *Taiwan Nichinichi Shimpô* 3 Sept. 1943, Taipei morning ed.: n.pag.

Sasayama, Takashi, Ronnie Mulryne, and Margaret Shewring, eds. *Shakespeare and the Japanese Stage*. Cambridge: Cambridge University Press, 1998.

Shashin Shûhô [Photographic Weekly]. Tokyo: Naikaku jôhôbu [Cabinet Information Board]. no. 257, 3 Feb. 1943, 5–6.

'Shidehara Hamlet' [Baron Shidehara as Hamlet]. Cartoon. *Asahi* 9 Dec. 1930, Tokyo morning ed.: 2.

Takemura, Satoru, *Nippon Eigaku Hattatsushi* [The development of English Studies in Japan]. Tokyo: Kenshu-sha, 1933.

Tozawa, Koya. 'Saô zenshû jo' [Introduction to the complete works of Shakespeare]. *Hamlet*. By William Shakespeare. Trans. Tozawa Koya and Asano Wasaburô. Saô Zenshû, vol. 1, Tokyo: Dainihon Tosho, 1905. p. 3. *Saô Zenshû* [The complete works of Shakespeare], 10 vols. Tokyo: Dainihon Tosho, 1905–08.

Watanabe, Mamoru. 'Yûyûtaru Doitsu Senryoku: sheikusupia no geki wo jôen' [The vast military potential of Germany: a Shakespeare play was produced]. *Yomiuri* 21 Jan. 1944, Tokyo morning ed.: 4.

Yamato, Yasuo. *Eibungaku no hanashi* [Tales of English literature]. Tokyo: Kembunsha, 1942.

Yoshihara, Yukari. 'Japan as "Half-Civilized": An Early Japanese Adaptation of Shakespeare's *The Merchant of Venice* and Japan's Construction of Its National Image in the Late Nineteenth Century.' *Performing Shakespeare in Japan*. Ed. Ryuta Minami, Ian Carruthers, and John Gillies. Cambridge: Cambridge University Press, 2001. 21–32.

9 'Warlike Noises': Jingoistic *Hamlet* during the Sino-Japanese Wars

ALEXANDER C.Y. HUANG

Some of the most fruitful interactions between the 'airy nothing' of a literary motif and its 'local habitation' – a physical and felt presence in a community – can be found in the radical adaptation of Shakespeare to the local exigencies.[1] In particular, wartime theatre puts the relationship between politics and art in flux. How should the politicization of aesthetics be historicized in relation to an academic culture that distrusts the notion of *l'art pour l'art* and insists on reading literature politically? How do theatre artists adapt Shakespearean localities to enhance the perceived value of the performance and its venue? Literary meanings, especially those associated with wars, are created between the locality where various conventions of authenticity are derived and the locality where the performance takes place. The unexpected twists and turns of history can give significant meanings to these localities, including the performance venue, the setting of the plays, and the audience's cultural locations. While *Hamlet* (unlike *Antony and Cleopatra* or *Henry V*) does not feature war as a thematic focus – except for occasional mentions of war in Horatio's and Claudius' comments such as 'that fair and warlike form,' 'this warlike state,' and Hamlet's last question before his death: 'What warlike noise is this?' – it has been staged in a wide variety of methods in many countries in the times of war. This chapter investigates a mid-twentieth-century site-specific interpretation of *Hamlet*: Jiao Juyin's production (1942) in a Confucian temple in China when the country was resisting the Japanese military invasion, and before the Chinese Communist Party (CCP) gained power. Figuring prominently in this case are collective cultural memory, local readings of Shakespeare informed by wartime ideologies, and the particularities of the site of performance.

The aesthetic practices of mid-twentieth-century China were punctuated by a keen sense of the political, and Shakespeare performances were increasingly informed by local knowledge. This is a period when Chinese theatre was in search of safe 'apolitical texts,' and also when the political turn in literary culture was alternately seen by different constituencies of the society as a left turn, a right turn, and a wrong turn, as Communist China began to lay claims of local 'ownership' on select sets of foreign ideas including Marxism, the Stanislavskian acting method, and Soviet social and cultural institutions. The dual canonicity of Shakespeare as an author widely read and performed gained additional purchase through Karl Marx, who cites Shakespeare at length to support his arguments, and through the Russian and Soviet traditions of political Shakespeare.[2]

Torn between various wars, mid-twentieth-century Chinese theatre artists opted for topicality and social relevance in their work. While literary production and theatre as public entertainment continued to thrive and acted as a repository for collective cultural memory, the preference for topicality came to define much of the artistic activity during this period. After two decades of improvisational performance, Shakespeare's plays were fast becoming part of the Chinese repertoire to train spoken drama actors in the 1930s, hence their popularity in drama academies and conservatories. Spoken drama (also known as *huaju*) is a new, Western-influenced theatre genre that emerged in early twentieth-century China but remains popular only among urban residents. *Huaju* may seem unintelligible, viewed from a distance in the West and separated by what seem to be insurmountable cultural differences, but this theatrical genre has been used as a tool for vocal training and articulation for a long time. It does not simply emphasize the corporeal or presentational fanfare – more common in Chinese opera – that has caught the attention of Western scholars.[3] Yu Shangyuan (1897–1970), the founding principal of the National Drama School, included Shakespeare in the repertoire of his new school and theatre, obviously following his Anglo-European contemporaries in eulogizing Shakespeare. He maintained that the reason to stage Shakespeare in China was that 'performance of Shakespeare has been an important criterion to measure success for theatres worldwide and not just in England' (28). Each graduating class was required to stage a Shakespeare play. During wartime, the requirement was not enforced every year, but the first, second, fifth, and fourteenth graduating classes did perform Shakespeare plays (Cao and Sun 99), including *The Merchant of Venice*

(1937), *Othello* (1938), and the production of *Hamlet* (1942) that is discussed in this essay. It is of interest to note that *The Merchant of Venice* is one of the most popular Shakespearean plays in China, and it was among the first Shakespearean works to be staged and filmed. When the Royal Shakespeare Company toured China for the first time in 2002, the play selected for the tour was *The Merchant of Venice*, in a production directed by Loveday Ingram. As noted by other contributors to the present volume, *The Merchant* holds the attention of twentieth-century audiences around the world for very different reasons. The play's reception in China follows the region's history of social and cultural modernization. Chinese directors and audiences have been attracted not to Shylock as an embodiment of ethnic and religious tensions in the modern world, but rather to Portia as a figure of the new woman. The local concerns revolving around cultural reform, the women's rights movement, and the emerging capitalist market in Shanghai have created a new lens for reading the play. Above all else, the outlandish plot involving a pound of human flesh also became a main draw, which is why some Chinese productions and translations were given such titles as *A Pound of Flesh* or *A Bond of Flesh* (Huang, *Chinese Shakespeares* 17, 69–70, 115–18; Fei and Sun 59).

Like *The Merchant, Hamlet* has had a long history of translation, rewriting, and performance in China. Two recent examples are *The Banquet* (2006, a martial arts period drama film in Mandarin, directed by Feng Xiaogang, and released in North America as *The Legend of the Black Scorpion*)[4] and *The Prince of the Himalayas* (2005, a Tibetan-language film, directed by Sherwood Hu, set and shot in Tibet, and later adapted for the stage in Mandarin in Shanghai). A recent documentary by the China Central Television Channel 10 even traces the Chinese tradition of performing *Hamlet* to Jiao's wartime *Hamlet*.[5] It is important to recognize the iconic status of Hamlet, the Ghost, and Ophelia in China. Contrary to what some scholars have assumed, Chinese moviegoers watching *The Banquet* or *The Prince* have had a great deal of exposure to Shakespeare and particularly to *Hamlet*.[6]

As helping to educate vigilant and patriotic citizens (according to whatever ideology was current) became the dominant mission of theatre, the locality of Chinese audiences was given primacy. One case in point is a *Hamlet* performance set in premodern Denmark and staged in a Confucian temple, directed by Jiao Juyin (1905–75). The production, first staged in Jiang'an in rural Sichuan for general audiences during the second Sino-Japanese War in June 1942, and later revived in

Chongqing, the provincial capital, married the foreign setting to local theatrical and allegorical spaces in a dialectical process that testified to the reciprocal impact on both the target and source cultures. The unique circumstances of this production may prompt two questions: Why theatre during the war, and why *Hamlet*? During a time when theatre was suspect, the Shakespearean canon was an obvious choice to avoid censorship by the Nationalist government. Theatre's function as a site for social education and its potential for propaganda were seen as compelling reasons to stage public performances that could provide entertaining relief, raise funds for military operations, and boost the audience's morale. These site-specific objectives derived from the performance venue and the cultural location of the production were inaccessible to American critics of the time. When the *New York Times* reviewed Jiao's production in 1942, the feature that drew Brooks Atkinson's attention was the actors' Western makeup and prosthetic noses, but what he missed was exactly what made the performance viable in the wartime environment in China. His review states that the actors 'have built up a series of proboscises fearful to behold. The king has a monstrous, pendulous nose that would serve valiantly in a burlesque show; Polonius has a pointed nose and sharply flaring mustache of the Hohenzollern type; Hamlet cuts his way through with a nose fashioned like a plowshare.' Atkinson concluded that 'sincere and painstaking though this *Hamlet* may be, it is not yet ready for Broadway' (38).

In addition to the prestige of performance associated with Shakespeare's stature, the ability to stage and attend plays during a time of war, when the entire town of Jiang'an had no electricity, was itself perceived as a victorious gesture. What was made propagandistic was not always only the play's allegorical dimension but also the act of staging the play itself. Wartime theatre can be highly allegorical in nature, representing the battlefield as a site where rival ideologies encounter each other, or presenting stereotypical caricatures of the enemy. In the context of a backwater community, the determination and ability to stage a theatrical production was itself an encouraging sign for the local residents running from Japanese bombings day in and day out. As Fu Xiangmo, a Jiang'an native and a journalist for the *Guomin gongbao* [Citizen's Gazette] and *Yishi bao* [Social Welfare], pointed out in his review of the Jiang'an performance, though he was a *huaju* lover, he had not seen many recent productions because 'nine out of ten amounted to nothing more than a piece of war propaganda.' He noted what a precious opportunity it was to be able to see a non-propaganda play during a time of war, and a good *huaju* production of Shakespeare in small town Jiang'an 'in a remote corner of China's hinterland' (115).

Jiao's *Hamlet* was staged in 1942 with playwright Cao Yu – often regarded as the father of modern Chinese drama – as the consultant, five years after the fall of Nanjing to the Japanese. Chiang Kai-shek (Jiang Jieshi, 1887–1975) and his Nationalist government moved the capital to Chongqing, which triggered a nationwide migration. Elites, bankers, scholars, artists, and members of other social classes who could afford to move all relocated to Sichuan Province, as did schools and universities. The realities of the new locality – backward economic conditions and frequent Japanese aerial attacks – lowered the morale of these Chinese refugees who had been uprooted from their hometowns and now found themselves in the Japanese occupation zone. Live theatre became a symbol of cultural life, and the presence of cultural life helped to maintain their dignity. The National Drama School, which had been founded in Nanjing in 1938, was relocated to Chongqing and to Jiang'an the following year, and then moved to Chongqing in 1945 before returning to Nanjing in 1946. The unexpected connection between the small town of Jiang'an and the National Drama School during its formative years marked an important phase in the history of modern Chinese theatre history, and has been commemorated by the National Drama School Museum and Archive, established in Jiang'an in 1988 (see fig. 9.1).

Yu, among his contemporaries, was invested in the symbolic value of wartime theatre. With his revival of the Jiang'an *Hamlet*, he wanted the performance to achieve two goals:

> [1] The social significance of *Hamlet* [to us] is Hamlet's progressive and revolutionary [*geming jinqu*] spirit, which is what the Chinese people need during the Anti-Japanese War ... Prince Hamlet resisted the destiny arranged by Fate, countered feudal oppressions, and sought liberation from an environment filled with licentious and corrupt individuals.
>
> [2] Those countries that produce the most high-quality Shakespearean productions are the countries with the highest cultural prestige ... Performing Shakespeare is a crucial step for our country to catch up and to join the countries with world-class cultural achievements. (Cao and Sun 105)

The pro-colonialist assumption of Yu's comments is striking. On the one hand, his goals demonstrate the imperatives of the cultural renewal project to establish Chinese self-esteem. As has been noted by scholars

9.1. 'The Cradle of Modern Chinese Theatre.' National Drama School Museum and Archive. Reproduced courtesy of the People's Government of Jiang'an County, China.

working on celebrations of Shakespeare in times of war, the domestication of Shakespeare's plays involves a dialectical process between the Bard's reception in Britain and elsewhere (Habicht 441). On the other hand, the assumption about the prestige of any Shakespearean performance defeats its purpose to celebrate indigenous Chinese values and exceptionality. The competing pull of admiration of Western theatre and Chinese nationalist sentiment constitute a local Shakespeare in the emerging postcolonial world. It is worth noting that this sentiment dominated mainland Chinese productions until as late as the 1980s. Zhang Qihong, director of the Chinese Youth Art Theatre's production of *The Merchant of Venice* (1980), made a similarly pro-colonialist comment at the first Shakespeare Society of China meeting in 1985. She invited Shakespeare, a 'god' of England, to descend to China and to display his 'profound critique of feudalism, great realism, humanism, and moral power' (Zhang 7; trans. Shen 29–30).

Yu's comments invite further speculation. The many contradictions and ideological positions have made Yu's reading of *Hamlet* opaque. For example, the destiny that Hamlet resists and the prince's 'revolutionary spirit' are never made clear. Instead, Yu's adaptation focuses on wartime exigencies. Unlike the rewriting of *Hamlet* by Lin Shu (1852–1924), which made the play conform to Confucian ethical codes (Huang, *Chinese Shakespeares* 82–4), Jiao's performance generally followed Shakespeare's text while turning the moral question into a wartime directive to the Chinese people. While Yu's interpretation was informed by the pre-1940s Chinese critical tradition of a 'Confucian Hamlet,' its primary task was to draw political analogies between a dislocated and historically undefined Denmark and modern China in crisis. Hamlet's virtues (his disdain for corruption), filial piety (demonstrated by his grief over his father's death), and patriotic spirit (as evidenced by – in various Chinese versions – his concern over the fate of Denmark) were regularly highlighted in the criticism of the period.

In their consideration of *Hamlet*, theatre artists and literary critics in mainland China have concentrated on selected themes that resonate with traditional Chinese literary culture and with Confucianism, such as usurpation, filial piety, and legitimacy of rulership. As Lu Gu-sun observed, 'to some of the early Chinese readers and critics of *Hamlet*, the … theme of the play was … conveniently in compliance with the Confucian ethical code demanding filial piety … and constant chastity, and with Buddhist tenets of karma' (56). For example, Tian Han (1898–1968), who wrote the first Chinese translation of *Hamlet* (1922), associated Hamlet's melancholy with 'patriotic' concerns ('The time is out of joint: O cursed spite / That ever I was born to set it right!' [1.5.188–9]) with *On Encountering Sorrow* (*Lisao*) by the Confucian poet Qu Yuan (ca. 339–ca. 278 BC) in his postscript to his translation (Cao and Sun 49). As with English-language Shakespeare scholarship and editions in the 1960s, Chinese scholarship emphasized moral criticism, though the Chinese preoccupation with morality lasted almost an entire century. As the first Shakespearean play to be translated into Chinese in its entirety, *Hamlet* holds a special place in Chinese visions of Shakespeare. There have been numerous Chinese adaptations and spin-offs, including Lao She's novella 'New Hamlet.' There were also non-Confucian engagements with *Hamlet*, including the play *Shamlet* by Lee Kuo-hsiu (Huang, 'Comical Tragedies,' 163–6), that challenged the tradition of Confucian criticism of Chinese and Western literary works.

This is not the first instance of a nation associating itself with positive or negative traits of various characters in *Hamlet*. Poets in other countries have taken to *Hamlet* for various reasons. For example, German poets and intellectuals have repeatedly identified Germany with Hamlet since the nineteenth century. In 1800 the Shakespeare translator Ludwig Tieck indicated that what was needed to begin Germany's own golden age of poetry (to follow in Shakespeare's footsteps) was a Fortinbras-like figure (Tieck; trans. Bate). In Ferdinand Freiligrath's poem 'Hamlet' (1844) the German dissident, poet, and Shakespeare translator declares, 'Germany is Hamlet!'[7] This analogy became so widely accepted that Horace Furness was compelled to dedicate the *Hamlet* volume of his 1877 New Variorum Edition of Shakespeare to the Deutsche Shakespeare-Gesellschaft on behalf of 'a people whose recent history has proven once and for all that Germany is not Hamlet,' alluding to the rise of the German empire under Bismarck as an indication that Germany was no longer hindered by self-doubt (Zimmermann). In China Hamlet's alleged Confucian virtues and nobility had become such a cliché by the 1930s that prolific writer Lao She (1899–1966) satirized the 'Chinese Hamlet syndromes' in his novella 'New Hamlet.' The story problematized the prince's 'self-righteous moral criticism' (Huang, *Chinese Shakespeares* 87–8).

This, however, is where the similarity ends. Director Jiao also highlights procrastination as the most important aspect of Hamlet's character, but he explains the negative trait away by arguing that 'Hamlet's hesitation is not caused by cowardice but his love for truth.' Jiao then turns to China's Hamlet syndrome: 'We Chinese people are often too cautious about everything, and as a result we lose courage. In the end we can do nothing' (107). But as Hamlet was being held as a negative example in China, he was also commended for his 'patriotism' and filial piety. In Jiao's production, Hamlet fully accepts the revenge mission as his undeniable duty as a son. The competing interpretations in the Chinese case complicate the reading of Hamlet. For Jiao and his audience, the Danish prince was at once a positive and a negative example. On the one hand, Hamlet's patriotic concern over the corrupt court made him particularly at home in a culture of filial duties and political loyalty. On the other hand, his inaction and irresolution resonated in the Chinese psyche. Jiao gave his wartime *Hamlet* a call-to-arms tone, but he did not resolve the essential paradox in these competing narratives. The pull of admiration for Hamlet as seeker of truth is countered by the production's localist bias and contextual underpinnings.

In this context, the wartime performance was already loaded with decidedly local connotations. Yu remarked that even though *Hamlet* is a tragedy, its wartime production was actually an uplifting experience, because the spirit was 'exactly what the Chinese people needed to resist the Japanese invasion' (qtd in Tian 453). This attitude reminds us of another prominent wartime Shakespearean performance from the same period, Laurence Olivier's *Henry V* (1944). Compared to Olivier's jingoistic and nationalist film, which was dedicated to the 'commandos and airborne troops of Great Britain,' however, the choice of a hesitating Hamlet motivated by personal causes – rather than a traditionally patriotic Shakespearean hero – is not surprising at a time when China, like Olivier's England, was at war. While Olivier's *Henry V* may exemplify what Walter Benjamin called 'the aestheticization of politics' (Rothwell 51), Jiao's *Hamlet* is an exercise in what Benjamin theorized as the politicization of art (Benjamin 235). In his essay on art and technology, 'The Work of Art in the Age of Mechanical Reproduction,' Benjamin focuses on the perils of fascist appropriation of the instrumental power of art, but his notion of the usefulness of art aptly captures the context of Jiao's wartime production. *Hamlet* became useful for the formulation of wartime demands and cultural politics. As the present volume shows, similar interpretive strategies inform the *Hamlet*s in Russian, Polish, Ukrainian, and other traditions.

The fortuitous site of performance added unexpected layers to the question of politics. This production was first staged in the temple in Jiang'an rather than Chongqing, because the school was located in Jiang'an. Located at a distance from the metropolitan culture of the provincial capital, this small town was tucked away in a pastoral other place where alternative political readings of *Hamlet* could find a ready home. The Confucian temple was chosen as the performance site not because it was attractive or more culturally significant than other temples or venues, but because, like many village temples in rural China, it functioned as a convenient and traditional gathering space in the town.[8] It was financially not feasible to construct a theatre during the all-out war of resistance against the Japanese, and the Confucian temple was one of the readily available architectural spaces to be found in many Chinese towns. The temple's architectural structure and allegorical space provided a ready site for such a performance and was used as a makeshift stage. In other words, the choice of performance venue inherited the accidents of history. In historical hindsight, the temple bears the marks of wartime exigencies and limitations. While temples and teahouses, among other informal performance spaces outside playhouses, were regularly used for public performances in China up to this time, the courtyards and the central halls of Confucian temples were used almost exclusively for dedicatory ritual performance (see fig. 9.2). Temples serve as sites for collective memories and gathering places, but

9.2. The courtyard of a Confucian temple in Zizhong, Sichuan. (This is one of the better-preserved Confucian temples in the province today). Reproduced courtesy of the People's Government of Jiang'an County, China.

the Confucian temple in particular has been regarded as a sacred site for Chinese intellectuals. Therefore, Jiao's *Hamlet* became a major public event not only because of its innovative stage design, but also because of its unconventional performance space for a Western-style spoken drama. Since the potential audiences in the small town could not afford theatre tickets but the National Drama School still needed some form of support to put on plays, many of the productions in Jiang'an during this period adopted an innovative scheme that allowed the audiences to gain admittance by donating daily necessities from household items to groceries (*pingwu kanxi*).

This is the historical context of Jiao's *Hamlet*. The production, accompanied by music (Handel's *Largo* and Beethoven's Minuet in G major), ran for three performances in Jiang'an but left a lasting impression on the audience, many of whom came from nearby rural areas for their first *huaju* experience (Atkinson 1:38). The communal experience also provided collective emotional support and reprieve from the Japanese bombings.

The performance was based on a popular translation, with cuts, rather than on a Sinicized adaptation. Jiao Juyin was a French-trained

Chinese director who would become one of the major figures in modern Chinese theatre. Having earned a doctorate from the Université Paris Sorbonne in 1938 with a thesis on his contemporary Chinese drama, Jiao returned to China just as the Sino-Japanese wars broke out. As one of the co-founders of Beijing People's Art Theatre (BPAT), he worked closely with Cao Yu, Ouyang Shanzun, and Zhao Qiyang to create the aesthetic style of BPAT. Modeled after the Moscow Art Theatre, BPAT established itself as one of the most important models for Chinese theatre artists interested in the *huaju* genre, and continues to hold the leadership position in today's China. Under Jiao's directorship, BPAT performed both Chinese *huaju* and Western realist plays with elements taken from the Stanislavsky system and from Jiao's own 'theory of mental images,' in which actors were trained to develop mental images of dramatic characters and situations before creating stage images. In addition to adaptations, Jiao is recognized for his productions of canonical modern Chinese plays such as Lao She's *Chaguan* [Teahouse], which was revived by the BPAT as part of a centennial celebration of Jiao's birthday in 2005. Premiered by the BPAT in 1958, this play is set in a traditional Beijing teahouse where conflicts among characters from all social classes arise. It is commonly regarded as one of the most successful plays offering a cross-sectional view of Chinese society from the end of the Qing dynasty in late nineteenth-century to the wars and revolutions in the mid-twentieth century.

Scripted rather than improvised as many early twentieth-century Chinese performances had been, this drama-school-initiated production was one of the earliest complete stagings of *Hamlet* in the spoken drama format.[9] The performance thus attracted both intellectuals and villagers, leading to a revival later that year in a formal indoor theatrical space (rather than a temple) in Chongqing, the biggest city in the province. The revival was part of the Ministry of Education's '[wartime] social education' campaign (Shehui jiaoyu kuoda xuanchuan zhou) in Chongqing, which was both the provincial capital of Sichuan and the temporary capital of China during the war. The slightly different title, *Danmai wangzi Hamuleite* [Danish Prince Hamlet], was likely chosen for its proximity to Shakespeare's title in the First Folio and for the purpose of attracting larger audiences who might otherwise not be familiar with *Hamlet*. The Chongquing performances took place at the Huangjiaya-kou Experimental Theatre on 17 November and in the Guotai Theatre [Guotai Da Xiyuan] 9–19 December 1942.

The 'social education' in this context was a wartime patriotic campaign. The choice to perform *Hamlet*, a work thought to represent Anglophone cultures (including China's ally, the United States), would certainly encourage support of China's Western allies. However, extant historical documents show that the director and promoters of the production were more interested in *Hamlet*'s symbolic capital and in the perceived prestige and significance of being able to stage Shakespeare under challenging wartime material conditions. It seems that they, and their audiences, had no investment in *Hamlet*'s cultural connection with China's Western allies during the war, athough the production, in the context of Yu's drama school, had a pronounced purpose to boost morale and confidence of the Chinese.

Much of the production's vitality lies in its ingenious use of the temple as an allegorical space under poor material conditions, including frequent power outages. The action took place on the balcony in front of the shrine to Confucius, while the audiences were seated in the courtyard looking up to the balcony at the end of a stone staircase. The temple had two wings and a central hall. The stage design took advantage of this preexisting structure, covering the red pillars with black cloth. The stage was nearly two hundred feet, with twenty-four-foot curtains on each side hanging between the pillars. These curtains were used to conceal or to reveal a combination of pillars and scene depth in order to dramatize the twists and turns and the haunted atmosphere in 'the sinful and perilous Danish court' (Cao and Sun 104). For example, Polonius gave his blessing and his advice to Laertes – 'Neither a borrower nor a lender [be]' (1.3.57–81) – as he followed Laertes back and forth around different pillars, moving toward the back of the hall, which, for lack of lighting, was dark. Similar movements around the pillars were used for his other scenes, highlighting his ill-received lengthy speeches and the unseen twists and turns of court politics. The performance area thus acquired the depth of a proscenium stage. The ghost entered from the deep and dark end of the path lined with pillars and curtains. The minimalist stage design – two chairs, a bed, and a table – worked well with the dim open space in creating a sense of mysteriousness.

The most striking instance in which the localities of *Hamlet* and of the performance venue were brought to confront each other was seen in the emotionally charged nunnery scene. Hamlet (played by Wen Xiying, age 17) was infuriated by the fact that Ophelia was sent by Polonius and that Polonius might be present during their conversation. The scene culminated in Hamlet's passionate outburst and retreat to the back of the stage (3.1.142–9). He exited slowly towards the end of the

9.3 Shrine and statue of Confucius in a Confucian temple in Zizhong, Sichuan. Reproduced courtesy of the People's Government of Jiang'an County, China.

hall, with the gradual drawing of the curtains following the rhythm of his heavy footsteps. The lonely Hamlet, moving in the dim two-hundred-foot corridor (Jiang 106) was only visible to the audience through a two-foot gap between the curtains.[10]

The shrine of Confucius, located at the end of the corridor, was not part of the set but was not removed for this performance (see fig. 9.3). The shrine was well known to the local audience and it intruded into the performance. Thus the temple existed simultaneously in different temporal and spatial dimensions of the fictional and real worlds, an existence that was complicated by the desire to produce an 'authentic' *Hamlet* in an authentic Confucian temple. Buried in his thoughts, Hamlet appeared to be heading toward the shrine – a space that existed outside both the Danish setting and the stage set – as if he now was seeking advice from the Chinese sage. It is not clear whether or how he found an answer, but the director and the audience eagerly provided a number of inspiring but sometimes conflicting answers to the question of wartime theatre. If nothing else, the shrine's accidental intrusion into the dramatic world signalled an emotional investment in the Chinese tradition that stood as a sign of the viability and vitality of the country.

Posed against the backdrop of the exigencies of this particular location, Hamlet's question – 'To be, or not to be' (3.1.55) – acquired personal and political urgencies for wartime Chinese audiences who rushed to air-raid shelters on a daily basis, seeking protection from Japanese aerial attacks. Attending theatre in the temple, much like time spent in air-raid shelters with neighbours and families, became a communal experience that provided temporary relief through entertainment and at the same time as a sober moment of reflection in the midst of the chaos of war. The remote world of Denmark, Fortinbras' resounding footsteps, and Hamlet's ontological question crossed the vast historical and cultural distance to form a 'patriotic' play. Performed for Chinese audiences against the backdrop of a Confucian temple, the 'foreignness' of Hamlet and his outlandish yet oddly familiar story became an apt expression of wartime anxieties about losses. On one hand, the play was peculiar because of the admonition of the Ghost and the revenge mission that has never been clearly defined. On the other hand, a gentleman prince torn between prioritizing his duties to the state and his emotional ties to his mother is not an unfamiliar dilemma in the Confucian classics. The ongoing Sino-Japanese War prompted Jiao to look for moral messages in *Hamlet*. In an essay written on 12 December 1942, before the revival of the production in Chongqing, Jiao related Hamlet's problems directly to the Chinese situation, highlighting the lessons to be learned from Hamlet's procrastination. He pointed out that in this context the aesthetics of the performance could only be secondary to the political message of the production:

> The character of Hamlet [contains] a lesson for us who are living in the period of the Anti-Japanese War ... and a stimulus to those who do not have faith in our ultimate victory. The Danish prince has seen clearly what he needs to do when confronted by political and familial crises; however, he hesitates and does not put his thought into action. This leads to ... failure and destruction. The victory of the Anti-Japanese War hinges upon immediate and synchronized actions by all the [Chinese] people. This is why we introduce *Hamlet* to the Chongqing audience. The success of [the troupe's] performing skills is secondary. (2:167–8)

This statement is intriguing because the intellectuals' apparent sympathy for Hamlet did not translate into admiration for his inaction. Hamlet's procrastination thus constituted a negative lesson in moral behaviour.[11] This interpretation creates the negative image of a hesitating Hamlet. There is another side of the coin. Though Jiao downplayed the importance of his actors' skills to accommodate the wartime propaganda, the audience responded enthusiastically and was mesmerized by the actors' performances, including Wen Xiying's Hamlet, Luo Shui's Ophelia, and Peng Houjun's Gertrude (Fu 118).

Jiao seemed to contradict himself when he tried to explain Hamlet's hesitation. Recognizing procrastination as Hamlet's most important characteristic, Jiao argued that Hamlet hesitated because of his 'love of truth,' not because of cowardice (Jiang 107). Yet, desperate to draw connections between the localities of *Hamlet* and his production, Jiao brushed aside Hamlet's 'love of truth' and asked his audience to heed the moral of the performance: procrastination and inaction pave the road to failure.

The Confucian moral contexts in this production appeared first by accident but were subsequently consciously deployed by both the director and the critics. But how could Hamlet be at once a Confucian hero, with an exemplary 'spirit' fit for a time of war, and a negative example of procrastination, teaching the Chinese audience a good lesson for war? Much ink has been spilt in the history of Chinese Shakespearean criticism over Hamlet's character and the qualities shared by Hamlet and the typical Confucian gentleman. Despite the popularity of earlier Confucian interpretations of *Hamlet*, Jiao's production was the first documented performance to take place in a Confucian temple. Up to the 1940s, before the Chinese Communist Party took over China and institutionalized Marxist-Leninism, most interpretations aligned Hamlet with historical and quasi-historical political figures who took it as their responsibility to set aright 'the time ... out of joint' (1.5.189). Their frustration at not being able to communicate or realize their moral and political ideals led to their melancholic state. Mainland Chinese criticism of the period did not give much attention to the problem of Hamlet's procrastination. When it was mentioned at all, Hamlet's insistence on seeking truth was used to explain away the inconsistency. Performed against the backdrop of a Confucian temple and a tradition of 'Confucian Hamlets,' Jiao's production might have downplayed Hamlet's procrastination were it not for the demands of wartime theatre. The obvious contradiction in the untimely death of a truth-seeking noble Confucian Hamlet prompted Jiao to extrapolate a moral lesson from Hamlet's negative example.

Most theatre historians agree that performance 'deserves to be judged by the impact it has in its own time, unaffected by changes in fashion – in styles of costume and haircuts, of vocal and gestural techniques' (Wells xx). This is especially true of interpretations that engage at once the fictional, cultural, and actual sites embedded within and beyond the plays themselves. The audience can become so invested in nostalgic enthusiasm that they refuse to accept changes in fashion or gestural techniques. The site-specific meanings have come to be fully embedded within the historical performance, which has been turned into an event itself.

Although certain meanings of the production will be associated with the performance style and plot, other meanings are produced by the clash of the associated cultural localities. In the case of the wartime *Hamlet* performance in a Confucian temple, the choice was accidental, imposed by historical exigencies or material conditions, gaining accidental additional purchase on the production value.

Notes

I thank Columbia University Press for permission to use material from chapter 5 of *Chinese Shakespeares: Two Centuries of Cultural Exchange*. The present essay is an expanded and updated study of Jiao Juyin's *Hamlet*.

1 'As imagination bodies forth / The forms of things unknown, the poet's pen / Turns them to shapes, and gives to airy nothing / A local habitation' (*A Midsummer Night's Dream*, 5.1.14–17).

2 Karl Marx often quotes from Aeschylus, Sophocles, Shakespeare, and Goethe. For example, Marx quotes the Schlegel-Tieck German translation of *Timon of Athens* (4.3) to support his argument about the power of money in bourgeois society. Marx's daughter Eleanor recalled in 1895 that 'Shakespeare was the Bible of [their] house, seldom out of our hands or mouths.' By the time she was six, she 'knew scene upon scene of Shakespeare by heart' (147). See also Tucker 80–1 and Marx and Engels, *Economic and Philosophic Manuscripts of 1844*.

3 'The fundamental difference between Shakespeare's dramaturgy and the theatrical systems of many Asian theatres is the respective emphases they place on the verbal and the corporeal' (Kennedy and Yong 17).

4 Multimedia essays with film clips are available in 'Asian Shakespeares on Screen: Two Films in Perspective,' Special issue, ed. Alexander C.Y. Huang, *Borrowers and Lenders: The Journal of Shakespeare and Appropriation* 4.2 (2009). http://www.borrowers.uga.edu/.

5 The episode can be viewed freely online: http://v.youku.com/v_show/id_XNTg1NDMzNjg=.html.
6 Ingo Berensmeyer erroneously assumes that Chinese moviegoers 'have had little or no exposure to Shakespeare's *Hamlet*.' Ingo Berensmeyer, 'Cultural Ecology and Chinese *Hamlets*,' *New Literary History* 42.3 (2011): 419–38, see 429.
7 Ferdinand Freiligrath, 'Deutschland ist Hamlet,' *Werke*, ed. Julius Schwering (Berlin: Bong, 1909) 2:71–3; English translation in Horace Howard Furness, ed., *Hamlet: A New Variorum Edition of Shakespeare* (London: Lippincott, 1877) 376–8. See also *Poems from the German of Ferdinand Freiligrath* (Leipzig: Bernhard Tauchnitz, 1871) 201–4.
8 Cf. *Sichuan wenmiao* [*Confucian Temples of Sichuan*], ed. Sichuan sheng wenwu kaogu yanjiu yuan [Sichuan Provincial Archeological Institute] (Beijing: Wenwu chubanshe, 2008).
9 The first documented performance of *Hamlet* in Chinese was a Chinese opera, rather than a spoken drama, staged by Ya'an *Chuanju* (Sichuan Opera) Theatre in 1914.
10 A short interview by Wen on how he played Hamlet and recollections by graduates of the School (such as director Xu Xiaozhong) of their days in Jiang'an are available in '3. Xiju yaolan' [Episode 3. The Cradle of Modern Chinese Theatre] of the China Central Television Channel 10 documentary *Guoli juzhuan zai Jiang'an* [The National Drama School in Jiang'an]. The documentary can be viewed freely online at http://v.youku.com/v_show/id_XNTg1NDMzNjg=.html or at http://www.tudou.com/programs/view/anS4qHeVCnI/.
11 This is a view shared by the former US Secretary of State George Schulz, who, in the 1980s, warned that the United States had become 'the Hamlet of nations, worrying endlessly over whether and how to respond' to terrorism (Johnson).

Works Cited

Atkinson, Brooks. 'The Play.' *New York Times* 18 December 1942: n.pag.
Benjamin, Walter. 'The Work of Art in the Age of Mechanical Reproduction.' *Illuminations*. Ed. Hannah Arendt. Trans. Harry Zorn. London: Pimlico, 1999. 211–44.
Cao, Shujun, and Sun Fuliang. *Shashibiya zai Zhongguo wutai shang*. Harbin: Ha'erbin chubanshe, 1989.
'Episode 3. Xiju yaolan.' *Guoli juzhuan zai Jiang'an*. Dir. Chen, Fan. China Central Television Channel 10, China, 2008.

Fei, Chunfang, and Sun Huizhu. 'Shakespeare and Beijing Opera: Two Cases of Appropriation.' *Shakespeare in Asia: Contemporary Performance*. Ed. Dennis Kennedy and Yong Li Lan. Cambridge: Cambridge University Press, 2010. 57–70.

Fu, Xiangmo. 'Guan Sha weng de shijie da beiju.' *Guoli xiju zhuanke xuexiao xiaoyou tongxun yuekan* 3.8 (18 June 1942). Reprinted in *Zhongguo zaoqi xiqu huakan*. Beijing: Quanguo tushuguan wenxian suowei fuzhi zhongxin, 2006. 37:115.

Habicht, Werner. 'Shakespeare Celebrations in Times of War.' *Shakespeare Quarterly* 52.4 (Winter 2001): 441–55.

Huang, Alexander C.Y. *Chinese Shakespeares: Two Centuries of Cultural Exchange*. New York: Columbia University Press, 2009.

– 'Comical Tragedies and Other Polygeneric Shakespeares in Contemporary China and Diasporic Chinese Culture.' *Shakespeare and Genre: From Early Modern Inheritances to Postmodern Legacies*. Ed. Anthony R. Guneratne. New York: Palgrave Macmillan, 2012. 157–72.

Guoli juzhuan: Jiang'an. Ed. Zhongguo renmin zhengzhi xieshang huiyi Sichuan sheng Jiang'an xian weiyuanhui and Wenshi ziliao yanjiu weiyuan hui. 1994.

Jiang, Tao. 'Lun Zhongguo Shaju wutai shang de daoyan yishu.' *Xiju* 3 (1996): 107.

Jiao, Juyin. 'Guanyu *Hamuleite*.' *Jiao Juyin wenji*. Beijing: Wenhua yishu chubanshe, 1988. 2:167–8.

Johnson, Boyd M. 'Executive Order 12333: The Permissibility of an American Assassination of a Foreign Leader.' *Cornell International Law Journal* 25 (1992): 421, n. 129.

Kennedy, Dennis, and Yong Li Lan. 'Introduction: Why Shakespeare?' *Shakespeare in Asia: Contemporary Performance*. Ed. Dennis Kennedy and Yong Li Lan. Cambridge: Cambridge University Press, 2010. 1–23.

Lao She. 'Xin Hanmuliede.' *Lao She xiaoshuo quanji*. Ed. Shu Ji and Shu Yi. Wuhan: Changjiang wenyi chubanshe, 2004. 10: 443–59.

Lu, Gu-sun, 'Hamlet Across Space and Time,' *Shakespeare Survey* 36 (1988): 56.

Marx, Eleanor. 'Recollections of Mohr.' *Marx and Engels on Literature and Art: A Selection of Writings*. Ed. Lee Baxandall and Stefan Morawski. St Louis: Telos Press, 1973.

Marx, Karl, and Frederick Engels. *Economic and Philosophic Manuscripts of 1844*. Trans. Martin Milligan. Buffalo: Prometheus Books, 1988.

Rothwell, Kenneth S. *A History of Shakespeare on Screen*. 2nd ed. Cambridge: Cambridge University Press, 2004.

Tian, Benxiang, *Zhongguo xiandai bijiao xiju shi*. Beijing: Wenhua yishu chubanshe, 1993.

Tieck, Ludwig. 'Bemerkungen über einige Charaktere im 'Hamlet', und über die Art, wie diese auf der Bühne dargestellt werden könnten.' *Kritische Schriften.* Leipzig: Brockhaus, 1848–52. 3:243–98. Trans. in *The Romantics on Shakespeare.* Ed. Jonathan Bate. London: Penguin, 1997. 326–35.

Tucker, Robert C., ed. *The Marx-Engels Reader.* New York: Norton, 1972.

Wells, Stanley. Foreword to *Shakespeare, Memory and Performance.* Ed. Peter Holland. Cambridge: Cambridge University Press, 2006. xx.

Xie, Zengshou and Zhang Tuoyuan. *Liuwang zhong de xijujia yaolan: cong Nanjing dao Jiang'an de Guoli juzhuan yanjiu.* Chengdu: Tiandi chubanshe, 2005.

Yu, Shangyuan. *Yu Shangyuan xiju lunwen ji.* Wuhan: Changjiang wenyi chubanshe, 1986.

Zhang, Qihong. 'Rang shangdi jianglin renjian: Zai Zhongguo Shashibiya Yanjiuhui chengli dahui shang de fayan.' *Qingnian yishu* 1 (1985): 7. Trans. Fan Shen. 'Shakespeare in China: *The Merchant of Venice.*' *Asian Theatre Journal* 5.1 (Spring 1988): 29–30.

Zimmermann, Heiner O. 'Is Hamlet Germany? On the Political Reception of Hamlet.' *New Essays on Hamlet.* Ed. Mark Thornton Burnett and John Manning. New York: AMS Press, 1994. 293–318.

10 Shakespeare, Stratford, and the Second World War

SIMON BARKER

A cartoon that appeared in the *Manchester Guardian* on Thursday, 21 February 1946,[1] shows William Shakespeare arriving with his suitcases at a Stratford-upon-Avon hotel during the Second World War. We know it is Shakespeare from the 'W.S.' printed on one of his two suitcases, as well as from his Elizabethan costume and his general demeanour: he is balding, bearded, and sexily English – imagined, perhaps, from the statue above his tomb in nearby Holy Trinity Church. We also understand from a label on a second suitcase that he is attempting to check in for the annual Shakespeare Festival. Lounging across the entrance to the hotel and blocking Shakespeare's way sits a bowler-hatted figure from the middle of the twentieth century – a caricature of a civil servant perhaps, or at least someone who has taken officialdom to heart in that he clearly does not acknowledge the celebrity of the figure he confronts. He is a picture of nonchalant self-importance: his hat is tilted forwards, his feet are propped up against the doorway, and he is more interested in his newspaper than in this new arrival. A dog sleeps nearby. The contrast with the upright, expectant Shakespeare is complete: enervation versus energy, complacency versus creativity. The hotel front is plastered with posters declaring that the building had been requisitioned during the emergency of 1939 and is now closed to the public. Although nothing in the scene itself hints of emergency, we know when it is set since the newspaper headline reads: 'Hitler invades Poland.' The caption of the cartoon gives a voice to the bowler-hatted guardian of the commandeered hotel, declaring to Shakespeare, in very bold type, 'Rooms? Rooms?? My good man, don't you know there's a war on?'

10.1 David Low, cartoon of 'wartime' Shakespeare. *The Manchester Guardian*, 21 February 1946. Reproduced with permission from Solo Syndication Limited.

The cartoonist's reflection on Stratford-upon-Avon during the Second World War accurately represented something of the crisis that faced the town. Anyone trying to book into a hotel in Stratford during the conflict may have been disappointed. Hotels were indeed requisitioned as government agencies were relocated to the town, and there were also, as we shall see, elaborate plans in place for the Shakespeare Memorial Theatre itself. What the cartoon does not reveal, since the image of the lounging civil servant and sleeping dog suggests a rather uninterested, even hostile, attitude to Shakespeare, is the enthusiasm with which those involved with Shakespearean production in Stratford-upon-Avon strove to keep the theatre alive during the hostilities. This chapter describes something of these efforts, as a salute to the persistence of these theatre practitioners, whilst also trying to determine the ideological sense of the productions that emerged in the context of wartime Stratford. What emerges is something of a contrast with other manifestations of Shakespeare during the 1930s and 1940s.

Shakespeare, War, and Hitler's Library

Over recent years an international body of research has grown which has addressed the abundant historical connections that can be made between Shakespeare and warfare.[2] Some scholars have focused on the particular relationship between Shakespeare and the Second World War. Others, understandably enough, and alongside theatre historians, directors, actors, and critics, have been concerned with the way that Shakespeare's plays can be reread and newly performed in order to address more recent or present-day military conflict. As far as the specifics of the Second World War are concerned, there are numerous instances of the way that Shakespeare's texts were employed during the years leading up to the war and throughout the period of hostilities itself. One example would be the use of *Coriolanus*. Hans Rothe's 1932 German translation, broadcast to an emerging Nazi Germany, led to his exile the following year because of the way that he had adapted Shakespeare's play as a critique of Adolf Hitler. Meanwhile, a French translation of the play by René-Louis Piachaud for a performance during the Christmas and New Year of 1933–4 led to royalist/fascist clashes with critical Parisian citizens in the streets around the theatre. In this instance, as a response to these disturbances, the director of the play was replaced by the chief of the Sûreté. In locations as far away from each other as Pasadena and Moscow there were corresponding left-wing, or anti-fascist productions.[3] Finally, though, *Coriolanus* enjoyed a firm place in the Nazi education machine throughout the Second World War, Shakespeare's text being deemed an exemplum of the virtues of the strong military leader.

Examples of an understanding of Shakespeare as somehow in tune with Nazi values are unsurprising given Hitler's own evaluation of the playwright's standing in relation to German culture – and this evaluation may even have contributed in part to the prevailing atmosphere in Stratford-upon-Avon during the war. In his compelling study, *Hitler's Private Library*, Timothy W. Ryback notes that Hitler's favourite books were '*Don Quixote* along with *Robinson Crusoe, Uncle Tom's Cabin* and *Gulliver's Travels*' and quotes Hitler as saying of these books, that 'each of them is a grandiose idea unto itself' (Ryback xi). In *Robinson Crusoe* Hitler apparently perceived 'the development of the entire history of mankind' (xi). Hitler's library of sixteen-thousand volumes also included the collected works of William Shakespeare, 'published in [a] German translation in 1925 by Georg Müller as part of a series intended to make great literature available to the general public' (xi). According to Ryback,

> [Hitler] considered Shakespeare superior to Goethe and Schiller in every respect. While Shakespeare had fuelled his imagination on the protean forces of the emerging British Empire, these two Teutonic playwright-poets squandered their talent on stories of midlife crises and sibling rivalry. Why was it, he once wondered, that the German Enlightenment produced *Nathan the Wise*,[4] the story of the rabbi who reconciles Christians, Muslims and Jews, while it had been left to Shakespeare to give the world *The Merchant of Venice* and Shylock?
>
> Hitler appears to have imbibed his Hamlet – favourite phrases included 'To be or not to be' and 'It is Hecuba to me' – and he was especially fond of *Julius Caesar*. In a 1926 sketchbook he drew a detailed stage set for the first act of the Shakespearean tragedy with sinister façades enclosing the forum where Caesar is cut down. 'We will meet again at Philippi,' he threatened an opponent on more than one occasion, plagiarizing the spectral warning to Brutus after Caesar's murder. He was said to have reserved the Ides of March for momentous decisions. (Ryback xi–xiii)

Hitler's interest in Shakespeare had existed for some time. With characteristic loathing for what he perceived as a narrowing of German culture, particularly under the influence of Jews, he had written in *Mein Kampf* of his desire to restore Shakespeare to his rightful place on the German stage (Hitler 236). In fact, however, despite Hitler's endorsement and the role of the texts within the state education system, Shakespeare struggled under Nazi rule as far as the live theatre was concerned. Gerwin Strobl has noted in *The Swastika and the Stage* that, once restored following early condemnation, Shakespeare probably only received attention in the theatre due to Hitler's personal support.

> Since the Führer took only an intermittent interest in the non-musical stage, control over German theatre essentially devolved to Joseph Goebbels. Goebbels was, however, overruled by Hitler on a number of occasions. These ranged from the appointment of prominent *Intendanten* [artistic and managing directors] to the issue of salaries for the Reich's theatrical stars. Once or twice, Hitler even intervened in repertoire policy: the initial ban on Shakespeare as an enemy dramatist after the outbreak of war, for instance, was lifted on the Führer's personal orders. Yet Goebbels

was left to implement the Führer's wishes, and thus enjoyed some leeway in interpreting Hitler's commands. In the case of Shakespeare, Goebbels instructed his own subordinates to limit all theatres to one play by the Bard per season, even though Hitler had not suggested any limitations; and Goebbels saw to it that his own order was enforced. (153)

As Werner Habicht and Zeno Ackermann have demonstrated in their essays for this volume, tension over the status of Shakespeare in the Nazi sphere of influence continued throughout the war, with competing agencies at work in determining both frequency of performances and the interpretation of the plays. The complexity of the ideological apparatus underpinning the staging of *Julius Caesar* and other Shakespeare plays is matched only by the brutality of the ideological aims that were to be fulfilled. Despite clear disagreements among those at work behind the scenes, Nazi aesthetics, with respect to Shakespeare in general and *The Merchant of Venice* in particular, seem ultimately to have been mediated by a recognition of Hitler's profound interest in the playwright.[5]

There are many other examples of the ways in which Shakespeare had a significant role in the years leading up to the Second World War and during the 1940s. In diverse contexts and national cultures, Shakespeare was recruited as a 'voice' in support of various contrasting political allegiances.[6] In Britain, there was the work of the academic George R. Wilson Knight (1897–1985) whose wartime production *This Sceptred Isle* was staged at the Westminster Theatre in London in 1941. This production was conceived as Shakespeare's contribution to the war effort, as Britain had stood for a while isolated but defiant in the face of German aggression. Its tone captured the spirit of much of the orthodox criticism of the 1930s and 1940s.[7] Knight had experienced war first hand, having served as a dispatch rider in Iraq in the First World War. His early theories about the relationship between Shakespeare and Empire were further developed during the years he spent teaching at the University of Toronto (1931–40).[8]

Laurence Olivier's enduring film version of *Henry V*, released in November 1944 and famously dedicated to 'the Commandos and Airborne Troops of Great Britain,' had developed from his performances of the play in the years before the war. Given the energetic and understandably propagandist nature of these largely metropolitan contributions to the war effort, it is surprising not to find an equivalent forthright approach to the performance of Shakespeare in Stratford itself.

Stratford's War and 'Operation HK'

As Timothy Ryback has commented, the contents of Hitler's library became clear to those beyond his immediate circle only after the war had ended, but his views on Shakespeare were known long before the beginning of hostilities. Thus a rumour to the effect that Hitler said that he would never bomb Stratford-upon-Avon because of the centrality of Shakespeare to Germany's national culture was of considerable importance to those living in the town in 1939. This rumour has to be seen in terms of wartime debate about mutual aerial bombing. There was, at first, some tacit agreement that cities and towns of significant cultural and architectural significance might be spared.[9] This quickly changed to a policy involving the deliberate bombing of such places on both sides, most notably Germany's 'Baedeker Blitz' of Bath, Canterbury, Exeter, Norwich, and York, seen by the German High Command as a reprisal for the British bombing of Lübeck. These targets were chosen from a guide to the most historically interesting British cities. Whatever the truth about Hitler's rumoured attitude to Stratford-upon-Avon (as somewhere apparently excluded from this policy) it is the case that the town remained surprisingly unscathed by enemy action.

It is tempting to think that the British authorities in London also held some belief in the idea that Stratford-upon-Avon was somehow exempt from the extreme dangers that faced other wartime communities. The town is, after all, not far from cities that suffered some of the most severe bombing of the early years of the war. Medieval Coventry was devastated by 'Operation Moonlight Sonata' in November 1940, and Birmingham suffered continual attacks during 1940, 1941, and 1942. Both cities were associated with industries that were critical to the British war effort; but Stratford, despite its reputation as a quintessential rural market town, was also the site of significant small-scale wartime production, particularly to do with aviation. This, and its proximity to the larger centres of manufacture, would hardly make Stratford an obvious place of safety, especially given the indiscriminate nature of so much of the nocturnal bombing principally aimed at nearby centres. Although a stray German bomb fell in Maidenhead Road on one occasion, and a plaque in Evesham Place still commemorates the two Fleet Air Arm personnel who were consumed by fire when their aeroplane crashed there in September 1941, Stratford's citizens largely escaped such airborne peril.[10]

It is a measure of how secure government officials considered the town that in the early years of the war Stratford-upon-Avon afforded a temporary home for children evacuated from urban areas. Yet, as was suggested by the *Manchester Guardian* cartoon, the war quickly brought other kinds of relocations. The town's main hotels, including the Shakespeare, the Falcon, the Arden, and the Swan's Nest were requisitioned by various government and military departments; surviving records, including personal accounts by hotel workers, reveal the elaborate and hasty contingencies that came into force.[11] The hotels were stripped of their furniture in favour of more functional office equipment; walls were reinforced, communication systems were installed, and coded notices signalling (to those that could interpret them) the accommodation's new significance were posted. For a while the town became a kind of extension of Whitehall as civil and military personnel arrived with lorry loads of files and the associated paraphernalia of wartime administration. Although the hotels could no longer accommodate what must have been but a meagre trickle of casual tourists and Shakespeare enthusiasts, the new occupants, and those who visited them on official business, provided ready audiences for the productions at the Memorial Theatre. The earlier playhouse, constructed in 1879, had been almost entirely destroyed by a fire in 1926. Elizabeth Scott's design for the replacement had been controversial, partly because the new building resembled a cinema, but also because of its limitations as a performance space. In some quarters, however, the facilities of the new theatre apparently found great favour. Archival records in the library of the House of Lords reveal the precise detail of secret manoeuvres to take place in case of an invasion that threatened London as the seat of the British Government. In such an event, parliamentary personnel were to be evacuated to Stratford-upon-Avon by special trains and buses that were kept prepared for the purpose; these papers include precise details of the mode of transport afforded to each type of traveller, according to his or her status. In Stratford itself, billets would be allocated according to the rank of each parliamentary member or official, with the best granted to those who would sit in the conference hall in the Memorial Theatre as the newly established alternative House of Lords. These plans, code-named 'Operation HK,' are of interest for their precise and even fussy attention to social class that would prevail despite the gravity of the situation that would see them activated.[12] I have written elsewhere of the image of members of Parliament making a last-ditch stand against an invading German army from within the very epicentre of Shakespearean production.[13] Yet, the plans speak seriously of the centrality of Stratford-upon-Avon in terms of its geographical situation at the 'heart of England' and, without doubt, of a cultural symbolism associated with the life and work of William Shakespeare. It is perhaps too fanciful to suggest that government planners also believed the rumour that Hitler would use every opportunity he could to avoid the destruction of a town so associated with a playwright considered central to his own view of German culture. It is significant, however, that the Rt Hon. Anthony Eden, a leading figure in the early wartime cabinet, had visited Stratford-upon-Avon to speak to Warwickshire hoteliers on 'the subject of commandeering of hotels'.[14]

The deployment of government officials to Stratford-upon-Avon during the war therefore provided one source of audiences for productions at the Memorial Theatre. Another was a constant stream of military personnel from the various camps and airforce bases established in the countryside around the town. As the war progressed the area became a significant point of mobilization for soldiers and aviators from Canada, the United States, and other Allied nations, and Canadian service personnel had, in fact, been visiting from the earliest months of the war. A newspaper cutting from the *Stratford-upon-Avon Herald* of 29 March 1940 has the headline 'Canadian Smiles.'

> About 40 members of the Canadian Expeditionary Force visited Stratford-on-Avon on Friday. Their first port of call was the picture gallery at the Shakespeare Memorial Theatre where they were met by the Mayor and Mayoress (Councillor and Mrs. T.N. Waldron), Sir Archie Flower (Chairman of the Governors), and Lady Flower. Having been shown around they went on to the Theatre, where, as a compliment to their hosts, they mounted the stage and gave a stirring rendering of their regimental song. They evinced great interested in the workings of the stage, which they examined thoroughly, even descending into the depths. They also 'took trips' on the rolling stage. They finished at the Theatre café, where coffee and sandwiches were served. The officers and men chatted with their hosts, one of them saying that he had been afraid to visit Stratford because he had heard it praised so highly by his own countrymen and he was certain it could not be all that it was 'cracked up' to be. 'Actually,' he added 'it has surpassed my expectations.' (*Herald* 29 March 1940: 3)

Thomas Holte's accompanying photograph of the Canadian soldiers is a compelling image. The kilted Canadians and their hosts are indeed smiling, and the article insists on a mutual interest in Shakespeare as

Flower 'contented' himself with a quotation from *King John*: 'Nought shall make us rue if England to itself do rest but true' (3).

As it turned out, these Canadian soldiers were pioneers in attempts to link activities at the theatre to the war effort. An article published in the *Herald* on 13 September 1940, quoting Flower, described the first wartime Shakespeare Festival held over the course of twenty weeks. Echoing his speech to the visiting Canadians earlier that year, Flower noted that the

> Governors were happy at the result of their experiment, and though there would be a loss, as was expected, they had the satisfaction of knowing that 80,000 had attended Shakespeare's plays. Those people had derived encouragement and recreation, and those who saw *King John*, and particularly the last act, must have gone away full of the idea of England at her very best. (qtd in *Herald* 13 Sept. 1940, 1)

Flower had also noted the practical difficulties faced by those involved with the productions due to the war.

> The War had given them a great deal of extra work. In the course of the 20 weeks between 20 and 30 of the staff had joined the Forces, and their places had to be filled, which entailed additional rehearsals. But the company had tackled it, and he believed they had enjoyed it. In addition, over thirty of them had joined the Home Guard. (1)[15]

Shortage of staff was not the only problem facing Sir Archibald, the Festival Governors, and the early wartime director, Ben Iden Payne. Productions had to be scheduled to fit in with blackout times and there is evidence of the way that plays were cut to accommodate these regulations. There were also restrictions on supplies for the creation of sets and costumes, leading to the recycling of materials from prewar productions. Shortages of fuel affected the management of the productions and, it was feared, threatened audience attendance. Despite these challenges, however, audiences for this (and subsequent wartime Festivals) were not in short supply. The *Herald* happily noted that: 'In conclusion, Sir Archie mentioned that many men of the Forces had been among the audiences, and there was now a prospect that the Company would have an opportunity of carrying Shakespeare to the troops in various parts of the country' (1).

Indeed, a few days earlier the *Herald* had reported that under the auspices of the Entertainments National Service Association (ENSA) the Festival Company was to tour garrison theatres with 'potted' productions of *The Merry Wives of Windsor* and *Twelfth Night*.

> The 20 weeks' Festival at Stratford-on-Avon will close to-morrow (Saturday) after a season that has fully justified the bold policy of the Governors. The audiences have included many members of the Forces, drawn from all the Services, from all ranks, and including representatives of the Empire contingents. This feature of the Festival led to the conception of a scheme for providing the troops with potted versions of Shakespeare ... Mr Iden Payne has already experimented along these lines, for a few years ago he presented 50-minute productions of Shakespeare to enthusiastic audiences in the Globe theatre at the Chicago World Fair ... The difficulties can well be imagined, especially when it is remembered that Mr Payne had a delicate task when he had to restrict this year's Festival productions to two-and-a-half hours. (*Herald* 6 Sept. 1940: 1)

By 1944 the Memorial Theatre was offering weekly 'leave courses' for Canadian and US forces, predicting during the five months from April 17 to mid-September,

> twenty Canadians and twenty Americans should arrive here on Monday evenings ... The programme would actually start the following morning with a reception by the Mayor and Mayoress at 10 o'clock. Afterwards there would be a talk on the history of Stratford by Mr. John Bird, and then the members of the Forces would have a free morning to visit the interesting buildings of the town. In the afternoon Mr Robert Atkins would give a talk on 'The Shakespearean Stage,' and afterwards tea would be taken with members of the Festival Company and staff of the Memorial Theatre. In the evening they would attend the performance. (*Herald* 14 Apr. 1944: 1)

Shakespeare and the Home Front

The Festivals and the attendant educational programs took place alongside the kinds of wartime morale boasting and fund-raising activities that were common in Britain during the war. Stratford-upon-Avon held events such as War Weapons Weeks, which celebrated the manufacture of weaponry and sought financial donations from citizens. The Shakespeare Birthday Trust Archive holds a collection of items, left by local undertaker Frank Organ, that includes a photograph of his shop window dressed especially 'for the War Effort' as well as a photograph of an aeroplane on display in front of the Memorial Theatre during one of these campaigns.[16] Anthony Eden returned to Stratford-up-Avon in February 1940 to make a long and widely reported speech on 'The Progress of the War.' This event took place at the Shakespeare Memorial Theatre before an audience of local dignitaries, citizens, theatre staff, performers, and an international contingent of correspondents invited to the town especially for the occasion (*Herald* 9 Feb. 1940, 1).[17] Eden's speech was important in itself as an official declaration for an international audience of British attitudes towards the conflict, but the location was also highly significant, chosen in order to allow Eden to draw upon Shakespeare and his work as a kind of guarantee of the worth of the campaign and as a bulwark of national and international (or Imperial) identity. As Dominions Secretary he addressed the 500 people attending the event on the 'unquiet mind' of 'Dr Goebbels' goblins' (the Nazi propaganda machine), the importance of war savings (in the form of Savings Certificates), and the 'true character' and idealism of the British Commonwealth. Central to his address, and this ideal, was an evocation of Shakespeare and Stratford: 'Tonight we are met in Shakespeare's theatre, in an atmosphere seeped with the traditions of our race. Here on this stage our history is enacted, our philosophy as a people is given expression, in plays which are the greatest gift of English genius to mankind. We stand at the very heart of England, and we can have little doubt what it is we must do battle to defend' (*Herald* 9 Feb. 1940: 2).

The evening concluded with a short vote of thanks from Sir Archibald Flower. From an early twenty-first-century perspective such speeches as these, invoking the spirit of Shakespeare in aid of a just war, seem propagandist (if understandably so) in their nature, and can be compared with similar wartime imperatives elsewhere in Europe and beyond. They certainly had a counterpart in the Soviet Union where, as readers of the *Herald* discovered in April 1942, Shakespeare was to be lauded for his anti-fascist values: 'Special meetings are to be held in Moscow to mark the 326th anniversary of Shakespeare's death. "The Humanism of Shakespeare, the Enemy of Fascism," "Shakespeare and the War," and "English Humour in Shakespeare's Works" are among the subjects to be discussed' ('Shakespeare: Enemy of Facism' 1).

There was, then, much urgent and varied activity in and around Stratford-upon-Avon, with its commitment to government and military agencies, visiting soldiers and aircrew, training courses, speeches, and pomp. The town's proximity to the deadly bombing of Britain's

industrial heartland made the long-established and continually reinforced symbolism of Stratford-upon-Avon as the birthplace of Shakespeare especially important in these troubled times. What then, of the
nature of the performances that took place within the Memorial Theatre itself?

Although 1940 marked the real start of the wartime Festivals, an anticipation of conflict hung in the air during the summer of 1939, seemingly
influencing the quality of the performances and certainly affecting audience numbers. Clearly, something of Sir Archibald's triumphal account
of the success of the 1940 Festival was due to a contrast that could be
made with the dismal 1939 season, which had unfortunately also been
the Memorial's Diamond Jubilee. In fact, the quality of performances
at Stratford-upon-Avon had been an issue for critics since at least 1937.
What started with comments by W.A. Darlington of the *Daily Telegraph*
became a sustained attack when he was joined by Charles Morgan of
The Times, St John Ervine of the *Observer*, and Ivor Brown, writing in the
Manchester Guardian. Although the criticism abated somewhat in 1939
(presumably even the critics had other things on their minds), everyone
seemed aware that standards in Stratford had been in decline for some
time. Records relating primarily to the organization of the 1940 Festival include sometimes heated correspondence among Flower, William
Slavery (general manager of the Stratford-upon-Avon Festival Company), Henry Tossell (manager of the Memorial Theatre), and Ben Iden
Payne (theatre director). The burden of the exchange is the particularly
poor showing of the 1939 season of plays, and in the background, a
proposed pro tempore amalgamation of the Shakespeare Memorial
Theatre and London's Old Vic, which at that time was under the directorship of Tyrone Guthrie.[18] Although it came to nothing, this proposal
(which many continued to find attractive for long after this period) was
characteristic of the uneasy relationship over Shakespeare that existed
at the time between London and Stratford-upon-Avon.[19] It is impossible
to summarize these discontents here, but it is clear that the Old Vic and
other London companies thought that Stratford lacked a sense of inter-
pretative adventure but believed (erroneously) that it enjoyed endless
financial support. In contrast, the Memorial Theatre prided itself on its
rural location, its claim on Shakespeare's life, and a misplaced adher-
ence to a sense of continuity, which the critics saw as conservatism.

During the war years, Stratford-upon-Avon saw almost sixty separate runs of works by Shakespeare, Sheridan, Goldsmith, and Jonson,
although the repetition of plays that were either popular or easily

revisited reduces the productions that may be considered truly original conceptions, conservative or not. (The list below does not include the 'potted' versions taken to garrisons, as these were sometimes reprised versions of productions from earlier seasons.) Within each season, the plays are listed in chronological order; the figures in brackets indicate the individual run against the total number of productions of that play during this period.

Full Productions at the Shakespeare Memorial Theatre 1939–45

1939
The Taming of the Shrew [1/5]
As You Like It [1/4]
Richard III [1/1]
Othello [1/3]
Twelfth Night [1/4]
Comedy of Errors [1/1]
Much Ado about Nothing [1/3]
Coriolanus [1/1]

1940
Measure for Measure [1/1]
As You Like It [2/4]
The Merry Wives of Windsor [1/3]
The Merchant of Venice [1/4]
Hamlet [1/3]
She Stoops to Conquer [1/2]
King John [1/1]
The Taming of the Shrew [2/5]

1941
Much Ado about Nothing [2/3]
Twelfth Night [2/4]
Julius Caesar [1/1]
The Taming of the Shrew [3/5]
The Rivals [1/1]
Richard II [1/2]
The Tempest [1/2]
Romeo and Juliet [1/2]
The Merchant of Venice [2/4]

1942

A Midsummer Night's Dream [1/3]
The Merchant of Venice [3/4]
Hamlet [2/3]
As You Like It [3/4]
The School for Scandal [1/1]
Macbeth [1/2]
The Tempest [2/2]
The Winter's Tale [1/2]
The Taming of the Shrew [4/5]

1943

Twelfth Night [3/4]
Othello [2/3]
A Midsummer Night's Dream [2/3]
Henry V [1/1]
The Merry Wives of Windsor [2/3]
King Lear [1/1]
The Winter's Tale [2/2]
The Critic [1/1]

1944

The Merchant of Venice [4/4]
The Taming of the Shrew [5/5]
Macbeth [2/2]
As You Like It [4/4]
Hamlet [3/3]
A Midsummer Night's Dream [3/3]
Richard II [2/2]
Volpone [1/1]

1945

Much Ado about Nothing [3/3]
The Merry Wives of Windsor [3/3]
Othello [3/3]
Twelfth Night [4/4]
Antony and Cleopatra [1/1]
She Stoops to Conquer [2/2]
Henry VIII [1/1]
Romeo and Juliet [2/2]

Given the shortage of materials, the conscription of performers and theatre staff into the armed forces, the financial difficulties (underestimated in London), and the sheer hardships of war, it would be fair to say that this sequence of productions represents an admirable success in maintaining 'business as usual.' Undoubtedly audiences were entertained and diverted from the greyness of wartime Britain, and visitors from overseas certainly came to know something more of the work of Britain's legendary dramatist. Yet by all accounts, despite a sequence of new directors and the engagement of some experienced and sophisticated actors, the overriding impression derived from reviews of these productions is of a universal blandness in their creative vision and delivery.[20] Sally Beauman, whose 1982 book on the Royal Shakespeare Company remains the most authoritative account of the early history of the RSC and its precursors, has evaluated the period thus:

> [The] function of theatre, to reinterpret and rediscover the classic plays by returning to the text and examining it without preconception or prejudice, was particularly vital at Stratford, where directors and companies were working almost exclusively on the plays of one dramatist. It was a function that Stratford generally failed to undertake. One of the most remarkable things about the Diamond Jubilee season and the Memorial's productions generally after sixty years of existence was the predictability of its directorial vision, which hampered even the most talented of its actors. Iden Payne, like Bridges-Adams before him, worked from old prompt-books when redirecting the same play, so that again and again cuts, transpositions and business used the first time he directed a play remained the same in all succeeding productions. (159)

For Beauman, 'business as usual' meant the perpetuation of a Shakespeare who remained somehow isolated from a contemporary world that cried out for his comment. Reflecting on the last production of the 1939 season, which rather set the tone for what was to come over the next six years, she wrote:

> This was *Coriolanus*, directed by Iden Payne, and it opened on 9 May, just three and a half months before Hitler ordered the invasion of Poland. By May conscription in Britain had already been introduced and war with Germany seemed inevitable. Of all the plays in the canon *Coriolanus*, with its complex and impassioned political arguments, its subtly balanced dialectic, its investigation of democracy and authoritarianism, was a play

that had obvious and immediate relevance to the events which were at that very moment dividing Europe. Yet Iden Payne's production appeared totally unrelated to and unaware of those events, and it was cocooned in theatrical traditions from the past. (160)[21]

Whatever one thinks of the highly politicized productions of Shakespeare staged elsewhere in Britain, and for that matter, elsewhere in the world during the 1930s and 1940s, those wartime productions testify to a contemporary relevance, not in the name of a 'timeless Shakespeare' but of the dynamics of interpretation. These dynamics do not rely on an obvious core of meaning. People forget, for example, that the much-discussed Olivier film of *Henry V* evolved along an uneven course from his early performances under Guthrie, who, according to Tony Howard, 'initially chose *Henry V* to attack jingoism: Olivier recalled, "I fought against the heroism by flattening and getting underneath the lines, no banner waving for me." They [Guthrie and Olivier] debunked the Church and the Salic Law and underlined Henry's conscience' (Howard 149).[22]

While the contingencies of war affected narrative value in cases such as Olivier's, the Memorial Theatre chose to rely on a poetics of patriotism drawn from the mere context in which productions were staged. Outside the Memorial Theatre it was war; inside the theatre it was as if the lazing man in the *Manchester Guardian* had it right in asking a wartime Shakespeare, 'My good man, don't you know there's a war on?'

A cartoon from the weekly *Das Reich* of 2 March 1941 seems to suggest that some in Germany also acknowledged a lack of recognition of Shakespeare's wartime potential. In this cartoon the ghostly spirits of Goethe, Wagner, and Shakespeare, in celestial Olympian splendour, are discussing their comparative posthumous reputations. Goethe and Wagner ask Shakespeare: 'Well, dear Master Shakespeare, you seem to be staged quite regularly in Germany. How are we faring in England?' Shakespeare (who is drawn as a figure not unlike that which appeared half a decade later in the *Manchester Guardian*) replies wistfully: 'Oh, we've long been treated equitably there: in England none of us is staged.'[23]

Notes

I am grateful for assistance with this essay to the staff of The Shakespeare Centre Library and Archive in Stratford-upon-Avon, and of the Martial Rose

Library at the University of Winchester, as well as to Lorna Scott, the Archivist at the University of Gloucestershire

1 Stratford Birthplace Trust Archive, DR885/1/6.
2 See Stephen Marx, 'Shakespeare's Pacifism,' *Renaissance Quarterly* 45 (1992): 49–95; Richard Courtney, *Shakespeare's World of War: The Early Histories* (Toronto: Simon & Pierre, 1994); Nick De Somogyi, *Shakespeare's Theatre of War* (Aldershot and Burlington: Ashgate, 1998); Bruce R. Smith, *Shakespeare and Masculinity* (Oxford: Oxford University Press, 2000); Nina Taunton, *1590s Drama and Militarism: Portrayals of War in Marlowe, Chapman and Shakespeare's Henry V* (Aldershot and Burlington: Ashgate, 2001); Alan Shephard, *Marlowe's Soldiers* (Aldershot: Ashgate, 2002); Patricia Cahill, *Unto the Breach* (Oxford: Oxford University Press, 2008); Paola Pugliatti, *Shakespeare and the Just War Tradition* (Aldershot and Burlington: Ashgate, 2010).
3 For a discussion of the further instances of the use of *Coriolanus* in the years leading up to the Second World War, see Simon Barker, 'Coriolanus: Texts and Histories,' *Assays: Critical Approaches to Medieval and Renaissance Texts*, ed. Peggy Knapp (Pittsburgh: University of Pittsburgh Press, 1986) 109–28.
4 *Nathan the Wise* (1779) is by Gotthold Lessing.
5 See Andrew G. Bonnell, *Shylock in Germany: Antisemitism in the German Theatre from the Enlightenment to the Nazis* (London: Taurus, 2008) 119–69.
6 I am thinking of other essays in this volume but also of those in Ros King and Paul Franssen, eds., *Shakespeare and War* (Basingstoke: Palgrave Macmillan, 2008).
7 See G.R. Wilson Knight, *This Sceptred Isle: Shakespeare's Message for England at War* (Oxford: Basil Blackwell, 1940); 'A Royal Propaganda, 1956. A Narrative Account of Work Devoted to the Cause of Great Britain During and After the Second World War,' MS, 11768.f.13, British Library (1964); and *Shakespearean Production* (London: Faber and Faber, 1964). For a discussion of Shakespearean critics of the 1940s and their relation to the war, see Graham Holderness, *Visual Shakespeare* (Hatfield: Hertfordshire University Press, 2002) especially chapter 5. For his own account of his war service, see Knight, *Atlantic Crossing: An Autobiographical Design* (London: Dent, 1934).
8 Knight, *The Imperial Theme* (London: Oxford University Press, 1931) was published in the year he took up his post in Toronto.
9 For discussions about the bombing, see Paul Addison and Jeremy Crang, eds., *Firestorm: The Bombing of Dresden, 1945* (London: Pimlico, 2006); and

A.C. Grayling, *Among the Dead Cities: Was the Allied Bombing of Civilians in World War II a Necessity or a Crime?* (London: Bloomsbury, 2006).

10 Documents held in the Stratford Birthplace Trust Archive (DR755) detail a claim made by Mr D.W. Newport to the War Damage Commission in respect of 'damage to ... Wincott Close as a result of a bomb falling in the neighbouring fields on 13 September 1940.' The extent of the paperwork perhaps gives a clue to the rarity of such events compared with similar episodes in nearby cities.

11 See the typescript recollection by Mrs Kate Higgins of the requisitioning of the Royal Shakespeare Hotel held in the Shakespeare Birthplace Trust Archive: DR730/6 and the typescript account from His Majesty's Office of Works: DR595/150. Many details of the requisitions survive. For example, the RAF occupied the Red Horse Hotel in Bridge Street and the Arden Hotel in Waterside, the WRAC occupied White Gates in St Gregory's Road, and the Welcombe Hotel was given to civil servants from the Treasury.

12 The Stratford Birthplace Trust Archive holds a copy (PR254/8) of 'a secret memorandum outlining the plans for evacuating the House of Lords to Stratford-upon-Avon, utilizing the Conference Hall at the Shakespeare Memorial Theatre, and the Shakespeare and Falcon Hotels.' Members of the House of Lords ('A grade' personnel) were to be billeted in the hotels or private houses; B and C grade people were allocated to boarding houses. The new Parliamentary Office was to be housed in the Shakespeare Hotel. See House of Lords Record Office Papers No 313/23.

13 See Simon Barker, *War and Nation in the Theatre of Shakespeare and his Contemporaries* (Edinburgh: Edinburgh University Press, 2007) 4–5.

14 Stratford Birthplace Trust Archive, DR595/51.

15 John Laurie, a leading actor at Stratford-upon-Avon during the war, was one of those who joined the Home Guard. Ironically he later played the part of a Home Guard private in the BBC's long-running comedy series *Dad's Army*.

16 Stratford Birthplace Trust Archive, DR611/79.

17 Stratford Birthplace Trust Archive, ER25/3/34/4).

18 Guthrie and others had long envisaged a permanent alliance between Stratford-upon-Avon and the Old Vic (as a kind of National Theatre) but Guthrie contributed his ideas about a temporary arrangement in a letter of 31 October 1939, presumably in a spirit of wartime conciliation.

19 Stratford Birthplace Trust Archive, DR1108/1/7. Other notable correspondents on the issue of the 1939 season and the festival to come were Victoria Powell, Robert Atkins, and Dame Edith Lyttleton.

20 When Payne took up a lecturing post in the United States he was replaced

by Milton Rosner, who was followed by Robert Atkins, who in turn
resigned in 1945, making way for Sir Barry Jackson and a new era at the
Memorial Theatre. Notable actors during the war included Baliol Hol-
loway, James Dale, Alex Clunes, John Laurie, and Claire Luce; apparently
Luce was responsible for a record attendance of 250,000 in the 1945 season.

21 Beauman gives an excellent account of the very different ethos that
emerged in Stratford-upon-Avon in the postwar years.

22 See also Laurence Olivier, *On Acting* (London: Weidenfeld and Nicholson,
1986), 60.

23 This drawing is reproduced in Strobl 211.

Works Cited

Beauman, Sally. *The Royal Shakespeare Company: A History of Ten Decades*.
Oxford: Oxford University Press, 1982.

Hitler, Adolf. *Mein Kampf*. Trans. Ralph Mannheim. London: Pimlico, 1992.

Howard, Tony. 'Shakespeare in the 1930s.' Ed. Clive Barker and Maggie B.
Gale. *British Theatre between the Wars, 1918–1939*. Cambridge: Cambridge
University Press, 2000. 135–61.

Ryback, Timothy W. *Hitler's Private Library*. London: Bodley Head, 2009.

Stratford-upon-Avon Herald, 9 February 1940: 1–2.

Stratford-upon-Avon Herald, 'Canadian Smiles,' 29 March 1940: 3.

Stratford-upon-Avon Herald, 6 September 1940: 1.

Stratford-upon-Avon Herald, 13 September 1940: 1.

Stratford-upon-Avon Herald, 'Shakespeare: Enemy of Fascism,' 17 April 1942: 1.

Stratford-upon-Avon Herald, 14 April 1944: 1.

Strobl, Gerwin. *The Swastika and the Stage: German Theatre and Society, 1933–
1945*. Cambridge: Cambridge University Press, 2009.

11 Rosalinds, Violas, and Other Sentimental Friendships: The Osiris Players and Shakespeare, 1939–1945

PETER BILLINGHAM

In act 2, scene 4, of Shakespeare's problematic comedy *Twelfth Night* (1602) the female character Viola, in role-disguise as the young man Cesario, is in dialogue with her/his newly found patron, the Duke Orsino:

VIOLA: My father had a daughter loved a man
   As it might be, perhaps were I a woman
   I should your Lordship.
ORSINO: And what's her history?
VIOLA: A blank my lord. She never told her love,
   But let concealment, like a worm i'th'bud,
   Feed on her damask cheek. She pined in thought,
   And with a green and yellow melancholy
   She sat like patience on a monument,
   Smiling at grief. Was not this love indeed? ...
ORSINO: But died thy sister of her love, my boy?
VIOLA: I am all the daughters of my father's house,
   And all the brothers too; and yet I know not. (107–20)

This short extract embodies some of the key themes and issues surrounding the unique but little-known touring British theatre company: the all-female Osiris Players, founded by a woman of impressive tenacity and commitment to the social and cultural value of theatre, Nancy Hewins (1902–78) (see fig. 11.1).

This company toured Shakespeare principally though not exclusively throughout the Second World War to villages and small towns, quite often playing in non-standard and even non-theatre venues to

11.1. Nancy Hewins as General Burgoyne in the Osiris production of Shaw's *The Devil's Disciple*. Photograph reproduced from Marie Crispin's copy of an Osiris promotional brochure. Photographer unknown.

war-torn communities throughout the west midlands of England. In doing so they reversed in gender terms the original performance conventions of the Elizabethan and Jacobean periods. They also demonstrated a remarkable commitment to a belief in the intrinsic cultural and restorative value of theatre and especially, canonically, the plays of Shakespeare. I first came across the Osiris Players as a minor, virtually forgotten footnote of British theatre history whilst researching my doctoral thesis from the late 1980s through into the early 1990s. My research, published under the title *Theatres of Conscience*, examined and discussed the work of four small British touring theatre companies during the Second World War and the two decades following 1945. The four companies were the Pilgrim Players, the Adelphi Players, the Compass Players, and the Century Theatre.

The Pilgrim Players were formed by Elliot Martin Browne, who was a close friend of T.S. Eliot and directed the premieres of all Eliot's verse dramas. Browne was also a friend and associate of George Bell, the Bishop of Chichester and an ardent and courageous public voice against the blanket-bombing of German cities in the latter part of the war, fearful of the mass numbers of German civilians that would suffer through this strategy. Bell was also in sympathetic and regular contact with the German liberal theologian Dietrich Bonheoffer, who was executed by the Nazis in April 1945 for his involvement in the unsuccessful plot to assassinate Hitler. Richard Heron Ward, the founder of the Adelphi Players, also had significant wider political and radical religious associations in that he was an activist in the Peace Pledge Union, which was founded in the mid-1930s in Britain as a cross-political if largely left-liberal anti-war coalition. Ward worked as a personal assistant to Canon Dick Shepherd, priest of St Martins in the Fields.[1] Both the Pilgrim Players and the Adelphi Players were committed to a vision of taking theatre to the people and especially so under the traumatic socio-cultural conditions of war. They were not in any sense propagandists in intention or repertoire but rather believed in the innate value of theatre to enrich and transform lives.

The important sense in which the conditions of war facilitated a renewed interest in cultural activities is central to a wider understanding of why companies such as the Osiris Players were necessary for public morale. It furthermore explains why their work was so welcomed, even if the quality and standard of production and acting was varied. The conditions of wartime undoubtedly highlighted that sense of cultural heritage in the darkness of those times. Of course there were other individuals and companies who contributed to and were committed to the therapeutic value of culture in wartime Britain. The Old Vic was a major presence both in London and the regions, although its charismatic founder Lillian Bayliss had passed away in 1937; Tyrone Guthrie took over her mantle and through the 1939–40 season his commitment to casting an 'all-star' company (including Robert Donat, John Gielgud, Lewis Casson, Cathleen Nesbitt, and Fay Compton) helped provide high-quality theatre in the opening year of the war. In November 1940 the Old Vic's Governing Council took the much criticized decision of moving the company out of London to a regional base, the Victoria Theatre in Burnley, Lancashire. Throughout the war Donald Wolfit, the legendary actor-manager made famous posthumously by Ronald Harwood's play *The Dresser*,[2] continued to perform in London and also toured the provinces.

I came across the existence also of the Osiris Players through the chance comments of a former actor with the Adelphi Players I had interviewed in 1986; it transpired that the Osiris had toured some of the same venues as the Adelphi. In the autumn of 2008 in another chance conversation, this time with Dr Philip Crispin of the drama department at the University of Hull, England, I mentioned my intention of trying to unearth details about the Osiris, possibly for an article or conference paper. He told me that his mother, Mrs Marie Crispin, a retired professional actress, had begun her acting career with the Osiris Players more than fifty years previously. While Marie Crispin did not join Osiris until 1955, the core company, which dated back to its prewar origins, was still in place, and she was thus able to share with me first-hand accounts related to working and living conditions with the prewar and wartime companies. In the postwar years theatre companies with the word 'Players' in their title were increasingly seen as 'amateur' in status,' so it is not surprising therefore that the Osiris Players were rechristened the Osiris Repertory Company in the post-1945 period.

I made arrangements to meet with Marie Crispin and interview her about her time with the Osiris Players. It was through this meeting that I began to find out more about this unique company. Equally importantly I gained access to a small but invaluable documentary collection of photographs, posters, and programs that she had kept over the years.[3] In this relatively short essay I can only hope to introduce the Osiris Players and place them in the wider context of touring theatre in Britain between 1939 and 1945. To that end, I will continue by returning to a short overview of other companies, including the Adelphi Players, the Pilgrim Players, and the Compass Players, and the values and ideals that inspired their work. The rest of this discussion will be devoted to an exploration of the Osiris, their origins, ideals, and challenging life on the road performing Shakespeare under the social, economic, and cultural conditions of wartime Britain.

The decade prior to the start of the Second World War had seen the emergence of what historians of the liberal left subsequently called the Popular Front in British social, cultural, and political life. It was a somewhat eclectic network, rather than a formal movement, with relatively fluid connections in places that embraced liberal and radical Anglican Christians such as Bishop Bell and Canon Shepherd. The Popular Front was also facilitated through individuals such as the publisher Victor Gollancz and his Left Book Review and Left Book Club. Socialists and pacifists within the Labour Party and the rapid rise in membership and

activity of the British Communist Party in the 1930s were other important signifiers of organized opposition to rising militarism and the
threat of fascism in Europe. In theatre the former association of amateur
working-class agit-prop groups known as the Workers' Theatre Movement coalesced into the Unity Theatre.[4] English choreographer Rupert
Doone (a former lover of Diaghilev) and his London-based Group
Theatre also played a significant role, utilizing talents and involvement
of W.H. Auden, Christopher Isherwood, and Benjamin Britten among
others. This company of principally gay artists with broadly left-wing
political aims and sympathies was also significant in a period when
homosexuality itself was illegal. While it would be simplistic to suggest
any deeper connection between the two companies, there is nevertheless some wider historical of evidence of artists creating work from an
effectively 'hidden' and counter-cultural position during this period.

It was out of these disparate strands that people such as the novelist and playwright Richard Ward founded the Adelphi Players and
the artist and anarchist-communist John Crockett established the Compass Players. Along with these two companies, Browne, who had also
directed the premiere of *Murder in the Cathedral*, went on to form the Pilgrim Players. The impetus for this touring theatre company was Bell's
founding of the Religious Drama Society of Great Britain in the late
1920s. At the outbreak of war, the British government, recognizing the
morale-boosting value of the arts, decided to support and facilitate the
performing arts – especially theatre, music, and dance – for the wartime population. The formation of the Council for the Encouragement
of Music and the Arts (CEMA) represents the first state-sponsored arts
production in Britain. At the close of the war the CEMA metamor-
phosed into the Arts Council of Great Britain. During the war CEMA
was able to facilitate the essential infrastructure for the provision and
organization of venues, subsidies for petrol vouchers (without which
motorized transport for touring would have been impossible), as well
as advertising and publicity. A total of seventeen other touring theatre
and dance companies supported by the Council for Education Music
and the Arts during the war years have been identified, including Joan
Littlewood's Theatre Workshop and the Ballet Joos, a contemporary
dance company of exiled Dutch dancers.

Not surprisingly in propaganda terms, the war against Germany in
particular was presented as a war and struggle for hearts and minds
between the traditional values of a Christian-oriented Western civilization and a similarly defined English cultural history against an ideology

that was violently opposed to such cultural and historical narratives. In this wider context Shakespeare as a dramatist and furthermore as a cultural icon of privileged values of 'humanity,' 'Christianity,' 'valour,' and 'truth' was the preeminent playwright to be supported and promoted by the authorities.

Universal suffrage for women was not achieved until 1928, eleven years prior to the outbreak of war, and prewar British society was also patriarchal and reactionary, demanding that women who were trained as teachers and nurses withdraw from these professions on becoming married. Against this social, cultural, and political backdrop, the emergence and existence of the Osiris Players constituted a remarkable paradox and contradiction. Here was a company of women committed to the mission of producing Shakespeare – but also playwrights such as Ibsen, Shaw, and Congreve – on their own terms. The initial and crucial drive and energy and the material means for the realization of this vision came from a young woman with a well-to-do, upper-class background named Nancy Hewins. The other young women who joined her idiosyncratic artistic crusade were also inevitably from the middle and upper-middle classes. This core of long-standing personnel included Kay Jones, ex-Somerville College, who had trained at the Old Vic and who served both as principal male lead and as Hewins's long-suffering personal assistant; she was also fellow lesbian (though not Hewins's lover). The class-demographics of the Osiris reflected the fact that in the prewar period educational opportunities for working-class women were basic, to say the least, providing at best a working literacy and numeracy and training in traditional 'female skills' such as cooking. In this crucial respect, the anti-patriarchal credo of the Osiris was as much if not more reflective of a degree of personal liberty dependent upon economic privilege as upon the wider emancipation of women. Unlike the later ground-breaking feminist theatre companies of postwar Britain – such as Monstrous Regiment and Clean Break, who embodied, fused, and questioned the politics of gender, sexuality, and the left – Osiris did not see itself in organized political opposition to reactionary or patriarchal views of women. While Hewins was undoubtedly a classic example of the kind of broadly progressive, university-educated, upper-class women of the period known as Bluestockings,[5] she saw her theatre work as principally an expression of the possibilities and potential of the theatre and of women; Hewins and her confederates were proud bearers of that term and its associations.

While it is true that the self-confessed 'revolutionary pacifist' of the 1930s Richard Ward sought not to conflate art and politics, the absence of any wider political sensibility in Hewins's vision and practice remains intriguing. As potentially and radically problematic and unsettling as the theatrical convention of 'boys-as-girls' in Elizabethan public playhouses undoubtedly was, Hewins's mid-twentieth-century 'girls-as-boys' equally, if without conscious self-regard, provoked the quasi-Freudian anxiety buried in the collective unconscious of the social establishment. Without wishing to attribute or privilege special meaning to a single character in one Shakespeare play, I would suggest that there is a kind of collective, socially and culturally constructed Freudian slip in Viola/Cesario's poignant existential paradox: 'I am all the daughters of my father's house and all my brothers too.' Here is a 'breeching' of the dominant conventions of the performance of gender roles: an anxiety of what unjust power relations were concealed and might be revealed.

If the fluidity and relativity of gender-formations implicit within that paradox were to provoke and necessitate social, economic, and political reality in mid-twentieth-century Britain, then who would iron the costumes and place them on their hangers in the stage that is the world? Furthermore, and possibly even more troublingly, who would decide who should wear which costumes and – embarrassment upon confusion – who would know who was kissing whom? What employment would chaperones find in such a world turned upside down? Might there indeed be an emerging world in which the very idea of a chaperone might not be needed and would become extinct?

The Osiris company was founded in 1927 as the Isis Players – an amateur theatre group committed to performing Shakespeare to the tough inner-city children of London's infamous East End. These two names are fascinating in terms of mythic connotations: the nature-goddess Isis was associated as both the wife of the Egyptian god Osiris but also though her own cult as the enactment of the destruction and resurrection of Osiris. One can only speculate as to the potential significance of the naming of the all-female professional company arising out of the origins of its amateur, female-named antecedent. Might Hewins have subconsciously imagined, notwithstanding the emancipation of women in the year following the new company's foundation, that a male-oriented name might subdue their all-female identity in a socially and culturally useful way?

Hewins continued to lead Osiris until its demise in 1963. Throughout its long existence' Osiris was based in her large country house in

11.2. Osiris company members loading the van with costumes and props in wartime Britain. Photograph reproduced from Marie Crispin's copy of an Osiris promotional brochure. Photographer unknown.

the Worcestershire countryside, a county adjoining onto Warwickshire: the birthplace and final resting place of course of William Shakespeare. There was a large barn in the grounds of her house, and it was here that the company not only rehearsed but also slept in the haystacks, regardless of the weather or time of the year. Before and after the war, they travelled in a Rolls-Royce and an Austin Healey, both motor-cultural indicators of class, wealth and esteem. The Austin towed a truck containing properties and costumes (see fig. 11.2), while the Rolls, always driven by Hewins, towed her personal caravan in which she lived a life of almost regal isolation. The fact that her car could accommodate seven passengers was the sole criteria in defining the size of the company. In the postwar years this seclusion was interrupted on a fortnightly basis when two actresses from the company would, on a strict rota system, cook for Hewins; as recompense they were allowed to sleep on bunkbeds in a curtained-off area of the caravan – a tangible reward considered against the deprivations of sleeping on the floors of church halls or in bales of hay in barns. During the war, however, owing to the severe and necessary rationing of petrol, Hewins, like Ward, was most suspicious of the interference that might accompany state support for their respective enterprises. While Ward partially compromised by accepting petrol vouchers to enable his company to travel further afield and reach even more theatre-starved communities, he refused to accept an annual payment from CEMA of fifty pounds (a significant amount of money at that time). Hewins would not compromise on either account; her company travelled, with some eccentricity, by horse and dray throughout the towns and villages of the Cotswolds from their base near Worcester. It was not until after the end of the war that the Rolls-Royce and the caravan were resurrected from their garages.

When Marie Crispin first came upon the company in 1955, she was just over twenty years of age and had completed training as a teacher, her first choice of actor-training having been discouraged by her parents. Nevertheless, having secured the employment security of her teacher's qualification, she was encouraged to explore any possibilities that might exist to find work as an actor. At that time Osiris, with a sublime audacity characteristic of Hewins throughout her very active life, was playing all-female, open-air Shakespeare in a public park in Stratford, only a stone's throw from the Stratford Memorial Theatre, with all of its associations of the high-cultural establishment. Crispin saw a performance and asked if she might be auditioned for the company. No audition was required; she joined in the late summer of that year and toured with them until May 1956. In the process she gained her Equity card – an absolute necessity if she was to earn her living as an actor.

Unlike Ward's Adelphi Players or Crockett's Compass Players, of the same era and however fractious or imperfect they proved in practice, there was no question of company meetings with the Osiris; furthermore, there was neither the will on the part of its founder nor the means in terms casts limited to seven performers, to discuss repertoire. Hewins ran the company as an essentially benign if sometimes bad-tempered autocrat. She ruthlessly 'edited' the plays they performed (long-standing Shakespeare favourites included *As You Like It*, *Macbeth*, *Julius Caesar*, and *Henry V*) but even these pragmatically abridged versions still necessitated multiple casting and playing. As Marie Crispin observed, one of the finest lessons she learned through her time with the Osiris was the 'fine art of the quick change.' Costumes and sets were fairly rudimentary and although Crispin remembers that, 'we made the language work reasonably well,' she also recollected, though not without fondness, that 'once invited to perform, there was seldom an invitation to return.'

As the journalist Paul Barker observed, 'The war was Hewins's finest hour. Osiris put on 1,534 performances of 33 plays, 16 of them

Shakespeare. For reasons of economy, the company was never larger than seven women. Everybody did everything: acting, props, cooking, changing tyres. On stage, scenes were cut and transposed to make the doubling work' (16).[6] Barker went on to describe their production of *Macbeth*, which he had seen as a child in a local West Yorkshire co-operative hall: 'Hewins played Lady Macbeth in a ferocious red wig, changing her make-up at top speed so that she could become the Porter within a few lines. By the time the company closed, in 1963, Hewins reckoned she had taken 129 parts herself, in 55 plays' (16).

Such ingenious adaptations of plays and re-editing of scenes to accommodate a small company was a common and regular necessity amongst other touring companies of the period; examples include Crockett's Compass production of Marlowe's *Dr Faustus* and Richard Ward's *Flora Whitely*, an assemblage of scenes and characters from Shakespeare. Ward, recognizing that wartime audiences had an insatiable appetite for Shakespeare but lacking the personnel or means to produce an additional, even abbreviated play, essentially employed a collage approach. Possessing two very strong actresses with prewar professional training and credits, Ward created a fictional older actress – Flora Whiteley – who in nostalgic reflection relives some of the major speeches from her career as a Shakeapearean actor. The play was very popular with audiences, providing a reassuring assemblage of familiar and well-loved speeches from Shakespeare's plays.

Like Hewins, Ward and Crockett also came from wealthy upper-class English backgrounds and all three were committed to an aim of 'theatre for the people' long before this phrase became the mantra of many left-wing theatre companies of the 1960s and 1970s, such as Red Ladder, Belt and Braces, and The General Will. Hewins's father was the first director of the London School of Economics and her godmother was the socialist activist and writer Beatrice Webb. She was educated at St Hugh's College, Oxford, in the 1920s, where she threw herself into the Drama Society (OUDS) with more enthusiasm than she showed for her studies, although although she did graduate with an Honours degree. Social class and economics combined with the perfect timing of a donation of forty pounds from her father's friend, the newspaper magnate Lord Rothersmere, enabled the fledgling Isis amateurs to turn professional with the inaugural Osiris production of *The Merchant of Venice* in December 1927. We know that this production toured schools in London's economically and socially infamous East End, but unfortunately there are no further details of specific venues or cast lists.

It was in the company's production of *As You Like It* in Kent, during the first decade after the Second World War that Marie Crispin made her first appearance with the company, and indeed her first professional acting role of any kind, playing Rosalind. Crispin recalled that the dramatic relationships of such characters mirrored what she termed many 'sentimental friendships' that inevitably grew in an all-female company living under such intense conditions. Such 'sentimental friendships' ranged from her own deep but platonic friendship with another new young actress (they had joined at the same time) to relationships that were clearly intimate and lesbian. Crispin commented that this spectrum of relationships rarely if ever created problems within the company, and remembered that should a romantic or emotional crisis temporarily flare up, Hewins's usual remedy was a teaspoon of brandy and a 'maternal' confidential chat. Hewins herself seems to have directed all of her own energies into the running of her beloved company and her own passionate commitment to acting: this passion was, however, of questionable and certainly erratic quality. Like her male counterpart of that generation, the legendary actor-manager Donald Wolfit, she led by autocratic example and brooked no dissent. Wolfit, unlike Hewins, was an actor of undoubted power and charisma, but both leaders shared a view that there was a central spotlight on them in whatever principal role they were performing. The sole task of the rest of the cast was to remain outside its illuminating radiance.

In later years Hewins said, in explanation of not marrying, that: 'I always loathed being tied in any way and couldn't have run a career and a household' (qtd by Crispin). In a period when male homosexuality was a criminal offence and many men lived in terrible fear and guilt, lesbianism endured rather disturbing invisibility, both socially and culturally; in British society it was not so much 'the love that dare not speak its name' but rather the love that had no name to speak of.

As Marie Crispin clearly recalls, the company's sole commitment was to the play itself and especially to Shakespeare, with Hewins's often repeated assertion that 'the play must come alive and speak directly.' A concrete instance of this strong sense of the immediacy and materiality of theatre and of Shakespeare came in a production of *Macbeth*: Marie Crispin (cast as both the Porter and one of the Three Witches) playing to a school audience in rural West Ireland was nervously touched by a young boy who announced, astonished, to his friends 'She's real you know!' The Osiris toured south and west in the Republic of Ireland with increasing frequency in the post-1945 years. This reflected a substantial demand for productions of Shakespeare in schools in Ireland, a principally rural country outside of a relatively small number of cities and towns. At the same time the demand for touring theatre in England that had been present in wartime was now shrinking, a reflection of the sudden return to more traditional models of employment as women were encouraged to return to or remain in the home as domestic providers. Furthermore it was evidence of the seminal Arts Council's policy decision in the first decade after the war to support building-based theatres and limit if not discourage touring theatre. Osiris toured schools and Catholic seminaries principally; it is hoped that further research will facilitate a more detailed tracing of touring routes and venues.

Osiris was to all intents and purposes, like the Adelphi, Pilgrim, and Compass Players, a cooperative with shareholders limited to current members of the company. In wartime the Adelphi Players paid themselves what they called the 'Tommy rate' of £2 per week,[7] regardless of role or status within the company. After the war, Actors' Equity (the actor's union) insisted on an actor's minimum wage. Marie Crispin and the others were paid ten shillings a week plus 'all found' (that is, board and lodging, however basic, provided free of charge). During the war, to eke out their meagre payment and also, no doubt, to further demonstrate their war-labour commitment, actors in the company made gas-mask cases and took jobs in Cotswold shops, always pooling their money and eating a great deal of black pudding, a common wartime dish.[8]

In June 2004 *We Happy Few*, a play inspired by the Osiris company, written by and starring Imogen Stubbs, opened in London's West End at the Gielgud Theatre. While Hewins, no doubt, would have been pleased that her company and lifelong vision had not been consigned to the dusty lower shelves of English theatre history, she would equally certainly have been as unconvinced by the play's rather idealized account of the sepia-tinted past. Unfortunately *We Happy Few* endured very mixed reviews, resulting in a short run, and it disappeared with depressing speed.

In conclusion, the Osiris actors were not motivated or driven by any overt or explicit ideological or left-liberal feminist values or aspirations. Nevertheless, in supporting the national war effort by bringing their productions of Shakespeare to many communities who previously might not have seen either his or any other plays, I believe that the Osiris company was waging another equally crucial if 'secret' war, a war against reactionary hearts and minds in British society of that time regarding the role, status, and legitimate aspirations of women. Just as working-class women, such as my own mother, discovered a new economic and personal independence through doing 'men's work' in factories during the Second World War, the Osiris actors were also doing 'men's work' while reversing the politics of representation of the late sixteenth- and early to mid-seventeenth-century stage. It is interesting, in this respect, that Marie Crispin remembers that Hewins did not see the company as 'women-playing-men' but rather as actors playing Shakespeare, with zeal and to the best of their intentions. The standard of acting was varied and the necessities of touring theatre under such conditions meant that sets and costumes were basic and often improvised, but Nancy Hewins and the others were breaking exciting new ground.

Who ironed the costumes, who chose which ones to wear, and who kissed whom, and who had the empowerment of enacted gender and social status to *choose* whom to kiss was an existential, political, and social challenge lived by millions of women (and homosexual men) long after the Osiris actors had taken their costumes off for the final time. Government and state propaganda in the immediate postwar period was powerful and unrelenting in its insistence upon women returning to their 'natural' place in the home and their equally 'natural' role as homemakers. For any woman who had the opportunity to see the Osiris in production, might not their performances have suggested at least a passing thought that there could be yet other 'unnatural' opportunities for them as women? If it were 'unnatural' for women to love women, and men to love men, and for women to 'become men' in these robust Shakespearean productions, then what kind of 'natural law' or morality had authorized men to 'become women' five hundred years before?

The fact that women were increasingly and ultimately able to begin to answer that question for themselves and on their own terms, and to consider 'her story' as well as the 'his story' of patriarchal readings of social, cultural, and political change, was contributed to in no small measure by the pioneering work of Nancy Hewins and the actors of the Osiris Players. The artistic quality of the company was undoubtedly varied, although it included some fine individual performances from those who had received professional training. Nancy Hewins herself (a 'large Lady Macbeth in a bright red wig' as Marie Crispin fondly recalled) was almost certainly more successful in her real-life role as entrepreneurial visionary than in any role she played on stage.

Orsino asks 'Cesario' of his sister: 'What was her history?' It was of course a hidden and secret history that societal pressures and prejudices required to be disguised, even as Viola could only find a public voice by adopting a fictional male persona. It was also a history that would inevitably form my post-Marxist cultural materialist reading of human history and evolution, a narrative that would welcome and encompass others who are marginalized, whether in terms of race, ethnicity, sexual orientation, or class. For every Cesario there was also a Caliban or Bianca.

It is a history that is still being written and we should remember and express our thanks to those women of the Osiris across the three decades of the company's existence for writing a small but key passage of progressive change through their efforts: truly a labour of love. As for me – pass me that iron! Let's 'press' on!

Notes

1 St Martins in the Fields, London, is a handsome neo-Classical church designed by Sir Christopher Wren, architect of St Paul's Cathedral.
2 *The Dresser* was later made into a film starring Tom Courtenay and Albert Finney.
3 This essay and the further research I intend to carry out on Osiris could not have happened without her enthusiasm and willingness to be interviewed and share her memories. All quotations and other information from Marie Crispin come from personal interviews I conducted with her in December 2008. I dedicate this essay to her and to that intrepid band of female actors and their indomitable leader and founder, Nancy Hewins.
4 In 1939 Richard Ward commented that the Unity Theatre had 'died of propaganda.'
5 The term Bluestocking, used to refer to an intellectual or literary woman, has its origins in mid to late eighteenth-century London society. A social group formed in England's capital city in 1750 by three women – Hannah More, Elizabeth Montagu, and Elizabeth Carter – met for literary discussions. Certain progressive-minded male scholars and writers also attended, and it was the fashionably informal blue woollen stockings worn by Benjamin Stillingfeet that gave the group its enduring name.
6 Barker's article, published in the English liberal-left newspaper *The Guardian* in 2004, was only the second article about the Osiris ever to appear.
7 The so-called Tommy rate was the weekly wage received by an army infantry man or 'Tommy.'

8 Black pudding (sometimes called pig's pudding) is an old, traditional form of inexpensive meat produce. In appearance it resembles a large sausage, coloured black with a white mosaic pattern through it. As it provided a very cheap form of meat and protein it was always associated with the urban and rural working class. In recent years it has enjoyed a wholly unexpected revival in the context of a resurgence of 'traditional' English foods and menus.

Works Cited

Barker, Paul. 'Shakespeare's Sisters.' *The Guardian* 26 June 2004: 16.

Billingham, P. *Theatres of Conscience 1939–53: A Study of Four Touring British Community Theatres*. London: Routledge Harwood, 2002.

Shakespeare, William. *Twelfth Night*. Oxford: Oxford University Press, 1994.

12 Maurice Evans's *G.I. Hamlet*: Analogy, Authority, and Adaptation

ANNE RUSSELL

The best known American Shakespeare production of the war years, Paul Robeson's *Othello*, has received much attention, overshadowing Maurice Evans's widely publicized production of *Hamlet* for US Army troops in Hawaii in 1944, a period of intense fighting throughout the Pacific.[1] Evans's shortened version of *Hamlet* was performed from 28 October 1944 to 9 December 1944 at two theatres, one in Honolulu and one at Schofield Barracks, a few miles north of Honolulu. Evans had planned to tour the production to non-traditional locations, writing, 'Some of our theatres would be open to the sky too, a sky interlaced with searchlights and tracer bullets' (Preface 15), but the only performance of *Hamlet* in 'field conditions' that has been documented by military historian Jack Shulimson took place on 18 December with basic staging (263). In 1945–6, Michael Todd produced Evans's adaptation as *The G.I. Hamlet* on Broadway for a total of 147 performances, followed by a coast-to coast tour.[2] The script – *Maurice Evans' G.I. Production of Hamlet by William Shakespeare: Acting Edition* – was published with a preface by Evans in 1947. The New York production of *The G.I. Hamlet* facilitated Evans's postwar prestige as a producer and actor, providing a launching pad for the next stage of his civilian career.[3]

In the preface to the *Acting Edition* Evans emphasizes that he drastically shortened the script for his military audience because of the limited free time available to soldiers. In deciding how to cut the play, Evans wanted to emphasize elements that he believed could raise 'troop morale' by an 'oblique approach' (22). He wanted the play to seem topical and immediate for the audience of soldiers, many of whom had never seen Shakespeare. The costuming was largely military, and the detailed stage directions prescribe movements and tones of voice emphasizing a martial and active interpretation of some lines and characters. Evans authorizes his most striking alteration – the complete omission of the graveyard scene in act 5 – by stressing that he was following the example set by the eighteenth-century actor and adaptor of Shakespeare, David Garrick, and further justifies his changes by invoking the presumed authority and approval of Shakespeare himself. While asserting that Shakespeare's works are universal and for all time, Evans also felt it necessary to make significant cuts for an audience of American soldiers in the Pacific campaign.

Before examining this production more closely, a few words should be said about Shakespeare's role in American culture. Shakespeare's status had long been contested in the United States. While the Bard's works had the prestige of high art, they were also criticized for representing hierarchical, monarchical, and English perspectives that were regarded as alien to a republic. Thomas Cartelli and Kim C. Sturgess, among others, have noted that, as Cartelli puts it, 'for many nineteenth-century Americans, Shakespeare functioned as a privileged medium through which a self-consciously postcolonial society could both address and construct its differences from the society which had preceded it' (30). Documenting some of the many ways nineteenth-century American performers parodied and appropriated Shakespeare in performances and adaptations, Sturgess sees not only differences but recognition of similarities, suggesting that Shakespeare was frequently performed in part because the plot and action of many of his plays could be read from specifically American perspectives.[4] By the 1930s, as Michael Bristol has shown, Shakespeare was institutionalized and Americanized to a considerable degree, most evidently by Henry Clay Folger's symbolically-sited Shakespeare Library on Capitol Hill in Washington (opened in 1932), which made Shakespeare 'a crucial link or point of mediation within what is now conceived as a historically unified Anglo-American culture' (76).

Hamlet's role within American culture similarly shifted and changed as Shakespeare's significance was continuously reread throughout the course of the nineteenth and twentieth centuries. As Shakespeare became 'Americanized,' so did Hamlet. The idea of Shakespeare as representing essentially American values coincided with scholarly efforts 'to restore Hamlet as an active hero' (Foakes 30) by reconfiguring him as an active figure in search of good (rather than as a vacillating and weak Prince).[5] The tension between old and new perspectives of Hamlet – as an indecisive figure whose faults lie deep within himself, and as a more morally aware and dynamic figure who confronts a corrupt society – play out in criticism in the first few decades of the twentieth century;[6] some of these ideas seem to have influenced Evans's full-length production of *Hamlet* on Broadway in 1938. By 1944, when the Americans were fully engaged in the Second World War and had experienced the disaster at Pearl Harbor, Evans had new reasons to make his Hamlet particularly heroic, masculine, and American. But, in order to construct this vision of Hamlet, Evans needed to cut significant passages from the play.

In explaining his reasons for revising *Hamlet* as he did, Evans begins with practical arguments. He needed to keep the running time to two hours and forty-five minutes so that the soldiers could return to base at the required time (Preface 9). Evans's two-act adaptation (with seven and eight scenes respectively) makes many of the traditional or conventional cuts to the play with which he was familiar (10–11), but he could not reduce the play to the required length until he decided to omit the gravedigger scene.[7] In discussing this omission, Evans alludes to several issues of aesthetics and authority that he does not explicitly acknowledge or analyse. As a performer who had played Hamlet many times, his familiarity with the play and its stage traditions may have occluded his understanding of the challenges the play might pose to soldiers not familiar with the high art tradition associated with Shakespeare and *Hamlet*. Throughout the preface, Evans is direct about his desire to raise 'troop morale' by the performance, yet reticent about aspects of the play that might resist his morale-building intentions. His particularly evasive discussion of the graveyard scene suggests he had unacknowledged anxieties about presenting this play, and this scene in particular, to a military audience in wartime.

There were three distinct contexts and audiences for the production of Evans's *Hamlet*. Soldiers at the performances in Honolulu attended relatively conventional theatres, in a staging zone for the war in the Pacific, close to the ruins of Pearl Harbor but largely removed from immediate fighting. These theatres had proscenium stages, sets, lighting, and ushers. A few civilians also attended, and the performance was discussed in the local press and featured in a piece by Quentin Reynolds in *Colliers Magazine* on 24 March 1945 (Shulimson 263). The one known audience in 'field conditions' included soldiers in a camp closer to combat zones, of which there were many: by late 1944, US troops in the Pacific were involved in major ground fighting on Leyte, naval battles, and airstrikes to prepare for future invasions. Evans does not discuss this outdoor performance in the 1947 preface to the acting text, but his 1987 memoir describes the soldiers at this camp as 'a mixture of troops brought for rest from the fighting … and those preparing to be shipped out' (177). But the largest audience by far was for the postwar Broadway production and subsequent tour, which producer Michael Todd named *The G.I. Hamlet* (*Memoir* 181). These varied contexts are relevant in understanding the gaps and differences in accounts of the play's reception and reputation. The few available accounts of the Hawaii performances suggest that in its wartime context and locations *Hamlet* was not as unambiguously successful with soldier audiences as Evans had hoped. In contrast, *The G.I. Hamlet* was very successful in New York and on the country-wide tour, as the postwar audience appreciated the production from the secure perspective of victory and peace.

Maurice Evans had been acting in the USA since 1935 and had taken citizenship in 1941. In 1942, after receiving a preliminary draft notice, he contacted 'influential military people' and offered to bring the Broadway production of *Macbeth*, in which he was currently playing with Judith Anderson, to Fort Meade, Maryland for three performances (*Memoir* 155). The production was considered successful; and one result was that Evans was offered a commission in the Army Specialist Corps to help organize military entertainment (*Memoir* 156; Shulimson 256–8). A few months later Evans was sent to Hawaii where he was responsible for organizing comedies, variety shows, satirical reviews, and other entertainments (Preface 23). Shulimson notes that 'to service the more isolated outposts, Evans formed small musical units, dubbed 'Five Jerks and a Jeep,' which performed throughout the Pacific' (259). In his memoir Evans recounts asking a chaplain who disapproved of the sexual innuendo in one review 'if he would rather see us doing something more uplifting … Shakespeare, for instance? … So it was with the church's blessing that we plunged into a play about the powers of darkness, murder, and violence' (162–3). After this conversation, Evans was authorized to bring the earlier *Macbeth* production with Judith Anderson to Hawaii, where he told a reporter that he wanted to produce *Macbeth* 'because it had so many parallels for the present' without elaborating what parallels he found important (qtd in Shulimson 260).[8] In his 1947 preface, Evans says that he chose *Macbeth* and then *Hamlet* for production 'to leaven the otherwise giddy fare in which we … indulged with occasional productions of somewhat more substantial character' (9) and to provide 'a little spiritual refreshment' (22) with the aim of representing 'Shakespeare's eternal verities in the spirit of these times' (24). Evans's retrospective account of his discussion with the chaplain suggests that the cultural authority of Shakespeare played a significant role in making *Macbeth*'s violent content acceptable to the military hierarchy; the success of *Macbeth* in Hawaii was one element in Evans's decision to produce another Shakespeare tragedy, *Hamlet*, for the military.

Evans was already familiar with the role of Hamlet, which he had played in London in 1935 and again in 1938, when he produced a complete version of *Hamlet* on Broadway; the performance was so long that it had a dinner break catered by Sardi's restaurant. In his memoir he proudly quotes a review of 13 October 1938 in the *New York Post* by John Mason Brown praising him in this production as 'the first entirely masculine Hamlet' (134). Though Evans does not say so specifically, an army production was an ideal chance to further develop a 'masculine' interpretation of the character.

In the preface to the acting edition, in contrast to his apparent confidence about the relevance of *Macbeth*, Evans's comments on *Hamlet* seem sensitive to the possibility of political misreading or misinterpretation. He stresses the unfamiliarity of the play to much of his soldier audience when discussing why he chose to retain or cut particular passages. For example, in the first scenes, he cut references to Fortinbras and the discussion of the 'political background' because he wanted 'alternative means ... of suggesting visually the threat of war which Shakespeare was stressing in these political speeches' (10). The first appearance of Fortinbras comes in act 2, scene 6, marching across Denmark to attack Poland (150); here, soon after the defeat of the Warsaw uprising, the ensuing discussion of battles over 'a little patch of ground' would seem to make the play seem more relevant to the war in Europe, as would Fortinbras's return 'from the Polack wars' in the final scene. But Evans appeared either uninterested or unwilling to develop this political reading by emphasizing references to the war in Poland and to Fortinbras's role as the military commander who would take over after Hamlet's death. Instead, Evans wanted to make the play 'intrinsically entertaining' (15) and to make 'action ... the keynote of our production' (16). He saw Hamlet as unquestioningly heroic, yet also as 'a character in whom every G.I. would see himself vaguely reflected – a man compelled to champion his conception of right in a world threatened by the domination of evil,' a man 'thoroughly normal' (16). The well-known convention of representing Hamlet as a 'princely philosopher ... incapable of wreaking the revenge urged by the ghost' was 'too special, too abnormal for our purpose' (17). A Freudian reading would not succeed because 'a G.I. who brooded too much ... soon found himself behind the padded doors' (18). Evans cuts lines 'dangerous for a soldier audience' such as 'Something is rotten in the state of Denmark' without giving a reason (11). It is 'wiser' to omit Ophelia's description of Hamlet, which 'includes "his knees knocking together"' (11). The acting version also silently omitted other passages that might make Hamlet unstable or not sufficiently 'normal,' such as Claudius's description of Hamlet's 'unmanly grief.'

Cuts such as these indicate that Evans was aware that the character of a Hamlet representing an American soldier must be made less complex and contradictory than a Hamlet in Shakespeare's text in order to fulfil the production's political purpose of representing Hamlet as 'thoroughly normal,' moral, and straightforward, a virtuous and soldierly character with whom the soldiers could identify; in other words, a 'regular G.I.':

> Our audiences were composed entirely of men on the eve of going into battle or those who were staggering with fatigue and confusion after their first encounter with the enemy. Each of them was in his own way a Hamlet, bewildered by the uninvited circumstances in which he found himself and groping for the moral justification and the physical courage demanded of him. (Preface 17)

Yet in so explicitly expecting individual audience members to respond to the play by seeing Hamlet's experience as analogous to their own situations, Evans apparently recognized the possibility that some analogical readings would be 'dangerous for a soldier audience.' In spite of his efforts to revise the play to enhance the soldiers' sense of 'moral justification' for their roles in battle, the play's complex elements offer much material that is not particularly amenable to confidence and self-assurance. In order to deemphasize some of these elements, Evans used sets and costumes, as well as significant cuts, to make the play more accessible to the soldier audiences.

The costuming was primarily military. After seeing an officer on the street 'in the full-dress uniform of a South American naval attaché,' Evans decided that by dressing characters in military uniforms of different periods and ranks 'the comparative timelessness of uniforms ... [would] remove the play from any specific period' (Preface 20). He decided that the guards in the first scene should wear uniforms 'so close in general design to a modern soldier's greatcoat and cap that one would think for a moment that the play was being performed in modern times' (21). Overall, he wanted to 'suggest visually the imminence of war' in Denmark and to 'emphasize for our soldier audience the immediacy of the happenings' (21). Many of the musical cues are for trumpets or '*March music*' (43), thus adding to the military atmosphere.

In the acting edition, the first stage direction for act 1, scene 1 describes '*Francisco, a young officer muffled in greatcoat and wearing a sword*'; all the other characters in this scene are described as '*in uniform*' (30). A long stage direction at the beginning of scene 2 describes Claudius's courtiers '*in full dress uniform*' surrounding Claudius, '*resplendent in a gorgeous uniform*' (38) and accompanying Gertrude, '*bejeweled and handsome*' (39). Polonius '*in black knee breeches and swallowtail coat*' (39) accompanies them. In contrast, Hamlet's later self-description of his 'customary suits of solemn black' is signalled with a stage direction describing him as '*a solitary figure dressed in a black uniform*' (38). The set is dominated by '*two throne chairs*' and '*jubilant music*' is playing (38). The many different styles of dress, vivid colours, and music contrasted with the black-uniformed Hamlet to emphasize his isolation. Laertes's costume in scene 2 is not described, but in scene 3 he is presented as younger and less mature than Hamlet by virtue of '*a suit which suggests the garb of a student of a military college*' with a '*vizored cap*' (52) and '*cape*' (54). Ophelia is '*simply and demurely dressed … plying her needle*' (52). When Rosencrantz and Guildenstern arrive at a party scene at the beginning of act 1, scene 6, they are excluded from military seriousness: '*by their appearance, one would judge [they] are college students*' (80).

Many of the explicit stage directions in Evans's acting text indicate Hamlet's motives, suppress ambiguity, and present him as a character blocked by external circumstances – rather than doubt – from his morally righteous revenge. (Righteous revenge might be a familiar emotion for audiences so close to Pearl Harbor.) Stage directions for Claudius and Laertes emphasize their anger, hastiness, and treachery. Gertrude is not given much attention in the early stage directions, and is relatively unimportant until the closet scene, in which Hamlet completely dominates her. Stage directions for Ophelia's truncated part make much of her submissiveness, and represent her as almost childlike in the mad scene. Overall, Hamlet as the central character is represented as betrayed by everyone except his few male confidantes. He is certain of Claudius's guilt from the beginning, and does not seriously seem to seek evidence of the Ghost's claims, in spite of the staging of the play-within-a-play. His response to learning of Ophelia's knowledge that they are being spied on is angry and bitter. One consequence of the omission of the gravedigger scene is that Hamlet does not learn of Ophelia's death, so there is no quarrel with Laertes as to who claims to have loved her best. Gertrude's death is also barely acknowledged by Hamlet and his endorsement of Fortinbras in the final scene, removed from the context of their fathers' rivalries, seems to be merely a change of command rather than a marking of the extinction of two families and a royal dynasty.

Hamlet's first soliloquy is introduced with the stage direction '*he regards the empty thrones and speaks in a tone of bitter disgust*' (43). Throughout the soliloquy he moves between window, table, and thrones, addressing 'Hyperion to a satyr' and 'Frailty thy name is woman' directly to the thrones, the last '*angrily*' (44). The anger of Hamlet is also emphasized in act 2, scene 4, shortly after the Ghost's 'adieu.' The lines 'That one may smile, and smile, and be a villain! / At least I'm sure it may be so in Denmark. / So uncle, there you are!' are followed by the stage direction '*With his sword hilt carves the initial 'C' on the battlement wall, then viciously eradicates this symbol with an 'X'*' (67). This vicious and symbolic obliteration of Claudius emphasizes Hamlet's immediate will to revenge, and is reinforced a few lines later when '*Pressing the hilt of his sword to his lip,*' he says, 'So be it' (68).

Other stage directions indicate Hamlet's anger and drive. He '*shouts*' at Polonius (89) and later '*snatches*' a letter from Guildenstern (92). Just before the soliloquy beginning 'O what a rogue and peasant slave am I,' the stage direction indicates that his tone is '*bitter self-denunciation*' (100), and in the course of the soliloquy he '*raises a clenched fist over the King's throne*' and a few lines later '*strikes the back of the throne*' (101). After the king calls for light during the staging of the play-within-a-play, Hamlet '*leaps on the throne which Claudius has vacated, shouting*' (122). He is no less angry with Ophelia, throwing her letters to the floor '*with a bitter ejaculation* (108). Many other stage directions emphasize Hamlet's resentment, energy, and violent temper.

Before the duel in the final scene begins, Laertes is even angrier than Hamlet. Returning to court after Polonius's death, he first attacks the guard outside as '*A burst of rapid rifle fire is heard*' followed by the sound of a door being broken down. '*Advancing, sword drawn,*' he cries, 'Give me my father.' It is Gertrude who '*hurls herself in his path*' and later '*restrains him*' from using his sword on Claudius (159). In these and other stage directions, Laertes is represented as especially dangerous, an interpretation developed in the duel scene between Hamlet and Laertes when, at Osric's line 'Nothing, either way,' Laertes '*strikes Hamlet in the back. Stung by this treachery, Hamlet advances*' (182) and a few lines later '*rushes furiously at Laertes, beating down his defence, and stabs him*' (183). Claudius is '*stabbed by the onrushing Hamlet*' (184). After Fortinbras's arrival from the Polack wars to 'embrace my fortune,' Horatio asks him to 'give order that this body / High on a stage be placed to the view' (186). Evans's text here alters Horatio's reference to 'these bodies' to place the focus squarely on Hamlet, disregarding the 'collateral damage' represented by the bodies strewn on the stage. The final tableau of the play is of '*Scarlet clad captains ... bearing Hamlet on their shoulders.*' The last stage direction reads, '*The roar of distant cannon punctuates the triumphant crescendo in the music as the soldiers raise the body into a shaft of dazzling light. The curtain falls*' (187).

The apotheosis of Hamlet to the sound of cannon and triumphant music raises questions about how the soldiers in the audience, considered by Evans as in many ways analogous to Hamlet, might have responded. Hamlet's sacrifice is praised and elevated, but he himself does not survive. If a soldier had come to regard Hamlet's position as analogous to his own, the death of his alter ego in the play might compromise Evans's aim to boost morale. The corpses of the other characters on stage are disregarded, as the staging shifts from a focus on multiple deaths to the concentration on one death. The uncertain implication for the soldiers of the death by treachery of the hero who represents them is only one of the ways in which the material of *Hamlet* might be resistant to a morale-building aim.

However, the most troubling part of the play for morale-building is the gravedigger scene. Although Evans is often explicit about his politically grounded decisions for making changes to the play, his argument for eliminating the entire graveyard scene is less than straightforward. He devotes more discussion to the cutting of the graveyard scene than to any other issue, and he offers several arguments, none of which explicitly allude to the political and military issues that otherwise occupy him. In a production so insistently claiming wartime relevance, it is paradoxical, yet also understandable, to omit a scene representing the materiality of death and burial. But rather than acknowledging these troubling themes, Evans invokes aesthetics, theatrical precedents, and imagination.

He begins his long explanation for eliminating the graveyard scene by stressing that because of the early curfew for the soldiers he had to find a way to take another fifteen minutes out of a performance that he had already cut as much as he thought possible. While consulting other acting editions, Evans 'lighted on an old prompt script of David Garrick's *Hamlet*' and 'felt emboldened to follow his example and strike out altogether the graveyard scene' (Preface 12). One of the happy consequences of this cut is its conformity to the presumed aesthetic expectations of the audience, since 'our warrior audiences had very fixed ideas about comedy, and considered themselves authorities upon what was funny and what was not' (13). Since some unnamed 'radio comedians' had not been popular with the troops, the gravediggers' jokes would be condemned as 'corny' (13). However, Evans does not avoid corny humour at other points in the production. He keeps some of Polonius's inadvertent jokes and retains much of Hamlet's sardonic wit and all of his coarse punning to Ophelia before the play-within-a-play. In the exchange between Hamlet and Osric, stage directions that would be at home in vaudeville have Osric take his hat on or off whenever Hamlet changes his mind about the weather (173). Evans's implicit association of radio comedy, the gravedigger scene, and low comedy distracts attention from more serious aspects of the scene that might quite legitimately disturb an audience of soldiers, such as discussions of 'pocky corses,' varying rates of decomposition, and the smell of mortality. These elements, as well as Hamlet's meditation on Yorick's skull, and Laertes's and Hamlet's leaps into Ophelia's grave, might be expected to remind army audiences of some of the grim material conditions of the war they were fighting, diverting them from a proper appreciation of Hamlet's romanticized, soldierly death at the end of the play. It is likely that Evans was worried not so much by corny comedy as by the particularly grotesque implications for soldiers of some of the props, jokes, and actions in the scene.

Although he begins his detailed justification for omitting the graveyard scene by stressing how conveniently it solved his problem with performance time and conformed to soldiers' generic expectations of comedy, Evans also invokes two authorities of the past – David Garrick, the eighteenth-century actor-manager who specialized in Hamlet, and William Shakespeare himself. Evans explains that he cut the graveyard scene after he 'lighted on an old prompt script of David Garrick's.' Like many other eighteenth-century critics, including Samuel Johnson and George Steevens, both of whom had edited Shakespeare,

Garrick disapproved of the mixture of comedy and tragedy in *Hamlet*, particularly the gravediggers and Osric (Tomarken 26–7). Garrick published an acting version of *Hamlet* in 1763 that omitted part of the gravedigger scene, and in 1772 he staged a production that completely cut the gravediggers and 'all the rubbish of the fifth act' (Garrick; qtd in Johnson 14), a production he repeated over the next seven years (Stone 904–5). Most discussions of Garrick's life and career make reference to this famous adaptation, in which Hamlet asks Laertes and Horatio to rule after his death. (Evans does not follow Garrick to save Laertes.)[9]

Evans's appeal to Garrick's authority and example indicates that the two actor/adaptors share several aesthetic judgments about *Hamlet*, though these judgments are not clearly articulated by Evans. Like Garrick and many other eighteenth-century critics, Evans seems to disapprove of the mixture of the comic and the serious at key points in the play. Evans's understanding of the character of Hamlet also has much in common with Garrick's. One critical assessment of Garrick's representation of Hamlet is that, as Leigh Woods puts it, 'Hamlet as a hero is 'scaled down' by Garrick's decision to present the character ... as a man of affairs, a collaborator, and an equal' (72).[10] This description of Garrick's practice has much in common with Evans's intentions, as expressed in his preface, to present Hamlet as 'thoroughly normal.' Garrick's cuts, like Evans's, also tend to focus attention on Hamlet (and the star actor) at the expense of other characters, though Evans does not acknowledge this effect.[11]

Garrick is not the only authority Evans invokes to justify cutting the graveyard scene. He repeatedly asserts that Shakespeare would have agreed with his revisions of the play in general as well as with his thinking on the graveyard scene in particular. Evans makes several references to his intention to 'reaffirm the eternal truth of Shakespeare's vision' (Preface 7), asserting that 'every age ... has been able to stage his plays according to the fashion of the moment, without departing materially from the original text or intention' (8). While acknowledging that he 'must speak in a voice understandable to our own time' (9), Evans also claims common ground with Shakespeare himself since, like Shakespeare, Evans had to stage plays in noisy open-air spaces (15). There are other ways in which he believes his situation is like Shakespeare's: 'As a poet, of course, his vision was timeless, but as a playwright, in this instance, he emphasized the modernity of the theme of his play in order to illustrate the universality of the tragedy' (16). Yet in attempting to make the play modern, relevant, applicable to a GI audience, and also 'universal,' Evans complicates the idea of universality he claims. If that universality could be achieved only by significant cuts of the text, which would seem to be a definition of 'departing materially from the original text,' how can the play as a whole still have claims to universality?

Evans makes even more specific claims that he understands Shakespeare's intentions in writing the play, arguing that the gravedigger scene includes inconsistencies particularly apparent to the actor of Hamlet, especially the transition from his 'frenzied' exit from the graveyard to his entrance 'only seven lines later, chatting blithely with Horatio,' a transition Evans finds difficult 'to make with any kind of grace or conviction' (12). So dissatisfied is Evans with the effects of this scene that he states: 'I believe there are very real grounds for guessing that the graveyard scene was an addition to the original text, and that it was written in for some reason as simple as that Shakespeare had forgotten to include a part for the Globe's favorite comedian' (12–13). The suggestion that Shakespeare would forget to include a part for the company's comedian is another sign of Evans's uneasiness about the appropriateness of the comic aspects of *Hamlet*. In spite of his argument that the play should be generically consistent, terms such as 'believe' and 'guessing' suggest discomfort with his speculative arguments. Later Evans refers to his theory that the scene is 'a Shakespearean afterthought' as 'an actor's hunch' which is 'comforting' (13). Evans's uneasiness about his 'guess' may also indicate a displaced anxiety about the overall effect of *Hamlet* on the troops, since he devotes far more space to justifying the cut of the graveyard scene than he does to any other aspect of his adaptation.

The Honolulu production of the '*G.I. Hamlet*' ran for seven weeks (*Memoir* 176) with a total of 44 performances for about 52,000 audience members (Shulimson 263). There is little specific contemporary information on its reception in Hawaii and the Pacific in 1944 other than Quentin Reynolds's comment that, 'Evans the consummate artist was never greater. The khaki-clad audience followed every word of the soliloquy' (qtd in Shulimson 263). In 1990 Richard Gilman recalled his own attendance as a soldier at a performance in Hawaii, observing that Evans 'pared the play … on the assumption, one supposes, that military men, for whom Evans largely intended it, had an attention span no longer than that. Evans, by the way, was a rather overripe Hamlet' ('Stage View'). In a letter responding to Gilman, Joe Coogan, cast as 'Player Villain,' described the opening night response:

as I remember, on opening night 'Hamlet' seemed like a flop. There was barely a murmur of response from the house, and a fair amount of gloom backstage. We were later told that the audience had been reminded that this was not some cheap skin show but a classic, and that they were to show respect for Shakespeare and for Hamlet, who happened to be, by God, an officer in the United States army. With this misunderstanding cleared up, future audiences became more enthusiastic. (Letter)

The official warning against seeing the play as a 'cheap skin show' suggests the audience might not have been completely attentive and engaged, and suggests how unusual the production would have been for many audience members. The instruction that audiences 'respect' Hamlet as an officer makes Evans's hope that the soldiers would recognize themselves in Hamlet explicit rather than philosophical, but Hamlet himself is conflated with Evans, 'an officer in the United States army' who is owed 'respect.'

Evans's preface indicates that he expected to tour the production beyond Hawaii to forward bases, but no tour took place. Shulimson briefly describes the only performance under 'field conditions' on 18 December 1944, at 'one of the more isolated camps on Oahu ... The male members of the cast were dressed in army fatigues, while the women wore long black robes. They performed on a rough board stage devoid of scenery and stage lighting' (263). Evans's brief account of this performance in his memoir notes there was no 'special lighting' for this stripped down production, which started in moonlight and had, as a lighting effect, only a searchlight mounted on a tower (*Memoir* 177). A review of the performance in the *Honolulu Star-Bulletin* (19 December 1944) observes that there were some catcalls at first, but 'then the thing caught fire and the drama of the story combined with the unbeatable language of Shakespeare held a silent audience' ('No Costumes' 2; qtd in Shulimson 263). This review suggests that while the early part of the performance was received rowdily, the conclusion was greeted with silence. There are several possible but contradictory implications of that silence – that the play itself was not appreciated, or perhaps that the death of Hamlet reminded the audience only too clearly of its own situation. Evans was later reported as saying that soldiers preferred to attend a 'real theater with their own tickets ... seated by young usherettes' (qtd in Fisher 6; qtd in Shulimson 263), implying that *Hamlet* had a more enthusiastic reception under relatively normalized conditions than in the isolated camp, where the fatigues and bare stage made the plight of Hamlet and other characters much more closely allied to the soldiers' risk and isolation. It seems that soldiers wanted theatre to be an escape rather than an analogy to their own precarious situations. The physical experience of seeing the play in a modern theatre, rather than in an isolated camp, might thus partially insulate soldiers from the most direct analogical readings of the play.

Evans's duties in Hawaii ended on 30 June 1945, after VE Day. Although American forces were fighting on many fronts, and making considerable advances against the Japanese, at this point 'there seemed little prospect of a speedy end to the hostilities in the Pacific' (*Memoir* 178). Soon after he returned to the United States he was contacted by Michael Todd, who, having read Reynold's article in *Colliers* (Shulimson 264), was interested in bringing the production to New York, where it opened on 13 December. The show that Todd marketed as *The G.I. Hamlet* was very popular and had a much longer run than the original play in wartime Hawaii. Some of the enthusiastic critical responses to the Broadway performance indicate Evans's success in representing his vision of Hamlet as 'masculine' and normal. A *Life* pictorial calls his Hamlet a 'rough-and-ready extrovert, delayed in avenging his father's murder more by force of circumstance than by his own pigeon liver' ('The G.I. Hamlet' 57).[12] John Mason Brown, who had seen Evans's 1935 Hamlet as 'masculine,' described him in the *Saturday Review* as 'a Yankee Doodle Hamlet' who is 'virile' and 'all male' (qtd in *Memoir* 186). These reviewers admire the simple, uncomplicated, masculine, American, soldierly courage of *The G.I. Hamlet* in accord with Americans' postwar pride in their part in the victory.

Not all critics approved of the performance, however. Eric Bentley described Evans's adaptation as 'calculated to disprove the rumor that the play is famous, let alone great ... a nineteenth-century battle piece written for twentieth-century GIs' (316). Rosamund Gilder regarded Evans's Hamlet as 'consistently uncomplex,' played 'as though Hamlet is already a mature man' (76). She missed passion, doubt, and 'irregularity of mood' – elements that might not have contributed to Evans's desire to raise troop morale. Both Bentley and Gilder point to an old-fashioned element of the production, which failed to take into account the complexity of the character. American audiences, only months after the nuclear bombings of Hiroshima and Nagasaki that ended the war, may well have preferred a simple and patriotic representation of Hamlet.

There are a few hints in some reviews of the postwar production that the omission of the gravedigger scene was the subject of rumour and speculation. The pictorial feature in *Life* notes that the gravedigger scene was omitted because it was 'corny' ('The G.I. Hamlet' 57). Given that Evans uses this argument and term in the preface to the acting edition published the next year, it seems likely that this was an explanation he often gave. Gilder observes that 'Report has it that G.I. audiences would not "take" the grave-digger humors; that by-play with skulls was out of place' (76). It is easy to imagine why 'by-play with skulls' would not seem appropriate. It seems that Evans was so anxious about the effects of a comic scene with stage business involving bones and skulls, followed by the fight between Hamlet and Laertes in Ophelia's grave, that he was unwilling, even after the war's end, to articulate the problem the scene poses for an analogical reading of a play in which soldier audiences are invited to see themselves as Hamlet. In his preface Evans said he anticipated that, like Shakespeare who had 'trouble with the groundlings ... so might we' (15). A number of elements in the scene might well disturb the 'groundlings' Evans was sent to entertain.

For all Evans's cuts of elements 'dangerous for a soldier audience,' parts of the play that he retained also pose potential problems in understanding Hamlet as unquestionably heroic. For example, Evans keeps Hamlet's line after he kills Polonius – 'I'll lug the guts into the neighbour room' (140) – and also retains Hamlet's hiding of Polonius's body and the dialogue on the decomposition of bodies climaxing in the line 'a king may go a progress through the guts of a beggar' (147–8). These words and actions might undercut the normality Evans wanted soldiers to see in Hamlet. Another problem in asking a soldier to see himself reflected in Hamlet is posed by Hamlet's final representation in the play – a dead hero raised in a beam of light, while cannons shoot and triumphant music plays. Coogan's comment about the silence of the first-night audience in Honolulu suggests the possibility of that audience's unease with the events of the narrative and Hamlet's death. Only after instructions from the authorities were the soldiers sufficiently 'enthusiastic,' as Coogan puts it. The performance of *Hamlet* in 'field conditions,' played in fatigues with no lighting, might well represent a grim reminder of the possibility of violent death that confronted soldiers in the Pacific in 1944. The theatricality and intensity of this final tableau could be more easily accepted by postwar Broadway audiences than by the soldier audiences in Hawaii who might well have been uneasy about the death of the figure with whom they had been asked to identify.

A question that Evans never considers explicitly is whether and how tragedy itself could be good for morale in the midst of war. A more recent director of Shakespeare in a brief period of postwar reconstruction in Afghanistan in 2005 chose to produce a comedy, *Love's Labour's Lost*. Corinne Jaber 'noted that the Afghan actors she met did not want to do tragedies, after more than twenty years of war, so that left the comedies' (qtd in Carroll 443–4). In wartime Hawaii it seems that the military hierarchy saw the cultural status of Shakespeare and tragedy as sufficient reason for the production of Shakespeare. Through most of his preface Evans is explicit about his strategies for cutting *Hamlet* in order to make the plot and situation relevant to soldiers in the midst of a war, but his evasive discussion of the graveyard scene is striking. His oblique imputation of Shakespeare's own authorization to cut the scene also functions as an implicit defence of Garrick and the other neoclassical adaptors of Shakespeare who removed inconsistencies such as ambiguity of character and mixing of genres from Shakespeare's works. However, Evans's elision of the thematic implications of the gravedigger scene for soldiers in the Pacific in 1944 suggests that the matter of *Hamlet* was much more resistant to his intended use than he had anticipated, or could admit. By contrast, the success of the *G.I. Hamlet* in the postwar United States shows that Evans's deployment of neoclassical aesthetic conventions to focus and simplify genre and characterization was to some degree an effective strategy in adapting *Hamlet* for a postwar context and civilian audience. The play's success soon after the war indicates the attraction of a single-minded, revengeful Hamlet who could represent America's power and ultimate victory.

Notes

1 Maurice Evans (1901–89) was born in Dorchester, England; he began his acting career in England in 1926 before going to the United States, where he played many Shakespearean roles on Broadway, including Hamlet and Macbeth. He became a US citizen in 1941. In the late 1940s and through the 1950s, he continued to play Shakespeare and a series of Shavian roles on Broadway. From the 1960s through to the 1980s he had film and television parts in addition to stage roles.

2 *The G.I. Hamlet* ran for 131 performances at the Columbus Circle Theater

between 13 December 1945 and 7 April 1946. There were 16 more performances at the City Center starting on 3 June 1946. The production then
toured the country. In all, Evans says there were 452 performances in the
US (Evans, *Memoir* 183).

3 Other members of the Hawaii production groups – George Schaefer (director), Allen Ludden, Carl Reiner, and Werner Klemperer – also continued
careers in stage and film.

4 *Hamlet, Macbeth, Richard III,* and *Othello* were among the most performed
Shakespeare tragedies in the nineteenth-century (Sturgess 16–18).

5 On Hamlet in Europe and the United States, see Foakes 12–44.

6 Foakes cites J.W. Draper's defence of Hamlet as heroic, in contrast with
critics such as L.C. Knight and George Santayana who focused on Hamlet's weakness and lack of direction (30–4).

7 This essay does not address the contested question of adaptation and
appropriation in Shakespeare. Michael Dobson, *The Making of the National
Poet: Shakespeare, Adaptation and Authorship, 1660-1769* (Oxford: Clarendon
Press, 1992) esp. pp. 166–76 and Terence Hawkes, *Meaning by Shakespeare*
(Routledge: London and New York, 1992), esp. 1–10, discuss appropriation
in general with some references to *Hamlet.* For a detailed survey of stage
and film productions of *Hamlet,* see Marvin Rosenberg, *The Masks of Hamlet*
(Newark: University of Delaware Press, 1992).

8 Shulimson discusses the 1942 production of *Macbeth* at Fort Meade (256–7)
as well as the run of 70 performances by Evans and Anderson in Hawaii in
1943 (259–60). Comment cards distributed to the audience at Fort Meade
indicated that '1,512 soldiers stated that they had enjoyed the play; 3
said they had not' (Shulimson 257). Evans does not mention making any
changes to *Macbeth* for political reasons, though on Broadway he had omitted the final scene with Macbeth's severed head (*Memoir* 151).

9 Garrick's adaptation is reprinted by Pedicord and Bergman; see also Jef-
frey Lawson Lawrence Johnson, 'Sweeping up Shakespeare's "Rubbish":
Garrick's Condensation of Acts IV and V of *Hamlet,*' esp. pp. 16 and 24n7.
For the 1763 version, see vol. 3 of *The Plays of David Garrick,* ed. Gerald
M. Berkowitz. As George Winchester Stone pointed out in 1934, Garrick's
'Alteration was never printed, and had never been seen in its true form by
any of its commentators' until Stone himself transcribed the last act (892).
Since Stone had transcribed the alterations in Garrick's hand in the Folger
Shakespeare Library, it could not have been Garrick's own promptbook
that Evans saw in Hawaii in 1944. A prompter's version of Garrick's adaptation (rather than Garrick's own promptbook) was printed in 1777 and
reprinted in 1825 in Boaden's *Life of Kemble* (Stone 891–2; 901). Either of

these texts might have been the 'old prompt script of David Garrick' that Evans 'lighted on' (Preface 12).

10 Woods notes that Garrick makes use of contemporary references in his 'qualification of static and generalized "Neoclassicized" heroes' (71).

11 Johnson argues that Garrick cut lines in plays 'to provide space for his explosively emotional visual additions of his own' (15).

12 *Life* magazine was the dominant American venue for news photography and news stories in mid-century America. The *G.I. Hamlet* pictorial feature indicates the prestige of the production, and also provided invaluable publicity for the Broadway run and the subsequent national tour.

Works Cited

Bentley, Eric. 'Broadway Today.' *The Sewanee Review* 54.2 (Apr.–Jun. 1946): 314–16.

Bristol, Michael D. *Shakespeare's America, America's Shakespeare.* London and New York: Routledge, 1990.

Carroll, William C. '*Love's Labour's Lost* in Afghanistan.' *Shakespeare Bulletin* 28.4 (Winter 2010): 443–58.

Cartelli, Thomas. *Repositioning Shakespeare: National Formations, Postcolonial Appropriations.* Routledge: London and New York, 1999.

Coogan, Joe. Letter to *New York Times* 27 May 1990: n.pag.

Evans, Maurice. *All This … and Evans Too! A Memoir.* Columbia: University of South Carolina Press, 1987.

– Preface. *Maurice Evans' G.I. Production of 'Hamlet' by William Shakespeare. Acting Edition.* New York: Doubleday, 1947.

Fisher, Joe. 'Show Circuit Covering All Pacific Seen.' *Stars and Stripes*, Pacific Oceans Area 21 June 1945: 6.

Foakes, R.A. *Hamlet versus Lear: Cultural Politics and Shakespeare's Art.* Cambridge: Cambridge University Press, 1993.

Garrick, David. *Hamlet. The Plays of David Garrick.* Vol. 3. Ed. Gerald M. Berkowitz. New York: Garland, 1981.

– *Hamlet. The Plays of David Garrick.* Vol. 4. Ed. Harry William Pedicord and Fredrick Louis Bergman. Carbondale: Southern Illinois University Press, 1981.

Gilder, Rosamond. 'Matter and Art: Broadway in Review.' *Theatre Arts* 30 (Fall 1946): 73–82.

Gilman, Richard. 'Stage View; Tales of Hamlets Then and Now.' *New York Times* 6 May 1990: n.pag.

Johnson, Jeffrey Lawson Lawrence. 'Sweeping up Shakespeare's 'Rubbish':

Garrick's Condensation of Acts IV and V of *Hamlet*.' *Eighteenth Century Life* 8:3 (May 1983): 14–25.

'No Costumes or Scenery Needed for a Fine Hamlet.' *Honolulu Star-Bulletin* 19 Dec. 1944: 2.

Shakespeare, William. *Hamlet. The Riverside Shakespeare*. Ed. G. Blakemore Evans. Boston: Houghton Mifflin, 1974: 1135–97.

Shulimson, Jack. 'Maurice Evans, Shakespeare and the U.S. Army.' *Journal of Popular Culture* 10.2 (Fall 1976): 255–66.

Stone, George Winchester Jr. 'Garrick's Long Lost Alteration of *Hamlet*.' *PMLA* 49 (1934): 890–921.

Sturgess, Kim C. *Shakespeare and the American Nation*. Cambridge: Cambridge University Press, 2004.

'The G.I. Hamlet: Broadway sees how Maurice Evans made Shakespeare a Soldier Hit.' *Life* 7 Jan. 1946: 57–8, 60.

Tomarken, Edward. 'The Comedy of the Graveyard Scene in *Hamlet:* Samuel Johnson Mediates between the Eighteenth and Twentieth Centuries.' *Eighteenth Century Life* 8:3 (May 1983): 26–33.

Woods, Leigh. 'Crowns of Straw on Little Men: Garrick's New Heroes.' *Shakespeare Quarterly* 32:1 (Spring 1981): 69–79.

13 The War at 'Home': Representations of Canada and of the Second World War in *Star Crossed*

MARISSA McHUGH

Canadians and the War Overseas

For many Canadians, the Second World War was, and remains, a foundational – even mythic – event integral to the building of a mature Canadian nation state and people.[1] It was also generally understood as a 'good war': a valiant crusade against a tyrannical, barbaric ideology.[2] Prime Minister MacKenzie King declared Canada's war on Germany on 10 September 1939, one week after England, a delay that was generally perceived as an affirmation of national sovereignty.[3] Many Canadians of English descent felt a strong sense of loyalty to and kinship with Britain, the mother country, and thus quickly came to her defence by answering the call to arms. Other recruits perceived war as a means of ending the Depression, which had left millions on social security.[4] But there was also a substantial number reluctant to enter the war. For some, the horrors of trench warfare and the tragic loss of life during the First World War were still fresh memories.[5] Furthermore, the Second World War at once raised the possibility of a divided nation; although the First World War had begun the process of establishing a distinct Canadian identity, this war had also created enormous friction between French and English Canada, especially during the conscription crisis of 1916.[6]

By the end of the Second World War, however, the Canadian contribution to the Allied war effort was, in comparison to its population, fairly significant; from a population of 11.5 million, approximately 1.1 million Canadians served in the Second World War.[7] Canadian troops quickly distinguished themselves in military action,[8] most notably in the liberation of the Netherlands (September 1944 to April 1945); to this day, the Dutch–Canadian bond continues to be a special one, as annual memorial events attest.[9]

Canadians and the War at Home

Unlike Americans, Canadians did not experience the physically destructive effects of war on home soil. However, in addition to the usual privations, Canadians did experience extensive intra-communal infighting and suspicion that led to significant social divisions within the nation.[10] Canadians of Japanese, German, Austrian, and Italian descent, for example, were designated 'enemy aliens' and were forced to report regularly to authorities throughout the duration of the war. They were also subjected to mistreatment, persecution, dispossession, internment, and deportation.[11] The enemy was thus not only 'over there,' but was perceived to be 'here,' at home, and thus even more dangerous.

Canada's unique wartime experience may explain why Canadian theatrical responses to war – and to wartime Shakespeare – were markedly different from those of other countries examined in this volume.[12] There are no published records of Canadian productions of Shakespeare during the war years,[13] and there is no scholarship on this subject – despite the fact that Shakespeare was (and remains) one of Canada's most revered playwrights. The most notable Shakespearean events of the war were G. Wilson Knight's patriotic lectures – interspersed with rousing Shakespearean quotations – which were published in 1944 and radio adaptations of Shakespeare plays broadcast by the Canadian Broadcasting Corporation (CBC).[14]

An Interrogation of Positive Representations of Canadians at War

Star Crossed (ca. 1950) is a Canadian adaptation of William Shakespeare's *Romeo and Juliet* set in North Brabant in the German-occupied Netherlands: this area was one of the first liberated by Canadian soldiers during the Second World War and was thus specifically associated with one of their notable achievements. As an adaptation, *Star Crossed* adheres to the lengthy, creative, and dominant Canadian tradition of treating Shakespeare in adapted or even parodic form.[15] This little-known unpublished script problematizes idealized celebrations of the Second World War while also simultaneously embracing Allied victory and Canadian military achievements as significant and worthy of memorialization. The Shakespearean scaffolding of the play permits the author, writing in a period of postwar mythologizing, to examine war in such a complex fashion. More particularly, *Star Crossed* looks at the way in which war extends well beyond battlefields, infecting and devastating social-domestic spaces and times seemingly far removed from its horror.[16] The sustained focus on the tragedy of a Dutch family positioned within a domestic space during and shortly after the Second World War also enables the play to offer a counternarrative to traditional war discourse by presenting the war's pervasive presence at 'home' in contrast with the masculine battlefield experience.[17] To date, *Star Crossed* is the only playtext extant that adapts Shakespeare in order to comment on the Canadian experience of the Second World War. Despite its publication on the Canadian Adaptations of Shakespeare Project website, the play continues to be relatively unknown.[18]

At the foreground of the play is a *Romeo and Juliet* motif that charts the development of the 'death-marked love' (Prologue 9) between the Dutch Anna Heerdinck and the German Captain Folkert Busch, a Nazi Intelligence Officer.[19] A second, contrapuntal, narrative of the Canadian victory in the Netherlands remains outside of this main dramatic action, occurring in the violent public world of warfare. Radio broadcasts and visitors to the Heerdinck home report parts of this second military narrative, but the Heerdincks and the audience of the play never witness it. The first act dramatizes the Heerdincks' war efforts, namely their attempt to adopt and maintain Dutch nationalistic and anti-German discourse within the family home and to shelter an English airman named Edwards. This later task is made difficult by the presence of Folkert, who billets in an upstairs room. The second act features both the developing romantic relationship between Anna and Folkert and the Heerdincks' anticipation of the arrival of Allied (Canadian) troops. The third act culminates in the announcement of the liberation of North Brabant by Canadian soldiers. The celebratory atmosphere of peacetime is quickly undercut, however, by the graphic deaths of Folkert and Anna: Dirk, Anna's brother and a member of the Dutch Resistance, assassinates Folkert, and Anna, after hearing this news, commits suicide.

Authorship and Production History

To date, the authorship and production history of *Star Crossed* remain contestable. Library and Archives Canada (LAC) houses what seems to be an original, editorially annotated copy of the play that attributes authorship to Patrick Bentley (or possibly Patrick Bentket)[20] and includes what appears to be editorial credit to Clarence Malone. On the first page of the script, Bentley's name is crossed out and Malone's name is written below. However, Bentley is credited as the primary playwright on the page containing the list of characters. In 'Appendix II: List of Plays Donated' (held at LAC in the Dominion Drama Festival folder), the play is listed under Malone ('Malone, Clarence P. *Star Crossed*: a play by Patrick Bentley' [141]). Most of the plays in this list are alphabetically ordered by authorial name; however, the non-Canadian plays appear to be listed by director or producer – in the manner of the Malone/Bentley entry.

Various searches (including birth, death, and military records) at the Canadian Genealogical Centre yielded no results for either Clarence P. Malone or Patrick Bentley.[21] William S. Milne's *Canadian Full-Length Plays in English,* an annotated catalogue of the Canadian Dominion Drama Festival plays, lists Malone as the playwright both for *Star Crossed* and for a second unpublished play entitled *The Heart of My Mystery*, which focuses on a Shakespeare Society 'about to see a play purporting to prove a new theory of who wrote Shakespeare's play' (30). In his supplement, *Canadian Full-Length Plays in English (II)*, Milne includes a third entry for a 'Malone, C. *Patrick*' (emphasis added 22): an unpublished script of a comedy, entitled *A Great Day,* 'involving all Canadian "identity" problem clichés' (22).[22]

Daniel Fischlin's research, summarized on the *Canadian Adaptations of Shakespeare* website, led him to conclude that though *Star Crossed* 'has uncertain [authorial] attribution,' Bentley 'appears to have been [the play's] author' (1). He notes, however, that, '[t]he affiliation between Malone and Bentley/Bentket suggests a rather interesting mystery. Was Malone brought in to edit Bentley/Bentket's play as a function of his already having worked on a local, amateur piece involving a form of Shakespeare adaptation?' (1). Though this may have been the case, the focus on Shakespeare in *The Heart of My Mystery* and the authorship issues for that script (as suggested by Milne), along with the complete lack of information on Bentley, Malone's playwriting history, and the fact that Malone's middle name is Patrick all seem to suggest that there may not have been an affiliation, but rather that 'Patrick Bentley' was Malone's pen name. The parallel between the controversy of the authorship of Shakespeare's plays and the ambiguity surrounding the authorship of *Star Crossed* also suggests Malone may have been contriving the debate about authorship as another layer of allusion.[23] The limited information on either Bentley or Malone, however, makes it difficult to fully formulate any final conclusions as to the play's author, national identity,[24] affiliations, and/or intentions. The lack of information certainly raises questions about the playwright's identity, whether it was purposely shrouded and, if so, why this was the case.

Fischlin also contends that there is no concrete evidence detailing the play's genesis or production history, but he speculates that 'the dates for *Star Crossed* fall between the end of World War II and its mention by Milne in 1964' and speculates that 'the play was written in the 1950s' (1). The LAC records indicate that their housed script originated from the Dominion Drama Festival archives; considering that the Festival only produced full-length plays after 1950, it seems likely that *Star Crossed* was written and produced within Fischlin's estimations. The date of the play in the LAC catalogue – '[196-]' – is likely the date of acquisition rather than the production date.[25]

Though *Star Crossed's* place on a Dominion Drama Festival program cannot be located,[26] the material at LAC makes it abundantly clear that the play was staged at the Festival. The Dominion Drama Festival (DDF; 1932–9, 1947–78) was an annual bilingual amateur theatre competition[27] that aimed to foster the development of Canadian theatre. Though the DDF 'served as Canada's national theatre,' it later came to be critiqued for 'perpetuating elitist and colonial values' (Gardner), as well as for fostering a conservative approach. Socially disruptive material occasionally surfaced at the Festival, as was the case in 1937 with the Theatre of Action production of *Bury the Dead*, an anti-war play by American playwright Irwin Shaw; however, political plays remained uncommon and uncelebrated (Whittaker 145). Thus, the subtle critique of war and intolerance found in *Star Crossed* may have been couched in well-known Shakespearean intertext as a means of securing both audience favour and critical acceptance.

Shakespeare's presence was largely encouraged and was widely accepted as a symbol of cultural authority and the measure of high dramatic art both at the Festival and throughout mid-century Canada. Ric Knowles explains that the term 'Shakespeare' at mid-century remained 'representative of British high culture, an agent of either cultural improvement or imperialist nationalism and class dominance' (12). The first Dominion Drama Festival took place on Shakespeare's birth date, and Shakespearean content frequently appeared at the yearly competitions. Throughout Canada Shakespeare also remained mainstream, produced in little theatres across the country and frequently aired on CBC radio.[28] The most significant indication of Shakespeare's popularity and cultural authority in Canada, however, came in the form of a national theatre with the founding of the Stratford Festival in 1952.[29]

An Evocation of Shakespeare in the Canadian Postwar Climate

Star Crossed openly gestures to Shakespeare in numerous ways: most prominently in its title, in the epigraph, in character parallels (Anna/ Juliet, Folkert/Romeo, Elizabeth/Nurse, Father Lambertus/Friar Laurence, Dirk/Tybalt), and in dramatic action, which culminates in the tragic deaths of the lovers. These gestures to Shakespeare may have not only garnered the play's popularity but also enabled the play's subtle critique of war at a time when many Canadians, having just endured its hardships, sought to focus on the Canadian gains of war, 'the birth of the nation,' as a means of coping with the trauma of loss. The domestic tragedy of *Romeo and Juliet*, relocated into the Netherlands, subtly offers the audience a means to consider the cost of war on social-domestic relations and calls attention to the similar public conflicts affecting the social-domestic worlds of Italy (Verona), Europe (Holland), and Canada – without undermining the importance of the Second World War for Canada and without overtly offending patriotic sensibilities.

The ideological feuds experienced in Verona and in the Netherlands may also have invited Canadians to consider the remnants of war within their own existing social relations. Just as Shakespeare frequently set his plays in different locales as a means of subtly commenting upon English issues and conflicts, so Malone/Bentley (re)locates Canada to the Netherlands in order to achieve a similar end – to reflect upon the Canadian/German-Canadian conflict in Canada. Prior to the Second World War German Canadians made up a significant and integral part of the Canadian population;[30] however, this changed in the wake of the Second World War. 800 German Canadian 'enemy aliens' were interned, and those who had entered Canada after 1922 were forced to report regularly to authorities (Schreyer 26).[31] Wartime measures resulted in extensive social division and left a legacy of anti-German sentiment within the nation, a sentiment that was further heightened after Nazi atrocities were brought to light during the Nuremberg trials. *Star Crossed* critiques this legacy of hatred within the 'home' space (the Allied domestic space and the Canadian home front) in a manner reminiscent of Shakespeare's *Romeo and Juliet*. Bentley/Malone achieves this end by comparing the Montague/Capulet conflict in *Romeo and Juliet* to the Dutch/German conflict in the Netherlands and the Canadian/German-Canadian conflict in Canada: domestic conflicts all produced from public war discourse.[32]

A Counter-discursive War Narrative

Ultimately, *Star Crossed*'s transposition and portrayal of the ideological struggle against 'Germans' at 'home' suggests, in a manner oppositional to traditional hegemonic histories, that the Second World War extended past its public boundaries into domestic civilian spaces. In a 'total war,' as military theorist Carl von Clausewitz explains, a belligerent utilizes all possible resources, including all human ones, to obtain victory. Thus, all aspects of life, including all discourse, become occupied by forms of warfare, making it impossible to have any 'neutral space' (von Clausewitz 582). Early in *Star Crossed*, Malone/Bentley illustrates this concept by situating war squarely within the Heerdinck home, conflating the antithetical war front/home front and soldier/civilian categories often presumed by war discourse. Father Lambertus, the family priest and a frequent visitor in the Heerdinck home, explains, '[T]hese modern wars leave few alone. I think we'll all be in the front line. We'll all be soldiers – women, children, all of us' (7).[33] Here, this 'us,' possibly addressed on stage to a Canadian audience, suggests not only the conflation of war front/home front and soldier/civilian within the Heerdinck home but also a conflation of the Netherlands and Canada.

Star Crossed not only collapses soldier/civilian and war front/home front dichotomies but also blurs gender demarcations assumed by war discourse. When German soldiers come to suspect that the Heerdincks harboured Edwards, an English airman, Willem prepares his family for the questioning that is to come. He asks Elizabeth to assume a traditionalist, wartime feminine role, saying, 'Remember, you are a woman of peace and know nothing about the war' (30). Here, Willem asks Elizabeth to play what Jean Bethke Elshtain deems 'the non-combatant female': a woman 'embodying values and virtues at odds with war's destructiveness' and 'representing home and hearth' (xiii). Though Elizabeth certainly voices anti-war sentiment throughout the play (10, 18, 31),[34] she is not entirely 'at odds with war's destructiveness,' having actively engaged in the sheltering and escape plan for Edwards. Her constant domestic activities (dramatized in the form of meal preparation) merge with her war efforts and offer the reader/audience a graphic example of the 'combatant female' within the home space.

Willem also affords Anna an active role within the civilian war, further illustrating the conflation of the civilian/soldier division within their home. He interpolates her into the Dutch war effort and into her combatant role, saying, 'Anna, you may be called upon to be very brave. You will be a good soldier, I know' (30). Although Willem's implication appears to be that Anna will not confess the family's harbouring of a war pilot under the pressures of German interrogation, the use of the word 'good' recalls the, at times, ironic quality of soldiering in the Second World War. Earlier in the play Father Lambertus offers Willem a definition of what it means to be a 'good' soldier. He notes that it involves 'discipline,' the suppression of 'softer more human thoughts' in regards to the German enemy, 'hating,' and a hardening of oneself (20). He includes civilians and soldiers alike under his definition of the term 'soldier,' saying, '[W]e are all soldiers now, Willem, there are no civilians' (20). The implication, here, is that in this 'Last Good War,' a war supposedly involving 'an unambiguous struggle between good and evil' (Nelan 120), 'good' soldiering took the form of discrimination against 'Germanness' – in an ironic reversal for an Allied country.

For the Heerdincks, Father Lambertus's war rhetoric is initially – as Willem explains – 'difficult to maintain' (20), perhaps partially as a result of prewar 'German' associations. Prior to the Second World War, the national division between the Netherlands and Germany appears to have been more geographically than ideologically based – though a sense of anti-German sentiment had previously surfaced as a result of both Hitler's rise to power in 1933 and the Dutch Princess Juliana's marriage to the German-born Count Bernhard in 1936. During the First World War, the Netherlands had maintained its status as a neutral country, and when the Second World War broke out, the Netherlands once again declared its neutrality. However, the German army invaded nonetheless and bombed the Netherlands on 10 May 1940, prompting a new, antagonistic relationship between the Dutch and the Germans. To a certain extent this situation parallels that in Canada, where the Second World War prompted a similar shift in social relations. Though anti-German sentiment in Canada had emerged during the First World War, a wave of German immigrants arrived during the interwar years, contributing extensively to the nation-building project in the settlement and development of Western Canada. Despite this contribution, however, anti-German sentiment resurfaced with the advent of the war.

Elizabeth – who explains that prior to the outbreak of war in the Netherlands: 'All of Europe has been my home. Paris, Berlin, London! I love them all!' (8) – finds it difficult to adopt and maintain an antithetical conception of Folkert, whom she finds to be 'a very pleasant young man' (12) and 'the most interesting person' she has met in the last four years (13). To Elizabeth, Folkert is highly unsettling; he wears a Nazi uniform, yet he is far from the brutal, barbaric, cold-blooded 'Hun' featured in wartime propaganda. She confesses, 'Sometimes I almost forget he is a German, which, of course, I should not do' (12). Although Anna systematically responds, 'No, we must always remember that' (12) in an affirmation of her national alliance, her subsequent revelation that they 'have played the piano and talked a little, mostly about music' (12) reveals a weakening of her soldierly resolve.

Star Crossed specifically utilizes music to counter the nationalistic wartime rhetoric espoused and vocalized primarily by Father Lambertus, the character most frequently navigating between the sheltered Heerdinck private domestic space[35] and the violent public world of warfare. As Anna sits at the piano, playing Austrian composer Franz Schubert's setting of German poet Ludwig Holtz's poem 'Seligkeit' [Happiness] (15), she is joined by Folkert who questions whether she is playing a composition by Robert Schumann, a German composer with whom Anna is familiar (16).[36] This reference to Schumann calls attention to a specific instance of a 'German' transcending anti-German sentiment. Though a sense of Germanophobia lingered in the postwar Americas, Schumann, one of the most famous and influential composers of the nineteenth century, was still memorialized and acclaimed in the early postwar period in the American film *Song of Love* (1947). Through musical engagement, Folkert, like Schumann, momentarily transcends the anti-German sentiment of his environment. His love of music combined with his comic banter and his sharing of a cigarette enables Anna, here, to begin to conceive of him in less reductive terms than those proposed by the war discourse around her.[37] The scene also subtly celebrates artistic inter-culturality in its fusion of Shakespeare, Holtz, Schumann, and Schubert.

Prior to his placement in the Heerdinck home, Folkert, as Dirk later explains, was a 'very capable German Officer' (46) and an active persecutor of members of the Dutch Resistance (50); however, as *Star Crossed* shows, music and his developing love for Anna prompt his deracination from military activities and from war discourse. Wartime atrocities certainly make this process more difficult for Anna who, after hearing about a starving Dutch family, finds herself unable to reciprocate Folkert's affection: 'When I hear about them [those suffering at the hands of German soldiers] – I don't think I can …' (25). Folkert's request to

Anna, 'We must not hate each other' (25), seems a simple antidote, but to Anna, who equates 'hatred' with her nation's military success, 'love' is not a viable option. She responds, expressing her continued national alliance, 'I cannot be sure we should not. Can I forget that I am a Netherlander and you are a German?' (25).

Folkert, in a manner reminiscent of Romeo who 'tender[s]' (3.1.70) his enemy's name 'as dearly as [his] own' (3.1.71), comes to 'forget' his national alliances as a result of his fidelity to Anna and her family. When a German Colonel places Willem under arrest, Folkert blackmails the Colonel in order to secure Willem's release (34–7). Just as Mercutio sees Romeo's extension of 'love' (3.1.68) to Tybalt as a 'dishonorable, vile submission!' (3.1.72), so the Colonel perceives Folkert's behaviour – which he suspects stems from Folkert's love of the 'beautiful Anna' (36) – in a similar manner, condemning it as 'treasonable' (37). He reminds Folkert, 'You are risking your career – your life – for a contemptible reason' (36). Though Folkert acknowledges that his actions are self-serving and 'selfish' (39), he also recognizes that his 'imagined community,'[38] as formulated in war, 'is rushing to disaster' (37).

The kindness Folkert extends to Willem does not mitigate Dirk's view of 'Germans,' nor does it elucidate the contradictions within his static understanding of them. Willem informs Dirk that they have maintained a friendly relationship with Folkert and that he has acted as their 'protector' (45), a comment which prompts Dirk's surprised response of 'Father, he's a German!' (45). Though Willem attempts to explain that 'the circumstances are unusual' (45), Dirk refuses to consider Folkert in ambiguous terms and remains resolute in his assassination plot. His bitter argument, 'How are we to fight them, if we are not as hard and brutal as they are?'(46), epitomizes the growing resemblance between his mentality and that of the Nazis.[39] Dirk attempts to share this mentality with Anna, whom he reproaches for not being 'strong enough to hate' (50). He presses her to 'forget Captain Busch' (50) and, rather, to 'remember what he is': one of the many 'Germans' that 'invaded our country, ruined our cities, killed, imprisoned, tortured us' (50). Dirk's use of 'our' and 'us' suggests his continued inclusion of Anna within their 'imagined community' in a surprising act of kindness that would not have been easy or commonplace in the climate of the Second World War.

The Second World War prompted a widespread demonizing and dehumanization of the enemy that was often extended to those who associated with them. Kjersti Ericsson explains that the Second World

War 'was not only a war over territories, resources and narrow national interests,' but also 'a war over ideas and values, good pitted against evil' (3). This, she explains, 'gave an added impetus to a process by no means exclusive to World War II: that of demonizing of the enemy' and of 'everybody with the slightest connection to the Nazis' (3). Following the liberation of the Netherlands, Dutch women who had relations with German soldiers were frequently deemed 'moffenhoeren' and 'Kraut-whores,' and '[i]t was assumed that they knew no solidarity or sense of honour and their actions were solely directed at satisfying their self-interest and greed' (Diederichs 151).[40] Members of the Dutch community and the Dutch Resistance accused these women of treason and punished them by shaving off their hair in public venues (157), an act that physically marked them as outsiders within the nation.

Anna is aware of the social stigmatization that could potentially befall her, and this awareness informs her interactions with Folkert.[41] She warns him, 'If the others knew, they would…' (24), but he insists, 'They shan't know' (24). When Anna discovers that Folkert enabled her father's release from the German Colonel, she, once again, considers the possibility of public castigation. She questions Folkert, saying, 'You did'nt [sic] … ' (38), and Folkert, again, assures her, 'No I did'nt [sic] use your name. I would'nt [sic] do that' (38). Anna's relationship also concerns her family, who are conscious of their own positions within the war discourse around them. To Willem, Elizabeth explains, 'You know very well the stigma attached to those who have been friendly to the Germans. They will never be forgiven … Some friends of the Germans will be punished, but they'll all be despised. You will despise them and so will I. It's a brand that won't wear off' (56). *Star Crossed*'s apt evocation of an image of permanence, of 'brand[ing],' intimates the civilian conflicts that will follow the signing of the Second World War's armistices. This awareness may also have been experienced by the author, as he appears to have a keen understanding of such 'branding.'

Anna and Folkert recognize that their relationship is unsustainable and unsafe outside the temporal limits of war and of the spatial limits of the Heerdinck home. In their final discussion, Anna asks Folkert to 'surrender as a prisoner of war' (59), but he refuses, explaining that it 'would be weak and cowardly' (59). He chooses to reassume his national 'duty' and to retreat with his army (59). Though Folkert believes 'that someday [he] will return' to the Netherlands for her (60), Anna, withholding her knowledge of Dirk's assassination plot in an act suggesting her own return to 'duty,' ominously explains that '[t]here will be no future for us' (60). Unlike Romeo and Juliet, they admit, 'We are enemies' (60), part, and attempt to reintegrate into their respective communities. Here, Bentley's play differs greatly from Shakespeare's *Romeo and Juliet*, in which Juliet places love above all other considerations, even the murder of a close relative. Ultimately, Bentley is less optimistic about what love can achieve.

A Celebration of Canadian Achievements in War

While seemingly critiquing the way in which the Second World War prompted a devastating process of 'othering,' *Star Crossed* simultaneously celebrates Canada's wartime achievements and national development in war. Initially, the play dramatizes the way in which the Heerdincks envision the Allies as a single, unified group: this group bearing the title of 'the British.' Elizabeth carefully asks a German officer whether 'there is any "danger" ... of the British ... "capturing" the village' (14), and Willem uses 'the British' as an overarching term referring to the Allied troops reported to be approaching (40). As the actual troops (including both British and Canadian infantry) draw near, however, a slight demarcation between the British forces and the Canadian troops develops. A BBC report celebrates both the accomplishments of British infantry and of British troops of the 1st Canadian army: 'Mighty British infantry and armored forces plunged across the sodden Netherlands countryside tonight in a race to trap the German 19th army in the lowlands of southwest Holland after British troops of the 1st Canadian Army made a daring amphibious landing on the Scheldt Estuary Island of South Beveland and British forces to the east captured Tilburg, keystone bastion on the west flank of the Allied Netherlands salient' (40).

Then, in the first scene of act 3, Dirk returns home and informs his family, 'The Canadians will be here soon' (61). As the liberation draws nearer the Heerdinck household comes to conceive of the Canadians as an entity separate from the British, with Father Lambertus informing Elizabeth that 'the troops who are relieving are Canadian, not English' (65). When the Canadian troops appear outside of their window, confirming Father Lambertus' information, Willem concludes that the Canadians will 'be idolized! And well they deserve it!' (65). In its return to a highly celebrated time in Canadian history that enabled the forging of a distinct national identity, *Star Crossed* also subtly calls attention to problems inherent in the nation's development: the Canadians' war effort was predicated upon the 'othering' and defeat of 'Germans,' as well as on the systematic exclusion of an integral part of its own population.

Star Crossed also dramatizes the lasting, devastating effects of war on domestic relations. It specifically focuses on the loss of Marguerita, Willem's wife, and the way in which this particular loss informs Willem's conception of peace. Though Marguerita appears in the prologue, she is hauntingly absent for the subsequent three acts, having died in a Rotterdam air raid (23). In the theatre the 'absent body' can be experienced 'as a palpable, "embodied presence,"' in a manner, as Helen Gilbert and Joanne Tompkins explain, that can be highly 'unsettling' (230). The Heerdincks' frequent sorrowful references to Marguerita (14, 23, 49, 50, 57, 64) enable this tragic sense of 'absence-presence' throughout the play and highlight the way in which war losses infect peacetime. Willem explains, 'I look forward to freedom with dread,' as it will not bring back his wife, nor will he have the wartime diversions from his sorrow (23). The announcement of liberation also prompts Elizabeth to consider Willem's losses and to further the play's deconstruction of peace as an assumed category. She reflects that Willem will experience a 'glooming peace' (5.3.305) and 'have time now to think of what he has lost ... His wife, his son, his daughter' (64).

The play's epigraph, 'From forth the [*sic*] loins of these two fatal [*sic*] foes/ A pair of star-crossed lovers take their life' (1), a slight reworking of *Romeo and Juliet*'s ominous prologue (1.1.5–6), suggests that the play will also counter the celebratory atmosphere of liberation with the tragic deaths of the lovers. Despite Anna's pleas and the German army's retreat, Dirk assassinates Folkert and informs his family of this fact, noting that it was Folkert who started 'the blood flowing' in his persecution of members of the Dutch Resistance and in his execution of Philip, Dirk's best friend (62). Dirk's murder of Folkert is thus reminiscent of Romeo's murder of Tybalt, the character responsible for the death of his best friend, Mercutio. This moment in *Star Crossed* also seemingly evokes Macbeth's reflection, 'Blood will have blood' (3.4.121), and draws attention to the cyclical nature of violence and war. Anna's recognition, '[n]o one is to blame' (62), implies that she has come to fathom Folkert's death as war's casualty, rather than as Dirk's, in a manner enabling her to forgive her brother.

Though at first 'overwhelmed' (62) by the announcement of Folkert's death, Anna soon becomes 'detached' and 'faraway' (62), descriptors that suggest her sudden dislocation from those around her. Though Anna, here, appears to experience a private moment of social disassociation, other Dutch 'collaborators' experience the process of alienation publicly. As Dirk '[s]oberly' reports, 'Some collaborators have been rounded up. I saw one – a girl. They were clipping her hair' (66). Anna never comes to experience this form of public 'retribution' (66); however, her private act of suicide, which closes the play, achieves the same end. Her death represents a graphic instance of 'retribution' and of the fight against 'Germans' and those associated with 'Germans' directed at the self. It also illustrates the impossibility of reconciling private desires with communal imperatives.

Star Crossed frequently gestures to Shakespeare throughout the play in order to highlight the similarities between the Capulet/Montague conflict and those in postwar 1950s Canada. *Star Crossed*, however, deviates from *Romeo and Juliet* in its conclusion in order to call attention to the problematic notion of 'peacetime' in 1945 – when the official armistices had been signed but hatred and intolerance still lingered. *Romeo and Juliet* closes with the full resolution of the Capulet/Montague conflict. The deaths of Romeo and Juliet bring about a new, peaceable order, and their love, as Janette Dillon explains, 'is seen to have had value, indeed power to change the world' (51). *Star Crossed*, however, complicates *Romeo and Juliet*'s resolution, showing the way in which 'blood continues to beget blood' despite public settlement. Although open warfare is brought to an end, peace is not achieved, and the deaths of the lovers come to incite further social-domestic hatred. Anna's death prompts Willem to blame himself for not having rigidly enforced the fight against 'Germans' within his home, an act he assumes would have enabled the maintenance of Anna's Dutch identity and her continued safety. As the 'cheering' of the masses 'bursts forth' from outside (67), Willem declares, 'We are to blame, Elizabeth. We did not hate them enough! We did not hate enough!' (67). *Star Crossed* thus closes ambiguously, balancing a tragic domestic scene with a celebration of Canada's war effort; in doing so, it succeeds in memorializing the achievements of the Canadian soldiers in the Netherlands without glorifying war.

Notes

1 In *Our Century*, for example, Canadian historians Robert Bothwell and J.L. Granatstein contend that the Second World War initiated the nation's second 'coming of age,' a time of growth when Canada further consolidated its identity as a strong, independent nation and gained a reputation as a

'middle power' within the world as a result of its extensive contribution to the war effort (128).

2 The popular, romantic remembrance of Canada's engagement in a 'good war' has been interrogated in recent years, most notably by Canadian historian Jeff Keshen in *Saints, Sinners, and Soldiers: Canada's Second World War*, which acknowledges and historicizes the little-known aspects of Canada's war effort. The numerous historical accounts of Canada's internment and deportation of Japanese Canadians (1941–6) also undermine the conventional, heroic treatment of the Second World War.

3 Canadian popular historian Pierre Berton argues that 'King, for all his vacillating, knew quite well that when Britain went to war with Germany, Canada would follow. Public opinion demanded that he simulate his country's independence. But public opinion also demanded that when Hitler rejected the British ultimatum and plunged the world into a new global conflict on September 3, 1939, Canada would be part of it' (322).

4 Berton notes that '[i]n 1939, a million Canadians were still on relief. Hunger as much as patriotism drove [Canadian men] to the recruiting stations' (327).

5 Keshen notes that there were actually veterans who downplayed the war's horror and encouraged young men to fight.

6 There were other reasons for not welcoming the war: the recollection of the debilitating spread of the Spanish influenza throughout Canada in 1917–18, and, postwar, the high national debt stemming from Canada's participation in the war.

7 This includes 106,000 in the Royal Canadian Navy and 200,000 in the Royal Canadian Air Force (Hillis, 'Facts'); 41.15% of the male population enlisted (Hillis, 'Facts'), and approximately 46,998 military personal died (Hillis, 'Canadian Military'). Canadian industries on the home front also contributed to the war effort; they manufactured over '800,000 military transport vehicles, 50,000 tanks, 40,000 field, naval, and anti-aircraft guns, and 1,700,000 small arms' for the Allied troops overseas (Hillis, 'The Canadian War Industry').

8 Other major battles at which Canadians distinguished themselves include the Battle of the Atlantic (1939–45); the Battle of Hong Kong (18–25 December 1941); the Battle of Dieppe (19 August 1942); the Battle of Ortona (21–8 December 1943); the Juno Beach, Normandy Landing (6 June 1944); and the Battle of the Scheldt (1 October to 8 November 1944).

9 This is certainly the case in the Netherlands where Canadian veterans are – arguably – more honoured than even in their own country. Canada's choice to harbour the pregnant Dutch Princess Juliana during the war also cemented Dutch–Canadian relations.

10 English-French relations became strained after Prime Minister MacKenzie King imposed conscription in 1944, despite Quebec's resistance to this measure. For more information on the conscription crisis of 1944, see J.L. Granatstein and J.M. Hitsman, *Broken Promises: A History of Conscription in Canada* (Toronto: Oxford University Press, 1977).

11 The situation for Japanese Canadians became especially grave after the bombing of Pearl Harbor in 1941. Many Japanese Canadians were moved inland from British Columbia and/or interned in camps throughout British Columbia as a means of safeguarding the coast from potential Japanese invaders. Most Japanese Canadians were stripped of their rights and possessions, forced to do manual labour, and issued special clothing. On 22 September 1988 Prime Minister Brian Mulroney formally apologized to Japanese Canadians on behalf of the Canadian government; surviving internees were issued a compensation of $21,000, and those who had been deported to Japan were reinstated as Canadian citizens.

12 Canadian theatrical responses to the Second World War have been decidedly delayed. Only in recent years has an efflorescence of plays appeared on the theatrical scene. These include (but are not limited to) Tom Hendry's *Fifteen Miles of Broken Glass* (1975), John Murrell's *Waiting for the Parade* (1980), Peter Cooley's *You'll Get Used To It: The War Show* (1982), Kenneth Brown and Stephen Scriver's *Letters in Wartime* (1994), Irene Kirstein Watts's *Goodbye Marianne* (1995), Jason Sherman's *None Is Too Many* (1997), Michael Healey's *The Drawer Boy* (2002), Norah Harding's *Sometime, Never* (2002), and John Mighton's *Half Life* (2005). These plays reveal a significant preoccupation with recovering the Second World War from a distinctly Canadian perspective. Interestingly, almost all of them allude to Shakespeare.

13 The *Canadian Adaptations of Shakespeare Project* at the University of Guelph has attempted to collect and compile all Canadian adaptations of Shakespeare. According to their research, *Star Crossed* is the only play centred on the events of the Second World War. See http://www.canadianshakespeares.ca/Production_Shakespeare/SearchPublic.cfm.

14 Knight's collection, first published in 1940 as *This Sceptred Isle*, was revised and re-published under the title *The Olive and the Sword: A Study of England's Shakespeare* (London: Oxford University Press, 1944). Shakespeare plays were aired on CBC radio throughout the war years; see Marta Straznicky, '"A Stage for the Word": Shakespeare on CBC Radio, 1947–1955.'

15 Shakespeare adaptations have been hailed a distinctive feature of Canadian drama and one of the most utilized, celebrated, and creative approaches

on the Canadian theatrical scene. Irena R. Makaryk notes that 'Shakespeare's influence [in Canada] ... has been responsible for initiating the extremely fertile and distinct subgenres of Shakespearean parodies and serious adaptations' (35). She also argues that '[a]s a settler/invader colony founded on displacements, Canada has been well positioned to deal with revisions and rewritings of canonical works ... In Canada's case, a growing desire for equality with, not complete separation from, Britain marks its historical development' (35). Fischlin echoes this argument, noting that though 'Shakespearean presence is a function of Canada's colonial heritage with its dependency on immigrant cultures, it is also a function of how a new and emergent culture has sought to define itself in dialogue (and frequently against) the Shakespearean tradition' ('Welcome').

16 A bolder claim could be made about this play as a kind of allegory or an oblique critique of the way in which war produces xenophobia and hate everywhere, even in Canada.

17 Donna Coates, in an analysis of Canadian literary representations of women and the Second World War, argues that 'war has traditionally been considered a male experience and the tale of the battlefield the privileged war story' (251). Though this is certainly true of most 'hegemonic histories' and 'dominant war drama[s],' which 'concentrate on battles, politico-military strategy, and changes in maps and boundaries' and centre on 'male experience at the battlefront' (Tylee, Turner, Cardinal 1), it is not necessarily reflective of Shakespeare's plays, which frequently feature the perspectives of women on war. See, for example, the Histories and, perhaps especially, *Troilus and Cressida*.

18 For Fischlin's introduction to *Star Crossed* and a PDF link to the script, please see http://www.canadianshakespeares.ca/a_starcrossed.cfm.

19 This relationship would have paralleled many in Canada, namely those between German Canadians and Canadians of Allied descent, which would have been acceptable in prewar Canada but not in wartime.

20 Fischlin explains that Library and Archives Canada notes two spellings for the author of *Star Crossed* – Patrick Bentley and Patrick Bentket ('Star-Crossed: A Play'). I have been unable to find 'Bentket' anywhere on the LAC copy of *Star Crossed*.

21 There are no Canadian First World War service records for Malone or Bentley, nor are there records of their deaths in either the First or the Second World Wars. Service records for living Second World War veterans remain confidential and inaccessible to the general public. Many veterans, however, remained in contact with the Legion following the War, and the deaths of these veterans can be found in public Legion files. No conclusive

Legion files were found either for Bentley or for Malone; however, there is one general record of death for a Clarence P. Malone, who was born in 1906 in Guelph, Ontario, and was married to Edna (Kaiser) Malone. Given *Star Crossed*'s romantic conflict, Edna's German maiden name may offer a clue both to Malone's identity and to the need to suppress it.

22 I have not been able to locate either *The Heart of My Mystery* or *A Great Day*.

23 This name shifting also recalls the situation in the First World War, where German Canadians changed their names and ethnic affiliations as a result of anti-German sentiment in Canada. For more information, see Edward Schreyer, *The Role of German-Canadian Settlers in Canada – Past and Present* (Saskatoon: Saskatchewan German Council, 1990), 22. Town names in Canada were also subject to change. For example, the Ontario town of Berlin became Kitchener. For more information, see Patricia P. McKegney, *The Kaiser's Bust: A Study in War-time Propaganda in Berlin, Ontario 1914–1918* (St Jacobs: Bamberg Press, 1991). In Western Canada, the towns of Koblenz, Bremen, Prussia, and Kaiser were also renamed as a means of affirming community patriotic alliances.

24 The inclusion of Malone in Milne's catalogues and the content of *A Great Day* strongly suggest Malone's Canadian citizenship.

25 Archivists at LAC report that there may have been an acquisition form, but that this form cannot be found. Within the Dominion Drama Festival file, there is a note explaining that all scripts were received between 1961 and 1970.

26 Programs from each year have not survived. *Star Crossed* is not listed in the LAC collection of programs.

27 The Dominion Drama Festival was initially created in 1932 by the standing Governor General of Canada, the 9th Earl of Bessborough Sir Vere Brabazon Ponsonby, along with a number of well-placed theatre practitioners and 'enthusiasts' including lawyer, diplomat, and later Governor General of Canada (1952–9) Vincent Massey and playwright Herman Voaden (Whittaker 144).

28 Between 1944 and 1955 CBC adaptations of Shakespeare were frequently featured on radio programs such as *National School Broadcast*, *Stage*, and *Wednesday Night* (Straznicky, '"A Stage for the Word"').

29 The Stratford Festival was legally founded in October 1952. The first production took place in 1953 in a large canvas tent, and the Festival Theatre was officially opened in 1957.

30 The last national census before the Second World War took place in 1931. Of the total Canadian population of 10,376,786, Germans accounted for 39,163 (Statistics Canada).

31 Schreyer contends that the First World War incited a greater ideological war against 'Germanness' than the Second World War. During the First World War the government suppressed all German language newspapers and schools. Furthermore, towns with German names were renamed and many German Canadians changed their surnames, adopting new ethnic identities in the process (27–8). Malone would have been aware of this history at the time of the play's writing and production, especially if he was married to a woman of German descent.

32 All of the conflicts appear to focus on Juliet's question, 'What's in a name?' (2.1.87), and on the way in which hatred is blindly attributed to particular ideological categories.

33 Similarly, in Shakespeare's play – although not a war play – the young protagonists are unable to escape the conflict-ridden confines of the omnipresent and destructive feud between the Capulets and the Montagues, a sort of civil war.

34 Elizabeth conveys much of the play's anti-war sentiment in lines such as 'Don't tell me war is not ridiculous!' (10), 'Even the German's must be convinced now that war is stupid' (18), and 'War! War! How preposterous!' (31).

35 Though *Star Crossed* situates the Heerdincks in a war-torn country, their position within an isolated home in a 'secluded' village, 'off the main roads, and of no military importance' (7), enables their partial escape from the horror of war. Their situation thus parallels that of Canadians on the home front.

36 Busch's Schumann/Schubert mistake could be read as an indication of the play's date. Though it could be merely coincidental, in 1956, East Germany issued a pair of postage stamps with Schumann's picture at the foreground and Schubert's music in the background. The stamps were later reissued with both Schumann's picture and his music.

37 The history of the song 'Lilli Marlene' also suggests the place of music as a counter-current to war. This song, which describes the anguish of a soldier separated from his girlfriend, transcended battle lines and reminded soldiers of their common experience of war. The song bridged not only soldiers but also civilians from the Americas and other nations. In America, in particular, the widespread popularity of German American Marlene Dietrich's English version, combined with her anti-Nazi campaign, served to foster American and German-American relations and to prompt a reconsideration of the wartime conception of the 'German.' For more information, see Liel Leibovitz and Matthew Miller, *Lilli Marlene: The Soldiers' Song of World War II* (New York: Norton, 2008).

38 In *Imagined Communities* (1983) Benedict Anderson argues that a nation

is a social construct imagined by the people who perceive themselves as belonging it to it (6–7).

39 Although I suggest that Dirk comes to adopt discriminatory practices reminiscent of those of the Nazis, my intention is not minimize the significant disparities between his actions, representative of the Dutch Resistance, and those of the Nazi regime.

40 There is a subtle parallel between Juliet and the 'moffenhoerens.' Juliet's transgression of social rules, in her of refusal of her father's choice of a marriage partner and her preference for an enemy Montague, 'signals her resolute privileging of her own desire' (Léon Alfar 69–70) over the needs of the community around her. This leads Capulet to condemn Juliet to 'hang, beg, starve, die in the streets!' (3.5.192).

41 The significant erasure of German culture in Canada by Canadians of German descent suggests that they also feared stigmatization.

Works Cited

Anderson, Benedict. *Imagined Communities: Reflections on the Origin and Spread of Nationalism*. London: Verso, 1983.

'Appendix II: List of Plays Donated.' *Dominion Drama Festival*. Library and Archives Canada.

Berton, Pierre. *Marching as to War: Canada's Turbulent Years, 1899–1953*. Toronto: Doubleday Canada, 2001.

Bothwell, Robert, and J.L. Grantstein. *Our Century: The Canadian Journey in the Twentieth Century*. Toronto: McArthur, 2000.

Coates, Donna. 'Wish Me Luck as You Wave Me Goodbye: Representations of War Brides in Canadian Fiction and Drama by Margaret Atwood, Mavis Gallant, Norah Harding, Margaret Hollingsworth, Joyce Marshall, Suzette Mayr, Aritha van Herk, Rachel Wyatt.' *Back to Peace: Reconciliation and Retribution in the Postwar Period*. Ed. Aránzazu Usandizaga and Andrew Monnickendam. Notre Dame: University of Notre Dame Press, 2000. 250–71.

Diederichs, Monika. 'Stigma and Silence: Dutch Women, German Soldiers and their Children.' *Children of World War II: The Hidden Enemy Legacy*. Ed. Kjersti Ericsson and Eva Simonsen. Oxford: Berg, 2005. 151–64.

Dillon, Janette. *The Cambridge Introduction to Shakespeare's Tragedies*. Cambridge: Cambridge University Press, 2007.

Elshtain, Jean Bethke. *Women and War*. New York: Basic Books, 1987.

Ericsson, Kjersti. 'Introduction.' *Children of World War II: The Hidden Enemy Legacy*. Ed. Kjersti Ericsson and Eva Simonsen. Oxford: Berg, 2005. 1–12.

Fischlin, Daniel. 'Star Crossed: A Play.' *Canadian Adaptations of Shakespeare*

Project. University of Guelph. n.d. 5 Mar. 2010. http://www.canadianshake-speares.ca/a_starcrossed.cfm.

– 'Welcome to the Canadian Adaptations of Shakespeare Project.' *Canadian Adaptations of Shakespeare Project.* University of Guelph. Aug. 2007. 5 Mar. 2010. http//www.canadianshakespeares.ca/main.cfm.

Gardner, David. 'Dominion Drama Festival.' *The Canadian Encyclopedia.* Historica-Dominion Institute. n.d. 5 Mar. 2010. http//www.thecanadianen-cyclopedia.com/index.cfm?PgNm=TCE&Params=A1ARTA0002346.

Gilbert, Helen, and Joanne Tompkins. *Post-colonial Drama: Theory, Practice, Politics.* London: Routledge, 1996.

Hillis, Erik. 'Canadian Military Personnel Killed.' *Canada at War.* n.d. 20 Dec. 2010. http://wwii.ca/index.php.

– 'Facts and Information.' *Canada at War.* 4 July 2009. 20 Dec. 2010. http://wwii.ca/content-7/world-war-ii/facts-and-information/.

– 'The Canadian War Industry.' *Canada at War.* 17 Sept. 2007. 20 Dec. 2010. http:wwii.ca/content-17/world-war-ii/canadian-war-industry/.

Keshen, Jeff. *Saints, Sinners, and Soldiers: Canada's Second World War.* Vancouver: University of British Columbia Press, 2004.

Knowles, Ric. *Shakespeare and Canada: Essays on Production, Translation, and Adaptation.* Brussels: P.I.E. – Peter Lang, 2004.

Léon Alfar, Christina. *Fantasies of Female Evil: The Dynamics of Gender and Power in Shakespearean Tragedy.* London: Associated University Presses, 2003.

Makaryk, Irena R. 'Introduction: Shakespeare in Canada: "a world else-where?"' *Shakespeare in Canada.* Ed. Diana Brydon and Irena R. Makaryk. Toronto: University of Toronto Press, 2002. 3–41.

Malone, Clarence. *Star Crossed. Canadian Adaptations of Shakespeare Project.* University of Guelph. N.d. 5 Mar. 2010. http://www.canadianshakespeares. ca/anthology/star.pdf.

Milne, William S. *Canadian Full-Length Plays in English: A Preliminary Annotated Catalogue.* Ottawa: Dominion Drama Festival, 1964.

– *Canadian Full-Length Plays in English (II): A Supplement to the Preliminary Annotated Catalogue.* Ottawa: Dominion Drama Festival, 1966.

Nelan, Bruce W. 'The Last Good War.' *Time* (151) 9 March 1998: 120–6.

Schreyer, Edward. *The Role of German Canadian Settlers in Canada – Past and Present.* Saskatoon: Saskatchewan German Council, 1990.

'Shakespeare.' *Canadian Theatre Encyclopedia.* Athabasca University. 12 Aug. 2009. 20 Dec. 2010. http://www.canadiantheatre.com/dict. pl?term=Shakespeare.

Shakespeare, William. *Macbeth. The Norton Shakespeare: Tragedies.* Ed. Stephen Greenblatt et al. New York: Norton, 1997.

– *Romeo and Juliet*. Ed. Jill L. Levenson. Oxford: Oxford University Press, 2000.

Straznicky, Marta. '"A Stage for the Word": Shakespeare on CBC Radio, 1947–1955.' *Shakespeare in Canada: A World Elsewhere?* Ed. Diana Brydon and Irena R. Makaryk. Toronto: University of Toronto Press, 2002. 92–107.

Statistics Canada. 'Table 26: Birthplace of the population by quinquennial age groups and sex.' *Population Overview: Volume 1. Canada and Provinces 1931 Census.*

Tylee, Claire M., Elaine Turner, and Agnès Cardinal, eds. 'General Introduction.' *War Plays by Women: An International Anthology*. London: Routlege, 1999. 1–15.

von Clausewitz, Carl. *On War*. Trans. and ed. Michael Howard and Peter Paret. Princeton: Princeton University Press, 1984.

Whittaker, Herbert. 'Dominion Drama Festival.' *The Oxford Companion to Canadian Theatre*. Ed. Eugene Benson and L.W. Conolly. Toronto: Oxford University Press, 1989. 144–5.

14 Shakespeare's Merchant of Venice in Auschwitz

TIBOR EGERVARI

I am Jewish. I was born in Budapest in 1938, two months after the Anschluss. The fact that I survived is either a miracle or a stroke of luck, depending on your beliefs. The Stalinist regime that saw to much of my schooling had little interest in the Shoah. At home, we spoke about it only in roundabout ways and in hushed tones. In any case, my mother, who had lost a son and a husband, categorically refused to discuss it. And I felt no vocation to bear witness.[1]

While I am not a Shakespeare scholar in the academic sense of the term (by trade, I am a theatre director), I have been familiar with the Bard since my childhood in Budapest. Nearly all of Shakespeare's plays could be seen in Stalinist Hungary, but not *The Merchant of Venice*. In the same way that the regime 'settled' the anti-Semitism problem by purging it from the official rhetoric, it simply eliminated any plays that could not be given a 'correct' Marxist interpretation from the repertory. A performance of *The Merchant* no doubt would have disturbed the established order of ideas. As a result, I did not see *The Merchant* until 1970, at the Stratford Festival in Ontario. What struck me most about that production was its failure to grasp the Jewish questions in the play, which to me were obvious. I was not alone in this reaction. Theatre critic Arnold Edinborough echoed my response in his article 'A Gallic Romp through Shakespeare': 'Though Donald Davis is a fine actor and his presence on the stage unmistakable in its authority, [Jean] Gascon [the director] made him present his character as that of a man who merely drives a hard bargain, not as a Jew … There was no ultimate degradation of the Jew when he was forced to convert to Christianity' (459).

I will limit my remarks to two points related to Jewishness that the production patently ignored. First, for Shylock, who is a widower, losing his only daughter to a Christian amounts to both the death of his daughter and the end of his lineage: a tragedy coupled with breaking the commandments. The text is clear in this regard: 'I would my daughter were dead at my foot, and the jewels in her ear! Would she were hearsed at my foot, and the ducats in her coffin!' (*Merchant*, 3.1.91–4). As in other productions I saw later, the references to the jewels were interpreted as further proof of Shylock's cupidity without noting that those ornaments pertain to Jessica and Jessica only. The dowry ornaments – for marriage to a Jew, of course – are an integral part of his daughter and therefore must die with her.

The other point pertains to the blood that Portia forbids Shylock to shed by taking the pound of Antonio's flesh to which he is 'entitled.' Obviously, blood spilled by a Jew, especially in the late sixteenth century, recalls the medieval persecution of Jews for supposedly using Christian blood, and what's worse, from young children, in making their Passover matzo. This ignominious accusation played an important role in the resurgence of anti-Semitism in the nineteenth century. It also can be seen in relation to the kosher food rules that prohibit Jews from consuming blood in any form. To me, Portia's cruel allusion seemed sufficiently clear to warrant attention in even a minimally thoughtful staging. Edinborough again had it right: 'There was thus no pathos in the Court scene – just Portia's triumph' (Edinborough 459). Having made these observations, I felt quite sure I had identified the fundamental issue of the play and the flagrant errors of the production. I also took note to address them should I direct the play.

A few years later, I found myself heading a large theatre in Bussang, in the Vosges region of eastern France – a 'people's theatre,' or *thé-âtre populaire* as the French call it. The Théâtre du Peuple was founded in 1895 by Maurice Pottecher, and until the early 1970s it performed his plays exclusively. On summer Sunday afternoons the vast wooden building with the stage back opened to reveal the landscape, unique in France, and welcomed audiences representing almost every level of French society. When I took over as artistic director, my first move was to change the repertory by adding several Shakespeare plays, because if anyone ever wrote for the people, it was the Bard. *The Merchant of Venice* was an obvious possibility, and I decided to study it with a view to production. I was in for a brutal shock. I knew that Shylock had 'usurped' the leading role, of course, but I had had no idea of the riches this usurpation was concealing. The first discovery was what I believe to be the main theme, which is the transactions or commerce, in the broad sense of the term, between and of men and women. As in all his major plays, Shakespeare has organized the dramatic structure of *The Merchant of Venice* to reflect the main theme, with each scene shedding light on one of the facets. A glance at act 1 confirms this:

Scene 1: The conversation between Antonio, Salanio, and Salarino basically revolves around the merchant's business; then Antonio's conversation with Bassanio leads to the possibility of acquiring Portia's fortune. Bassanio begins the description of his future wife – 'In Belmont is a lady richly left' (*Merchant*, 1.1.161) – and the deal is sealed. Antonio lends his name and reputation so that Bassanio can borrow the money he needs to capture the inheritance and the woman who comes with it. So goes the world where everything is bought and sold.

Scene 2: This scene could be compared to the famous portrait scene in Molière's *Misanthrope*, where Célimène ridicules her entourage,[2] but Shakespeare goes much further. Contrary to the young, financially independent widow Célimène, Portia, in principle immensely wealthy, is bound hand and foot by her dead father's wishes. In her conversation with Nerissa we learn how the father's will disposes of his daughter and his fortune without giving her a say in the matter. Her hand – I was going to say 'the goods' – is to go not to the highest bidder but to the man best able, in the father's mind, to manage the wealth and the wife.[3]

Scene 3: We are at the heart of the fable, at the meeting between Bassanio and Shylock (joined by Antonio), a famous scene that needs no description. The scene is most obviously driven by the central transaction in the play: 'Three thousand ducats, for three months and Antonio bound' (*Merchant*, 1.3.9–10). What is remarkable is Shylock's initial response. Caught off guard by Bassanio, he has had no time to prepare, but even so, he knows that Antonio 'is sufficient. Yet his means are in supposition. He hath an argosy bound to Tripolis, another to the Indies. I understand moreover, upon the Rialto, he hath a third at Mexico, a fourth for England, and other ventures he hath, squandered abroad' (*Merchant*, 1.3.17–22). There you have the banker at his best, fully informed about a potential client … in advance. Information is the banker's primary tool; it is required if a job must be done right. Shylock, however, is not just a good banker. While demonstrating an extraordinary memory that no doubt houses 'databases' of the entire Venetian merchant class, he pretends to be addled and asks about the terms of Bassanio's request again and again. Neither Antonio nor Bassanio recognizes the ruse, which is a fair indication of their poor business sense, to say the least.

In the same scene we see the fundamental confrontation of the two concepts of money: the medieval notion held by Antonio and the modern one held by Shylock. For Antonio, money is a mere signifier, or, if you like, a method of payment with no intrinsic value. Shylock, on the other hand, is already using money in the modern sense, if only of necessity, since usury (as all money-lending was then called) is his livelihood. Money had come to be a signifier as well, of value in and of itself. It was a commodity like any other, to be rented in exchange for payment – hence the French term *loyer de l'argent* (money rent), meaning interest rate.[4] As is often the case, Shakespeare's sympathy lies with the old, even as he knows the advent of the new is inevitable.

The main theme is sufficiently clear by now; going through the whole play would be tedious, but I cannot resist the temptation to add the scene in which Bassanio, having won the heiress's hand, declares his love, which Portia seems to share (*Merchant*, 3.2). The language here is decidedly peculiar.

BASSANIO: So, thrice-fair lady, stand I, even so,
  As doubtful whether what I see be true,
  Until confirmed, signed, ratified by you.
PORTIA: You see me, Lord Bassanio, where I stand,
  Such as I am. Though for myself alone
  I would not be ambitious in my wish,
  To wish myself much better; yet for you
  I would be trebled twenty times myself –
  A thousand times more fair, ten thousand times
  More rich –
  That only to stand high in your account,
  I might in virtues, beauties, livings, friends,
  Exceed account. But the full sum of me
  Is sum of something which, to term in gross ...   (*Merchant*, 3.2.147–60)

While the word 'account' can be understood in the sense of 'esteem,' the multiplications and the use of terms such as 'sum,' 'gross,' and 'livings' leave no room for doubt about the commercial dimension of human relations. However, the most striking example comes at the end of the scene, when Portia takes leave of her betrothed: 'Since you are dear-bought, I will love you dear' (*Merchant*, 3.2.316) – a theatrically splendid line if ever there was one.

Besides the powerful theme of commerce – again, to be understood in the broadest sense – the play presents other aspects, the most important of which, to my mind, is the role assigned to women in this transactional world. The two women who marry (I do not count Nerissa, who as a waiting-maid is simply imitating her mistress) are wealthy heiresses. Portia's hand and fortune are hidden in one of the three caskets, and once Bassanio chooses correctly, with the barely disguised help of Portia who, despite her protests is no stranger to deceit, everything becomes subject to the husband's control. Portia is simply the depositary or trustee of the casket, a mere conduit. Locked away out of her reach, the inheritance passes directly from father to son-in-law.

Jessica does not wait for her father to decide. She steals the casket containing a small fortune and – note the Shakespearean dramaturgy – tosses it down to Lorenzo before joining him in the street. She no doubt feels she has no right to keep it, even for the short time it takes to go downstairs. Shakespeare thus uses the same pattern and instrument to reveal the same demonstration of woman's role.

From a contemporary angle, *The Merchant of Venice* is not merely anti-Semitic; it is also profoundly xenophobic. Portia's suitors are mocked according to their ethnic characteristics. Ethnic jokes abound. And yet for ages, even centuries, all these theatrical riches meant to delight anyone with an interest in theatre have been swept under the rug in order to devote stagings and performances either to justifying or, more rarely, to condemning Shylock. As I thought about putting the play on, I was revolted that a work like this could be reduced to such a slight question. And what defence are we offered for a character that was obviously conceived to be a *villain*?

More often than not, this defence is based on one of the two best-known passages of the play: Shylock's tirade 'Hath not a Jew eyes?' (*Merchant*, 3.1.61). This speech comes at the beginning of act 3. He has just lost his daughter[5] and is honing the weapon of his vengeance, which he justifies in advance. He certainly is not going to call himself a crook, especially since he sincerely believes he is within his rights. The argument he makes is powerful: If you were in my place, you would do the same thing! This is not the Universal Declaration of Human Rights; it is the skilful defence of an unsympathetic, but not yet criminal, being. Moreover, he offers it in front of two characters that have absolutely no influence.[6]

This led me to the conclusion that, if I were to produce the play, I would have to attempt to restore its original value. Reversing the trend seemed to be a good place to start. I naively thought that putting Shylock back in his place, so to speak, would allow me to concentrate on the dramatic riches I described. All it would take was the courage to treat him as the *villain* he is, to take him out of the spotlight, and all would be well! I was much younger then, and I had the audacity to take my reasoning to the finish. It was clear that I could not do it, but what would happen, I wondered, if a real anti-Semite, someone without my scruples, were to produce the play? My next thought would have very heavy consequences, not for the universal history of theatre, but for my humble self.

So there I was with my bright idea, a director righter-of-wrongs, and I found the alter ego of my folly. I imagined an SS officer, intelligent and well versed in the theatre, who obtains permission to conduct the experiment of a lifetime with slave actors – something many directors dream of – in Auschwitz. Of course I know that there were cultural and artistic activities in Theresienstadt, and none except the orchestra in Auschwitz, but I was composing in fiction, not reconstruction. To say that I fell into my own trap would be an understatement.

My intelligent director was familiar with the play and understood its riches. Instead of doing what I asked him to do, that is, to skip over the Jewish question in order to restore the play's full meaning, he began to focus precisely on demonstrating what he considered Jewish baseness. In this he was behaving like most intelligent people who give themselves body and soul to an ideology: obsession, not to say madness, trumps reason. As the sorcerer's apprentice, I could do nothing but follow my creation – who decided to play Shylock himself. He explains why in trying to make the project clear to a German actress he has called in, who does not know what to expect:

SHYLOCK: You are here on official assignment. It's our duty to unveil the true face of this enemy race which the Führer has defined as a moral plague worse than the black plague of early times. Have you read *Mein Kampf*?
JESSICA: I ... well, not completely.
SHYLOCK: Well it doesn't make me laugh.

JESSICA: Forgive me ...

SHYLOCK: You will have time to read it ... all.

JESSICA: But since there are Jews here, why not have them do the Jews' parts? I could learn Portia in no time. My memory is excellent. Two weeks ago we found out that the grandmother of one of our actresses was Jewish. To think she performed all the great parts all those years. When the police arrested her, I learned her part overnight, it was ...

SHYLOCK: I'll let you know when I want your input. Do you honestly believe those Yids would project the image I wish to show of them? We're the only ones who can unveil their true identity. You're a professional actress, you should know that performing on stage means being someone other than yourself.

(Egervari 1.16)

Consequently, he casts the Venetians with Jewish prisoners selected for their appearance, history, and accent. He teaches these amateurs to act using highly dubious methods, including mental and physical torture, the worst, of course, being the obligation to emphasize their characters' anti-Semitism. For the two women of Belmont, he chooses two Roma women: after all, they too are foreigners. A prisoner, who is also a kapo (overseer) is to play Lancelot Gobbo, and another completes the cast as SS sergeant, stage manager, and Tubal.

They all live shut in a single room twenty-four hours a day: the prisoners in three cages (Venetians, women of Belmont, Lancelot Gobbo), the Jews in dressing rooms above them. Their routine includes warm-ups – as practiced in good theatre schools in the 1930s – humiliation sessions, corporal punishments, and rehearsals, all under the auspices of the National Socialist ideology with passages of *Mein Kampf*. The method also includes the systematic denigration of sacred texts, such as the Old Testament, and stories drawn from Jewish tradition, including an anecdote about Baal Shem Tov, founder of the Hassidic movement.[7]

In the play – mine, that is – the SS director leads rehearsals of Shakespeare's scenes, not in chronological order but close enough so that an audience unfamiliar with the original does not get lost. This gives the director the opportunity to develop a few aspects of the text, but mainly to perfect his rendering of Shylock. He is the only one in costume during rehearsals and he gradually changes his appearance until he resembles an ultra-orthodox Eastern European Jew. The others remain in their prison uniforms, with a few identifying marks here and there (see figs. 14.1, 14.2, and 14.3).

14.1 *The Merchant of Venice in Auschwitz*. From left to right: (on platform) Carole Bélanger as Portia, Carol Beaudry as Tubal; (on lower level) Mario Gendron as Shylock, Annick Léger as Bassanio, Robin Denault as Antonio, Mike Brunet as Gratiano, Dan McGarry as Salarino. Production photograph, Théâtre Distinct, 1993, directed by Tibor Egervari, set design by Margaret Coderre-Williams, costumes by Angela Haché.

14.2 *The Merchant of Venice in Auschwitz*. From left to right: Mario Gendron as Shylock (in dressing gown), Robin Denault as Antonio, Annick Léger as Bassanio. Production photograph, Théâtre Distinct, 1993, directed by Tibor Egervari, set design by Margaret Coderre-Williams, costumes by Angela Haché.

A basic costume of an orthodox Jewish boy is found for Jessica, since she disguised herself as a young man to escape from her father in Shakespeare's play.

At the beginning of the second part, Shylock announces that he wants to rehearse the court scene in act 4, even though it has not yet been blocked. The scene is fairly static, so he summarily indicates each group's position. He wants the scene to be 'improvised' and forbids anyone to interrupt the rehearsal for any reason whatsoever. Tubal plays the Duke in his SS sergeant uniform. Things go reasonably well, with the Venetians, played by Jews, railing against the increasingly hideous Shylock. Everything, however, stops when Portia enters. She is wearing an SS officer's hat and a Hitler-style moustache drawn with charcoal. General stupefaction gives way to the imperious wish of lord and master Shylock to continue, since he is totally into his role.

Portia delivers the famous 'The quality of mercy is not strained' passage like a Hitler speech, complete with intonations and gestures. (A word about this tirade: Most performers and directors seem to get carried away by the grand poetry of the text, without paying attention to its dramatic value. Barely five minutes after so superbly vaunting the virtues of mercy, Portia denies it to Shylock. And to boot, she reviles the Jew even more fiercely than the Venetians.)

After the performance by the prisoner playing Portia, the Venetians move closer and closer to Shylock, who is performing as if in ecstasy. Falling to his knees, he drops his knife. Antonio picks it up and, in a flash, kills Shylock, the hated SS, and even more hated ignoble image of the Jew that he projects. Tubal seizes his revolver and regains control of the situation. The Jews die singing 'Sh'ma Yisrael' (Hear (O) Israel),[8] the Gypsies reciting 'Ave Maria' in Latin, the kapo with a smile on his lips, and Jessica offering herself to the sergeant in an attempt to save her life – the last circle of Hell.

There have been three versions of the play. The first was performed in French by La Comédie des Deux Rives, the student troupe of the Department of Theatre at the University of Ottawa.

The second version had a run of performances in English and in French by Théâtre Distinct in 1993, in Ottawa and Montreal. In Montreal, it played at Théâtre le Gesù, concurrently with a production of Shakespeare's play at Théâtre du Nouveau Monde, a coincidence engineered by me that caused a minor uproar in the local theatre community. The third and final version was given a staged reading in a mixture of English and French at the University of Ottawa in 1998; this version was

14.3 *The Merchant of Venice in Auschwitz*. From left to right: Carol Beaudry as Tubal, Andre Perrier as Lancelot, Nadine Desrochers as Jessica. Production photograph, Théâtre Distinct, 1993, directed by Tibor Egervari, set design by Margaret Coderre-Williams, costumes by Angela Haché.

also published in English by Playwrights Press Canada in an anthology of adaptations of Shakespeare in Francophone Canada edited by Leanore Lieblein. This endeavour, which took more than two decades, was my only foray into playwriting – unintentional playwriting, that is, since I just wanted to give a magnificent play a proper staging. Even if my failure resulted in a new play, I wish I could have achieved my original goal. Artistically and intellectually it would have been more satisfying than the actual outcome, but it was impossible. In the second part of the twentieth century a number of small orchestras and individual soloists started introducing original baroque instruments to interpret music of that period. Audiences have reacted with great enthusiasm. At the same time, several stage directors attempted to apply similar treatments to plays of the past. Everything, from archaic pronunciation to set designs that imitate original physical environments, has been used to bring back the original flavour of centuries-old theatrical events. But theatre is more than reproduction; it is always a living relationship with a given audience – a *hic et nunc* audience.

Contemporary audiences have already inherited several strong interpretations of *The Merchant of Venice*. Those who never saw or read the play at least know Shylock's name and its associations. While it is impossible to ignore the history of anti-Semitism of the last several hundreds years, one cannot just push a reset button to cancel or change cultural references. And no 'director's notes' in theatre programs will have the slightest influence on the mindset of any member of the audience. On the one hand, it is fortunate that there is no limit to the research a scholar or a director can undertake about a play, an author, or a period; but on the other hand, unfortunately, there can be serious limitations to the staging of their findings. I was under the impression that, in the case of *The Merchant of Venice*, these limitations were so extreme that I felt compelled to write a new play. As I have mentioned, artistically and intellectually, this was meant to be just an ersatz that I could have chosen not to write. However, the idea of this new play was not just any idea. It brought about the story I would not, I could not, speak of in any other form.

There are things that sooner or later one must do, notwithstanding the quality of the deed. If one is, as I am, a procrastinator, this necessary action can take a long time. There are people who write masterpieces in a matter of weeks or even days; others can take twenty years to produce a mediocre play. I am convinced that I will never belong in the former category and I cannot but hope not to be part of the latter. Nonetheless, I know my limitations as a playwright. That is why I was so frustrated not having realized the staging I dreamt of, and why I thought that my 'brilliant idea' had such heavy consequences for my humble self. Instead of doing something I thought I was quite capable of, I had to struggle with a form I did not master. This happened to millions before me, except that people used to give it a simple name: duty.

Translated from French by Marcia Couëlle.

Notes

1 It was not until much later that I realized that I am part of the last generation to have 'been there,' and that one does not refuse this responsibility without good reason.
2 She similarly insults her suitors at the end of the play, but this time in letters.

3 An attentive reading reveals that Portia cheats by helping Bassanio choose the right casket, thus foiling her father's plan.

4 Today interest-free loans are considered highly suspect; in fact, a former French Prime Minister committed suicide after being accused of such borrowing.

5 Very religious Jews often sit shiva (observe the mourning rite) when a child converts.

6 One could even imagine that he is rehearsing for the trial and that, seeing the demonstration leave his listeners cold, he decides not to use it later.

7 This passage is taken from *Célébrations hassidiques* by Elie Wiesel.

8 'Hear (O) Israel' is a basic prayer of the Jewish faith to be recited in the morning and in the evening and by a dying person.

Works Cited

Edinborough, Arnold. 'A Gallic Romp through Shakespeare: An Account of the 1970 Season at Ontario's Stratford Festival.' *Shakespeare Quarterly* 21.4 (1970): 457–9.

Egervari, Tibor. *Shakespeare's The Merchant of Venice in Auschwitz. A Certain William: Adapting Shakespeare in Francophone Canada.* Ed. Leanore Lieblein. Toronto: Playwrights Canada Press, 2009. 107–84.

Shakespeare, William. *The Merchant of Venice. The Complete Works.* Ed. G.B. Harrison. New York. Barnes and Noble, 1966.

15 Appropriating Shakespeare in Defeat: *Hamlet* and the Contemporary Polish Vision of War

KATARZYNA KWAPISZ WILLIAMS

> In looking at their history and identity the Poles show a clear tendency to highlight sufferings as the key to the nation's philosophy of history. For more than three centuries suffering has been a constant historical determinant of Poland and the price paid for patriotism. Suffering can mean defeat; it can be regarded as proof of the absence or impotence of God. Polish spirituality, however, puts suffering in a different perspective. Suffering is seen as a sign of chosenness and the specific mission of Poles. The notion of chosenness is historically rooted. It explains all events in the light of the role and position of the Polish nation in God's plans.
>
> Chrostowski, 'The Suffering, Chosenness and
> Mission of the Polish Nation'

The image of Poland's 'chosenness' and messianic role has been recycled and reused by Poles in different historical contexts over the centuries to alleviate the pain of defeat they have suffered at various hands. The belief that Poles as a nation are exceptional in comparison to other nations was adopted from the messianic doctrine popular in Europe as early as the sixteenth century, further developed as a response to the long and unsuccessful struggle for independence, especially during the partition of Poland (1772–1918), and recycled in the coming years of occupation (Chrostowski).[1] Polish Romantics, writing in the aftermath of the failure of the 1830 Uprising against Russia, most effectively evoked the image of Poland as 'a Christ of Nations.' There have been many examples of literary works created since the Romantic period in which the motif of an uprising, struggle for independence, and the idea of suffering and heroism of the Polish nation is prominently exhibited.[2] This collective, national martyrology continued during the Second World War, enforcing the self-image of Poles as simultaneously betrayed victims and heroes. The failure of the last national uprising before the end – at least for most nations – of the Second World War, plus the following years under the Soviet rule, enforced the position of the myth of heroic struggle for freedom in Polish culture. Finally, in post-Soviet Poland, the growing number of museums and monuments – an imperative of living memory – changed, as Małgorzata Sugiera claims, from a 'necessary and slow process of mourning into automatic and institutionally encouraged duty of remembering' (14).[3]

Stories of the 1944 Warsaw Uprising, one of the most tragic and least known episodes of the Second World War, are told in numerous ways and contexts. Since 2006, to commemorate the anniversary of the Uprising, the Warsaw Uprising Museum has organized annual performances that celebrate the memory of war and retell the events of 1944 in, as they claim, 'a modern way.' According to the Museum's official sources, its objective is to 'universalise the experiences of war, occupation and the Uprising itself through classical literature,' and to question the way that the Warsaw Uprising is usually presented and understood in Poland, that is, 'either as a tiresome Polish martyrdom, or as an experience sanctifying Poland … [more] than any other nation' ('Odczytać Powstanie'). Although the Museum's efforts, closely aligned with the conservative political party Prawo i Sprawiedliwość (Law and Justice), imply institutionalisation of national memory and continuation of national mythology, the productions organized and sponsored by the Museum function in a rather unexpected way: by questioning what Sugiera has called the 'privileged ways of representing the past' (14). Moreover, young directors with unconventional approaches to art and history have used diversified forms of expression that attract young audiences.[4]

The audience that gathered in the Warsaw Uprising Museum on 1 August 2008 to watch Paweł Passini's stage play *Hamlet'44* was encouraged by the production to reflect on the heroism of fighting and dying for one's country, to consider death, its purpose and meaning, but also to think about Polish war history in universal terms, as existential experiences of freedom and fear known from philosophy and world literature ('Odczytać Powstanie'). Most probably Passini's audience anticipated, maybe even desired, the repetition of certain motifs used in 'modern Shakespeare' productions. Yet, they were perhaps surprised to hear the famous 'To be or not to be' soliloquy recited by a group of young actors

15.1 Maciej Wyczański (Hamlet) and Łukasz Lewandowski (Horatio) in
Hamlet'44, directed by Paweł Passini, Museum of the Warsaw Uprising, 2008.
Photograph by Julia Sielicka-Jastrzębska, reproduced courtesy of the Museum
of the Warsaw Uprising, Warsaw.

portraying insurgents who fall dead on the gravel under the fire of a Nazi squad, get up immediately, and then fall again. And get up and fall again. And get up and fall again. Reused and reclaimed in numerous cultural, social, and political circumstances, Shakespeare proved that the best way to understand his texts is by appropriating them to the local context. There may also be no better way to comprehend the terrifying events of war than by exposure, repetition, recycling.

The Warsaw Uprising (1 August to 3 October 1944) was organized as a part of 'Operation Tempest' by the Polish resistance movement – the Home Army (Armia Krajowa) – in the hope that, with Allied air-drops of supplies (weapons and food) and the military support of the advancing Red Army, Warsaw could be liberated from Nazi occupation and that the authorities of what became known as the 'Polish Underground State' could seize power in Poland before the Soviets did so.[5] However, the expected support did not arrive and, after sixty-three days of struggle, the Polish forces surrendered. During the Uprising the city of Warsaw was razed; between 130,000 and 180,000 civilians died,[6] and 16,000 Home Army soldiers were killed or reported missing.

The Uprising has always been a controversial and sensitive issue. After 1945, once the Communists seized power in Poland, reference to the Uprising became unpopular because it cast the Communists in a bad light, drawing attention to their failure to lend assistance to the Poles during the fighting. The legend of the Uprising remained; it lived underground and provided an arena for a struggle against Communism. Following the fall of the USSR in 1989, Polish history, which had been so often an uncomfortable topic, began to be reinvestigated and retold. Yet, the Uprising became a difficult 'myth' to cultivate. The young and the intellectuals died, as some say, 'without weapons and without reason,' but – as it is officially proclaimed – having achieved 'moral victory' (Sidorowicz 47).

For today's culture of sorting and separating, reusing and recycling, refashioning myths, the process of retelling stories and revaluating history does not seem problematic. In 2008, on the occasion of the sixty-fourth anniversary of the Warsaw Uprising and as part of the project 'Reading the Uprising – Theatre/Museum,' Paweł Passini directed *Hamlet'44*. Through Shakespeare, Passini presented a contemporary interpretation of the Second World War's tragic events and the struggle of young insurgents during the Uprising.[7]

One of the most violent periods in human history became a perfect age for Shakespeare to comment on. After all, Shakespeare was

15.2 Tomasz Dedek (Claudius), Paweł Pabisiak (Guildenstern), and Michał Czachor (Rosencrantz) in *Hamlet'44*, directed by Paweł Passini, Museum of the Warsaw Uprising, 2008. Photograph by Julia Sielicka-Jastrzębska, reproduced courtesy of the Museum of the Warsaw Uprising, Warsaw.

familiar with wars: 'warfare is everywhere in Shakespeare,' as Charles Edelman observed; his history plays are all about battles and even in 'the most non-military comedies … there is a great deal of military imagery' (1–2). In addition, his works have always functioned as reusable goods.[8] During the war Shakespeare was 'repossessed' by secret and military theatres, by theatres in exile, salvaged in prisoner of war camps and concentration camps, recovered by those who witnessed the evil of war, as some of the essays in this volume reveal. It is no surprise, then, that after the war he also became a part of the postmodern discourse of recycling the past, its values, and myths – a discourse that promotes 'a narrative of cultural production and progress that negates the idea of significant loss' (Kendall and Koster). He became a part of the process of modern cultural production that is often defined by such notions as 'bricolage,' 'différance,' 'simulacrum,' and, most frequently as 'appropriation' and 'recycling.' Shakespeare is 'already disseminated, scattered, appropriated, part of the cultural language, high and low' (Garber 7). As Garber claims, 'the word "Shakespearean" today has taken on its own set of connotations,' while modern Shakespeare 'often becomes a standardized plot, a stereotypical character, and, especially, a moral or ethical choice – not to mention the ubiquitous favorite, "a voice of authority."' He appears in journalistic jargon, is often sampled 'in forms from advertising to cartoon captions,' and his plays are now being used, 'regularly and with success, to teach corporate executives lessons about business' (4–7). Shakespeare also proved that recycling, after all, 'can make you feel good' (Hawkins 95).

Shakespeare's works have always functioned as re-usable goods, even for the playwright himself.[9] He was already 'recycled' in the Restoration period and then, for centuries, his texts were modified to please the tastes of the reading public and critics. The eighteenth century taste for adaptation, for cuts and additions, modernization of language, simplification of plot, changing characters and scenes, for interludes, afterpieces and *divertissements,* evinces extravagant if not violent ways of materializing Shakespeare both on stage and page.[10] Though adaptations were traditionally criticised as 'a symptom of a diseased popular taste' (Marsden 7) or as a 'deterioration and degradation of Shakespeare's art' (Bristol 65), they have been often preferred over the original text, because they were informed by contemporary life.

Modern adaptations obviously assume various degrees of distance from the original, but they all attempt to reclaim Shakespeare for the present. We have finally accepted the fact that literary works, canonical works especially, in spite of all their universality and timelessness, are like other products of modern culture – they are products with a limited useful life: each culture and generation must recover them for further use of their own. Especially after Jan Kott's *Shakespeare, Our Contemporary* (1965), many theatre directors were inspired to recycle Shakespeare and relate him to present audiences. One of them, Charles Marowitz, who authored very bold recensions of Shakespeare's works (see his *The Marowitz Shakespeare*), believes that 'recycling' enables the contemporizing of Shakespeare, but it also allows one to produce true art, keep theatre alive, and challenge 'the assumptions of the past' ('Improving').[11]

Hamlet'44 was one such attempt to challenge the 'assumption of the past,' to recycle the old play, together with Poland's history and memory. The war does not appear in allusions only; the performance was all about war and war drama; some scenes even confront the audience with projected images from the actual war. The play was staged outdoors, in the park surrounding the Warsaw Uprising Museum, located in the city district (Wola) where the fighting had been particularly fierce and where mass executions once took place. Some elements of the performance were projected on the Memorial Wall on which the names of thousands of insurgents who died during the Uprising are engraved. Thus the stage became a space marked with a very special meaning: it was the place of a real battlefield and a war grave.

As with other nations, in Poland *Hamlet* was often a vehicle for social and political commentary. During the long struggle for independence under various occupants, debates about freedom raged, and Hamlet was used and regarded as representative of the Polish nation, an 'intellectual, prisoner, and fighter' (Sułkowski 171): 'the Polish Prince.' With the end of Communism in Eastern Europe in 1989 and the end of 'the struggle for the national cause,' the play became less attractive and less useful, giving way to *Macbeth*, which brought a different vision of war – not a national heroic struggle, but a global conflict and a universal culture of war. Now, in 2008, *Hamlet* returned but served a different function. The play was recycled to comment on sensitive matters of the past, of political and ideological implications, to help find new myths in a different, new Europe. It was recycled to refresh our memory, free it from banalities and simplifications. It was staged to encourage contemplation of the fact that reality is never black or white.

Since the Uprising became a legend in Poland and 'the myth of the heroic dash of [the citizens of] the Capital' to liberate Warsaw from Nazi German occupation is still alive in Polish society (Sidorowicz 46), *Hamlet'44* seemed to make an attempt to measure its strength against the official interpretation of the Uprising: that it was necessary, unavoidable, heroic, and in some respect, even successful.[12] In the 1990s, Bogusław Sułkowski conducted sociological research on the Polish reinterpretation of *Hamlet* on an audience who 'has not personally experienced the totality of war ... the first generation whose physical existence has not been endangered.' He concluded that modern artists and audiences must revaluate history and develop new tools for interpreting reality; in doing so they are to be inspired by Shakespeare, and 'they, in turn, inspire Shakespeare' (222) – that is, they appropriate his texts for their individual use. However, since Shakespeare's text in *Hamlet'44* has been significantly rewritten and extended with many additional lines and plot elements, some reviewers wondered why Shakespeare was used here at all. They considered whether the only reason for this production was the fact that the director found a soldier with the pseudonym 'Hamlet' on the list of dead insurgents (Drewniak). Some insisted that introducing the themes of war into the play was rather artificial and unjustified, as well as an abuse of Shakespeare's genius (Bończa-Szabłowski). Other reviewers believed that inserting *Hamlet* into the heroic history of the Warsaw Uprising seemed quite natural, since that was the time when Poles faced Hamlet's dilemma: deciding whether 'to be or not to be' symbolically, as a nation, or, literally, as individuals. For the director of the performance and the organizers of the 'Reading the Uprising – Theatre/Museum' project, Shakespeare was to help to tell the war story, narrate the Uprising 'without [mental] complexes, or even with some vigour and spirit' ('Powstańcy u Szekspira'). Recycling *Hamlet*, as the director clarified, was to help to extract the tragic dimension of the Uprising (Kopciński 19) to the utmost, to present its appalling and grievous facts, but also to reflect its complex nature, which still offers no simple interpretation. Adam Zamoyski explained that, for Poles, the Warsaw Uprising is

> the subject of a never-ending conundrum – was the rising an act of heroic if doomed self-defence, a historical imperative, or was launching it an act of criminal recklessness, resulting in the death of hundreds of thousands and the destruction of the capital? ... The issue will not go away because it has affected and continues to affect life in Poland ... Despite the meticulous reconstructions, one cannot walk around Warsaw today without being aware that one is walking over a battlefield.

Undoubtedly, recycling old images and stories and looking at complex events and situations through familiar lenses helps to understand the past that lives only in these stories. Shakespeare is constantly refashioned and recycled 'for the same reasons that we are constantly reinterpreting history, re-evaluating the lives of its leading figures, and revising the significance of its most seminal events; trying always to dig deeper and learn more than the generations before us' (Marowitz, 'Improving'). The play, and Hamlet's dilemma in particular, inspired interpretations that, in the Polish context, have become vital comments on war and its dimensions.[13] On the one hand, Hamlet's dilemma became a metaphor of a moral dilemma: 'to fight or not to fight,' raising the question of moral paralysis, the inability to act. On the other hand, it expressed the extremities of the situation, a unanimous war cry, without restraint, without doubts, and was *not* posed as a question. Though the theme of hesitation and inability to act has usually been present in Polish appropriations of the play, the phrase 'To be or not to be' became a symbol of a moral duty: to fight for the country's independence or die as a nation. Jacek Trznadel observes that '[t]he myth of Polish Hamlet testifies to ... the vitality of a certain idea and the ethos of a hero who wants to act, even in the most difficult conditions, in the name of truth and justice' (310). This hero 'who wants to act' remained the strongest Shakespearean image associated with Poland's struggle for independence.

Polish Hamlet has never faced a real interpretive alternative; 'To be' usually meant the struggle of the repressed Polish nation for freedom – for survival – while 'not to be' meant not fighting, as Kott claimed in his influential text 'Hamlet po XX zjeździe' [Hamlet after the Twentieth Congress] (1956: 3).[14] It may at first appear that the production of *Hamlet'44* continued this rhetoric of fighting for a national cause as the main dilemma of the Prince and one also shared by other characters. In such a view, the question is seemingly simple: whether or not to take part in the national struggle, to fight or not to fight. However, in the context of the Uprising, which, as many commentators and survivors believe,[15] was bound to fail from the beginning, the question 'To be or not to be' becomes quite complex: does 'to be' mean 'to fight and die achieving moral victory' or rather 'not to fight and survive.' Passini explained that 'in our performance "to be" means, for them [the insurgents], "to go"' (qtd in Kopciński 19), to fight and sacrifice one's life. The performance, however, showed that it is difficult, if not impossible, to provide *the right* answer to the question.

The phrase 'to be or not to be' was repeated three times during the production. It first appeared in a song sung by young boys in a pub, galvanizing them to fight. Then it was spoken by Hamlet himself. The third time, it was recited by young soldiers standing and falling in front of an invisible firing squad. The scenes, presenting various attitudes and convictions as equally valid, proved that Hamlet's moral dilemma is still today a dilemma without a solution, as it juxtaposes the national tradition of a myth of devotion and heroism in the face of war with individual and very subjective feelings, fears, and desires. Hamlet's father (seen as a monumental image projected on one of the museum's walls) is a distinguished Polish officer who has no doubts about the response to the question, nor does he have sympathy for those who have second thoughts.

15.3. Maciej Wyczański (Hamlet) and Jan Englert (Ghost) in *Hamlet'44*, directed by Paweł Passini, Museum of the Warsaw Uprising, 2008. Photograph by Julia Sielicka-Jastrzębska, reproduced courtesy of the Museum of the Warsaw Uprising, Warsaw.

He does not even take into account the possibility that his son could hesitate; he focuses on explaining in detail how to fire a rifle, how to fight. Undoubtedly the father, played by Jan Englert (dressed in the same Polish officer uniform he wore in Andrzej Wajda's Oscar-nominated 2007 film *Katyń*) represents the old myth of unflinching Polish heroism in an indisputably glorified struggle for independence. Polonius, unlike Hamlet's father, represents the survival instinct. He trembles for his children's lives, he is aware of danger and does not want them to die, even for the so-called right cause: 'reaching for a weapon, you join the madness' (*Hamlet'44*). Yet, Laertes plunges into the maelstrom of war and Ophelia also joins the insurgents. Polonius is not the only tormented parent. Gertrude explains that she married Claudius, who works for the Gestapo, only to save her son's life, as 'Claudius breathes for us all' (*Hamlet'44*).

Hamlet's dilemma, as well as Polonius's and Gertrude's decisions,

15.4. Maria Niklińska (Ophelia) and Władysław Kowalski (Polonius) in *Hamlet'44*, directed by Paweł Passini, Museum of the Warsaw Uprising, 2008. Photograph by Julia Sielicka-Jastrzębska, reproduced courtesy of the Museum of the Warsaw Uprising, Warsaw.

provides an important perspective for looking at war, a possible new interpretive scenario. Horatio, a synonym for honour, for whom 'to be' means 'to be *in* the war,' presents a real 'fragment' of war: he introduces to the audience two elderly people, a man and a woman, real-life insurgents who tell their story on the stage. This is the most poignant fragment of the production and, as Drewniak noted in his review, for a moment the audience's judgment is humbled; it is not theatre any more. The survivors tell stories that are tragic but somehow straightforward, simple, and unpretentious. By contrast, the characters in the play 'really want to play their own heroic death, grow up to the role in the national drama. Bowing down like [performers] on a stage, they die – individually, in groups' (Drewniak).

The image of the 'real' war becomes quite vivid with the testimony of these survivors, with the reading of the insurgents' letters to their family, and with the descriptions of executions of civilians. This image of war recreated on stage provokes difficult questions and raises anxiety:

> Real insurgents – not those who pinned the Home Army Crosses on [their own chests] in the 1990s, because there are many of those, but those who were on the barricades – were very critical of the Uprising. They had the feeling that they were a deceived generation. The civilians also felt harmed. We do not write about this, because it is not proper, it is not politically correct. (Wieczorkiewicz 9)

It may seem that the production managed to present the Polish tragedy in all its complexity and that it moved well beyond the simplistic polarity of right and wrong. Yet, the border between real life and stage was quite delicate in the performance. Telling their stories, the insurgents entered the stage as the actors of 'The Mousetrap.' Horatio introduced them: 'the actors arrived.' On the one hand, this scene destroyed the illusion of the performance; on the other hand, it forced the insurgents to be viewed through 'a theatrical metaphor' (Paprocka 26). The former insurgents who had attended the rehearsals also wanted the actors to dress up, 'change into their [the insurgents'] old clothes, battledresses. To try [them] on' (Kopciński 18). The theatrical nature of the scene was carried through at the end of *Hamlet'44*, which concluded with a fragment from Wyspiański's *Studium o 'Hamlecie'* [Study of Hamlet], a bold attempt to examine and define the essence of theatre – its objectives, ideal stage, actors.[16] Through these various devices, Passini also encouraged such a theatrical perspective of the Uprising itself (Mościcki).

One of the reviewers observed that this interpretation of the Warsaw Uprising is highly inappropriate because at that time people did not treat the Uprising as theatre, nor did they 'hamletise' – that is, philosophise or hesitate; they were not in a quandary, but did make decisions and gather up their courage (Mościcki). It is not, however, at the reconstruction of real wartime events that the production took aim. Wyspiański provides a clue: discussing his ideal theatre, he desired to revive the past by selecting details and transplanting them into the present, creating theatre that does not reconstruct or pretend, but remains a synthesis of reality. Similarly, Passini wanted his performance to encourage discussion about the 'continuation' of the Uprising, about its topicality. The performance was, he mentioned, an attempt to transform 'this myth into one's own experience' (Kopciński 19). But perhaps the rhetoric of theatre also allows for an open interpretation, without any pretensions to truth and without imposing any judgment; the Uprising did not arouse the world's conscience in 1944, as its leaders had hoped, but it should arouse the conscience of each individual now.

Passini used the word 'recycling' to refer to his production and to similar projects. He seemed to understand recycling as recovering those thoughts and concepts whose value is too obvious or customary to still influence reality today (Kopciński 18).[17] By recycling both Shakespeare (refreshed by the context of current dilemmas concerning how to interpret and remember the past) and the Warsaw Uprising (retold in a new institutionalized context), the war was contemplated once again in its complexity and terror. Even if Shakespeare may not necessarily require any new reading to be understood in a contemporary context, the Uprising actually needs rereading in order to be understood at all. *Hamlet'44* did not repeat the traditional 'parochial Polish conundrum' of whether it was right or wrong to launch the Uprising, but tried to show the everyday life of those who were there – whether by choice or by accident. Passini explained: 'There are no Germans in this performance. Because for us the most important [thing to show] was what happens between people in the streets and those behind a curtain' (qtd in Kraj). In order to make the war meaningful, give meaning to the event that was often seen as 'a useless commitment, vain effort, wasted sacrifice' (Stępień 266), one has to try to understand decisions, perhaps even dare to make some themselves – recycle history and memory, reconstitute the story.

The concept of recycling, a crucial element of postmodern culture, seems to be accepted by Shakespearean scholars, who with or without objection have to put up with modernized versions of the plays, pastiches, collages, and local appropriations. After all, as Marjorie Garber observed, 'We might say that Shakespeare is already not modern but postmodern: a simulacrum, a replicant, a montage, a bricolage. A collection of found objects repurposed as art' (5). There is even, as Marowitz asserts writing about free adaptations of Shakespeare, 'something culturally satisfying about toppling the idols we inherited from our forebears' ('Improving Shakespeare'). War, however, somehow resists this kind of rhetoric of reusing, modifying, or overthrowing the accepted interpretations. Reflecting on the past and coming to terms with the atrocities of war through recycling the themes of the

Second World War arouses objections. This is because in Polish culture the concept of war and struggle is idealized; talking about war brings to the fore a myth of freedom and sacrifice indispensable to our understanding of the nation, its messianic role, and its martyr's sufferings. Even though during the Second World War recycling, as it is literally understood, was an important element of national security – not only because it responded to the great need for materials and resources but also because it fostered a feeling of being active, useful, and motivated – the modern metaphor of reusing and salvaging implies something of a lower quality and value, waste to be recovered, something only deceptively 'the same.' By contrast, the tradition demands protection, demands to be unchangeable.

In times when myths are outdated, when grand narratives are assumed to no longer depict the past, when the confidence with which history is conceptualized is challenged, reconsidering war experiences becomes difficult: 'collective mythology is a dangerous romanticism which takes away freedom from an individual and forces him to die' (Kopciński 19). Now we *do* have doubts, 'which then the insurgents probably did not have,' explained Maciej Wyczański (the actor playing Hamlet), '[b]ecause I – born in 1981 – don't know how it is to fight, be afraid of death, to take risks' (qtd in Kraj). Thus, his Hamlet hesitates: 'both answers are wrong. To be, that is to survive. What for? Not to be? That is to fight. In the name of what? To survive? This is a choice without choice' (*Hamlet'44*). With these words, Hamlet blurs this clear meaning of a national myth. He is not an insurgent fighting for freedom; he is a contemporary, free man who wants to make an independent decision. He wants to have a choice that his father denies him.

Hamlet's father seems to be tradition's guardian; he is a ghost of all the soldiers/insurgents in all Polish uprisings and demands revenge for the wrong done to the whole nation. He doesn't hesitate; Ophelia, Laertes, and Horatio follow him. In the production his monologue was reinforced and expanded with a fragment from Władysław Bełza's patriotic poem drawn from a collection titled *Catechism of a Polish Child*, familiar to every Polish child. The fragment of the poem used in the performance included only the first two lines: 'Who are you?/ I'm a little Pole.' The audience, however, is well aware of the verses that follow: 'What is this land?/ My motherland./ ... Who are you for Poland?/ A grateful child./ What do you owe her?/ To sacrifice my life' (Bełza 1). This poem, written before the First World War, became a part of the national myth, a source of patriotic feelings for future generations, including the Warsaw Uprising insurgents. The poem, however, complicates the interpretation of the otherwise clear voice of tradition in *Hamlet'44*. On the one hand, the 'correct' answer to the questions posed is obvious; every child, every patriot would know what to do. On the other hand, the senseless repetition of the poem's lines (whose jingoistic meaning is presumably lost on most children preferring rhymes to sense) brings to mind this irrational drive to fight, to embrace a heroic death that adds splendour to the Polish myth of war. Perhaps it is this difficulty of not knowing, the difficulty of making independent decisions that is the main theme of *Hamlet'44*. Or perhaps it is the way of coping with the burden of the 'correct' answer that is the theme of the production. The final scene, when Horatio speaks directly to the audience convinced that the motherland is always the most important issue in one's life, does not provide a simple solution either. Horatio's direct message is disturbed by an image of insurgents lying dead on the ground and by the projection of the real insurgents' names. The myth of heroic war – this helpless faith in its success, the allure of heroism – is contrasted with an ordinary fear (the desire to survive in the most physical, simple sense), but also with a fear of feeling remorse or blame (for not going to fight, for living, as well as its opposite – for going and killing). Hamlet asks Ophelia, who is eager to fight, 'Have you ever killed a man?' (*Hamlet'44*), implying that the right and just fight also causes destruction and burdens conscience.

Criticized for being 'something like a comic book or action movie' (Mościcki), Passini's *Hamlet'44* was actually meant to elevate the Uprising in cultural discourse. Though considered neither a very successful interpretation of Shakespeare nor a proper comment on war, the production did, however, stir 'Polish fears, [open] wounds, prejudices, desires, expectations, phobias' (Kopciński 20). *Hamlet'44*, presenting a specifically Polish national approach to war, combined the theme of war with the feelings of responsibility, guilt, and helplessness in the face of its chaos; it drew attention to the actions taken and *not* taken. It complicated the view of war and confused the dilemmas and problems of an individual faced with human depravity. Sixty-four years after the Warsaw Uprising, from a safe temporal distance, Passini emphasized the problems of volition and solitude; he recycled memory and myth, paid homage to national heroes and provided a space for contemplating national defeat.

With Poland's re-entry into Western Europe, which led to the partial forsaking of the myth of Poland as a martyr and hero in favour of the vision of a common European future, such a production seems rather uncommon. A 'Polish Prince' has laid down arms; the play has already started to function successfully outside political allusions, focusing on its universal message and the modern globalized world, rather than on Poland's history alone.[18] The iconography of war and evil has also changed and the focus shifted from examining past experience to analysing the general concept of evil and contemporary political conflict.[19] After the Nazis and Soviets, evil is now identified with terrorism and war in the Middle East. Looking at war through the prism of Shakespeare's texts has, however, remained a potent way to deal with extreme social tensions and appalling conditions, although it is perhaps getting more difficult to present war and violence in theatre.

In the first week of the Second World War all theatres in Poland were closed. The National Theatre in Warsaw was destroyed in September 1939 and the remaining theatres through the coming years; but theatrical activity did not cease. Throughout the war, theatre, often the classics and Shakespeare in particular, continued to foster culture and lift spirits, as Krystyna Kujawińska Courtney has shown in an essay in this volume. Authors of critical and analytical texts published at that time tried to analyse the tragedy of war through the use of Shakespearean metaphors.[20] Today, even more than before, directors put Shakespeare to their own uses as they see an urgent need to revive and question cultural memory, reconstitute cultural values, and voice unresolved, silenced, or new doubts and questions. To find a *new* role for Shakespeare in the modern world, his works have had to be recycled and reused, but (to use Michael Thompson's term) they appear rather more durable than transient or 'rubbish.'[21] Appropriating and recycling Shakespeare anew in a specific Polish milieu ensures that the lost war – as it was for Poles[22] – does not become a lost memory, that the nationally vital cultural themes such as heroic war are not melted 'into the anonymous mass of an unrecognizable culture,' while interpreting Shakespeare from the modern perspective of war prevents his works from '"(bio)degrad[ing]" in the common compost of a memory' (Derrida 821).

Notes

1 During the seventeenth century the idea that the Polish nation played a special role in the history of Europe was presented by Wespazjan Kochowski (1633–1700), a noted historian and a poet of Polish Baroque,

in his psalms. The partitions of Poland by the Russian Empire, Kingdom of Prussia and Habsburg Austria, from the eighteenth till the twentieth century, became perceived in Poland as a Polish sacrifice for the salvation of Western civilization (Prizel 41).

2 Adam Mickiewicz focused on the image of Poland as 'a Christ of Nations' in *Books of the Polish Nation and Polish Pilgrimage*. In his drama *Dziady*, Mickiewicz presented Poland as a martyr nation that is suffering and dying for other nations. Juliusz Słowacki, though disputing Mickiewicz's idea of messianic devotion, also emphasized patriotism as the highest value (*Kordian*, 1833). Similarly, Zygmunt Krasiński focused on the problem of the enslavement of Poland and its struggle for liberation (*Nie-boska komedia*, 1833). Towards the end of the nineteenth century the motif of the uprising was continued by the writers who pondered on the reasons for Poland's failure in the January Uprising (1863–5) (for example, Bolesław Prus, *Lalka*, 1890; Eliza Orzeszkowa, *Nad Niemnem*), or tried to raise the nation's hopes for future freedom (for example, Henryk Sienkiewicz's historical novels, *Trylogia*, 1884–8, *Quo Vadis*, 1895, and *Krzyżacy*, 1900). At the beginning of the twentieth century, Stanisław Wyspiański wrote one of the greatest dramas in Polish literature, *Wesele* (1901), in which he claimed that the Polish nation was not prepared to fight for independence. The list of literary works devoted or referring to the Polish struggle for freedom is very long and cannot be presented here.

3 All translations, if not indicated otherwise, are mine.

4 In a televised reproduction of the performance the young composition of the audience is emphasized, suggesting the continued relevance of the events of 1944 to Polish youth and the continuing institutionalization of national memory.

5 The Warsaw Uprising is sometimes confused with the Warsaw Ghetto Uprising (1943), the Jewish resistance that arose in the Warsaw Ghetto to oppose Nazi Germany's plans concerning transportation of the ghetto population to extermination camps.

6 The number of casualties in the Warsaw Uprising is only roughly estimated by historians as no accurate documents exist in the public domain. For twenty years following the war the number of civilian causalities was considered to be 200,000, and during the 1960s, historians suggested that 250,000 civilians died, yet today they tend to agree on lower numbers, ca. 130,000 (Baliszewski).

7 In *Hamlet'44* the major scenes from Shakespeare's *Hamlet* (Claudius announcing his marriage to Gertrude, Hamlet meeting with the Ghost, Hamlet accusing Gertrude of betrayal, Hamlet rejecting Ophelia, the

Mousetrap, and Claudius admitting his guilt) are set within the context of the Warsaw Uprising. The plot centres on Hamlet, who mourns the death of his father and becomes anxious after hearing of Claudius's marriage to Gertrude. Though the ghost of Hamlet's father openly asks him to avenge his death and Ophelia encourages him to fight, Hamlet remains hesitant to act and pushes both the Ghost and Ophelia away. Laertes, in contrast to Hamlet, has a very precise plan: he wants to go to battle, despite Polonius's attempts to convince him otherwise. As the play continues, it becomes more and more focused on the theme of war and on Hamlet and Laertes' differing responses to the wartime conflict. The play closes rather ambiguously with Horatio contemplating and defending Hamlet's choice while projected images of marching army, tanks, and fluttering swastika flags suggest Warsaw's capitulation.

8 See, for example, Bristol; Marsden; Krystyna Kujawińska Courtney, *Królestwo na scenie: Sztuki Szekspira o historii Anglii na scenie angielskiej* (Łódź: Łódź University Press, 1997); Krystyna Kujawińska Courtney, 'Der polnische Prinz: Rezeption und Appropriation des *Hamlet* in Polen,' *Shakespeare-Jahrbuch* (1995): 82–92; Kujawińska Courtney, K. and K. Kwapisz Williams, '"The Polish Prince": Studies in Cultural Appropriation of Shakespeare's *Hamlet* in Poland,' *Hamlet Works*, ed. B.W. Kliman (www.hamletworks.org), 2009.

9 See, for example, Wolfgang G. Müller, 'Interfigurality: A Study on the Interdependence of Literary Figures,' *Intertextuality*, ed. Heinrich F. Plett (Berlin: Walter de Gruyter, 1991), especially 113–14, who draws attention to Shakespeare's reusing of characters in various plays.

10 See, for example, Bristol; Marsden; Krystyna Kujawińska Courtney, *Królestwo na scenie: Sztuki Szekspira o historii Anglii na scenie angielskiej* (Łódź: Łódź University Press, 1997).

11 See also Charles Marowitz, *Recycling Shakespeare* (New York: Applause, 1991).

12 The Soviet Red Army was usually blamed for the failure of the Warsaw Uprising because on the first day they held positions less than ten kilometres from the Warsaw city centre but did not advance or provide promised (and expected) support to the insurgents. Therefore, during the era of Communist domination of Poland, the Warsaw Uprising was presented as a reckless and foolish endeavour that caused much damage to the country, while the soldiers of the Home Army were legally persecuted by the Communists. After the fall of Communism, historians tried to reassess the facts. Though 'from the 1950s on, Polish propaganda depicted the soldiers of the Uprising as brave, but the officers as treacherous, reactionary, and charac-

terized by disregard of the losses' (Sawicki 230; Davies 521–2), the tendency was to construct and support a Warsaw Uprising cult or myth. Criticism of the Uprising was not welcome in Poland after 1989, as it was considered to continue Communist propaganda. Since then it has been unpopular (in press and academic review) to claim that the Uprising was poorly organized, with no strategic planning and, as a result, hundreds of thousands of people died and none of the military or political aims were achieved.

13 Different interpretations of *Hamlet* all considered the play to be a tool or weapon in the struggle against foreign oppressors and focused on Hamlet's ambivalence and 'existential anguish.' Tomasz Łubieński emphasized the importance of the dilemma for the Polish nation in his book on the history of Polish national uprisings, *Bić się czy nie bić. O polskich powstaniach* [To Fight or not to Fight: On Polish Uprisings] (Cracow: Wydawnictwo Literackie, 1978). See also Kieniewicz 347.

14 This is how Kott titled his review of the 1956 production of *Hamlet* by Roman Zawistowski. The review was initially published in the periodical *Przegląd Kulturalny* 41 (1956): 3, and later reprinted with modifications as 'Hamlet połowy wieku' [Hamlet of the Mid-Century] in *Shakespeare Our Contemporary* (72–85). For Kott, Zawistowski's *Hamlet* remained the most important production of the play, very contemporary and politically meaningful. It was staged when Khrushchev presented his secret report on Stalin's crimes during the Twentieth Congress of the Soviet Communist Party. Thus, the production symbolized the beginning of a change in the political climate: 'At first people whispered about the crimes on the throne, later they spoke loudly' (Kott, 'Listy o Hamlecie' 111).

15 See, for example, Sidorowicz; Władysław Pobóg-Malinowski, *Najnowsza Historia Polityczna Polski* (Warsaw: Krajowa Agencja Wydawnicza, 1990); Jan Ciechanowski, *Powstanie Warszawskie* (Warsaw: Państwowy Instytut Wydawniczy, 1989); Janusz Kazimierz Zawodny, *Uczestnicy i Świadkowie Powstania Warszawskiego – Wywiady* (Warsaw: Instytut Pamięci Narodowej, 2004), and *Powstanie Warszawskie w Walce i Dyplomacji* (Warsaw: Instytut Pamięci Narodowej, 2005); Lech Mażewski, *Powstańczy szantaż. Od Konfederacji Barskiej do stanu wojennego* (Elbląg: Elbląska Oficyna Wydawnicza, 2001); Tomasz Łubieński, *Ani tryumf ani zgon* (Warsaw: Wydawnictwo Nowy Świat, 2009).

16 Wyspiański considered himself a Polish heir of Shakespeare. He rewrote *Hamlet*, interpreting the play in the Polish political, social, and cultural contexts. This was 'one of the first attempts of a theatrical exegesis of Shakespeare's text in Europe' (Gibińska et al. 51), very influential for future Polish interpretations of the play. Additionally, his work, known as

Studium o'Hamlecie' was dedicated to 'Polish actors' and its aim was to provide a vision of ideal theatre that would 'hold a mirror up to nature.' See K. Kujawińska Courtney and K. Kwapisz Williams, '"The Polish Prince": Studies in Cultural Appropriation of Shakespeare's *Hamlet* in Poland,' *Hamlet Works*, ed. B.W. Kliman (www.hamletworks.org), 2009; and E. Miodońska-Brookes, *'Mam ten dar bowiem: patrzę inaczej': Szkice o twórczości Stanisława Wyspiańskiego* (Cracow: Universitas, 1997).

17 See also Agata Diduszko-Zyglewska, 'Jestem Jak Janko Muzykant. Wywiad z Pawłem Passinim' [I am like Janko Muzykant. Interview with Paweł Passini], *Dwutygodnik. Strona kultury* 5 (2009), 30 May 2009. http://www.dwutygodnik.com.pl/artykul/194-jestem-jak-janko-muzykant.html.

18 See, for example, *Hamlet* by Krzysztof Warlikowski (1999), *Hamlet* by Tomasz Mędrzak (2001), *Hamlet, książę Danii* [Hamlet, Prince of Denmark] by Krzysztof Kopka (2001), or Łukasz Barczyk's television theatre production of *Hamlet* (2004).

19 Recent Polish productions of *Macbeth* either horrify with scenes of intense staged violence and images of dead bodies, or present war with a game like appearance. In 2005 *Macbeth* dominated the Polish stage with six premieres, including productions by Andrzej Wajda, Grzegorz Jarzyna, Piotr Kruszczyński, and Maja Kleczewska.

20 See, for example, Stefania Zahorska's article '"Makbet" na emigracji' ["Macbeth" in Exile] published in London's *Wiadomości Polskie* [Polish News] in 1942, or Stanisław Cat-Mackiewicz's pamphlet 'Lady Macbeth myje ręce' [Lady Macbeth washes her hands], published in London in 1945.

21 In Michael Thompson's 'rubbish theory,' any cultural object transforms and changes its categorization according to the functions it plays in a society and the way people react to it; it can thus be transient (entertainment), rubbish, or durable. See Thompson.

22 Following the end of the Second World War, Poland was occupied by Soviet Russia for more than fifty years, resulting in the common understanding that Poland lost the war, even though the Allies won.

Works Cited

Baliszewski, Dariusz. 'Zakazana historia i zakazane liczby.' *PIO – Polityka, Internet, Opinie* 13 May 2007. 20 Feb 2010. http://unicorn.ricoroco.com/nucleo/index.php?itemid=82.

Bełza, W. *Katechizm polskiego dziecka. Wiersze.* Lvov: n.p., 1901.

Bończa-Szabłowski, J. 'Hamlet pełen wątpliwości.' *Rzeczpospolita* 181 (2008); n.pag. 10 Aug. 2009. http://www.e-teatr.pl/pl/artykuly/58430.html.

Bristol, Michael D. *Big-time Shakespeare*. London, New York: Routledge, 1996.

Chrostowski, W. 'The Suffering, Chosenness and Mission of the Polish Nation.' *Occasional Papers on Religion in Eastern Europe* 10. 3 (1993). n.pag. 26 May 2010. http://www.georgefox.edu/academics/undergrad/departments/socswk/ree/Chrostowski_Suffering_articles_previous.pdf.

Davies, Norman. *Rising '44. The Battle for Warsaw*. London: Pan Books, 2004.

Derrida, J. 'Biodegradables: Seven Diary Fragments.' Trans. Peggy Kamuf. *Critical Inquiry* 15 (Summer 1989): 812–73.

Drewniak, Ł 'Ostatnia wódka Hamleta.' *Przekrój* 34 (2008). n.pag. 10 Aug. 2010. http://www.e-teatr.pl/pl/artykuly/58962.html .

Edelman, Charles. *Shakespeare's Military Language: A Dictionary*. Athlone Shakespeare Dictionary Series. London: Athlone Press, 2000.

Garber, M. *Shakespeare and Modern Culture*. New York: Pantheon, 2008.

Gibińska, M., et al. *Szekspir. Leksykon*. Cracow: Znak, 2003.

Hamlet'44. By Magdalena Fertacz and Artur Pałyga. Dir. Paweł Passini. Warsaw Uprising Museum, Warsaw. 1 Aug. 2008.

Hawkins, Gay. *The Ethics of Waste: How We Relate to Rubbish*. Lanham: Rowman and Litttlefield, 2006.

Kendall, Tina, and Kristin Koster. 'Critical Approaches to Cultural Recycling: Introduction.' *Other Voices* 3.1 (May 2007): n.pag. 10 Feb 2010. http://www.othervoices.org/3.1/guesteditors/index.php.

Kieniewicz, S. *Historyjk a świadomość narodowa*. Warsaw: Czytelnik, 1982.

Kopciński, J. 'Robimy powstanie!' *Teatr* 10 (2008): 18–22.

Kott, J. 'Listy o Hamlecie.' *Kamienny potok. Szkice*. Warsaw: Nowa, 1981.

– *Szekspir współczesny* (1965). Cracow: Wydawnictwo Literackie, 1997.

Kraj, I. 'Wszyscy jesteśmy Hamletami.' *Rzeczpospolita* 179 (2008): n.pag. 10 Aug. 2009. http://www.e-teatr.pl/pl/artykuly/58388.html.

Marowitz, Charles. 'Improving Shakespeare.' *Swans Commentary* 10 April 2006. 17 Feb. 2010. http://www.swans.com/library/art12/cmarow43.html.

– ed. *The Marowitz Shakespeare: Adaptations and Collages of Hamlet, Macbeth, The Taming of the Shrew, Measure for Measure, and The Merchant of Venice*. New York: Drama Book Specialists, 1978.

Marsden, Jean. *The Re-imagined Text: Shakespeare, Adaptation, and Eighteenth-Century Literary Theory*. Lexington, Kentucky: University Press of Kentucky, 1995.

Mościcki, T. 'Rocznicowe głupstwa zamiast hołdu.' *Dziennik* 183 (2008): n.pag. 10 Aug. 2009. http://www.e-teatr.pl/pl/artykuly/58481.html.

'Odczytać Powstanie.' *Kultura polska: Portal kultury polskiej*. Instytut Adama Mickiewicza. 27 July –10 Aug. 2008. 14 May 2010. http://www.culture.pl/pl/culture/artykuly/wy_in_odczytac_powstanie_2008.

Paprocka, K. 'Powstanie Tu i Teraz. Wywiad z P. Passinim.' *Teatr* 10 (2008): 23–7.

'Powstańcy u Szekspira.' *Raporty. 64. rocznica Powstania Warszawskiego.* Portal TVN24.pl. 1 Aug. 2008. 10 Aug. 2009. http://www.e-teatr.pl/pl/artykuly/58410.html.

Prizel, I. *National Identity and Foreign Policy: Nationalism and Leadership in Poland.* Cambridge: Cambridge University Press, 1998.

Sawicki, J.Z. *Bitwa o prawdę: Historia zmagań o pamięć Powstania Warszawskiego 1944–1989.* Warsaw: Wydawnictwo 'DiG,' 2005.

Sidorowicz, J, ed. *Kulisy Katastrofy Powstania Warszawskiego 1944. Wybrane Publikacje i Dokumenty.* New York: Nieformalna grupa b. Powstańców Warszawskich, 2009.

Stępień, M. 'Największe nieszczęście i wyraźna zbrodnia.' *Kulisy Katastrofy Powstania Warszawskiego 1944. Wybrane Publikacje i Dokumenty.* Ed. Jan Sidorowicz. New York: Nieformalna grupa b. Powstańców Warszawskich, 2009. 261–6.

Sugiera, M. *Upiory i inne potwory. Pamięć-historia-dramat.* Cracow: Księgarnia Akademicka, 2006.

Sułkowski, B. *Hamletyzowanie nasze: socjologia sztuki, polityki i codziennosci.* Łódź: Wydawnictwo Uniwersytetu Łódzkiego, 1993.

Thompson, M. *Rubbish Theory: The Creation and Destruction of Value.* Oxford: Oxford University Press, 1979.

Trznadel, J. *Polski Hamlet. Kłopoty z działaniem.* Paris: Libella, 1988.

Wieczorkiewicz, P. Interview by Rafał Jabłoński. 'Obłąkana koncepcja Powstania.' Sidorowicz 7–14.

Wyspiański, S. *The Tragicall Historie of 'Hamlet,' Prince of Denmarke, By William Shakespeare. Wedlug tekstu Jozefa Paszkowskiego, swiezo przeczytana i przemyslana przez St. Wyspianskiego.* Cracow: Drukarnia Uniwersytetu Jagiellonskiego, 1905.

Zamoyski, A. 'Solving the Polish conundrum. Rising '44: The Battle for Warsaw by Norman Davies.' *The Spectator* 1 Nov. 2003. 10 Aug. 2009. http://findarticles.com/p/articles/mi_qa3724/is_200311/ai_n9331048/.

Appendix: List of Productions

1944, film, Britain, adaptation and dir. Laurence Olivier (188, 214)

Henry VIII
1945, Shakespeare Memorial Theatre, Stratford-upon-Avon (212)

Julius Caesar
1935, Basilica of Maxentius, Rome, Fascist adaptation (92–6, 103n10)
1936, *Giulio Cesare*, operatic adaptation by Gian Francesco Malipiero, Teatro Carlo Felice, Genoa (96–8)
1937, Mercury Theatre, New York, Orson Welles (99)
1939, *Cesare*, adaptation by Benito Mussolini and Giovacchino Forzano, Teatro Argentino, Rome (98–9)
1939, *Giulio Cesare, drama*, adaptation by Nino Guglielmi (103n13)
1940–50s, all-female adaptation, Osiris Players, England, dir. Nancy Hewins (226)
1941, Berlin Staatstheater (27)
1941, Shakespeare Memorial Theatre, Stratford-upon-Avon (211)
1953, film by Joseph Mankiewicz (10, 99–101)

King John
1940, Shakespeare Memorial Theatre, Stratford-upon-Avon (207, 211)

King Lear
1940, Deutsches Theater, Berlin (27)
1943, Shakespeare Memorial Theatre, Stratford-upon-Avon (212)

Love's Labour's Lost
2005, Kabul, Afghanistan, dir. Corinne Jaber (18n12, 248)

Macbeth
1940–50s, all-female adaptation, Osiris Players, England, dir. Nancy Hewins (226, 227, 228)
1942, 1944, Shakespeare Memorial Theatre, Stratford-upon-Avon (212)
1942, New York, then Fort Meade, Maryland, and Hawaii, starring Maurice Evans and Judith Anderson (236–7, 249n8)
1942, Piccadilly Theatre, London, John Gielgud as Macbeth (136)
1942, Residenztheater, Munich, dir. Schweikart (25)
1942, *Poprawki do 'Makbeta'* [Corrections to 'Macbeth'], adaptation by Adam Bunsch (11, 134–6, 140n23)
1945, Kammerspiele, Munich (209)

Measure for Measure
1940, Berlin Staatstheater (27)
1940, Shakespeare Memorial Theatre, Stratford-upon-Avon (211)

Merchant of Venice, The
1905, dir. Max Reinhardt, Rudolf Schildkraut as Shylock (44)
1920, Munich playhouse, Alexander Granach as Shylock (43)
1921, dir. Max Reinhardt, Werner Krauss as Shylock (38, 52)
1924, Theater in der Josefstadt, Vienna, dir. Max Reinhardt, Fritz Kort-
    ner as Shylock (45)
1924, Volksbühne, Berlin, dir. Fritz Holl, Alexander Granach as Shy-
    lock (42–4)
1927, dir. Jürgen Fehling, Fritz Kortner as Shylock (44, 46, 47)
1929, London, all-female adaptation, Osiris Players, dir. Nancy
    Hewins (227)
1932, Deutsches Theater am Rhein, Cologne, dir. Fritz Holl, Walther
    Richter as Shylock (41–2)
1936, Habimah Theatre, Tel Aviv, dir. Leopold Jessner (9, 63, 65–7, 78,
    79–80)
1940, 1941, 1942, 1944, Shakespeare Memorial Theatre, Stratford-upon-
    Avon (211–12)
1941, *The Merchant of Warsaw,* adaptation by Roman Brandstaetter, Tel
    Aviv (136)
1942, Rose Theatre, Berlin, dir. Paul Rose, Georg August Koch as Shy-
    lock (36, 48–51)
1943, Burgtheater, Vienna, dir. Lothar Müthel, Werner Krauss as Shy-
    lock (36–7, 52–4, 171)
1943, Minsk German Theatre (55–6)
1943, Murnau prisoner-of-war camp, Germany (59n20, 129, 131–3,
    139–40n17)
1944 (planned), film by Viet Harlan, Germany (36, 56–7, 59n20)
1944, Tatura Camp 3, Victoria, Australia (59n19)
1945, *The New Shylock / Shyluck Al-Jadid,* adaptation by Ali Ahmed
    Bakathir (9, 63, 71–9)
1970, Stratford Festival, Ontario, Canada, dir. Jean Gascon, Donald
    Davis as Shylock (15, 274)
1980, Chinese Youth Art Theatre, dir. Zhang Qihong (185)
1993, *Shakespeare's Merchant of Venice in Auschwitz,* adaptation by Tibor
    Egervari, Ottawa and Montreal (15, 279–83)
2002, Royal Shakespeare Company, China tour, dir. Loveday Ingram (182)

The Merry Wives of Windsor
1937, Shin Tsukiji, Japan, dir. Senda Koreya (172*t*)
1940, 1943, 1945, Shakespeare Memorial Theatre, Stratford-upon-Avon
(211–12)
1941, Berlin Staatstheater (27)
1942, Residenztheater, Munich, dir. Hans Schweikart (25)

A Midsummer Night's Dream
1940, Deutsches Theater, Berlin (27)
1940, Kammerspiele, Munich, dir. Otto Falckenberg (25, 29)
1940, Takarazuka Revue Company, Japan, dir. Katô Tadamatsu (173*t*)
1942, 1943, 1944, Shakespeare Memorial Theatre, Stratford-upon-Avon
(212)
1950s, Germany, dir. Gustav Rudolf Sellner (31)

Much Ado about Nothing
1939, 1941, 1945, Shakespeare Memorial Theatre, Stratford-upon-Avon
(211–12)

Othello
1937–8, Rose Theatre, Berlin (36)
1938, National Drama School, China (182)
1939, 1943, 1945, Shakespeare Memorial Theatre, Stratford-upon-Avon
(211–12)
1940s (cancelled), Theatre of Revolution (Mayakovsky Theatre), Moscow, trans. Boris Pasternak (157)
1942, Cotopouli Theatre, Athens, dir. and role of Othello Dimitris
Myrat (11, 107–17)
1942, Kammerspiele Theatre, Munich, dir. Otto Falckenberg (25)
1944, Berlin Staatstheater (27)
1944–5 (planned), Landestheater, Cobourg (30)
1951, Cotopouli Theatre, Athens, dir. and role of Othello Dimitris
Myrat (118n9)

Richard II
1939–40, Berlin. dir. Jürgen Fehling, Gustaf Gründgens as Richard
(27)
1939–40, Berlin, dir. Heinz Hilpert, Rudolf Forster as Richard (27)
1941, 1944, Shakespeare Memorial Theatre, Stratford-upon-Avon
(211–12)

Richard III
1937, Berlin Staatstheater, dir. Jürgen Fehling, Werner Krauss as
    Richard (26, 33n5)
1939, Shakespeare Memorial Theatre, Stratford-upon-Avon (211)
1940s, Switzerland, anti-Nazi staging (30)
1960, dir. Włodzimierz Woszczerowicz (planned during the war) (126,
    139n12)

Romeo and Juliet
1941, 1945, Shakespeare Memorial Theatre, Stratford-upon-Avon
    (211–12)
1940s (cancelled), Malyi Theatre, Moscow, trans. Boris Pasternak (157)
1950, *Star Crossed*, adaptation by Patrick Bentley[?] (14–15, 253–65)

The Taming of the Shrew
1939, 1940, 1941, 1942, 1944, Shakespeare Memorial Theatre, Stratford-
    upon-Avon (211–12)
1942, Berlin Staatstheater (27)

The Tempest
1941, 1942, Shakespeare Memorial Theatre, Stratford-upon-Avon
    (211–12)

Troilus and Cressida
1925, Kammerspiele, Munich, dir. Otto Falckenberg (25)
1936, Kammerspiele, Munich, dir. Otto Falckenberg (25)
1940s, Switzerland, anti-Nazi staging (30)

Twelfth Night
1939, 1941, 1943, 1945, Shakespeare Memorial Theatre, Stratford-upon-
    Avon (208, 211–12)
1941, Państwowy Teatr Dramatyczny, Vilnius (123–6)
1941, Residenztheater, Munich, dir. Hans Schweikart (25)
1943, Murnau prisoner-or-war camp, Germany (127, 129–30, 140n18)

The Winter's Tale
1942, 1943, Shakespeare Memorial Theatre, Stratford-upon-Avon
    (211–12)
1944, Deutsches Theater, Berlin (27, 31)
1946, provincial theatre in Germany, dir. Heinz Hilpert (31)

Contributors

Zeno Ackermann is research associate at Freie Universität Berlin, where he teaches English literature and cultural studies. He participates in a project on the German reception of *The Merchant of Venice* post-1945. His interests also include literary memory in twentieth-century Britain, antebellum American literature, and the interrelationships of rock music and cultural criticism.

Simon Barker is professor of English literature at the University of Lincoln in the United Kingdom. His publications include *The Routledge Anthology of Renaissance Drama* (2003); *Shakespeare's Problem Plays* (Palgrave Macmillan, 2005); *The Gentle Craft* (Ashgate, 2007); *War and Nation in the Theatre of Shakespeare and His Contemporaries* (Edinburgh University Press, 2007); and edited with Jo Gill, *Literature as History: Essays in Honour of Peter Widdowson* (Continuum, 2010).

Mark Bayer is assistant professor of English at the University of Texas at San Antonio. His publications include *Theatre, Community, and Civic Engagement in Jacobean London* (University of Iowa Press, 2011), and numerous articles on early modern literature and culture and on the long-term global cultural authority of Shakespeare's plays.

Peter Billingham is Head of Performing Arts at the University of Winchester and is both an authority on the plays of Edward Bond and a successful playwright. His most recent play, *Gifted,* was critically acclaimed in its London premiere (2010) and his book *At the Sharp End: Uncovering the Work of Five Contemporary Dramatists* (Methuen, 2007) was nominated for the The Writer's Guild Theatre Book Prize.

Tibor Egervari, born in Budapest into a Jewish family before the Second World War, escaped the fate of many members of his family who perished during the Shoah. He studied stage directing in Strasbourg where he began his career. Since 1960 he has been directing and teaching in both Canada and France. He is currently emeritus professor of theatre at the University of Ottawa.

Werner Habicht is a professor emeritus of English at the University of Würzburg, Germany, and the author of studies on medieval literature, Renaissance and modern drama, and nineteenth- and twentieth-century Shakespeare reception in Germany. He is a former editor of the *Shakespeare Jahrbuch* and *English and American Studies in German*, and the co-editor of a literary encyclopedia (*Literatur Brockhaus*) and several volumes of essays.

Alexander C.Y. Huang is associate professor of English and director of the Dean's Scholars in Shakespeare Program at George Washington University, and a research affiliate in literature at MIT. He is the general editor of *The Shakespearean International Yearbook* and a co-founder and co-editor of *Global Shakespeares* (http://globalshakespeares.org/). His recent book, *Chinese Shakespeares: Two Centuries of Cultural Exchange* (Columbia University Press, 2009), received the Aldo and Jeanne Scaglione Prize (MLA) and an honourable mention for the Joe A. Callaway Prize (New York University).

Nancy Isenberg is associate professor of English literature at the Università degli Studi Roma Tre, Italy. Her research on Shakespeare focuses mainly but not exclusively on his dramatic works in relation to dance and to early modern culture. She is co-editor of *La posa eroica di Ofelia* (Edizioni di Storia e Letteratura, 2003), essays on female characters on the Elizabethan stage, and *Questioning Bodies in Shakespeare's Rome* (Vandenhoeck and Ruprecht Unipress, 2010). In relation to her other main area of research, Italian-English connections in the eighteenth century, she published *Caro Memmo, mon cher frère* (Elzeviro, 2010), a critical edition of love letters by the Anglo-Venetian writer Giustiniana Wynne to Andrea Memmo (1758–60).

Tina Krontiris is professor of Renaissance literature and drama at Aristotle University of Thessaloniki in northern Greece. She has published internationally on Renaissance women writers and Shakespeare's reception in Greece. Her publications, local and international, include *Oppositional Voices* (London, 1992), *Shakespeare in Wartime, 1940–1950* (Athens, GR, 2007; in Greek) and (ed.) *Shakespeare Worldwide and the Idea of an Audience*, vol. 15 of the journal *GRAMMA* (2007).

Krystyna Kujawińska Courtney is associate professor at the University of Łódź, Poland, where she chairs the British and Commonwealth Studies Department and serves as vice-dean at the Faculty of International and Politological Studies. She has authored numerous articles and monographs on Shakespeare, is a member of the World Shakespeare Bibliography, and a co-editor of *Multicultural Shakespeare: Translation, Appropriation, Performance*. Her latest two monographs (in Polish and in English) are devoted to Ira Aldridge (2009).

Katarzyna Kwapisz Williams is an adjunct at the British and Commonwealth Studies Department at the University of Łódź, Poland, and the managing editor of the international journal *Multicultural Shakespeare: Translation, Appropriation and Performance*. Her research interests include literary theory, Renaissance culture, and utopian studies. Her recent monograph is entitled *Deforming Shakespeare: Investigations in Textuality and Digital Media* (2009).

Irena R. Makaryk is professor of English, cross-appointed to Theatre, and Vice-Dean, Faculty of Graduate and Postdoctoral Studies, at the University of Ottawa. Among her many publications are *Modernism in Kyiv* (2010, with Virlana Tkacz) and *Shakespeare in the Worlds of Communism and Socialism* (2006, with Joseph G. Price). *Shakespeare in the Undiscovered Bourn: Les Kurbas, Ukrainian Modernism, and Early Soviet Cultural Politics* (2004) was the runner-up for the Raymond Klibansky Prize for the best book published in the humanities in Canada (ASPP) and, in translation, was Book of the Year in the category of literary criticism in Ukraine (2010). She was named Professor of the Year, Faculty of Arts (2010), and received the F. Konowal V.C. Award for Lifetime Achievement in Ukrainian Studies (2009).

Marissa McHugh is a PhD candidate and a sessional instructor at the University of Ottawa. Her dissertation focuses on contemporary Canadian plays about the First World War. Other research interests include Canadian adaptations of Shakespeare and Canadian theatrical representations of war.

Ryuta Minami is professor of English at Shirayuri College. He has published extensively on Shakespeare performance in Japan, Shakespeare in Asia, and early modern English drama. He co-edited *Performing Shakespeare in Japan* (Cambridge University Press, 2001), *English Studies in Asia* (Malaysia, Silverfish, 2007), and *Re-playing Shakespeare in Asia* (Routledge, 2010).

Anne Russell is associate professor at Wilfrid Laurier University in Waterloo, Ontario. Her research interests include early modern drama and the performance history of Shakespeare's plays. She has edited Aphra Behn's *The Rover* (Broadview Press, 1994; 1999), and co-edited, with Viviana Comensoli, *Enacting Gender on the English Renaissance Stage* (University of Illinois Press, 1999).

Aleksei Semenenko is a research fellow at the Department of Slavic Languages and Literatures at Stockholm University. His PhD dissertation has been published as *Hamlet the Sign: Russian Translations of Hamlet and Literary Canon Formation* (2007). He has also published articles on Russian literature and translation. His most recent monograph is entitled *The Texture of Culture: An Introduction to Yuri Lotman's Semiotic Theory* (Palgrave Macmillan, 2012).

Index

An italic *f* following a page reference indicates an illustration; an italic *t* indicates a table. Please note that the Appendix on pp. 309–14 lists all the Shakespeare productions discussed in this book by title and year, with details and relevant page references.

Brandstaetter, Roman: *The Merchant of Warsaw*, 136
Braun, Kazimierz, 139n11
Brecht, Bertholt, 24
Bridges-Adams, William, 213
Bristol, Michael, 234
Britain: Canadian soldiers in, 206–7, 208; censorship priorities in, 106; liberal left, 220, 221–2; national theatre in, 13; Operation HK, 205–6; policy on Palestine and Middle East, 64–5, 69–70, 74–80; Polish soldiers in, 11, 132–8, 140n18; postwar theatre developments, 223, 227, 229; Royal Shakespeare Company, 182, 213; touring theatre companies, 13, 208, 211, 218–31; wartime bombing, 13, 204. *See also* Stratford-upon-Avon
British Communist Party, 222
Britten, Benjamin, 222
Browne, Elliot Martin, 219–20, 222
Brown, John Mason, 237, 246
Brunet, Mike, 281*f*
Bunsch, Adam: *Poprawki do 'Makbeta*, 11, 134–6, 140n23
Burgtheater (Vienna): *Merchant of Venice* at, 36, 37*f*, 38, 52–6, 53*f*, 171
Burte, Hermann, 28
Bykov, Dmitri, 157

Caesar, Gaius Julius: Caesarism, 85; Fascist portrayals of, 10, 86–8, 89*f*, 92–6, 98–100; as Germanic hero, 23; march to Rome, 83, 85, 102n2. *See also* Mussolini, Benito; Shakespeare, William: *Julius Caesar*
Calderón, Pedro: *El principe constante*, 153
Calvo, Clara, 17n4

Canada, 252–65; anti-German sentiment in, 15, 257–8, 269n23, 270n31; Dominion Drama Festival, 255–6, 269n27; production of *Merchant of Venice in Auschwitz* in, 282–3; responses to Second World War, 14–15, 267n12; role in Second World War, 15, 252, 257–8, 265–6nn1–8; (liberation of Netherlands), 15, 253, 254, 263, 266n9; Shakespeare adaptations in, 267–8n15; Shakespeare performances in, 256–7; soldiers in Britain, 206–7, 208; Stratford Festival, 15, 257, 269n29, 274
Canadian Adaptations of Shakespeare (website), 255
Canadian Broadcasting Corporation (CBC), 253, 257
Carlyle, Thomas, 169
Cartelli, Thomas, 234
cartoons: Baron Shidehara as Hamlet, 164, 165*f*; Shakespeare, Goethe, and Wagner, 214; Shakespeare in 'wartime' Stratford, 200*f*, 214
Casson, Lewis, 220
censorship: discourses or transcripts of, 107; faultlines in, 10, 114–15, 119n18; in occupied countries, 106–8; plays camouflaged to avoid, 108–9, 126; practices in Britain, 106; practices in China, 12, 183; practices in Germany, 40–1, 47–8, 107–8, 114, 119n17; practices in Greece, 10–11, 106–17; practices in Italy, 94–6, 108–9, 114, 119n17; practices in Poland, 123–4; priorities in, 106, 114; role of collaborators, 94–6, 113, 115; Shakespeare as an exception, 22, 24, 97, 113–15,